Education, Religion and Society

Education, Religion and Society celebrates the career of Professor John Hull, the internationally renowned religious educationist who has also achieved worldwide fame for his brilliant writings on his experience, mid-career, of total blindness. In his outstanding career he has been a leading figure in the transformation of religious education in English and Welsh state schools from Christian instruction to multi-faith religious education and was the co-founder of the International Seminar on Religious Education and Values. John Hull has also made major contributions to the theology of disability and the theological critique of the 'money culture'.

This volume brings together leading international scholars to honour John Hull's contribution, with a focus on furthering scholarship in the areas in which he has been active as a thinker. The book offers a critical appreciation of his contribution to religious education and practical theology, and goes on to explore the continuing debate about the role of religious education in promoting international understanding, intercultural education and human rights education. A possible basis for integrating Islamic education into Western education is suggested and the contribution of the philosophy of religion to pluralistic religious education is outlined. The contributors also deal with issues relating to indoctrination, racism and relationship, and examine aspects of the theology of social exclusion and disability.

This unique book, which includes a complete list of John Hull's writings up to the beginning of 2005, provides both an excellent introduction to contemporary issues in religious education in the West and the most complete critical account yet of the work of one of the great creative influences on religious education.

Dennis Bates is an honorary research fellow in the University of Birmingham School of Education, having recently retired from Manchester Metropolitan University where he had responsibility for religious studies. **Gloria Durka** is Professor of Religious Education at Fordham University, New York and has served as the President of the Association of Professors and Researchers in Religious Education. **Friedrich Schweitzer** is Professor of Religious Education and Practical Theology at the Protestant Faculty, Tübingen University.

Routledge research in education

Education, Religion and Society

Essays in honour of John M. Hull

**Edited by Dennis Bates, Gloria Durka
and Friedrich Schweitzer**

Routledge
Taylor & Francis Group

LONDON AND NEW YORK

First published 2006
by Routledge
2 Park Square, Milton Park, Abingdon, Oxon OX14 4RN

Simultaneously published in the USA and Canada
by Routledge
270 Madison Ave, New York, NY 10016

Routledge is an imprint of the Taylor & Francis Group

© 2006 selection and editorial matter, Dennis Bates, Gloria Durka
and Friedrich Schweitzer; individual chapters, the contributors

Typeset in Garamond by Wearset Ltd, Boldon, Tyne and Wear
Printed and bound in Great Britain by MPG Books Ltd, Bodmin

British Library Cataloguing in Publication Data
A catalogue record for this book is available from the British Library

Library of Congress Cataloging in Publication Data
A catalog record for this book has been requested

ISBN 0-415-36562-7

Professor John M. Hull (photograph by Dennis Bates).

Contents

Contributors

Dennis Bates has held positions of responsibility for religious studies, religious education and continuing professional teacher education in the former Humberside College of Higher Education (now the University of Lincoln) and Manchester Metropolitan University. A former doctoral student of Professor Ninian Smart and a contributor to Schools Council Working Paper 36, he has published articles on the history of religious education in the UK and religious education curriculum development in various journals including the *British Journal of Religious Education* and most recently, *Panorama* and *The Epworth Review*. Now retired, he is an honorary research fellow in the University of Birmingham School of Education.

Mary Beasley was a social worker in Birmingham for many years, latterly dealing with homelessness and alcohol and drug abuse. Now retired, her M.Phil. (Birmingham) dissertation was published under the title *Mission on the Margins* (Cambridge: Lutterworth Press 1997) and she is currently working for a Ph.D. (Birmingham) on factors underlying social exclusion and their theological implications with particular reference to the relevance of the findings of René Girard regarding scapegoating and parallels with Shia Islam.

Jerome Berryman has been Executive Director of the Centre for the Theology of Childhood, Houston, Texas since 1994. He graduated in Theology (Princeton), Law (Tulsa) and Education (Centre for Advanced Montessori Studies, Bergamo, Italy). An ordained priest in the Episcopal Church, he taught medical ethics and pastoral care of children at the Institute of Religion in the Texas Medical Center (1974–84) and was Canon (Education) at Christ Cathedral Houston 1984–94. He has published eight books and many articles on theology and religious education, most recently *The Complete Guide to Godly Play* (Denver, Colorado: Living the Good News 2003).

Reinhold Boschki is a Lecturer in Religious Education in the Roman Catholic Faculty of Theology in Tübingen University. His research interests include hermeneutical questions in religious education, ecumenical and inter-religious education, Jewish–Christian dialogue and a relationships approach to religious education, on the last of which he has recently written a major book – *'Bezeihung' als Leitbegriff der Religionspadagogik. Grundlegung einer Dialogisch-kreativen Religionsdidaktik* (Ostfildern: Schwabenverlag 2003). His most recent work in English is an article jointly written with Friedrich Schweitzer: 'What Children Need: Co-operative Religion in German Schools – Results from an Empirical Study', *British Journal of Religious Education*, 26: 33–44 March 2004.

Gloria Durka is Professor of Religious Education in the Graduate School of Religion and Religious Education at Fordham University, Bronx, New York. She is the author and editor of nine books, most recently *The Teacher's Calling* (New York: Paulist Press 2002), and numerous articles in academic and professional journals such as *The British Journal of Religious Education, Panorama*, and *Religious Education*. She has lectured throughout the USA, Canada, Europe and Australia and was a visiting research fellow in the School of Education, University of Birmingham. A past president of the Association of Professors and Researchers in Religious Education, she also serves on the editorial boards of several scholarly journals.

Liam Gearon is Reader in Education and Director of the Centre for Research in Human Rights at the University of Surrey, Roehampton. He is author and editor of fourteen books including recently: *Landscapes of Encounter: the Portrayal of Catholicism in the Novels of Brian Moore* (Calgary: University of Calgary Press 2002), *Education in the United Kingdom: Structures and Organisation* (London: David Fulton 2002), *Human Rights and Religion: a Reader* (Brighton and Portland: Sussex Academic Press 2002), and *Learning to teach Citizenship in the Secondary School* (London: Routledge 2003).

John Hick is Danforth Professor of Philosophy of Religion, Emeritus, Claremont Graduate University, California; H.G. Wood Professor of Theology, Emeritus, University of Birmingham, UK; an Honorary Professor of the University of Wales, UK; Fellow of the Institute for Advanced Research in Arts and Social Sciences, University of Birmingham, UK; Vice President of the British Society for Philosophy of Religion and Vice President of the World Congress of Faiths. He is one of the most distinguished living philosophers of religion and the author or editor of twenty-nine books, eighteen of which are still in print. His most recent book is *John Hick: an Autobiography* (Oxford: Oneworld 2003)

Robert Jackson is Professor of Education and Director of Graduate Studies at the University of Warwick, UK where he is also Director of the Warwick Religions and Education Research Unit. He is editor in chief of the *British Journal of Religious Education* and recently edited *International*

Perspectives on Citizenship, Education and Religious Diversity (London: Routledge Falmer 2003). He is also the author of many articles and several books including *Religious Education: an Interpretive Approach* (London: Hodder & Stoughton 1997) and *Rethinking Religious Education and Plurality: Issues in Diversity and Pedagogy* (London: RoutledgeFalmer 2004).

Fedor Kozyrev has a scientific background in biology and soil science but later undertook theological and teacher training in St. Petersburg Theological Academy and became a teacher in a state gymnasium. He then entered teacher training and is now Director of the Religious Pedagogy Centre at the Inter-Church Partnership and Head of the Department of Religious Pedagogy at the Russian Christian Humanitarian Institute. He is currently undertaking doctoral studies at the Herzen State Pedagogical University on the subject of non-confessional religious education in Russia and has published a number of articles on theology and religious education.

Wilna Meijer is Senior Lecturer in Philosophy of Education in the State University of Gröningen, Netherlands. Her most recent publications include a chapter on the rights of children (in F. Heyting, D. Lenzen and J. White (eds) *Methods in Philosophy of Education* (London and New York: Routledge 2001) and articles on the literary arts tradition and the mass media (2001) and the relevance of literature to life (2002). A recent prominent interest has been the culture of education in Islam and 'the West' which is the focus of her contribution to this book and on which she has also lectured and published elsewhere.

Charles Melchert was, until his recent retirement, Professor of Education and Religion at the Presbyterian School of Christian Education in Richmond, Virginia, USA where he was also Dean of the Faculty and later Director of the Doctoral Programme. He is now Adjunct Professor at Lancaster Theological Seminary in Lancaster, Pennsylvania. Among his recent major publications is *Wise Teaching: Biblical Wisdom and Educational Ministry* (Trinity Press International 1998). He is currently working on a book with the provisional title *Practice What you Teach: Patterns of Truth and Self-Deception in Education and Ministry.*

Gabriel Moran is Professor in the Department of Humanities and the Social Sciences and Director of the Graduate Program of Religious Education at New York University. One of the most distinguished and influential religious educationists in the USA, he has published twenty books, most of them on aspects of religious education, the most recent being: *Both Sides: The Story of Revelation* (New York: Paulist Press 2002). His teaching today is mainly in the field of ethics.

Wayne Morris is Lecturer in Theology and Religious Studies at University College, Chester, UK, and was until recently National Co-ordinator of

Church Action on Disability. He is co-author (with Roy McCloughry) of *Making a World of Difference: Christian Reflections on Disability* (London: SPCK 2002), and has published articles in the *Journal of Theological Education* and *Viewpoints*. He has been involved with the Deaf church in the Diocese of Birmingham since 1995 and has recently been awarded a University of Birmingham Ph.D. on the subject 'Theology and the Deaf Community'.

Karl Ernst Nipkow is Professor Emeritus of Practical Theology (Religious Education) in the Faculty of Protestant Theology and is also a member of the Faculty of Behavioural and Social Sciences in the University of Tübingen. He was a commissioner in the World Council of Churches (1968–83) and chairperson of the Commission for Education (1978–83); and in 1991 he was a co-founder of the International Academy of Practical Theology (IAPT). In his long and distinguished career, he has written and edited many books and articles on religious education and theology, most recently *God, Human Nature and Education for Peace* (Aldershot: Ashgate 2003).

Anthony Reddie is a Research Fellow and Research Consultant in Christian Education at the Queens Foundation for Theological Education in Birmingham, UK, and is also an honorary lecturer in the University of Birmingham. After working with the Afro-Caribbean and Asian communities as a Community Development Officer in Bradford and as a Youth and Community Worker in Birmingham, he became Christian Education Development Officer for the Birmingham Initiative, an ecumenical research project aiming to develop a new theory and methodology for the Christian education of Afro-Caribbean children in Birmingham's inner city churches. He is the author of a number of articles and books, most recently *Nobodies to Somebodies: A Practical Theology for Education and Liberation* (Peterborough: Epworth Press 2003).

K. Helmut Reich trained and worked as a physicist for twenty-eight years before turning to psychology of religion and religious education. He has worked in these areas in the School of Education of the University of Fribourg, Switzerland since 1984 and in 1994 was appointed Professor in the School of Consciousness Studies and Sacred Traditions in Stratford International University. In 1997, he received the William James Award of the American Psychological Association for his work in the psychology of religion. He is the author of many books and articles, most recently *Developing the Horizons of the Mind: Relational and Contextual Reasoning and the Resolution of Cognitive Conflict* (Cambridge: Cambridge University Press 2002).

Friedrich Schweitzer is Professor of Practical Theology (Religious Education) in the Faculty of Evangelical Theology in the University of Tübingen. Among his many professional roles, he was President of the

International Academy of Practical Theology from 1997–99 and is President of the Academic Society of Theology. In 2000 he delivered the Stone Lectures at Princeton Theological Seminary where in 1997 he was resident Fellow in the Centre for Theological Inquiry. He is editor of the German *Journal of Education and Theology* and of the *Yearbook of Education* and has written and edited many books, most recently *Religious Education Between Modernization and Globalization* (with R.R. Osmer) (Grand Rapids: W. Eerdmans 2003) and *Stages of Life in a Postmodern World* (St. Louis: Chalice Press 2004).

Geir Skeie is Associate Professor in Stavanger University College, Norway where he is also currently Dean of the Faculty of Humanities and teaches religious studies and religious education. His research interests are mainly in the field of the philosophy of religious education in relation particularly to modernity, pluralism and identity issues. Among his recent publications in English are: 'The Concept of Plurality and its Meaning for Religious Education', *British Journal of Religious Education*, 25: 47–59 and 'Nationalism, Religiosity and Citizenship in Norwegian Majority and Minority Discourses', in R. Jackson (ed.) *International Perspectives on Citizenship, Education and Religious Diversity* (London: RoutledgeFalmer 2003).

Heinz Streib is Professor of Religious Education and Ecumenical Theology in the University of Bielefeld, Germany where he has established the Research Centre for Biographical Studies in Contemporary Religion. His research interests include conversion to, and withdrawal from, new religious movements and fundamentalist theological orientations, faith development, and inter-religious classroom communication. He has written a good number of articles and his books include *Hermeneutics of Metaphor: Symbol and Narrative in Faith Development Theory* (Frankfurt: Peter Lang 1991) and most recently (with Albrecht Scholl) *Wege der Entzauberung* (Munster: Lit-Verlag 2000).

Acknowledgements

Thanks are due to the publishers and editors of *Panorama: International Journal of Comparative Religious Education and Values* for permission to include as the introductory chapter of this volume a revised and enlarged version of the article 'In Celebration of Professor John Hull: Christian Theologian and Educationist' first published in Volume 14:1 of that journal, Summer 2002. Thanks are also due to Professor Brian Gates of St. Martin's University College, Lancaster, UK, for his helpful critical comments on drafts of the introductory chapter.

General introduction

This book honours the contribution made by John M. Hull, Emeritus Professor of Religious Education in the University of Birmingham UK, to religious education and practical theology both in the UK and internationally over a period of more than three decades. It is written and edited by an international and ecumenical body of scholars all of whom have had some association with John Hull over his long career and wish to register their esteem for him and his work in the year he has celebrated his seventieth birthday. Those who know him will never use the word 'retirement' in his hearing – except perhaps in relation to themselves. Professor Hull has recently moved from the University of Birmingham School of Education, his location for thirty-six years, to the post of Honorary Professor in Practical Theology in the Queen's Foundation for Ecumenical Theological Education a short distance away where he will be able to pursue his wider teaching and research interests in theology.

This move is eminently appropriate. Although a committed educationist, John Hull has always seen himself first as a Christian practical theologian applying his theology to the theory and practice of religious education and, more recently, also to disability and the money culture. Writing in the early 1980s, he defined 'practical theology' as 'theology seeking to be related to the problems and possibilities of human life both inside and outside the community of faith' (Hull 1984: 208). Throughout his career, he has endeavoured to bring religious education into the mainstream of educational thought and practice by arguing for the replacement of a Christian nurturing approach to the subject by a secular, multifaith approach in state or 'county', now 'community', schools and the replacement of legally compulsory daily school worship by secular assemblies.

To many, the paradox is that he has advocated these changes on Christian theological grounds not only on educational grounds. Furthermore, he has also argued that it is necessary for the Christian churches to adopt the same critical, reflective approach to nurturing their children into the faith; and he has worked to produce viable syllabuses and curriculum materials in both community and church sectors. As will be seen in the critical appreciation below, it is this contribution to religious education both in the church and state sectors based on an overt Christian commitment that has made his thinking of such interest not only in the UK but to religious educationists in other countries in which the religious denominations often retain responsibility for religious education in state schools or run their own educational institutions.

The term 'practical theology' is now coming to be used more often in the UK and certainly reflects more accurately the purview of John Hull's work which extends well beyond religious education. He has written movingly and powerfully about his own traumatic personal experience of total blindness, and is working towards the forging of a theology of disability. He has also written extensively on the distorting influence of the 'money culture' and the imperialist legacy on theology, religious belief and religious experience in western societies. It will be interesting to see where Professor Hull's interests will take him in his new position.

In planning this festschrift, it was felt that he would be most honoured by a book in which respected colleagues wrote on their present research interests in the areas to which he has devoted and continues to devote his professional life. The majority of contributors chose to write on various aspects of religion and education in which he has such a well-established reputation but three essays in Part 2 reflect aspects of his later interests – disability and self deception. The result is a book which offers valuable insights into the current concerns and interests of religious educationists and theologians from a number of cultural and religio-educational contexts in Europe (including Russia) and the USA, as they grapple with the problems which the post-modern cultural ethos is posing across the developed world.

Many of the contributors are members of the International Seminar on Religious Education and Values (ISREV), an ecumenical and inter-faith organization jointly founded in 1977 by John Hull and Professor J.R. Peatling to promote international exchange between religious educationists. ISREV meets biennially in various locations throughout the world, most recently in Philadelphia 2004, and its deliberations and the continuing debates of its members between conferences are often published in leading journals, notably the *British Journal of Religious Education, Panorama* and *Religious Education*. Freidrich Schweitzer and Gloria Durka are long-standing members of ISREV and offer the following reflections on the impact of John Hull's work in Germany and the USA respectively:

John Hull and religious education in Germany

From a German perspective – and similar remarks could undoubtedly be made from the perspective of other countries in central and northern Europe – John Hull has been by far the most influential theorist of religious education from another country. The evidence for this is plentiful; John Hull's bibliography includes an exceptional number of articles translated into German and two of his monographs are available in German translation

(Hull 1992, 1997) as are two volumes of edited extracts from his writings (Hull 2000a, 2000b). Through ISREV as well as through other organizations, conferences, lectures, etc. he has been in personal touch with most of the leading figures in German religious education over the last twenty-five years. In 1995 he received an honorary doctorate from the University of Frankfurt which indicates that his leading role has been acknowledged well beyond personal impressions.

John Hull's publications are used by many religious educationists in this country and are regarded with great respect. This is quite remarkable because national discussions still play a major role in religious education due to its relation to national regulations for schools and education. Consequently, attention to writers from other countries tends to be limited and translations are rare. From a German perspective, John Hull stands for a modern type of religious education which is based on educational rather than on catechetical criteria. In this sense, his work is in line with similar attempts of German religious educators of his generation like Karl Ernst Nipkow. Many German religious educators also respect him as a key figure in the process of internationalizing religious education as an academic discipline; his work as editor of the *British Journal of Religious Education* testifies to this through its many international contributions, often resulting from John's personal invitation or encouragement.

Most recently, his decisive involvement with the development of an interfaith approach to religious education has received much attention. Many religious educators in Germany perceive the Birmingham approach as the model from which they have received inspiration for their own attempts in Germany. John Hull's participation in the Nuremburg Forums on intercultural and inter-religious education has been especially important in this respect. Beyond this, the Birmingham approach has been an important point of reference for most German writers interested in making religious education more inclusive of religions other than Christianity.

John Hull and religious education in the USA

John Hull is known in the United States (US) as a theologian of education. His thinking was first introduced to academic circles in the 1970s through the *British Journal of Religious Education*. This period was one of rapid growth and development for the profession of religious education in the US. The Association of Professors and Researchers of Religious Education, formed in the late 1960s, was gaining membership and its annual meetings were becoming forums for lively conversation and academic debate on the theory and practice of religious education. The Religious Education Association, founded in 1903, was the sponsor of the journal *Religious Education*, a forum for interfaith dialogue.

Working in an environment of separation of church and state, US religious educators in a variety of institutions were drawn to John Hull's description of the nature of religious education. His edited collection, *New Directions in Religious Education* (Falmer Press 1982), not only helped US religious educators to identify the key issues surrounding religious education in Britain but brought together significant articles on the nature of religious education, religious education in a pluralistic society, the design of the curriculum and methods in teaching religion. John Hull's own introductory essay expressed his interest in developing an approach that is not restricted to the learning of observable facts about religion, but one in which 'pupils should learn from religion in ways which will enrich them and deepen their humanity, rather than merely informing them' (Hull 1982: xv).

John Hull's concerns resonated with that of many US religious education theorists, and their interest was enhanced by the founding of ISREV. An invitational seminar to encourage the exchange of thinking and research, ISREV first met in the US in Schenectady, New York in 1980. It was here that scholars from the US and other countries had the opportunity to meet John Hull in person, listen to his lecture on the theme 'Christian Nurture and Critical Openness', and probe it in depth in a variety of working sessions. His lecture was later published and made available to a wider audience (cf. *Understanding Christian Nurture*, British Council of Churches 1981). Many US religious educators became members and were able to initiate regular exchanges of ideas and concerns with John Hull whose writings became more widely read in the 1980s. His book *What Prevents Christian Adults from Learning* (SCM 1985 and Trinity Press International 1991) appeared on required reading lists of university and theological school courses, thereby introducing his thinking to scores of students who began to seek out his other writings. Practitioners also became familiar with John Hull as they were drawn to his works on teaching children and young people such as *God-talk with Young Children* (Trinity Press International 1991) and curriculum projects, for example, *A Gift to the Child* (Simon and Schuster 1991). Teachers were impressed by the fact that his work drew from his own experience as teacher, scholar, writer and thinker.

It was no surprise, and most appropriate, when in 1992 John Hull was honoured in the US by the presentation to him of the William Rainey Harper award of the Religious Education Association of the USA and Canada. By then he was recognized as one of the most influential religious education scholars in the English-speaking world whose work had enhanced US religious education theory and practice. John's keynote address at the Conference, 'Adult Learners: Making Critical Connections', personally introduced him to professional religious educators who were moved by his passion, wit, commitment and courage in the face of his blindness. What he wrote about in *Touching the Rock: An Experience of Blindness* (SPCK 1990) was known to many, but his presence at this meeting gave compelling witness to his remarkable career and vocation.

The structure of the book

After the introductory section, the book is divided into three parts: the first, reflecting the interest of John Hull in socio-political and educational issues worldwide, deals primarily with international, intercultural and philosophical dimensions of religious education; the second examines important topics in the theology of education, disability and social exclusion; and the third explores significant recent developments in the theory and practice of religious education. The contents of the three major parts of the book are discussed in more detail in their respective introductions.

References

Hull, J. (1984) *Studies in Religion and Education*, Lewes, Sussex: Falmer Press.
—— (1982) *New Directions in Religious Education*, Lewes, Sussex: Falmer Press.
—— (1992) *Im Dunkeln Sehen Erfahrungen Eines Blinden* trans. Silvia Morawetz, Munich: C.H. Beck'sche Verlagsbuchhandlung.
—— (1997) *Wie Kinder über Gott Reden: Ein Ratgeber fur Eltern und Etziehende*, Gütersloh: Gütersloher Verlaghaus (with a Foreword by Friedrich Schweitzer).
—— (2000a) *Glaube und Bildung {Ausgewahlte Schriften Band 1}* trans. Susanne Naumann and Sieglinde Denzel with an introduction by Prof. Dr Werner Kramer, Zurich: KIK Verlag.
—— (2000b) *Gott und Geld {Ausgewahlte Schriften Band 2}* trans. Silvia Morawetz, Berg am Irchel: KIK Verlag.

Dennis Bates, Gloria Durka, Friedrich Schweitzer

John Hull

A critical appreciation

Dennis Bates

This introductory chapter gives an overview of John Hull's career, including brief outlines of his thinking in the major areas in which he has been engaged; this also includes curriculum development work undertaken by and with his colleague of many years, Michael Grimmitt. The essay concludes with a critical assessment of his work to date including those aspects of it shared by Michael Grimmitt and others.

Upbringing, education and early career

Born in 1935 in the state of Victoria in Australia, John Hull trained as a teacher in the University of Melbourne and taught for three years (1956–59) in a Melbourne Church of England grammar school. His father was a Methodist minister of conservative evangelical persuasion and it was in such a faith that John was brought up. The centrality of the Bible to Christian faith in these formative years left an indelible imprint on him. In 1959 he came to Britain to study theology and his traumatic encounter with the 'higher criticism' of the Bible at Cambridge University (1959–62) caused a 'crisis of faith' (Hull 1997: 6). As a result of this his conservative evangelicalism gave way to a theology strongly influenced by the then current 'New Theology' with its utilization of the language of depth psychology and its embracement of secularity as part of God's purposes for humanity 'come of age'.

Rather than undermining the centrality of the Bible to his faith, however, this fresh orientation seems to have enhanced it. For him the Bible continued to be the primary reference point for Christian belief and his expository gifts and sheer pleasure in working with the text are reflected in many of his writings, but brilliantly so in his recent book *In the Beginning There was Darkness* (SCM Press 2001). After Cambridge, he resumed his teaching career for four years, teaching religious education in a London grammar school. During this time, he also undertook part-time doctoral research in New Testament Studies at London University. His thesis, which was completed at the University of Birmingham, was later published under the title *Hellenistic Magic and the Synoptic Tradition* (SCM Press 1974).

In 1966 Hull was appointed lecturer in divinity at the free church sponsored Westhill College of Education in Birmingham and in 1968 succeeded Edwin Cox as lecturer in religious education in the School of Education at the University of Birmingham. During his two years at Westhill he worked closely with Edwin Cox, who was one of several religious educationists, among them Harold Loukes, Ronald Goldman and J.W.D. Smith, who were rethinking the character and aims of Biblically focused Christian religious education in face of research evidence of poor learning in the subject and an increasingly secular and pluralistic social environment. Cox argued for a more child centred, 'open ended' approach to a subject which would still 'largely involve teaching of the sources and faith of Christianity' (Cox 1966: 68), albeit with 'some consideration' of the teaching of other religions and even secular philosophies. John Hull learned much from Edwin Cox as his warm dedication of a recent book to him indicates (Hull 1998: viii), but his own thinking was soon to go well beyond that of his colleague.

The real transformation of religious education which occurred during the following decade and in which Hull was to play a crucial role, owed much to the thinking of Professor Ninian Smart who, in the year that John Hull was appointed to Westhill College, had resigned from his chair of Christian Theology at the University of Birmingham, to become founding professor in the Department of Religious Studies at the new University of Lancaster. In his Heslington lectures (Smart 1968), Ninian Smart called for the abandonment of faith-nurturing aims in state school religious education and their replacement by 'a sensitive induction into religious studies, not with the aim of evangelizing but with the aim of creating certain capacities to understand and think about religion' (ibid. 97). On a shrinking globe and in an increasingly pluralistic as well as an 'open and religiously uncommitted society' (ibid. 91), Ninian Smart held that Christianity should be studied alongside the other great world faiths which should no longer be presented in the light of Christian missionary theology (as the agreed syllabuses had presented them to date) but empathetically and fairly using phenomenological methodology. In a review article published in 1970, John Hull concludes that 'we must have the type of neutral religious education advocated by Ninian Smart . . . and . . . this approach is *consistent with* the nature of Christian thought' (Hull 1984: 96).

Christian education and secular education

If Ninian Smart's thinking was the major inspiration behind the transformation of religious education, John Hull was the driving force behind securing its wider acceptance. Unlike Ninian Smart, who was seen by many teachers as an academic with unrealistic notions of what was feasible in schools, John Hull was an 'insider', a trained teacher, a religious educationist and prominent member of the Christian Education Movement (CEM) which had long been the major organization supporting teachers of religious education in UK schools. Most important, he became editor in 1971 of the CEM journal *Learning for Living* (renamed the *British Journal of Religious Education* (BJRE) in 1978), the only British religious education journal of any standing; this role gave him a unique platform from which to influence thinking.

Hull was in broad agreement with the suggestions of the Lancaster Schools Council project working paper (Schools Council 1971) which combined the child centred experiential methods of 1960s liberal Christian religious education with Ninian Smart's phenomenological method and six dimensional typology of religions. However, he had already shown tentative concern in 1970 about how far Smart's approach took account of 'the personal growth of the pupil' (Hull 1984: 96); and after the surge of the world religions movement during the 1970s he became concerned during the early 1980s that RE was seeing 'an exaggerated emphasis upon the observable facts about religion' (Hull 1982: xv). Not surprisingly, religious education in the University of Birmingham became increasingly focused on pupil centred 'learning from' religion as will be seen below. However, the early 1970s saw John Hull involved in another crucial debate which was to have a major impact on his thinking about religious education in all areas. It was Paul Hirst, one of a group of philosophers of education based in London University, whose thinking was a dominant influence in UK philosophy of education during the 1960s and 1970s, who provided the spur for Hull to develop his own Christian theology of education, religious education and Christian nurture.

Hirst had called for an objective, secular approach to the study of religion in state schools in an important article published in the mid-sixties (Hirst 1965); but in an article in *Learning for Living* (Hirst 1972) which formed the substance of a chapter in his later book *Moral Education in a Secular Society* (1974), he went further, arguing that the very notion of 'Christian education' was 'a contradiction in terms' since education is essentially a rational, critical process that cannot presuppose the truth of the beliefs of any religion or ideology. The aim of education was the 'development of people who are rational, autonomous beings in every area of life' (Hirst 1974: 81). In an editorial discussion of this in the BJRE (Winter 1975), John Hull argues that, contrary to Hirst's contention, it is possible to generate and support a 'free, open and enquiring' view of education from within Christian theology (Hull 1998: 20). In a series of articles written from the mid-1970s to the early 1980s and in his work on Christian nurture for the British Council of Churches (BCC 1976, 1981) Hull builds upon his thinking in *School Worship: an Obituary* (1975) and develops his case for a Christian theology of education, religious education and Christian nurture which embodies the critical principles of contemporary educational theory. The approaches he adopts to religious education in state schools and Christian nurture in the churches are very similar: in a BJRE editorial published in 1972, John argues that: 'the day of closed nurture is over and the churches in all their educational work, including that which takes place on Sundays, must accept the risks of a critical education' (Hull 1998: 8).

John Hull finds a basis for a Christian theology of 'critically open' education from a number of sources: most fundamentally, it derives from the Christian doctrine of God as 'Person', authoritative but not authoritarian: 'a God who gives himself in covenant relationship with men and women whom he calls to walk before him, not as slaves but as sons and daughters, advancing in love and trust and responsibility with him' (Hull 1984: 203). As he puts it in another article: 'Critical openness is the pedagogical technique adopted by a God who is personal and desires us to be persons' (ibid. 216). He also contends that 'the spirit of critical openness ... is central in New Testament Christianity' (ibid. 201), citing as evidence, for example, the many 'appeals to Christians to maintain an alert, watchful, vigilant, inquiring and discriminating spirit' (ibid.) to distinguish between true and false Messiahs, prophets, miracles etc. In the 'in-between age' after the coming of the Messiah and before his second coming 'nothing was clear and sharp' (ibid.). We shall return to Hull's theological justification for critically open religious education and Christian nurture below.

School worship and education

The issue of daily worship in state schools, compulsory under the 1944 Education Act, was John Hull's earliest major research topic in religious education. His interest in it dated back to his having to organize it in the south London grammar school in which he taught in the early 1960s. He had already written several articles on the subject, in the earliest of which, published in 1969 (cf. Hull 1984: 5–16) he had suggested that it be abandoned. In an important book (Hull 1975) he brings his thinking together in a focused and incisive way, exploring the subject historically and conceptually in some depth. In essence, he contends that worship on the one hand, which assumes belief in its object, and education on the other, which subjects all things to critical scrutiny, are mutually incompatible (ibid. 89). How can state schools have open, critical, multifaith religious education and at the same time have daily acts of Christian worship? Worship should therefore be discontinued in state schools and replaced by school assemblies the content of which could relate directly to school activities and interests including the free, voluntary expression of the beliefs of different groups; but there would be no assumption of belief on the part of the whole school and therefore no need for any group or individual to feel the need to be excluded. John admits that this book was 'a hard book for a Christian to write' (ibid. ix); however, as the 1988 Education Reform Act was to show, his 'obituary' for school worship was to prove somewhat premature (cf. Francis and Davies 2002).

Religious education and Christian nurture

The 1970s, his last years with the faculty of sight, were years of intense activity and achievement for Hull. He was active in virtually all areas of religious education. In state school religious education he was a key member of the agreed syllabus conference which produced, after five years work, the controversial 1975 Birmingham Agreed Syllabus, the first truly multifaith syllabus to appear in Britain. The conference included representatives of all of the major faith communities in Birmingham and co-opted secular humanists onto working groups. In John Hull's view 'The result is a syllabus which can be taught by any well informed and enthusiastic teacher, regardless of his faith or lack of it, to any interested pupil, regardless of his faith, or lack of it' (Hull 1984: 114). The syllabus received much criticism and Hull wrote several articles and editorials defending and justifying its approach (ibid. Part II: 27ff.).

He also wrote many articles which dealt with problems facing religious education teachers as they grappled with the 'new RE', including thematic teaching (ibid. Part III: 123ff.) and the problem of the relation between teachers' personal beliefs and the teaching both of their own faith and faiths or 'stances for living' to which they were not committed (ibid. Part IV: 175ff.). His distinction between 'convergent' teaching and 'divergent' teaching, with its recognition that both those who wished to teach from their faith stance (convergently) in the context of nurture and those who wished to teach neutrally (divergently) in secular education could be equally 'professional' and 'confessional' in their motivation and practice, was a useful corrective to more simplistic thinking. John was also a member of the working group which produced the Schools Council's *Groundplan for the Study of Religion* (1977), an important attempt to provide a framework of aims and objectives for the study of religion. During this period also he travelled widely, lecturing in Ireland, Australia, New Zealand, Canada and the USA. He found that 'the British problems were not isolated' (Hull 1984: 1) and one of John's most significant achievements during this hectic decade was his joint founding in 1977, together with Professor John R. Peatling, of the International Seminar on Religious Education and Values (ISREV).

In addition to his work in state schools, John Hull remained deeply interested and active in the Christian nurture of children and young people and adult Christian education in the churches, and made significant contributions to these areas. His thinking was a major influence on the British Council of Churches reports *The Child in the Church* (1976) and *Understanding Christian Nurture* (1981). He sought to rethink Christian nurture within the churches in the light of social and educational change. John's discussion in *School Worship: an Obituary* encapsulates the essence of his thinking. Nurture is not indoctrination; a true Christian nurture is a 'womb' not a 'straitjacket', it is open as education is open (Hull 1975: 108). A child nurtured in the Christian way 'will be brought up in his native tradition in such a way as to enter into dialogue with it, to become aware of it, so that he may appropriate it or reject it' (ibid.).

At the root of John's thinking both about Christian nurture and religious education is his conviction of the centrality of respect for personhood to the Christian view of humanity: 'autonomy or critical openness is an essential attribute of personhood' (Hull 1984: 216). Created in God's image, 'God has called us into fellowship with himself, having made us mind as well as spirit' (ibid. 217). A nurture which claims to determine what the child will become – 'to finish a person' – denies 'the integrity, the uniqueness of that person' (Hull 1975: 107). The New Testament teaches 'the idea of Christian man as unfinished man . . . the achievement of personhood . . . is a life-long task' (Hull 1984: 202). In an important essay published in 1994 which takes account of discussion and criticism of the concept of 'critical openness', especially in relation to Paul Hirst's 'rational autonomy', Hull draws the following distinction between them:

> whereas autonomy could perhaps suggest a certain isolation, even a self enclosed independence, or it might suggest individualism, . . . critical openness is intended to suggest that one is in a community, a learning community, in which one both speaks and listens, being both critical and receptive.
>
> (Hull 1994: 253–4)

John Hull's contribution to the development of thinking about the nurture of children in the church was recognized by his twice being elected President of the National Christian Education Council – formerly the British Sunday School Union – most recently in 2002. For a closer examination of his theological justification of a 'critically open' approach to religious education, with a discussion of his Biblical hermeneutic, see Wilna Meijer's essay, Chapter 5 below.

Turning points

Two events, in 1979 and 1980 respectively, marked major changes to the political and social environment of religious education in Britain and to John Hull's life, professional interests and personal consciousness. These were the coming to power of a Conservative government under Margaret Thatcher in 1979; and, after a life in which he had experienced constant battles to retain his sight, the onset of total blindness in 1980. There can be no doubt that after successfully and remarkably adapting himself to the limitations imposed by his blindness during the early 1980s, Hull's life, thinking and professional interests developed in new directions clearly influenced by these changes. His work on his experience of blindness and the theology of disability; and on the money culture and its effects on religion, spirituality and education show this unequivocally.

A turning point of another kind occurred in 1979 when John Hull was joined by Michael Grimmitt, who came from the post of Director of the then 'RE Resources and In-Service Training Centre' located in Westhill College of Education and had worked with Hull since 1974 as reviews editor of *Learning for Living*. The author of a pioneering textbook for multifaith RE (Grimmitt 1973, 2nd edn 1978), Grimmitt came to the University of Birmingham with a strong commitment to a multifaith view of religious education and with extensive experience of RE curriculum development and initial and continuing professional teacher education. Sharing similar theological positions and philosophies of RE, and with complementary interests, John Hull and his new colleague formed a strong team which, under Hull's vigorous leadership and building on the previous work of both of them, was to establish the University of Birmingham's School of Education as an internationally reputed centre for teacher training and research in religious education, attracting research students from all over the world.

It was Grimmitt's contribution which was the major creative influence upon the curriculum development aspect of the work of the 'Birmingham team' as Trevor Cooling calls it (Cooling 1996: 168). His and John Hull's thinking were firmly in the tradition of the person centred liberal ecumenical Christian education of J.H. Oldham in the inter-war period and, in the 1960s, that of J.W.D. Smith, Harold Loukes and Ronald Goldman (cf. Bates 1984, 1986, 1992). As indicated above, it was the rethinking of Christian religious education along experiential and developmental lines by Loukes, Goldman and Smith which, together with Ninian Smart's phenomenological 'religious studies', formed the complementary facets of the Lancaster Secondary RE project's bipolar 'implicit/explicit' religion schema (Schools Council 1971). According to this, RE was to be 'a dialogue with experience and a dialogue with living religions so that the one can interpret and reinforce the other' (Schools Council 1971: 43). It is clear that this formula has strongly influenced Grimmitt's view of the nature of religious education up to the present (cf. Grimmitt 2000: 37–8). In his influential book of 1973, Grimmitt applied the Lancaster schema with changed terminology – 'existential' (personal 'quest for meaning') and 'dimensional' (phenomenological study of religions) – to classroom practice (Grimmitt 1973: Chapters 5 and 6). The 'existential' aspect was deeply informed by the 'new theology' and especially Paul Tillich's language of 'depth' and 'ultimacy'.

This was developed further in his work with Garth Read on the 'Christians Today' project at Westhill RE Centre in which the 'learning from' and 'learning about' distinction was first mooted (cf. Grimmitt and Read 1977: 7–8). It was also in his work on this project that he formulated his view of education as 'a process by, in and through which pupils may begin to explore what it is, and what it means to be human' (ibid. 20). In an essay published in 1982, it is clear that this human development focus of education is intended in part as a means of ameliorating the 'antipathy' of the ethnic minority religious communities, especially Muslims, 'towards the current stress on objectivity and openness in RE' (Grimmitt 1982: 140). He also expresses the view that 'other theological perspectives' (ibid. 141) than 1960s radical theology were necessary in order for the approach to be acceptable to these communities. The outcome of this second phase development was a rationale for multifaith RE which would be made acceptable to the major faith communities by basing it on the common ground of human development and avoiding any very overt Christian theological underpinning. 'Ultimate questions' however, retained distinctly Tillichian overtones.

Grimmitt develops his thinking fully in a major study which was primarily written to advocate the contribution of religious education to personal, social and moral education (Grimmitt 1987). In this, he outlines a revised bipolar curriculum strategy based around the interaction of 'Shared Human Experience' and 'Traditional Belief Systems'. It is the 'ultimate questions' of meaning and value arising from the former that have allegedly given rise to the beliefs and values of the latter. These 'ultimate questions' form the basis of the 'Adolescent life-world curriculum' which is intended to interact with the 'Religious life-world curriculum' which shows how five world faiths respond to these questions (ibid. Part 2: 267–388). However, RE is not simply 'learning about' religion; much more importantly, it is 'learning from' religion, that is 'what pupils learn from their studies in religion about themselves – about discerning ultimate questions and 'signals of transcendence' in their own experience and how they might respond to them' (ibid. 225). The overriding aim of the whole process is the pupils' personal development or their 'humanization' (cf. ibid. Chapter 2 and 230ff.) and the selection of curriculum content in RE should be determined by how far it facilitates this process. In order to achieve this:

> subject matter must be chosen which has the potentiality for reflection on, and re-evaluation and re-interpretation of the self . . . what is studied (and how it is studied) must have the capacity to prompt young people to ask: 'Who am I?'
>
> (ibid. 206)

The impartial role of the teacher is also emphasized by Grimmitt: 'Despite their title, "religious" educators are essentially "secular" educators concerned with the educational value of studying religion' (ibid. 258).

That John Hull shared this broad approach was clear early on in his work on the Birmingham Agreed Syllabus of 1975. As he writes in an article published in the year of the syllabus's publication, it incorporates alongside the study of religions and secular humanism an 'existential' aspect 'in that at each point an attempt is made to relate the material studied to the pupil's life' (Hull 1984: 114). His commitment to it became even more explicit later when he writes of the need for pupils to 'learn from religion in ways which will enrich them and deepen their humanity' (Hull 1982: xv). Most recently his support is further confirmed in his outline and discussion of the

Gift to the Child project on which he worked together with Michael Grimmitt and a team of teacher fellows (Hull 2000). In this, he writes that, reversing the common view that the purpose of RE was to enhance the children's understanding of religion, the team felt that 'the purpose of religious education was to make a contribution to the human and educational development of the child. . . . The end was the development of the child; the means was the study of religion' (ibid. 114).

Although this 'instrumental' view of the study of religion (Grimmitt 2000: 34) has not been without its critics (see the critical discussion below), the work of the 'Birmingham team' has had a major impact upon the theory and practice of religious education in the UK and other countries from the 1970s into the present. The 1980s however also saw multifaith RE faced with strong criticism, the proponents of which commanded political support within government circles. The culmination of this was the 1988 Education Reform Act and the debates surrounding it and subsequent government publications, notably DfE Circular 1/94.

The 1988 Education Reform Act

Although the 1988 Education Reform Act has strengthened the position of religious education in schools in England and Wales, the early stages of its preparation and its final wording were fraught with controversy. Prominent in this was its explicit mention of the central place of Christianity in both religious education (Section 8:3) and school worship (Section 7).These clauses were the result of pressure from a small but politically influential group of people who felt that Christianity was being sidelined in religious education practice and who opposed many of the features of multifaith religious education. They sought a return to a traditional nurturing model of religious education focused on Christianity, the religion of English cultural heritage, and to get rid of approaches to religious education and worship which included material from several religions (e.g. thematic teaching). The effect of such approaches, it was claimed, was confusion or 'mishmash' (cf. Hull 1991b). Since little seemed to change in the period immediately after 1988 because of ambiguities in the wording of the Act and widespread professional resistance, an attempt was made by this 'small and unrepresentative group of militant Christians' (Hull 1998: 119), to secure their objectives by directives from the DFE, notably Circular 1/94, and by arranging for the writing of 'model syllabuses' for the guidance of Local Education Authorities by the different faith groups under the auspices of the Schools Curriculum and Assessment Authority (SCAA).

John Hull's editorials in the *British Journal of Religious Education* (cf. Hull 1998: Chapter 3) and his articles and booklets (Hull 1989, 1991b, 1996a) were vociferous in their criticisms of the aims and policies of this pressure group and much of his time and energy was devoted to campaigning against them during the late 1980s and early 1990s. Such thinking, he argues, reflects a concern for the maintenance of the purity and integrity of the individual religions – especially Christianity – and the need to maintain that by teaching each faith separately and (ideally) only to the appropriate faith groups. Such an approach would lead to 'a sort of spiritual apartheid ... organised like a series of isolation wards' (Hull 1998: 116). In Hull's view, the 'horror of mish-mash is the horror of a threatened identity' (ibid. 117); however, he argues, 'Religious education must play its part in widening identity from the tribe and from the nation to all that is truly human' (ibid.).

He took this theme further in his response to Department for Education (DfE) Circular 1/94 in which he identified a 'theology of the DfE' which was characterized by careful separation of the religions and the predominance of Christianity 'which is to be regarded as the heritage of this country' (ibid. 125), with the implication that the members of other faith groups 'are not to regard themselves as part of this country's heritage' (ibid.). John Hull describes this divisive theology as 'religionism' – 'an adherence to a particular religion which involves the identity of the adherent so as to support tribalistic or nationalistic solidarity' (ibid. 55). He affirms his own position unequivocally: 'The United Kingdom belongs to all its people. Every man, woman and child, whatever his or her religion, is part of this country's ongoing heritage' (ibid. 126).

In view of his strong views on worship during the 1970s, Hull's treatment of the section (7:1) of the Act which required collective worship in schools to be 'wholly or mainly of a broadly Christian character' is predictably critical. In 1989 he felt that the Act's requirements may be 'unworkable' but all involved should 'try to make the best of it' (ibid. 142). In 1990, he tried to do this by stressing the educational character of collective worship (ibid. 143ff.). In 1995, he held that section 7 is 'deeply flawed' and should 'go' (ibid. 154), suggesting that schools should instead be 'required to hold acts of collective spirituality' (ibid.) supportive of the 1988 Act's requirement that education should contribute to the 'spiritual' development of children (for a recent critique of John Hull's case against school worship see Felderhof 1999 and 2000). Hull's work as campaigning editor and writer was enormously important in successfully limiting the religionists' influence.

Among John Hull's other significant contributions to the progress of RE at this time was his small but surprisingly influential booklet entitled *God-talk with Young Children* which he describes as an 'anecdotal study' (Hull 1991: 6). In this, he recounts and analyses conversations about God with his own children with a view to showing their ability to use and discuss religious concepts at an earlier age than syllabuses and curriculum materials written under the influence of earlier interpretations of Piagetian developmental theory allowed. This has been a stimulus for the emergence of the notion of 'children's theology' in Germany (see Chapter 12 below) and is cited as an exemplar for dialogical methodology in Russian schools (see

Chapter 15 below). During the 1990s, he also initiated a project based in the University of Birmingham School of Education, aiming to develop models of Islamic education utilizing methods which would accord more closely with commonly accepted British and European educational theory and practice but on clearly Islamic foundations – the Qur'an and Hadith (Sahin 2000). On the administrative front, he played a key role in the setting up in 1993 of the National Association of Standing Advisory Councils of Religious Education (NASACRE) to enable representatives of the local SACREs, given new powers under the 1988 Education Reform Act (cf. Taylor 1991), to meet together to discuss common problems with leading educationists. NASACRE celebrated its tenth anniversary in 2003 (cf. Hull 2003).

Blindness and the theology of disability

John Hull's writings on his experience of blindness have seen him emerge as a brilliant creative writer. His powerful and moving autobiographical writings (Hull 1990, 1997) have deepened sighted people's understanding and awareness of how the blind experience the world as well as inspiring blind people throughout the world by his indomitable spirit – *Touching the Rock* (1990) was translated into seven languages and was published in Australian and American editions; its second edition *On Sight and Insight* (1997) was translated into two further languages. That spirit saw him fighting and overcoming the limitations imposed by his blindness to the extent of his being appointed the first ever professor of religious education in an English university in 1989 and assuming the demanding administrative role of dean of his faculty in the University of Birmingham for three and a half years from 1990.

Coming to terms with his disability religiously and theologically was a long and difficult process. As a person who was blind, he became aware as never before of the negative images associated with blindness and the blind in the Bible, especially in its use of the images of darkness and blindness for the forces of evil and lack of faith. Hull asks why, for example, Jesus called the religious leaders of his day 'blind fools' and 'blind guides' and comments 'Yes, I know that you only meant it metaphorically, but it is not very nice to be regarded as a metaphor for sin and unbelief' (Hull 2002a: 161). He also questions the clear causal connection in the Bible between sin and unbelief and blindness. He finally finds comfort in Jesus's own experience of blindness when he was blindfolded and taunted after his arrest, thus sharing something of the experience of being a 'blind fool'; this leads Hull to acknowledge that his 'questions are silenced. You have become a partner in my world, one who shares my condition, my blind brother' (ibid. 170).

John Hull goes on to outline the elements of a 'theology of blindness' which he describes as 'a theology of states or conditions' similar to feminist and black theologies. This would include the exposure and denunciation of

the negative imagery flowing from the sighted world; a positive interpretation of the metaphor of blindness for 'the characteristics of the life of faith';
and a revised, more inclusive notion of 'normality' which would lead to a
critique of other forms of exclusion, especially that of the poor by the rich
(ibid. 177). Hull not only wrote about blindness but took positive steps to
improve the quality of life of all people with disabilities. In 1992 he was a
founder of 'Ability Net' an organization dedicated to providing computer
assistance to the disabled. He also initiated the 'Cathedrals through Touch
and Hearing' project which placed large models of English cathedrals inside
them to enable the blind to gain by the use of other senses an impression of
their shape and features. John Hull's inspirational writings on his experience
of blindness and its effect on his life, faith and theology have won him many
friends all over the world and spurred others on to develop greater public
awareness of how those with disabilities see themselves and wish to be seen
and treated by others. Mary Beasley's and Wayne Morris's contributions
below (Chapters 10 and 11) give pointed testimony to this.

Adult Christian education and the money culture

It was John Hull's work on the Christian nurture of children during the
1970s that led him to become interested in the education of Christian
adults. The result was his book *What Prevents Christian Adults from Learning?*
(1985, 1991) which he describes as an 'essay in practical theology' (Hull
1991: xi). Although we will not dwell in detail on its contents here, this is a
significant book first because it signals a shift of orientation in Hull's thinking towards a deeper examination of the social and ideological context of
adult learning, religion and education; and second because its preparation
and continued intensive reading in the social sciences after its publication
led him to insights which were to transform his thinking and enrich his
understanding of religion, spirituality and education. The key to this new
perspective was his reading of *Capital*, and in particular Karl Marx's theory
that it was the economic base of a society which generated its cultural
'superstructure' including to a large extent though not totally, the nature
and form of its religion and spirituality (Hull 1996, 1996a, 1997a). He
argues that *Capital* 'is the most sustained example of justice enquiry in the
social science literature, and . . . deals with money as the supreme enigma of
modernity' (Hull 1997: 23); it therefore becomes 'a suggestive resource for
the Christian educator' (ibid. 22).

The consequences of this are acknowledged in his preface to the American
edition of *What Prevents Christian Adults from Learning?* (1991). In this, he
frankly states how further reading and reflection have led him beyond the
position he adopted in the 1985 edition in which, despite an awareness of
ideology, 'the main focus of the educational analysis was still thought of as
being religious consciousness' (ibid. vi). He had come to the more radical
awareness that the 'conditions of late capitalism' and the money culture

which is intrinsic to it, have 'contaminated' Christian spirituality and theology with a 'false consciousness' (ibid. vii); the outcome is that religious experience and theology have become 'reifications' of the ideology of the money culture. In a lecture delivered in Edinburgh in 1996, he argues that 'in the United States, God is worshipped as money; in Europe, money is worshipped as God' (Hull 1996: 6) and it is necessary for all adults to understand the 'self deception' and 'unconscious distortion' which the money god induces. An obvious example of this is the 'prosperity gospel' in which increasing wealth and prosperity are seen as rewards for piety.

It is also evident in spirituality which has 'social origins . . . rooted in the concrete and material forms of our community life' (Hull 1996c: 35). Liberal capitalism produced 'the liberal individualistic type of spirituality' which is essentially a spirituality of self gratification characterized by a focus on inner feelings – for example, experience of the numinous and transcendent – which 'insulates the churchgoer . . . from confrontation with social reality' and thwarts 'the spirituality of justice and freedom' (Hull 1997a: 29). Hull rejects the traditional distinction between the 'spiritual' and the 'material' and also the 'aestheticisation' of spirituality which he describes as a 'pursuit of the refined classes'. He calls for an 'incarnational model of spirituality' – the 'materialisation of spirituality' (Hull 1999: 294) an 'embodied spirituality . . . which responds to human need and promotes human solidarity' (Hull 1996c: 42). With reference to education, he argues that: 'Spiritual education is that education which seeks to inspire children and young people to work for others . . . It is focused upon achieving a transformation of life in the direction of mutuality and sharing' (Hull 1999: 295).

Returning to adult Christian education in the west, Hull sees the task as one of 'illumination', removing the illusion brought about by the false consciousness created by the money culture. This is to be accomplished by rediscovering the values of 'the new society in the teaching of Jesus . . . the kingdom of God' (Hull 1997: 27) using the Bible as the major resource. In recent writings, he argues that the political power which accompanies economic power and produces imperialism and nationalism has also led to a false consciousness and self deception in theology. He illustrates this in the geo-political factors which led to the formation of the 'power theology of Europe' (Hull 2002: 17) and the nationalist and imperialist assumptions inherent in the theology behind the hymns of Isaac Watts (Hull 2002b, 2005). In its historical development the Christian movement was 'gradually transformed from a theology of sacrificial service into a theology of power and domination' (Hull 2002: 4) and the residue of this survives today in western Christianity. The task of adult Christian education is to sensitize people to this false consciousness by reference to Biblical teaching and 'theologies which have emerged from suffering and oppression' (ibid. 17). As will be seen below, Hull has recently brought these perspectives to bear on the role of European Christian churches in relation to religious education in certain countries in the contemporary period.

The work of John Hull: critical perspectives

No one person has had more influence on the development and promotion of religious education in virtually all of its aspects in the UK and internationally over the past thirty years of significant social, religious and educational change than John Hull.

His great achievement in the UK is to have been the thinker who led the movement to bring religious education into the mainstream of educational thought and practice by convincing many other leading educationists and large numbers of the predominantly Christian body of RE teachers that a secular, multifaith approach to RE in state schools was consistent with Christian theological principles. He achieved this at a time when the radical theology of the 1960s was still influential both among RE teachers and in the Christian Education Movement in which he became prominent. He transformed the CEM journal, the *British Journal of Religious Education*, over the twenty-five years of his editorship (1971–96), from a modest medium for the discussion of issues in (mainly) British religious education into an international academic journal.

On the international front, his joint creation of ISREV and his continuing secretaryship of the organization has contributed greatly to international professional dialogue, a broadening of perspectives and valuable co-operative research. Coupled with his outstanding work on his experience of blindness and the theologies of disability and the money culture for which he has also received international acclaim, he has shown himself to be a theologian and educationist of rare enterprise and distinction. Most recently, the Faculty of Psychology and Education of the Free University of Amsterdam has nominated him for the award in October 2005 of an honorary doctorate for 'exceptional academic achievements in the field of religious education, in particular [his] pioneering elaboration worldwide of a concept of interreligious education in public schools in theory and practice' (from the letter notifying John Hull of his award).

The critical discussion which follows focuses on Hull's and the 'Birmingham team's' work in religious education although in such a short space, treatment even of this has to be selective. John Hull's theologies of disability, the money culture and European power politics are still very much in process of maturation and await proper evaluation at a later time. However, as has been shown above, the changing emphases and insights of his theology as it has developed through his traumatic experience of total blindness and his realization of the full implications of Marx's theory of the economic base of cultural production has affected all areas of his thinking including religious education.

A few brief observations might be made at this point about some of the critical problems raised by Hull's theology. As with the many theologies which have drawn upon secular and/or non-Christian thought, it is a perennial matter of debate as to whether their substance and inspiration lies in the secular rather than the religious sources; and to what extent, if any, the integrity of Christian faith is compromised. John Hull's theology is orthodox but radical in its constant resort to the Biblical sources and its relative lack of reference to credal and historical authority. It probably belongs to Hans Frei's type three theology (Frei 1992) in which, according to David Ford, 'All sorts of philosophies or worldviews might help in doing Christian theology.' (Ford 1999: 27) and which, as Ford points out, is characterized by dialogue and correlation between Christian and other worldviews. John Hull's hermeneutic lies at the heart of this debate and there is interesting research to be undertaken here.

With regard to religious education, his contribution both individually and as a member of the 'Birmingham team' to its theory and practice has inevitably drawn criticism as well as support from his peers. John Hull and Michael Grimmitt have been among the leading figures weaning religious education away from its Christian nurturing past and both have seen a good measure of success; but John Hull's radicalism, particularly with regard to school worship, has often met with determined resistance. His notion of 'critical openness' and his strong affirmation of the secularity of RE were important in establishing the credentials of the subject in the educational community and thus elevating the status of RE; but they were not acceptable to many conservative Christians or to some in the ethnic minority religious communities for whom the open critical discussion of their faith was not culturally acceptable. Michael Grimmitt, as has been seen above, felt it necessary to move the foundations of multifaith RE onto more consensual ground and to give his 'learning from', pupil centred strategy a less overtly Christian theological rationale. Despite claims for the secularity of the subject, RE was never going to be thoroughly secularized (cf. Hull 1975: Chapter 4) in a situation in which the churches and, formally after 1988, the other major religious communities, were directly involved in the monitoring and development of RE syllabuses through SACREs and Agreed Syllabus conferences.

The Lancaster Schools Council project's 'implicit'/'explicit' religion framework, translated by Michael Grimmitt and others into the bipolar curriculum strategies outlined above, was able to accommodate both a religiously pluralistic educational approach and, through its liberal theological rationale, child centred religious nurturing elements. This has enabled it, in its changing forms, to dominate curriculum development in RE since the 1970s. There is no question that the broad framework of subject orientated and child orientated work which it has provided has given the subject the flexibility to incorporate various teaching styles and lesson content. It has given rise to much good religious education but the often complex, supposedly interactive curriculum programmes which, in its various forms, it has produced in agreed syllabuses and textbooks over the past thirty years have not always been perceived to cohere in practice and have often not been properly understood, particularly by non-specialist teachers. One result of this has been 'multi-fact RE' (Grimmitt 1987: 137) at one end of the spectrum and rather vapid thematic work at the other.

To a large extent, the problem lay in the secular theological premises which underpinned the schema both in its earlier and more recent forms and in relation to primary as well as secondary religious education (Bates 1992a). Those premises reflect 1960s radical secular theology (strongly informed by Paul Tillich's thought) which saw reflection 'in depth' on ordinary experience as leading to religious concepts and doctrines and (the aspect emphasized in Grimmitt's modified rationale of 1987) religious beliefs as constituting the answers humankind had formulated to the 'ultimate questions' about life's meaning and purpose arising from reflection 'in depth' on human life experience. The schema under consideration attempted to replicate these processes which in fact embody quite sophisticated adult religious experience (cf. Sealey 1985: 52ff.), in both primary schools and secondary schools. It did this by relating 'depth' themes to 'dimensional' themes (Grimmitt 1973) and later, by raising 'ultimate questions' with pupils through the units based on 'shared human experience' constituting the 'adolescent life world curriculum' (Grimmitt 1987: 272ff.) and relating these to the 'religious life-world curriculum'.

This 'learning from' aspect asked young people to work out answers to the 'ultimate questions' for themselves and then, introducing them to the various religious 'answers', asked them, through 'personal evaluation' and quite intense introspection (ibid. 226–8) involving the asking of 'autobiographical questions' (Grimmitt 2000: 35), to relate them to their own lives. This process has been described by Grimmitt as: 'to evaluate their understanding of religion in personal terms and evaluate their understanding of self in religious terms' (Grimmitt 1987: 213). In his earlier essay, Grimmitt describes this as 'the conscious reconstruction of self' (Grimmitt 1982: 144). Some have felt that behind what is justified as an open educational process engaged in 'human development' lies an essentially apologetic intention which seeks to commend the religious answers or at least to direct attention to them and to make sure, perhaps rather too intensely and intrusively, that pupils consider them in relation to their own lives. Grimmitt concedes that this may be open to the objection that it represents RE as 'a form of psychotherapy' (ibid.). In the absence of non-religious philosophical 'answers', it also has the appearance of a kind of religious nurture.

Religious educationists who are concerned to establish the academic credentials of RE vis-à-vis other curriculum subjects have expressed unease about the human development/learning from model. Thus, Robert Jackson, whilst welcoming the concern to engage the pupil, argues that 'the danger remains that a selection of material from a religion based on a theoretical framework imposed from outside it can result in a portrayal that adherents and specialist scholars alike regard as a distortion' (Jackson 1990: 112); and Peter Doble points out that there is no parallel to 'learning from' in other academic subjects and wonders whether it 'encourages the isolation (diminishment?) of RE?' (Doble 2001: 130).

The culmination of the curriculum development work of the 'Birmingham team' was the *Gift to the Child* project (Grimmitt *et al.* 1991), which adopts a new and imaginative strategy for introducing young children to religions (cf. Hans Streib's essay Chapter 13 below). The project puts aside the old bipolar structures and recognizes that: 'the direct study of religious content can encourage pupils to address significant questions of personal experience' (Grimmitt 2000: 37). However, it still retains the team's characteristic concern to make the child engage with religion in a personal way through the 'reflection' phase. It is seen to be through this process that the children will receive 'gifts' for their own personal development, including, in the case of 'believing children', to 'affirm them in their faith' (ibid. 37). Grimmitt sees this as embodying 'the concept of learning from religion [which] is the essential educational device which enables pupils to apply and personalise their learning about religion and religions to their own lives' (ibid. 38). The Birmingham team's contribution to curriculum development in RE has been outstanding and the 'learning about and learning from' strategy has been widely adopted (cf. Chapters 16–17 below); but, as the *Gift to the Child* project shows, there are other ways of applying the 'learning from' aspect which leave more initiative to the pupil and do not utilize a methodology with such apologetic theological associations.

This is also demonstrated by Robert Jackson's and his colleagues' work at the University of Warwick which draws its theory and methodology from social anthropology and relates it to classroom practice through materials derived from a detailed research programme. His and his colleagues' ethnographic studies of the lives of children from the major religious communities have been embodied in the materials of the Warwick RE Project which are intended for key stages 1–3 – children aged five to fourteen (Jackson 1997; cf. also Jackson 2000). Jackson argues that 'structured opportunities for reflection' are provided for pupils encountering through these materials the beliefs, practices and values of others. He contends that the 'activity of grasping another's way of life is inseparable in practice from pondering on the issues and questions raised by it' (Jackson 1997: 130ff.). Such 'pondering' or 'reflection' can lead to Rorty's (1980) notion of 'edification' – 'to be taken out of one's self'. Jackson continues: 'Through the challenge of "unpacking" another worldview, one can, in a sense, become a new person' (ibid. 130–1). This notion is similar to, but not identical with, 'learning from' (ibid. 132; cf. also Jackson 2000; 135); it arises from the application of the interpretive methods of ethnographic research to children's learning in religious education which involves both interchange of worldview and reflection on difference; and *may* lead to 'edification'. The best active learning methods typical of good thematic methodology in primary schools also lead to pupil involvement and varieties of expressive work which promote personal development (Bates 1992a).

Turning now specifically to John Hull; his most trenchant critics come from various standpoints within more conservative and theologically traditional Christian circles. Of these, Trevor Cooling's is by far the most detailed critique. Cooling, from an evangelical Christian, critical realist perspective attacks what he sees as the 'liberal ideal of rational autonomy, critical rationality, or critical openness' (Cooling 1994: 17) and its embodiment in the 'radical Christian liberalism' (ibid. 67) espoused by John Hull and Michael Grimmitt. His essential criticism of Hull is that his theology of education has effectively adopted the premises of rationalist philosophy (ibid. Chapter 4) which inevitably makes it intolerant of conservative Christianity and theological positions such as 'religionism'. He illustrates this intolerance from Hull's discussion in his book *What Prevents Christian Adults from Learning?* of the problems faced by adult Christians who find themselves baffled by the clash they perceive between their Christian beliefs and contemporary culture. Such people 'retreat into the safety of orthodoxy to protect their beliefs against decreasing plausibility rather than to respond to the challenge of learning generated by living in the modern world' (ibid. 11). Cooling claims that this condition of 'learning sickness' or 'ideological enclosure' as John Hull calls it, is equivalent to his later notion of 'religionism' which protects itself from the contamination of other faiths and worldviews by withdrawing into its own 'tribalistic' havens or enclaves. Rather than tolerating this 'ideological enclosure' or 'religionism' as one possible religious stance alongside others, Hull effectively declares war on it by advocating 'anti-religionist education' (ibid. 12). This antagonism, Cooling argues, effectively contradicts the liberal claim 'to be non-confessional and sympathetic to pluralism' (ibid. 15).

A further important criticism of liberal religious education advanced by Trevor Cooling is its 'theology of pluralism'. Again, he traces what he calls John Hull's 'universal, monotheistic faith' (ibid. 33) back to *What Prevents Christian Adults from Learning?* Utilizing Richard Niebuhr's description of three types of religious consciousness found in the modern world – Polytheism, Henotheism and Monotheism (Niebuhr 1960) – Hull writes of 'the universalist drive within Christianity' and argues that 'Christian adults are to be helped to move away from divided loyalty (polytheism) and limited tribalistic loyalty (henotheism) into the true monotheism of universal faith' (Hull 1985: 38). 'Henotheistic' Christians are religionists; 'monotheistic' Christians are people who have framed a theology which embraces 'all life and all being' (ibid. 36). With regard to the relativism of this universal faith (Cooling ibid. 33–4), Cooling cites the parable of the elephant and the blind men as typifying the liberal view that 'each religion has a true but partial insight into the nature of God' (ibid. 34) and John Hick's notion that each religion is a different culturally determined interpretation of a common religious experience (ibid. 35). The problem as Cooling sees it is that 'this theology of pluralism is not compatible with traditional forms of belief which see Christianity as uniquely true' (ibid. 34).

In a later publication, Cooling, writing of John Hull's and Michael Grimmitt's protests that the SCAA model syllabuses, which were drawn up under government direction, were an attempt to assert the faith communities' ownership of the material and were motivated by 'religionism', criticizes, both in this case and in the *Gift to the Child* materials, the elevation of the interests of education and children's personal development over the religious communities' right to represent their faiths in ways they choose (Cooling 1996). He regards it as 'unhelpful for secular educators to treat the content offered by the religions as booty to be raided and used for whatever purposes are deemed fit by them' (ibid. 180), advocating in another publication a 'content structured' and 'pupil related' rather than a 'pupil structured' approach (Cooling 2000: 163).

Writing from a critical realist, orthodox (though not evangelical) Christian standpoint, Andrew Wright, in a book published a year before that of Cooling (Wright 1993) also mounts a strong attack on aspects of the liberal religious education of the post-1970s period. Many of Cooling's criticisms are identical with those of Wright but seem to be independently conceived because no reference is made to Wright's work. However, Wright does not undertake the detailed critical analysis of both members of the 'Birmingham team' which Cooling offers. Indeed, in his highly generalized critique of 1993 (cf. also Wright 2000) he studiously avoids naming the exponents of the allegedly flawed liberal orthodoxy and, in a very limited bibliography, lists only Michael Grimmitt's book of 1987. In Wright's 1998 ISREV paper however, he includes specific criticisms of the work of John Hull.

Using terminology different from that of Trevor Cooling but meaning much the same thing, he sees a 'universal generic notion of religion' (Wright 2001: 209) as implicit within John Hull's counter attack on Baroness Cox's 'mishmash' criticism (Hull 1991b). Wright is also critical of what he, like Cooling, sees as Hull's illiberal attack on 'religionism': 'it fails to attend to the diversity of possible religious representations and in particular does not allow non-liberal representations a fair hearing' (Wright 2001: 210). In the more generalized critique of 2000, he contends that the dominant 'experiential/expressive' liberal model of religious education as he calls it, reflects a 'universal theology' according to which the great world faiths are based on a common universal religious experience of which they are all different but 'equally valid expressions' (Wright 2000: 172).

He contrasts this view with his own critical realist notion which sees the major faiths as each claiming to have received the revelation of eternal truths which in the case of some faiths inevitably involves them in being dogmatic and illiberal. For Wright, liberal religious education with its 'bracketing out truth claims ... carries with it the implication that realistic truth is not central to the concerns of believers' (Wright 2001: 208). Wright illustrates the stance of critical realism on this matter with reference to the case study of trinitarian Christianity in his 'Spiritual Education Project': 'The spiritual resources of Trinitarian Christianity begin not with inner subjectivity but with the objective reality of God, Father, Son and Holy Spirit' (Wright 2000: 175).

There can be no doubt that John Hull's thinking does bear the mark of several aspects of the liberal RE stereotype which both Cooling and Wright outline; but neither of them does full justice to his distinctive position which is radical rather than liberal. Thus, Hull recognizes the authority and inspiration of all of the world faiths ('They are to be treated in the full beauty of their holiness without trivialisation and invidious comparison' (Hull 1991b: 43), and it is clear both from this quotation and from his *Gift to the Child* essay that he has a belief in their shared quality of holiness. Rudolph Otto's concept of the 'numinous' is very much part of his and his colleagues' thinking (Hull 2000: 115); thus, he defines the 'numena' which are the focus of the project's materials as religious elements 'charged with the sacred beauty of faith and thus offering to the child something of the numinous' (ibid.). However, a caveat must be entered here; as we have seen above, John Hull also sees the 'liberal individualistic type of spirituality' embodying numinous and mystical experience as inferior to 'the spirituality of justice and freedom' which for him is the spirituality of the Kingdom of God.

Cooling and Wright are also correct in their contention that something resembling a 'universal monotheistic faith' or 'generic notion of religion' does figure in John Hull's thought, but they do not represent it fully or accurately enough. It has nothing to do with universal affective religious experience but with New Testament eschatology. In his inaugural lecture as professor of religious education in 1991, Hull affirms (citing Luke 6: 6–11) that the focus of the interest of 'the prophet from Nazareth' is not the beliefs and customs of religion but human life: 'the vision of a religion in the service of all humanity, a humanity which would transcend the distinctions between tribalized religions and which would lead eventually to a new kingdom' (Hull 1991c: 20). This 'universal/generic religion' finds further expression in *Mishmash*. In the light of Paul's teaching in Ephesians and Galatians, Hull affirms, 'the new humanity in Christ Jesus looks for the metaphorical or the spiritual in all literal religious traditions and does not become engrossed in the distinctions between Christianity and Judaism' (Hull 1991b: 41). Clearly, there is an embryonic theology of religions here although Hull never fully articulates such a theology; but it does not conform to Cooling's or Wright's liberal stereotypes. It is a vision of a coming faith which fulfils Jesus's teaching on the kingdom of God, embraces all humanity and transcends the religions as we know them. It is John Hull's fervent belief in the urgent need for the realization of this escha-tological vision that underlies most of what he writes and which partly lies behind his passionate attack on religionism.

Andrew Wright's own model of spiritual and religious education has at its heart a rigorous critical evaluation of the orthodox credal forms of actual religions and philosophies, taking full account of the (mainly doctrinal) differences within and between them and aiming at the achievement of 'religious literacy'. A central focus of the concerns of both Cooling and Wright is with the realistic portrayal of institutional religions (and in Wright's case, secular philosophies) and their not always liberal doctrines, beliefs and self understandings. John Hull has also been concerned with the accurate portrayal of religions and acknowledges that: 'It is certainly possible to interpret religious traditions in intolerant and exclusivist ways'; however, he adds, 'in a society like ours where the creation of tolerance and understanding must be rated as an important social goal, it seems unwise to take the risk' (Hull 1991b: 43). As can be seen in Robert Jackson's discussion (Chapter 2 below; cf. also Jackson 2004: Chapter 5), Wright sees any such social objectives as both unnecessary and threatening to the integrity of religious education. The attainment of 'religious literacy' is all that is necessary.

It is clear that both Cooling and Wright are focused upon certain present valued institutional and doctrinal realities of religions and philosophies – and especially Christianity. For John also, these are the greater part of what religious education should be about and are to be 'taken with full seriousness since they are part of the history that shapes the world' (Hull 1991b: 43); but through and beyond 'children and their faiths [living and learning] side by side' lies the 'building up of a new earth' (ibid.) which for John is the 'new humanity' of the 'kingdom of God'. Visionary perhaps but a vision which is at the heart of Judaeo-Christian and Islamic (cf. Chapter 10 below) hope and expectation and which, together with his Biblical grounding and theological justification of his notion of critical openness, is accorded no critical attention by either Cooling or Wright. It would seem that both of these Christian religious educationists fail to acknowledge the roots of Hull's proposed universal faith in the central conception of the teaching of Jesus. For many Christians, this is more central to their faith than the creeds.

It is the visionary, even prophetic character and quality of John Hull's thinking which marks him out from all other religious educationists of his generation in the UK. The penetrating directness and honesty of his writings took the somewhat staid world of UK religious education by storm during the 1970s and 80s and it is questionable as to whether the English ecclesiastical establishment has ever quite forgiven him for his criticisms of *The Fourth R* (1970) in *School Worship: an Obituary* (1975) and his argument for the abolition of school worship in state (community) schools. Hull's background in the decidedly non-deferential and plain-speaking social and cultural ethos of Australia and his strongly Protestant formative years in the Australian Methodist Church and the English Congregational/United Reformed Church may go some way to explain the fact that his notion of Christianity has no vestige of establishment mentality with the deference and compromise that this often entails. As he put it in his first editorial in *Learning for Living* in March 1971: 'Christians in education are not there to advance their own cause or to win selfish recognition for their own faith. They are there to serve.' (Hull 1998: 6). This conviction continues to be central to John Hull's thinking as can be seen in one of his most recent articles which illustrates his continued lively challenge to the status quo.

For him, the days of a Christian hegemony, however liberal, in state education in the UK and in other increasingly pluralistic and secular European societies should be over. The Christian churches no longer hold the positions of power and influence in society that they once did and which often corrupted their social and political consciousness and their theology. Together with other faiths and philosophies of life, they are now in a 'market place of educational ideas in modern Europe' (Hull 2004: 17–18). In a Europe 'come of age' (ibid. 17) a purely secular education is 'possible, plausible and viable' (ibid.) and the Christian churches and other major faiths have to show the 'value and relevance' (ibid. 18) of any contribution they have to make. The future lies in the various faiths rejecting 'narrow, tribalistic forms of religion' and becoming 'partners in humanization' (ibid. 16) or, in Biblical terms, in the 'flourishing' and 'growth' of individuals and communities (ibid. 18). The Christian faith should be 'willing to take up the basin and the towel and be a servant' (ibid. 15)

Not everyone shares this vision of the servant faith quite in John Hull's terms. In countries where certain churches and the state have an historic association, not least the UK, the maintenance of a Christian presence at the centres of power, or a privileged position in the administrative structures supporting religious education in state schools, is still sincerely seen by some as providing a valuable opportunity and surer base for serving the community. Inevitably, however, in times when the major denominational forms of institutional Christianity are suffering drastic decreases in membership and attendance at worship in the UK and in many parts of Europe (cf. Brown 2001; Bruce 2003; Davie 2000, 2002), there will inevitably be suspicions that the retention of legally enshrined rights of access to children in a nation's schools and the maintenance of traditional nurturing approaches – however 'educational' – may have other motivations. It should be recognized, however, that failure to attend churches need not be an indication that their presence in society is not esteemed. In many societies, not least the UK, the role of the churches in education may be perceived, for various reasons, as one of their most valued contributions. The relation between nations and their churches in Europe is complex. For example, in the highly secularized societies of Norway and Sweden in which low levels of church going and belief are combined with high levels of membership and financial support of the Lutheran state churches; 'belonging without believing' (Davie 2000, 2002) is more evident than 'believing without belonging' (Davie 1994).

In Germany, religious education in the schools of most states is still conceived as initiation into the Protestant or Roman Catholic faiths and some German educationists see this as also being in principle extendable to other faiths, notably Islam. The adoption of an open, critical approach to such religious education together with the development of dialogic methodology and 'inter-religious education' are seen by Karl Ernst Nipkow as guarding against indoctrination and offering a preferable model of response to religious pluralism to the multifaith approach adopted in England and Wales (cf. Chapter 6 below, Nipkow 1996 and Ziebertz 2003). John Hull sees the influence exerted by the churches in Germany and other countries as inhibiting the development of a broader RE curriculum which could, under secular educational control, more adequately meet the educational needs of pupils in religiously pluralist and secular societies (Hull 2005a). His support for the state of Brandenburg in taking control of religious education in its state schools and introducing a syllabus in world religions and ethics (cf. Hull 1998: 1 and 2005a; also Nipkow 1996) has caused some controversy. This debate is likely to continue for some time to come.

Although John Hull's peers inevitably do not always agree with him, few would deny that they have been made to think by his work or that they have come away from it without gaining some fresh insight or ideas. He has by turns inspired, infuriated and confounded his readers and hearers but has never bored them. Addressing John in an open letter, Karl Ernst Nipkow puts it thus: 'your life and your work, your person and your words, are powerful provocations' (Nipkow 2002: 48). There can be no doubt that John Hull's thinking has been the catalyst for the development of fresh ideas and perspectives which have enriched religious education and theology throughout the world. It is sometimes said that people can be judged by the friends they choose; John numbers among his friends people of all shades of theological stance and religious and non-religious allegiance from all continents, all skin colours and both genders. The champion of 'personhood' likes people and people tend to like and respect him even when they disagree with him. His outstanding contribution to religious education and practical theology is rightly celebrated in this festschrift and its editors and contributors together with many other friends and colleagues thank him and hope that he will continue to shock, inspire and provoke them all for many years to come.

References

Astley, J. and Francis, L.J. (eds) (1994) *Critical Perspectives on Christian Education: a reader on the aims, principles and philosophy of Christian education*, Leominster: Fowler Wright Books.

—— (1996) *Christian Theology and Religious Education: Connections and Contradictions*, London: SPCK.

Bates, D.J. (1984) 'Harold Loukes: Christian Educationist 1912–1980', *British Journal of Religious Education*, 6: 132–44.

—— (1986) 'Ecumenism and Religious Education between the Wars: the work of J.H. Oldham', *British Journal of Religious Education*, 8: 130–9.

—— (1992) 'Secularity, Agape and Religious Education – A Critical Appreciation of the Work of J.W.D. Smith', *British Journal of Religious Education*, 14: 132–44.

—— (1992a) 'Developing RE in Topic Based Approaches to Learning', in D. Bastide (ed.) *Good Practice in Primary Religious Education 4–11*, London: The Falmer Press.

British Council of Churches (1976) *The Child in the Church*, London: BCC.

—— (1981) *Understanding Christian Nurture*, London: BCC.

Brown, C.G. (2001) *The Death of Christian Britain: Understanding Secularisation 1800–2000*, London: Routledge.

Bruce, S. (2003) 'The demise of Christianity in Britain', in Grace Davie, Paul Heelas and Linda Woodhead (eds) *Predicting Religion: Mainstream and Margins in the West*, Aldershot: Ashgate.

Cooling, T. (1994) *A Christian Vision for State Education*, London: SPCK.

—— (1996) 'Education is the Point of RE – not Religion? – theological perspectives on the SCAA model syllabuses', in J. Astley and L.J. Francis (eds) *Christian Theology and Religious Education: Connections and Contradictions*, London: SPCK.

—— (2000) 'The Stapleford Project: Theology as the Basis for Religious Education', in M.H. Grimmitt (ed.) *Pedagogies of Religious Education*, Great Wakering, Essex: McCrimmons.

Cox, E. (1966) *Changing Aims in Religious Education*, London: Routledge and Kegan Paul.

Davie, G. (1994) *Religion in Britain Since 1945: Believing Without Belonging*, Oxford: Blackwell.

—— (2000) *European Religion: a Memory Mutates*, Oxford: Oxford University Press.

—— (2002) *Europe: the Exceptional Case. Parameters of Faith in the Modern World*, London: Darton, Longman and Todd.

Doble, P. (2001) Review of P.R. Hobson and J.S. Edwards (eds) *Religious Education in a Plural Society: The Key Philosophical Issues*, London: Woburn Press (1999), *British Journal of Religious Education*, 23: 129–30.

Durham Report, The (1970) *The Fourth R*, London: National Society/SPCK.

Felderhof, M.C. (1999) 'On Understanding Worship in School. Part 1: on schooling and education', *Journal of Beliefs and Values*, 20: 219–30.

—— (2000) 'On Understanding Worship in School. Part 2: on worship and education', *Journal of Beliefs and Values*, 21: 17–26.

Ford, D. (1999) *Theology: a Very Short Introduction*, Oxford: Oxford University Press.

Francis, L.J. and Davies, G. (2002) 'School worship in the primary school: a premature obituary?' *Panorama*, 14: 37–43.

Frei, H.W. (1992) *Types of Christian Theology*, G. Hunsinger and W.C. Placher (eds) Newhaven and London: Yale University Press.

Grimmitt, M.H. (1973) *What Can I Do in RE?*, Great Wakering, Essex: Mayhew McCrimmon.

—— (1982) 'World Religions and Personal Development', in R. Jackson (ed.) *Approaching World Religions*, London: John Murray.

—— (1987) *Religious Education and Human Development: Case Studies in the Research and Development of Good Pedagogic Practice in RE*, Great Wakering, Essex: McCrimmons.

Grimmitt, M.H. *et al.* (1991) *A Gift to the Child: Religious Education in the Primary School*, London: Simon and Schuster.

Grimmitt, M.H. (ed.) (2000) *Pedagogies of Religious Education*, Great Wakering, Essex: McCrimmons.

Grimmitt, M.H. and Read, G.T. (1977) *Teaching Christianity in RE*, Leigh on Sea, Essex: Kevin Mayhew.

Hirst, P.H. (1965) 'Morals, religion and the maintained school', *British Journal of Educational Studies*, 14: 5–18.

—— (1972) 'Christian Education: A Contradiction in Terms', *Learning for Living* 11: 6–11.

—— (1974) *Moral Education in a Secular Society*, London: University of London Press/National Children's Home.

Hull, J.M. (1974) *Hellenistic Magic and the Synoptic Tradition*, London: SCM Press.

—— (1975) *School Worship: an Obituary*, London: SCM Press.

—— (ed.) (1982) *New Directions in Religious Education*, Lewes, Sussex: Falmer Press.

—— (1984) *Studies in Religion and Education*, Lewes, Sussex: Falmer Press.

—— (1985) *What Prevents Christian Adults from Learning?* London: SCM Press; 2nd edn 1991, Philadelphia: Trinity Press International.

—— (1989) *The Act Unpacked: the Meaning of the 1988 Education Reform Act for Religious Education*, Derby: CEM.

—— (1990) *Touching the Rock: an Experience of Blindness*, London: SPCK.

—— (1991) *God-talk With Young Children: Notes for Parents and Teachers*, Derby: CEM.

—— (1991b) *Mishmash: Religious Education in Multi-cultural Britain: a Study in Metaphor*, Derby: CEM.

—— (1991c) *Religion, Education and Madness – a Modern Trinity*, CREDAR lecture series No. 2, Birmingham: University of Birmingham.

—— (1994) 'Critical Openness in Christian Nurture', in J. Astley and L.J. Francis (eds) *Critical Perspectives on Christian Education*, Leominster: Fowler Wright Books.

—— (1996) 'Educational Values in the Money Culture', a paper presented to an education conference, January 1996, CEM, Scotland.

—— (1996a) 'Christian Education in a Capitalist Society: Money and God', in D. Ford and D.L. Stamps (eds) *Essentials of Christian Community: Essays in Honour of Daniel W. Hardy*, Edinburgh: T. and T. Clark.

—— (1996b) 'A Critique of Christian Religionism in Recent British Religious Education', in J. Astley and L.J. Francis (eds) *Christian Theology and Religious Education*, London: SPCK.

—— (1996c) 'The Ambiguity of Spiritual Values', in J.M. Halstead and M. Taylor (eds) *Values in Education and Education in Values*, London: Falmer Press.

—— (1997) *On Sight and Insight*, Oxford: Oneworld.

—— (1997a) 'Karl Marx on Capital: Some Implications for Christian Adult Education', *Modern Believing*, XXXVIII: 22–31.

—— (1998) *Utopian Whispers: Moral, Religious and Spiritual Values in Schools*, London: Religious and Moral Education Press.

—— (1999) 'Spiritual Education, Religion and the Money Culture', in J.C. Conroy (ed.) *Catholic Education Inside-Out/Outside-In*, Dublin: Veritas.

—— (2000) 'Religion in the Service of the Child Project: the Gift Approach to Religious Education', in M.H. Grimmitt (ed.) *Pedagogies of Religious Education*, Great Wakering, Essex: McCrimmons.

—— (2001) *In the Beginning There was Darkness*, London: SCM Press.

—— (2002) 'Practical Theology in Context: The Case of Europe', in W. Gräb and B.Weyel (eds) *Praktische Theologie und Protestantische Kultur*, Gütersloh: Chr: Kaiser/Gütersloh Verlagshaus.

—— (2002a) 'Open Letter from a Blind Disciple to a Sighted Saviour', in M. O'Kane (ed.) *Borders, Boundaries and the Bible*, Sheffield: Sheffield Academic Press.

—— 2002b) 'From Experiential Educator to Nationalist Theologian: the Hymns of Isaac Watts', *Panorama*, 14: 91–106.

—— (2003) 'The National Association of SACREs: An Historical Note', *SACRE News* Special Issue 1993–2003, 2–3, Summer 2003.

—— (2004) 'Practical theology and religious education in a pluralist Europe', *British Journal of Religious Education*, 26: 7–19.

—— (2005) 'Isaac Watts and the Origins of British Imperial Theology', *International Congregational Journal*, 4: 2.

—— (2005a) 'Religious Education in England and Germany: the Recent Work of Hans-Georg Ziebertz', *British Journal of Religious Education*, 27: 5–13.

Jackson, R. (1990) 'Religious Studies and Developments in Religious Education in England and Wales', in U. King (ed.) *Turning Points in Religious Studies*, Edinburgh: T. and T. Clark.

—— (1997) *Religious Education: an interpretive approach*, London: Hodder and Stoughton.

—— (2000) 'The Warwick Religious Education Project; the Interpretive Approach to Religious Education', in M. Grimmitt (ed.) *Pedagogies of Religious Education*, Great Wakering, Essex: McCrimmons.

—— (2004) *Rethinking Religious Education and Plurality: Issues in diversity and pedagogy*, London and New York: RoutledgeFalmer.

Niebuhr, H. Richard (1960) *Radical Monotheism and Western Culture, with Supplementary Essays*, New York: RoutledgeFalmer.

Nipkow, K.E. (1996) 'Pluralism, Theology and Education: a German Perspective', in J. Astley and L.J. Francis (eds) *Christian Theology and Religious Education*, London: SPCK.

—— (2002) 'Importance of Personal Bridges', *Panorama* 14: 45–8.

Rorty, R. (1980) *Philosophy and the Mirror of Nature*, Oxford: Blackwell.

Sahin, A. (2000) 'Critical/Dialogic Islamic Education: Attitudes towards Islam and Modes of Religious Subjectivity among British Muslim Youth', unpublished Ph.D. thesis, University of Birmingham.

Schools Council (1971) *Religious Education in Secondary Schools*, London: Evans Methuen Educational.

—— (1977) *A Groundplan for the Study of Religion*, London: Schools Council.

Sealey, J. (1985) *Religious Education: Philosophical Perspectives*, London: Allen and Unwin.

Smart, R.N. (1968) *Secular Education and the Logic of Religion*, London: Faber and Faber.

Taylor, M.J. (1991) *SACREs: Their Formation, Composition, Operation and Role in RE and Worship*, Slough, Berkshire: National Foundation for Educational Research.

Wright, A. (1993) *Religious Education in the Secondary School: prospects for religious literacy*, London: David Fulton Publishers in association with the Roehampton Institute.

—— (2000) 'The Spiritual Education Project: Cultivating Spiritual and Religious Literacy through a Critical Pedagogy of Religious Education', in M.H. Grimmitt (ed.) *Pedagogies of Religious Education*, Great Wakering, Essex: McCrimmons.

—— (2001) 'Religious Literacy and Democratic Citizenship', in L.J. Francis, J. Astley and M. Robbins (eds) *The Fourth R for the Third Millennium*, Leamington Spa: Lindisfarne Books.

—— (2003) 'The Contours of Critical Religious Education: Knowledge, Wisdom, Truth', *British Journal of Religious Education*, 24: 279–91.

Ziebertz, H-G. (2003) *Religious Education in a Plural Western Society: Problems and Challenges*, London: LIT Verlag.

Part 1

Religious education, pluralism and global community

Introduction

Dennis Bates

It is one of the tragic ironies of the contemporary world that despite over half a century of the work of the United Nations, increasing religious pluralism and intercultural contact in many societies and unprecedented world travel, outbreaks of conflict in which race and religion are major causal factors are still frequent occurrences. The leading theme of Part 1 is the role that religious education could fulfil in helping to promote deeper inter-religious and intercultural understanding in order to undermine the racial and cultural stereotypes which have led to persecution, conflict and genocide in so many parts of the world. The first two essays argue that the need is for a religious education which can engender a deeper interpersonal understanding and respect between people of different faiths and cultures, recognizing the plurality which exists within each tradition. The subject should also (the fourth essay) communicate an awareness of the potential of religion to being used in the pursuit of often evil and inhuman political ends. Associated with these themes, the third essay explores the role of philosophy of religion in religious education in providing a forum for the rational discussion of religious beliefs by pupils and students of all faiths and none with a view to promoting dialogue and furthering understanding. Using John Hull's Christian theological justification of a critically open approach to religious education as an example, the fifth essay suggests a possible way by which there might be found a means of justifying from Islamic tradition, an open, critical study of religion, thus making possible a convergence of western and Islamic religious education and helping to resolve the present tensions between them.

In its first part, Gabriel Moran's essay (Chapter 1) reviews references to religion and religious education in key documents produced by the United Nations since its inception. Whilst the two human rights covenants recognize parental rights to choose the religious education of their children, the phrasing and terminology used in relation to the subject highlight common prejudices and questionable levels of understanding. These are directly addressed in the second part of the essay. Thus, for example, too rigid a distinction is made between, on the one hand, 'neutral and objective' history of religions as a legitimate study in public schools and, on the other, 'instruction' in one particular religion which is implicitly 'biased and subjective'. What matters, Moran argues, is whether the subject promotes an 'intersubjective' understanding of what it means to be religious in the various traditions present in societies. Such a religious education which is a lifelong requirement needed by all, and politicians most of all, could make all the difference to overcoming international, inter-religious and intercultural conflict.

Robert Jackson (Chapter 2), focusing on the UK context, takes up a related theme. Reviewing the earlier differences between multicultural education in Britain and anti-racist education, he highlights the importance of the case argued in the early 1990s for the coming together of multicultural education and anti-racist education in 'critical multiculturalism' or what is now increasingly designated 'intercultural education'. After a downturn in the 1980s and early 1990s, the fortunes of multicultural education revived in 1997 in the wake of the new government's policy to develop 'citizenship education' as a curriculum subject. The twin towers tragedy and race riots in the North of England lent awareness and urgency to the need to include the religious dimension of intercultural diversity in citizenship education. Citing an example of successful dialogic intercultural RE in a multicultural primary school, Jackson argues against the view that the instrumental aim of promoting social harmony diverts RE from its proper concern with understanding religion and necessarily leads to relativism and universalism. In his view, a religious education incorporating interpretive and dialogic approaches and thereby flexible enough to recognize individual and 'membership group' differences within religions could make an invaluable contribution to a critical and reflexive intercultural education.

Philosophy is beginning to figure in the school curriculum in many countries, and in UK schools, philosophy of religion has become a popular option in A level religious studies. John Hick (Chapter 3) commends the value of its contribution to religious education in the state schools of religiously and philosophically pluralist societies. It offers a non-partisan, open forum for the discussion of key religious topics and questions in which believers of various faiths and non-believers alike have equal status and opportunity to put forward their viewpoints. Hick illustrates his case with reference to some of the key areas of his subject – the problem of defining religion, the current status of the traditional arguments for the existence of God and finally the cognitive validity or otherwise of religious experience. The last issue receives particular attention, the key question being whether, in view of the contribution of the human mind to all forms of awareness, it is rational to trust such modes of experience as responsive as well as projective. The recognition and discussion of such issues should form part of a genuinely open religious education.

Liam Gearon's essay (Chapter 4) focuses on the urgent need for attention to be given in religious education to human rights education and especially to the continuing horror of genocide. Despite numerous United Nations pronouncements, genocide is still a common occurrence in various parts of the world, including Europe, as has been seen in Kosovo. Recognition of the important role of religion in conflict has been shown in more recent UN documents and a full account of these is given. It is argued that religious education has for too long demonstrated a 'benign neglect of the political' but that the appearance of citizenship education in the National Curriculum offers an opportunity for the subject to make a vital contribution to education in this pivotal issue in human rights.

Wilna Meijer's essay (Chapter 5) addresses the problem of the disjunction between western and Islamic approaches to religious education encountered in many western societies with large Muslim minorities and suggests a way forward. The earlier part of her essay explores John Hull's justification on Biblical and theological grounds of his concepts of 'critical openness' and 'divergent' teaching in a subject traditionally associated with uncritical, nurturing approaches and offers a defence of his hermeneutic. She then suggests that it may be possible for Muslim educationists similarly to find a basis in Islamic theology and tradition for an open and critical approach to the study of religion. She finds a possible exemplar of such an approach in the distinction pointed out by Makdisi between 'riwaya' (transmission) in hadith classes and 'diraya' (interpretation) in law classes in the early medieval madrasa of Baghdad. The disputations which occurred in the latter formed the basis of Islamic jurisprudence and since students were made party to the interpretations of the professors an inevitable element of critical assessment was introduced. Meijer tentatively suggests that this might offer a possible precedent for the development of an Islamic critically open religious education.

1   Religious education and international understanding

Gabriel Moran

The thesis of this essay might seem strange to some people. My claim is that religious education is one of the central issues of international understanding in today's world. Future peace and security depend not only on politics, economics and technology, but on the successful transformation of religious education. This claim does not get denied by political leaders or economic experts; they may never think about religious education. Indeed, even religious leaders and educational experts tend to think in very parochial terms about religious education. In some parts of the world, 'religious education' connotes initiation of the young into the Christian, Jewish or another religion. In other places, 'religious education' refers to a minor, often optional, subject in the school curriculum. Neither meaning can do justice to the task of relating the religious life of humankind and a lifelong process of education.

In the last half century there has been some progress in acknowledging that religion is central to international conflicts and that education is the key to resolving such conflicts. There has been less progress in tapping into the positive possibilities of religion for national identity and international cooperation. Here, too, education is needed for showing the tolerant and pacific side of each of the world's main religions. For the exploration of religious education in its political and economic implications, John Hull has probably been the most important person in the world. While exemplifying a deeply rooted Christian life, Hull has led the way toward an educational approach to the religions of the world. Not only in the United Kingdom but in many countries on every continent, John Hull's influence has been impressive; but as he would readily agree, we still have a long way to go in shifting the term 'religious education' so that it is recognized as a serious participant in worldwide struggles for peace, justice and freedom.

This essay has two sections. First, I will survey what has been accomplished to protect the right to practice and to teach one's religion. Second, I will examine the need for religious groups to achieve understanding and tolerance in their practice and teaching. In the first section, I will look at United Nations documents that deal with religion and religious education. The second section will take its lead from the ambiguities and inadequacies in the language of the United Nations documents. Those of us concerned with religious education have to work at improving the language. One cannot expect the United Nations or any national legislature to develop an adequate language for religious education.

Section 1: United Nations documents

The United Nations, without being aware of it, is a kind of religious education association; that is, it is regularly immersed in religious issues and in conflicts between religiously inspired groups. The United Nations is always in search of non-violent – or educational – means to reach understanding and avoid war. From its beginning, the United Nations has had a fragile existence; its ability to solve any problems has often been hopelessly compromised. Nation states jealously guard their 'sovereignty' which hampers every move that the United Nations makes. Nowhere is this more true than in the United States of America where the right wing has fought the United Nations from its inception and has become more stubbornly opposed in recent years, just when the United Nations might finally be effective.

Despite its limitations, the United Nations is the most visible and stable institution of international order. Much of its difficulty is simply the result of taking on problems that no one at present knows how to solve. The proliferation of United Nations documents often seems to undermine its credibility; the writing is inflated and sermonizing. Nevertheless, a few of the key documents form the basis of today's international law. I will summarize and comment on references to religion and religious education in five of these documents from 1948 to 1998:

The Universal Declaration of Human Rights (1948)

This document, which originated with the organization's founding, is the basis of human rights legislation. The importance of the document has continued to increase throughout the last half century. The fact that the document was composed, debated and approved in 1948 (without a negative vote and only eight abstentions) was an amazing accomplishment. Eleanor Roosevelt shepherded the document through the process but the authors were Lebanese, Canadian, Chinese and Chilean. When religious controversy arose during the writing, Roosevelt decreed that religion would be excluded. The decision may have been necessary to arrive at agreement but it merely postponed facing up to religious issues in the conduct of nations (Glendon 2001). A reference to God in the first article was explicitly rejected. However, there are four places in the document where religion does get referred to. Article 2 says that 'everyone is entitled to all the rights and freedoms set forth in the Declaration, without distinction of any kind, such as race, color, sex, language, religion . . .' I think that the use of the term 'distinction' here is peculiar and unfortunate. I will come back in Section 2 to comment on its significance.

The Declaration includes reference to religion in Article 18:

> Everyone has the right to freedom of thought, conscience and religion; this right includes freedom to change his religion or belief, and freedom, either alone or in community with others and, in public or private, to manifest his religion or belief in teaching, practice, worship and observance.

The wording here provided the standard formula used in subsequent documents: 'thought, conscience and religion'. The most crucial word in the article is 'manifest', the assertion of an individual's right to openly practise a religion.

The Krishnaswami Report (1959)

The first step to seeing that this right was observed came from the 'Subcommittee on Prevention of Discrimination and Protection of Minorities'. It appointed a committee, headed by Arcon Krishnaswami of India, to produce a study of religious rights. In 1959, Krishnaswami produced a careful and comprehensive report of eighty-two countries. Krishnaswami recognized the possible conflicts entailed by a right to 'manifest' one's religion. He noted that there are permissible limitations upon the right so long as a minority group is respected and the decisions further the freedom of the society as a whole. One group's right to 'disseminate' their religion can conflict with another group's right to maintain their own 'uncoerced opinions'. The Krishnaswami Report also catalogued a list of practices that might be included in the manifesting of one's religion: worship, pilgrimage, processions, holidays, marriage and divorce arrangements, dissemination of the religion and training of personnel. The last two items are of particular significance for the practice of religious education. Krishnaswami also made the important point that differential treatment of individuals or groups is not always evidence of unfair discrimination.

The International Covenant on Civil and Political Rights (1966)

While only a declaration was deemed possible in 1948, the plan was to give legal force to rights by way of an international covenant. That task proved to be long and difficult; because of conflict between the United States and the Soviet Union, two covenants eventually emerged. The *International Covenant on Civil and Political Rights* reaffirmed the *Universal Declaration*'s 'freedom of thought, conscience and religion'. It also named some of the reasons for limitation of this right: protection of public safety, order, health or the fundamental rights of others. National security is not listed as a reason.

Article 18 of the Covenant is of special importance here. It affirms the 'liberty of parents . . . to ensure the religious and moral education of their children in conformity with their own convictions'. A recognition of the right to religious education is remarkable progress. The drawback is that religious education is addressed only in the context of a parental right to choose for their children. I will suggest in Section 2 that the United Nations, having affirmed religious education, will have to discover the need for a lifelong religious education as included in a comprehensive 'freedom of thought, conscience and religion'. International peace and stability require nothing less. A committee clarification of the Covenant ruled that public school instruction 'related to the general history of religion and ethics is permitted if given in a neutral and objective' way. Instruction in a particular religion is not acceptable unless there are non-discriminatory exemptions or alternatives for those who want them (Lerner 2000: 18).

Declaration on the Elimination of All Forms of Intolerance and Discrimination Based on Religion and Belief (1981)

The unwieldy title of this document is indicative of the difficulty that existed in getting consensus on how to state the question. The United States and the Soviet Union squared off over whether the phrase 'religion and belief' covered atheism. The resulting compromise was to include the term 'whatever' before 'belief' in Article 1. This Declaration furthered the work of the *Universal Declaration* and the *International Covenant on Civil and Political Rights* in cataloguing the religious rights that need protection (Articles 1 and 6).

The document affirms that 'no one shall be subject to discrimination by any state, institution, persons, or groups of persons' (Article 2). At the same time, it recognizes that religious institutions need leeway in hiring personnel, mandating dress or organizing observances (Article 6). Progress is shown by the document's recognition that protection of rights has to be accorded to groups and communities, not only individuals. The *Universal Declaration of Human Rights* had placed its emphasis on the rights of individuals. Exclusive concern with individuals is insufficient for the maintenance of religious communities and their institutions. The *Declaration on Elimination of All Forms of Intolerance and Discrimination Based on Religion and Belief* is the most important international document for the protection of religious rights.

The Amor Reports

Finally, I would take note of the reports submitted by Special Rapporteur Abdelfattah Amor since 1994; the Report of 1998 is especially noteworthy. Amor surveyed 77 countries regarding the observance of religious rights. What he found was not very encouraging either in the protection of the right to practise one's religion or in the practice of religious education. Amor found that many states have compulsory religious instruction in the religion of the majority. Most states do not provide for any exemption from this instruction. There is a very limited teaching of what he calls 'comparative religion'; and minority religions often find it impossible to have their own religious institutions. Evidently, many states are oblivious of what constitutes religious coercion.

Section 2: religious understanding

Some of the language adopted by the United Nations can hinder the project of religious understanding. There may never be an entirely adequate language to cope with the differences among religions and the paradoxes within each religion. Trying to achieve a less inadequate language is a continuing challenge for the disciplines of religion and religious education. I will comment on five problems of language reflected in the documents cited above: general versus particular, distinction versus discrimination, objective versus subjective, one tolerance versus another tolerance, and pluralism versus relativism.

General versus particular

In the brief reference above to what is permissible and impermissible in the state school, the United Nations committee assumed an unhelpful dichotomy. The choice, they asserted, was between 'general history of religion' and 'instruction in a particular religion'. The former has to be done in a 'neutral and objective' way. The latter way of doing things is not described but one might infer that instruction in a particular religion is assumed to be 'biased and subjective'. The United Nations is not especially at fault here. It has adopted language that has floated through Western languages since the time of the European Enlightenment. Events of the last century should be enough to spark realization that our language is inadequate to deal with religion, especially the living religions of living people. The phrase 'history of religions' has made successful inroads within respected scholarship. Why is there no 'geography of religions' that would seriously examine the present along with the past?

A religious education that is adequate for the future has to examine religions in particular not in general; but one particular religion has to be related to other particular religions. This principle allows for considerable leeway in a lifelong and 'lifewide' process. A small child, for example, need not be exposed to a multiplicity of religions; that will come soon enough. The International Covenant is legitimately concerned that parents (rather than the state) have control of the religious education of their children. It can hardly be expected that Christian parents would choose other than Christianity as the religion which their children first experience; but as with all education, parents are the first but not the only educators. Schoolteachers become partners to parents in the education of their children. The school raises questions and stimulates inquiry in ways that most parents cannot. This partnership can run into problems if parents neglect their duties or if schools become too far separated from the communities that support them; but even in the best of cases, the young person's thinking should and does diverge from that of the parents. Religious education cannot be subsumed entirely under the right of the parents to 'ensure the religious and moral education in conformity with their own convictions'.

A number of parent groups have claimed on the basis of this statement in the *International Covenant* that the school's teaching violates their religious rights. The most common complaint is the school's teaching on homosexuality. Some Christian groups protest that an approval of homosexuality is in violation of biblical teaching and therefore an attack on their rights. This protest has not received much attention in the press but it is a lively movement made possible by the Internet. Families in Alberta, Canada are able to share strategy with parents in Tasmania, Australia. It is a fascinating development to see conservative groups asserting their rights by appealing to United Nations documents. Although such protests are upsetting to some schools, the positive possibilities are obvious. Why shouldn't there be a worldwide discussion of the rights of parents, the rights of school people, the basis of human rights, and the applications of the *International Covenant?*

Distinction versus discrimination

I noted one glaring inadequacy of language in the *Universal Declaration*: its use of 'distinction' in Article 2. The document says that all of the rights apply 'without distinction of any kind'. It then proceeds to list some of those distinctions, such as race, sex, nationality. One distinction that is not listed is age. I think it is obvious that age does make a difference in how rights are applied. The United Nations document, *Convention of the Rights of the Child*, does make a distinction between adult and child; but I would argue that that document still suffers from a lack of distinctions. It stipulates that 'child' means anyone below the age of eighteen. Surely one has to distinguish how rights apply differently at seven months, seven years and seventeen years.

I use the example of children as illustrative of the problem of saying 'without distinction of any kind'. Surely, making distinctions is necessary for any process of thinking. In dealing with religion, it is important to distinguish differences and respect the distinctions. To disallow distinctions is to pronounce that education is unnecessary. This peculiar modern approach to complex problems tries to get rid of the problem by declaring that there is no room for discussion; education is replaced by political lobbying. What the *Declaration* was presumably trying to oppose was not 'distinction' but 'discrimination'. The latter term has become fixed in the twentieth century as negative in meaning, even though 'discriminate' is sometimes used positively and 'discriminating' almost always so. It would probably be quixotic to try to rehabilitate 'discrimination' but the negative meaning of a term such as this one is what makes development of a language of religious education so difficult.

Objective versus subjective

The committee document refers to the teaching of religion that is 'objective and neutral'. Here, I think, there is an inbuilt ambiguity that cannot be entirely overcome but should be noticed. The claim that the public or state school instruction in religion should be 'objective' may seem self-evident. Surely, one cannot advocate a proselytizing or indoctrinating attitude? However, the choice of alternatives should be carefully considered. In many contexts, the term 'objective' represents the ideal to be achieved. In experimental science or in legal proceedings, one's feelings and private opinions should be put aside. They are considered 'subjective', an interference with seeing the situation as it is – seeing it objectively. This ideal is beyond dispute in those situations where the task is to see or measure an object, a thing, that stands before the examiner.

There are other situations, however, that demand a different, possibly opposite, attitude. If the 'object' is another subject, that is, another person, one achieves little understanding by looking and measuring or bracketing one's feelings. Sometimes understanding demands trying to put oneself into the place of another subject and listening to the person(s). British religious education, as early as the 1970s, struggled to overcome the dichotomy of objective and subjective; an influential publication interprets the 'objective' as 'critical and appreciative intersubjective understanding' (Schools Council 1971: 23). Sciences such as psychology, anthropology and sociology have struggled to include the inner dimension of human life along with their respective claims to be a modern science. Professions such as medicine have to live with the tension between scientifically objective research and the inescapably dialogic element of medical practice.

Objectivity in some situations can be horribly inappropriate (Price 1992). At Rudolf Eichmann's trial, his lawyer often made the point that Eichmann was proud of his objectivity (*Sachlichkeit*). Hannah Arendt brilliantly portrayed Eichmann as attending to all the details of his job with no feeling for the 'objects' of his decisions. Ironically, Arendt was herself criticized for her objectivity – for not passionately denouncing Eichmann as the incarnation of evil; but I think Arendt was trying to do a proper journalistic report amid emotions run rampant (Arendt 1992: 287). The understanding that is appropriate to religion is on the outer extreme of the tension between objective elements and the attitudes, feelings, motives and decisions of human subjects. The demand that religious education be 'objective' can collapse the tension into a single misleading dimension.

In a state school, there has to be emphasis upon the factual and a wide range of facts; but teachers and students still have to try to get inside the subjects involved. A Christian has to ask not only 'what do Muslims believe?' and answer with a text from the Qur'an. The Christian also has to ask 'what does it feel like to be a believing Muslim?' and 'Can I understand the world as a Muslim does?' In a religiously affiliated school, the objective elements may be narrowed so that teacher and student can mainly attend to one religion. The perceptions, beliefs and emotions of that religion's devotees may be specially emphasized. Nonetheless, the treatment should maintain the tension of objective elements and subjective life. A Christian cannot attend to details of the Christian religion without, for example, immediately encountering Jewish religion. The contemporary context (economic, political, military) of Christian belief and practice is indispensable in trying to understand the lives of Christians. In the course of study in a Christian school, a question might be 'how does Christianity appear to a Muslim?' or 'how do Jews view Christian attitudes to Judaism?' Instruction in a single religion is not necessarily 'indoctrination', which is one of the most damning words in educational literature. The danger is admittedly present in any Christian, Jewish or Muslim school but indoctrination is also a danger in the teaching of economics, political science or psychology.

Tolerance versus tolerance

The International Covenant on Economic, Social and Cultural Rights refers to 'understanding, tolerance and friendship among ... all religious groups' (Article 13). The insistence on friendship may be demanding too much; friendship cannot be mandated. However, the second term, 'tolerance', is a central concept of modern times that is linked to understanding and is a prerequisite of friendship. Tolerance has two quite distinct paths. What has largely triumphed in the Western world is a form of tolerance based on scepticism. We should tolerate different views because no one can be certain of the truth. This attitude can be refreshing in the midst of clashing certainties that have sparked religious wars in the past and continue to cause bloody conflicts. Isaiah Berlin is probably the best known exponent of a tolerance based on the limits of knowledge (Berlin 1991). Religion, in this view, is a problem because of its passionate claim to know the truth. Voltaire believed that

> with the decline in the strength of religious creeds there would be a concomitant decline in human hatreds, in the urge to destroy another man because he is the embodiment of evil or falsehood. Indifference would breed tolerance. The gruesome tale of torture, killing and hatred in the last century does not seem to bear this out.
>
> (Steiner 1971: 47)

Some of the intolerance of the twentieth century was religiously inspired; much of it was not. At least, Nazism, Communism or Fascism are not officially known as religions. Perhaps 'indifference would breed tolerance' if people did not have to interact with each other; but indifference is not an option for Palestinians and Israelis, for Christians and Muslims in the Balkans, for Indians and Pakistanis in Kashmir. In fact, given worldwide travel and communication, it is increasingly difficult to be indifferent to anyone who is intolerant of your very existence. There is a different path that tolerance could have taken and eventually must be developed, a toleration based on understanding rather than indifference. The earliest move toward toleration was not based on indifference. John Plamenatz notes that in Locke, Milton and others in the seventeenth century there was a religious underpinning to tolerance. The move was from 'faith is supremely import-ant, and therefore all men must have one true faith' to 'faith is supremely important, and therefore every man must be allowed to live by the faith which seems true to him'. Plamenatz concludes that 'liberty of conscience was born, not of indifference, not of scepticism, not of mere open-minded-ness, but of faith' (Plamenatz 1963: 50).

We cannot simply resurrect the seventeenth-century context but it might give us hints as to the direction needed today. The link between the two attitudes to tolerance is a humility about anyone possessing the whole truth. Faith can include a sceptical (questioning) element. Faith, if genuine, is based on the experience of trustworthiness. To believe in someone is to trust beyond the edge of rational certainty. I can tolerate differences if I can trust that the other is not out to destroy me. I can lessen the fear of difference if I can get some understanding of the difference. One ought to be sceptical about any formula that claims to be the final truth, but that is not equival-ent to giving up the search for truth and the conviction to live by the truth as one knows it. The inevitable occasions of conflict in differing views can then be the subject of negotiation, debate and compromise. A religious edu-cation not only requires this kind of tolerance. Religious education ought to be the practical embodiment of this attitude.

Pluralism versus relativism

In recent writing, 'pluralism' has been offered as the alternative to abso-lutism (only one truth) and relativism (no truth beyond statements relative to the immediate context). Pluralism is meant to be a recognition that the truth is found along many paths, not just one path. Isaiah Berlin and most writers who have followed his lead assert a distinction between pluralism and relativism (Berlin 1991); but in trying to avoid relativism, pluralism can become the one absolute. The question then has to be raised whether pluralism is plural. Is pluralism just another ideology that dictates that only one way of thinking is acceptable? That is a serious question for many reli-gious people who find that a secular pluralism has no place for them. For example, Diane Orentlicher, in an essay entitled 'Relativism and Religion', takes issue with Michael Ignatieff's pluralism in relation to human rights. While Ignatieff says that every voice has to be heard at the bargaining table, only religion seems to be excluded. Orentlicher rightly argues that human rights need to exist within religious traditions, not just against them (Orentlicher 2001: 149). The exclusion of religion from the discussion suggests that pluralism is not open to all plurality.

The choice between pluralism and relativism is itself problematic; two terms that end in ism do not provide a helpful starting point; but 'plural' and 'relative' are useful and clear; they belong together. 'Relativism' usually carries a negative connotation; it is the contention that something is true only in relation to one culture or one society or one group. The contrast is to absolute truths that are always and everywhere true, that is, not relative to time or place. But if the statement of any truth is related to conditions of time and place, then relation – being relative – is not a defect. In fact, the wider and deeper the relations, the greater the truthfulness. In such a 'relative' world, plural would describe these many relations. If a pluralistic approach to truth is to avoid despairing of finding certainty, the many parties claiming truth have to engage in dialogue or at least have an openness to dialogue. Far from excluding the relative, the plural requires it.

Many religious thinkers have latched on to 'pluralism' as the only acceptable place to be these days. Pluralism is said to be necessary for tolerance and ecumenism but the claim can nonetheless be heavy-handed. John Hick, for example, lists three approaches to religious study as exclusivism, inclusivism and pluralism. He clearly prefers pluralism but he cannot avoid the paradox that his pluralism is either exclusive of the other two or inclusive of both of them. In either case, his pluralism is insistent on only one approach being legitimate (Hick 1995). It might be more helpful to acknowledge that language always includes and excludes at the same time. Simple factual statements exclude other facts. There is nothing wrong with that element of exclusivity. Some language, however, can be very inclusive in seeing another level in ordinary experience. That kind of poetic language passionately affirms the particular while intimating the universal. The language of art, friendship and love are affirmations of the particular which point toward the universal. Northop Frye referring to Macbeth writes: 'If you wish to know the history of eleventh-century Scotland, look elsewhere; if you wish to know what it means to gain a kingdom and lose one's soul, look here' (Frye 1964: 64).

Religious language is both inclusive and exclusive; how the two are related determines whether the language is tolerant or intolerant. There can be a plurality or multiplicity of tolerant positions in which there are exclusive elements of religion, as well as an inclusive attitude. The term 'pluralism' can be helpful only if it does not flatten out the paradox, namely, that the exclusive and inclusive are not the alternatives to the plural but the inner working of the plural.

In the United Nations document cited above, religious education is to be allowed if given in a 'neutral' way. It is difficult to see how religion can be approached 'neutrally', that is, from neither side. The fear, once again, is a proselytizing attitude but one has to approach the teaching of any subject with a passion for getting it right. Asking a teacher not to take sides makes no sense. In a pluralistic attitude the teacher takes both sides: inside and outside. The principle holds whether one religion or several religions are at issue. The task is to provide appreciation of how the religion is actually practised, while at the same time providing a critical angle provided by a different religion or by secular society.

I think there is a lot of good religious education being practised, most of it outside the spotlight. One can find examples in every continent, at every school level, in religiously affiliated institutions and secular education. The biggest need is to break down some of the categories which encapsulate these efforts and which prevent people from finding partners in trying to help people live intelligent, free, peaceful, faithful, loving lives. I am not surprised that we are still at the beginning of religious education; its importance is still only emerging. In the future, religious education has to be inter-religious and international if it is to make sense of ordinary experience. Political leaders are going to need basic training in religious education to carry on the duties of national office.

References

Amor, A. (1998) *Civil and Political Rights, Including Freedom of Expression*, New York: UN.

Arendt, H. (1992) *Eichmann in Jerusalem*, Middlesex: Penguin Books.

Berlin, I. (1991) *The Crooked Timber of Humanity*, New York: Knopf.

Frye, N. (1964) *The Educated Imagination*, Bloomington: Indiana University Press.

Glendon, M.A. (2001) *A World Made New: Eleanor Roosevelt and the UHDR*, New York: Random House.

Hick, J. (1995) *A Christian Theology of Religions*, Louisville: Westminster John Knox.

Lerner, N. (2000) *Religion, Belief and International Human Rights*, Maryknoll: Orbis Books.

Orentlicher, D. (2001). 'Relativism and Religion', in M. Ignatieff *et al. Human Rights as Politics and Idolatry*, Princeton: Princeton University Press.

Plamenatz, J. (1963) *Man and Society*, Vol. I., London: Longman.

Price, R. (1992) *A Whole New Life*, New York: Atheneum.

Schools Council Working Paper No. 36 (1971) *Religious Education in Secondary Schools*, London: Evans-Methuen.

Steiner, G. (1971) *In Bluebeard's Castle*, New Haven: Yale University Press.

United Nations (1948) *The Universal Declaration of Human Rights*, New York: UN.

—— (1959) *Report of the Subcommittee on Prevention of Discrimination and Protection of Minorities*, New York: UN.

—— (1966) *International Covenant on Civil and Political Rights*, New York: UN.

—— (1981) *Declaration on the Elimination of All Forms of Intolerance and Discrimination Based on Religion and Belief*, New York: UN.

—— (1990) *Convention on the Rights of the Child*, New York: UN.

—— (1994) *Report of the Special Rapporteur of the Commission on Human Rights on Freedom of Religion or Belief*, New York: UN.

For further information consult the United Nations website *www.un.com*.

2 Intercultural education and religious education

A changing relationship

Robert Jackson

Religious education, multicultural or intercultural education and antiracist education have had an interesting relationship and varying fortunes over time in Britain.[1] In the late 1960s and early 1970s, while Ninian Smart and his team were introducing a global dimension to religious education through importing theory and method from the phenomenology of religion (Schools Council 1971), religious educators in some of Britain's increasingly multicultural towns and cities were beginning to use local religious diversity as a resource for their subject. They were also finding a role in promoting good community relations at the local level, and it is significant that one of the first books to explore religion in a multicultural and multifaith setting in Britain was published by a council for community relations (Cole 1972). Many teachers of religious education joined the National Association for Multiracial Education, and RE was commonly regarded as a valuable contributor to multicultural education.

Then there was a schism. This was between those with fundamentally 'antiracist' concerns and those emphasizing intercultural understanding (Mullard 1984). The antiracists argued that multiculturalists had treated cultural issues superficially, unnecessarily reifying cultures and inadvertently emphasizing difference (Troyna 1983). Rather than promoting understanding, it was argued, multiculturalists were playing into racist hands by creating stereotypes of distinct, separate cultures. These were allowed limited forms of expression by the beneficence of a tolerant national culture (McIntyre 1978). According to antiracists, multicultural education also avoided issues of power, explaining racism psychologically in terms of attitudes that could be changed through acquiring knowledge and learning tolerance, rather than through challenging accepted power structures within institutions. These inequalities of power were regarded as the real explanation for the perpetuation of inequality. Because of its concern with changing structures, antiracism gave limited attention to the curriculum, offering ideas to promote a critical awareness of 'institutional racism', for example, but not addressing issues of culture.

It was not until the early 1990s that some writers attempted to heal the schism, recognizing the need for an antiracist stance, but criticizing antiracists for their stridency and inflexibility and for underestimating the importance of issues of cultural and religious representation, transmission and change. These writers included Mal Leicester (e.g. Leicester 1992) and Ali Rattansi (Rattansi 1992), both appealing for reform through a synthesis of the two fields. Thus 'antiracist multicultural education' (Leicester 1992: 217), 'critical multiculturalism' (May 1999: 33) and 'reflexive multicultural-ism' (Rattansi 1999: 77) are critical of essentialist views of culture while acknowledging the role of power relations in cultural formation.[2]

Multicultural education in the 1990s

The developments introduced in the early 1990s remained unnoticed by politicians in government in Britain. Policy on the issue of multicultural education became clearly hard line during the latter part of the period of Conservative government between 1979 and 1997. In 1977, two years before the election of a Conservative government, the Department of Educa-tion and Science promoted the recognition of Britain as a multicultural society and education that recognized that fact. 'Our society is a multicul-tural and multiracial one, and the curriculum should reflect a sympathetic understanding of the different cultures and races that now make up our society' (DES 1977: 41). The policy was maintained during the early years of the Conservative administration. For example, student teachers received training to teach in a multicultural society, in-service training courses were made available to serving teachers and GCSE examination boards[3] had to take account of linguistic and cultural diversity. Moreover, money from central government was given to support projects on curriculum develop-ment for an ethnically diverse society (Tomlinson and Craft 1995). However, despite positive rhetoric from Government sources,[4] policies relat-ing to the implementation of the National Curriculum eroded work in mul-ticultural and antiracist education. Concern for equal opportunities and offering knowledge about minorities disappeared in favour of a drive to raise standards, market competition, a regulated National Curriculum and testing. In a climate in which lobbyists from the New Right were influential (Ball 1990), the *Times Educational Supplement* could judge that 'There seems to be a definite though unformulated intent to starve multicultural educa-tion of resources and let it wither on the vine' (*Times Educational Supplement* 1990: A23). The Prime Minister of the day, John Major, could declare at the 1992 Conservative Party Conference that 'primary teachers should learn how to teach children to read, not waste their time on the politics of gender, race and class'. A year later, the former Chief Executive of the National Curricu-lum Council (what today is the Qualifications and Curriculum Authority) revealed that there had been specific instructions to remove references to multicultural education from the National Curriculum (Graham 1993). Central Government's erosion of local education authority responsibilities for providing policy and financial support for what takes place in schools was also an important factor in the demise of multicultural education (Troyna 1995: 140).

There was a change in atmosphere with the election of a Labour Government in 1997, and a drive towards the development of citizenship education through the establishment of an Advisory Group on Citizenship. This group published the Crick Report during the following year (QCA 1998). The introduction of citizenship education in 2002 as an optional subject in primary schools and as a statutory part of the National Curriculum for secondary schools, has given a new impetus to multicultural education in England and Wales. Citizenship education in secondary schools requires knowledge and understanding of 'the diversity of national, regional, religious and ethnic identities in the United Kingdom and the need for mutual respect and understanding' (DfEE/QCA 1999a), while the non-statutory advice for primary schools encourages children to 'appreciate the range of national, regional, religious and ethnic identities in the United Kingdom' (DfEE/QCA 1999b). Thus, at last, a form of multicultural education has been incorporated into the curriculum, but it needs to be developed along the lines suggested by Leicester and Rattansi and must not lapse into the simplistic multiculturalism of the 1970s. There is a clear role for specialists in religious education to contribute to this form of education (Jackson 2003, 2004: Chapter 8).

Intercultural understanding, religion and social cohesion

The need for including the dimension of religious diversity in a critical multicultural education was reinforced by riots in the northern English towns and cities of Oldham, Burnley, Leeds and Bradford in the summer of 2001 in areas inhabited mainly by people of Pakistani and Bangladeshi Muslim origin (Home Office 2001a and b). The causes of the riots, which mainly involved young men, include social and economic deprivation in the areas involved as well as the political activity of the extreme right wing British National Party, which has for some time been expressing racist views in religious terms, especially through its vilification of Islam (McRoy 2001: 18–19). The Parekh Report on the future of multiethnic Britain draws attention to the use of religious categories in extreme right wing propaganda circulated in Britain, including a document appealing to the government to use troops to remove all mosques, temples and synagogues from 'this Christian land' (Runnymede Trust 2000 para 17.3: 237). This equation of national and Christian identity, associating all other religious identities with difference and otherness, is a version of what Tariq Modood has called 'cultural racism' (Modood 1992, 1997). Racism directed towards religious groups, or justified on religious grounds, prompts the writers of the Parekh report to argue that strategies for countering it need to recognize the distinctive and powerful nature of religious identity.

There had been riots in Bradford in 1995, and Lord Ouseley's report on the city of Bradford happened to be published at the same time as the 2001 riots. The Ouseley Report depressingly describes a city 'fragmenting along racial, cultural and faith lines' (Ouseley 2001: 6), and the 'virtual apartheid' of education (Ouseley 2001). Several reports on the 2001 riots were commissioned by the Home Office. The report of the Ministerial Group on Public Order and Community Cohesion concludes that lack of communication contributed to the unrest, and it appeals for the promotion of dialogue between the different groups (Home Office 2001a: para 2.16: 13). The second report by an independent review team into Community Cohesion – the Cantle Report – specifically recommends educational programmes promoting cross-cultural contact (Home Office 2001b: para 5.8.18: 36).

On a global scale, events such as those of 11 September, 2001 in the United States of America and their aftermath, including the atrocities in Bali in the autumn of 2002, in Casablanca in May 2003 and Jakarta in August 2003, and the wars in Afghanistan and Iraq, have also put religion on political, social and educational agendas internationally. Indeed, in the European context, directly as a response to the events of 11 September 2001 and their consequences, the Council of Europe is encouraging the addition of the dimension of religious diversity to intercultural education, including civic education, across Europe. A project on 'intercultural education and the challenge of religious diversity and dialogue' was approved by the education committee of the Council at the end of September 2002 (Jackson 2002). This aims to produce materials for policy makers and practitioners across more than forty member states by the end of 2004 (Jackson 2004: Chapter 10).

Motivated by a wish to establish international codes of human rights, an international project co-ordinated by the Oslo Coalition on Freedom of Religion or Belief is developing a global interdisciplinary network 'to encourage school education that increases understanding and respect between people of different religions or world views and that fosters knowledge about and respect for freedom of religion or belief as a human right'. Through this, the project aims 'to combat discrimination and intolerance based on religion or belief and prevent violations of the human right to freedom of religion or belief' (Jackson 2004: Chapter 10; Larsen and Plesner 2002).

Thus, the needs of citizenship education and responses to civil unrest in Britain, reactions to international terrorism in Europe, and attempts to apply codes of human rights globally, all invite forms of intercultural education that take full account of issues in religious diversity, promote communication and dialogue between pupils from different backgrounds, and foster social cohesion through the encouragement of tolerance, understanding and respect between peoples.

Religious education, social cohesion and tolerance

It seems fairly obvious that religious education has a great deal to offer towards the attainment of such goals. Yet some religious education specialists are sceptical about this, arguing that a focus on promoting tolerance and social cohesion diverts attention from the subject's primary aim as well as importing assumptions of relativism or of theological pluralism. For example, in discussing the aims of RE, Andrew Wright states that 'the aim of religious education need be no more complicated than the process of producing religiously literate individuals. This is an aim in itself that has intrinsic importance and has no further need of justification' (Wright 1993: 63). In a recent article, Wright has gone further than this, claiming that if 'religion is taught not as an end in itself, but as a tool for encouraging tolerance and mutual understanding in a culturally divided society', then there is a hidden assumption that 'religion is no more than a relativistic expression of culture whose primary function is to point beyond itself to our common humanity'. Wright also claims that 'concerns for social cohesion have often led to the conclusion that, insofar as religion is viewed as a human response to transcendence, the only valid theological option is that of a universal theology in which all traditions are regarded as being equally true' (Wright 2003: 287).

I want to argue against this position. First, it is impossible to establish a *necessary* connection between the instrumental goal of using religious education to promote tolerance and social cohesion and the adoption or propagation of relativism or theological pluralism. Second, there is some empirical evidence to show that there is no *tendency* towards relativism or theological pluralism among children taught RE that includes such instrumental goals. For example, Julia Ipgrave – who teaches religious education with both 'knowledge and understanding' and 'social cohesion' aims (Ipgrave 2003) – has conducted research on the inter-influence of children from Muslim, Hindu and Christian backgrounds in a Leicester primary school (Ipgrave 2002). Ipgrave notes three aspects of children's thinking evident in their dialogue. The first is the experience-led nature of their understanding. Experiences of religious plurality and religious rivalry (including experiences at school) influenced and informed their ideas in RE lessons. The second is the rational basis of their thinking about religion. The children provided many examples of bringing together ideas in an attempt to synthesize them into a coherent whole. However, although children adapted their personal views over time, there was no trend towards their abandoning the faith positions of their families and communities. A third feature is the underlying realism of much of children's discourse. Children adapted their views as a result of engagement with the religious languages of others but, rather than moving towards a relativist stance in the face of a variety of belief systems, many of the children maintained a realist view (Ipgrave 2002; see Jackson 2004: Chapter 7 for a discussion of Ipgrave's contribution to research and pedagogy).

Like Ipgrave, I would argue that a religious education that sets out *only* to promote tolerance or social cohesion is inadequate. Elsewhere I have argued that a key aim for RE is to develop an understanding of the grammar – the language and wider symbolic patterns – of religions and the interpretive skills necessary to gain that understanding (Jackson 1997: 129). Achieving this aim requires the development of critical skills which, when applied, raise issues of representation, interpretation, truth and meaning. I have also argued that the nature of learning in religious education is reflexive, with understanding and reflection being inseparable elements of the interpretive process. Students develop through reflecting upon encounters with new ideas and experiences. Religious education is thus a conversational process in which pupils, whatever their backgrounds, continuously interpret and reinterpret their own views in the light of what they study (cf. Meijer 1995). Moreover, this position seems consistent with Wright's three stage model for religious education which deals respectively with the child's own current perspective, the child's interaction with alternative spiritual stories and the expression of a well thought out, religiously literate viewpoint. 'From the start', says Wright, 'children are expected to identify, own and take responsibility for their own world-view narratives' (Wright 1999: 44).

My hope is that *through* the processes of critical engagement and reflection, interreligious and intercultural understanding will be fostered. But this does not imply a methodological assumption that religions are simply cultural facts or are equally true. Pupils will formulate a variety of views about the nature of religion and the relationship between the truth claims of religions, and the formation of these views will be influenced by various factors, many of them beyond the RE classroom.

I would want to add a cautionary note about the relationship between knowledge and attitudes. It is a mistake to assume that understanding and knowledge necessarily foster tolerance. There are some very well informed racists and bigots. Similarly, specialists in propaganda and 'spin' are aware that lies and misinformation can increase tolerance, sympathy and respect. I would argue, however, that knowledge and understanding are necessary but not sufficient conditions for the genuine removal of prejudice. Moreover, not everything learned about and understood will command respect – religious education requires an analysis of the negative as well as the positive influences of religion (Gearon 2002) – and there are also limits to tolerance.

Pedagogies of intercultural and religious education

A critical or reflexive intercultural education needs to present more sophisticated analyses of culture than the reifications found in the multicultural education of the 1970s. Numerous ethnographic studies have informed the debate about the concepts of 'culture' and 'cultures', and this debate needs to be reflected in intercultural education as well as religious education (Jackson 1997: Chapter 4).[5] Such studies reflect an analysis of plurality that incorporates both 'traditional' aspects, such as overt religious diversity, and 'modern' elements, such as competing rationalities and epistemologies and interpersonal contact enhanced by new technology (Jackson 2004: Chapter

1; Skeie 1995, 2002). Gerd Baumann's analysis of cultural discourse, based on his research in Southall, is particularly illuminating. Baumann distinguishes between what he calls 'dominant discourse' in which people reify views of cultures, religions and ethnic groups, and 'demotic discourse', the language of interaction with others at the personal level, which creates new culture. Of course, 'dominant discourse' in relation to culture and religion is habitually used by politicians and the media. However, Baumann found that, in certain contexts, individual inhabitants of Southall, in their own interests, also used 'dominant discourse, sometimes identifying themselves with categories such as Punjabi, Sikh or Asian. In other contexts, they interacted with others, creating cultural fusions and new cultural expressions. 'Southallians', says Baumann, 'engage the dominant discourse as well as the demotic one. They reify *cultures* while at the same time making culture' (Baumann 1996: 31). The reified categories are useful reference points, but they obscure the diversity, interaction and change that is the underlying reality. As Baumann puts it, 'Culture ... is not so much a photocopy machine but a concert or indeed a historically improvised jam session. It only exists in the act of being performed, and it can never stand still or repeat itself without changing its meaning' (Baumann 1999: 26). This second view of culture – culture as process – was absent from the multicultural education of the 1970s, and indeed from much religious education to date.

In combating the stereotypes that characterize racist language, intercultural education needs to ensure that generalized cultural categories are not taken to be uniform 'wholes'. The complexity and diversity of cultural interaction needs to be represented. Baumann gives the following advice:

> Try to unreify all accepted reifications by finding crosscutting cleavages. Whenever the reifying discourse talks about citizens or aliens, purple or green ethnics, believers or atheists, ask about rich or poor citizens, powerful or manipulated ethnics, married or sexual minority believers. Who are the minorities within majorities, who are the unseen majorities right across minorities? Combine every method of questioning to every possible category around you, for the permutations are endless when it comes to questioning reifications.
>
> (Baumann 1999: 141)

There are several pedagogical approaches to religious education that are consistent with Baumann's observations about cultural discourse. The interpretive approach aims to help children and young people to find their own positions within the key debates about religious plurality. Drawing on methodological ideas from ethnographic research, it recognizes the inner diversity, fuzzy-edgedness and contested nature of religious traditions as well as the complexity of cultural expression and change from social and individual perspectives (Jackson 1997). Individuals are seen as unique, but the group tied nature of religion is recognized, as is the role of the wider religious traditions in providing identity markers and reference points. Pedagogically, the approach develops skills of interpretation and provides opportunities for critical reflection in which pupils make a constructive critique of the material studied at a distance, re-assess their understanding of their own way of life in the light of their studies and review their own methods of learning. The interpretive approach has been adapted by others, to meet particular classroom needs (Jackson 2004: Chapter 6; Krisman 1997; O'Grady 2003).

Having much in common with the interpretive approach, is a group of dialogical approaches to religious education developed independently by Julia Ipgrave in Britain, Heid Leganger-Krogstad in Norway and Wolfram Weisse and his colleagues in Germany. All claim the relative autonomy of the individual, but recognize the contextual influence of social groupings, such as family, peer, ethnic and religious groups. There is common agreement that the personal knowledge and experience that young people bring to the classroom can provide important data for study, communication and reflection. All also introduce further source material; religious education does not only consist of the analysis and exchange of personal narratives.

Julia Ipgrave bases her approach on the research in her multicultural primary school in Leicester referred to above. Her pedagogy capitalizes on children's readiness to engage with religious questions and their ability to utilize religious language encountered through interacting with children from different backgrounds in school. The teacher often acts in the role of facilitator, prompting and clarifying questions, and considerable agency is given to pupils, who are regarded as collaborators in teaching and learning. Ipgrave finds that her approach raises children's self-esteem, provides opportunities to develop critical skills, allows underachievers to express themselves and generates a climate of moral seriousness through the discussion of basic human questions (Ipgrave 2001, 2003; Jackson 2004: Chapter 7).

Ipgrave's research project developed a threefold approach to dialogue which has been incorporated into the pedagogical work derived from it. Primary dialogue is the acceptance of diversity, difference and change. Secondary dialogue involves being open to and positive about difference — being willing to engage with difference and to learn from others. Tertiary dialogue is the actual verbal interchange between children. The basic activity here is discussion and debate. Throughout, the approach encourages personal engagement with ideas and concepts from different religious traditions and children are encouraged to reflect on their contributions and to justify their own opinions. They are also encouraged to consider how they arrived at their conclusions, to recognize the possibility of alternative viewpoints and to be open to the arguments of others.

Heid Leganger-Krogstad developed her dialogical approach in northern

Norway. RE moves between the child's personal experience and wider social experience and between the past – in terms of tradition and history, especially the children's own 'roots' – and the future. There is a gradual broadening of children's experience as they relate their personal concerns to selected cultural material, extending their horizons beyond family and locality to the region and nation and, in turn, to wider European and global issues. Pupils' individual concerns and questions are related to broader social and cultural issues, with 'local' issues acting as a bridge. Children's dialogue, whether 'within' their own culture – in recognizing its internal diversity – or 'between' cultures is seen as a key element in developing what Leganger-Krogstad calls metacultural competence, the ability to handle new and unfamiliar cultural material with skill and sensitivity (Jackson 2004: Chapter 7; Leganger-Krogstad 2000, 2001).

Developed in the multicultural city of Hamburg, Wolfram Weisse's approach to what he calls 'intercultural/interreligious learning', combines elements of religious education and education for citizenship (Weisse 1996a and b, 2003). Weisse's approach, ethically grounded in human rights codes, aims to foster communication within multicultural societies. Weisse sees issues such as relativism, undermining faith and challenging the absoluteness of Christianity as part of the debate that young people should engage in. Rather than leading to the relativism and theological pluralism feared by Wright, Weisse's approach tackles such issues head on:

> While the spectrum of topics points to the many similarities between the religions, dialogue in RE is also designed to demonstrate the differences between religious traditions. Individual positions are not found by mixing different views, but by comparing and contrasting them with one another. Religious education should make dialogue in the classroom possible by allowing participants to refer to their different religious backgrounds . . . Dialogue in the classroom fosters respect for other religious commitments, can confirm pupils' views or help them to make their own commitments whilst also allowing them to monitor their commitments critically.
>
> (Weisse 2003: 194)

Pupils practise the skills of listening, of comparing and contrasting their own views with those of others, and of empathy. Difference is recognized, and pupils are encouraged to find their own epistemological standpoint. Weisse recognizes that dialogue in school can lead to conflict. This is regarded as normal, and conflicts are worked through as part of religious education, with students sometimes having to agree and accept that differences cannot be resolved (Weisse 1996b: 275–6, 2003).

Conclusion

Both intercultural/multicultural education and religious education have changed significantly since the 1970s. Both now include theoretical frameworks and pedagogies that take account of the complexities of plurality and incorporate sophisticated analyses of culture. Tragic events within Britain and internationally have pointed to the need to give more attention to the religious dimension of social life in educational programmes. Home Office Reports following riots in England recognize the religious elements in the conflict and recommend the promotion of dialogue and cross-cultural contact in education.[6] The Council of Europe and Oslo Coalition projects also grasp the importance of the religious dimension to intercultural and human rights education. Interpretive and dialogical approaches to religious education are among those that can contribute positively and directly to intercultural education, through their underlying empirical research, theory and their pedagogies. Moreover, they can do this without promoting relativism or particular theories of theological pluralism.

Notes

1 The terms 'multicultural education' and 'intercultural education' have been used in a variety of ways by different writers and are sometimes used interchangeably. 'Multicultural education' gained currency in Britain and in the USA. Although the term 'multicultural' has been criticised for suggesting distinct and bounded cultures, many writers (e.g. Baumann 1999; Rattansi 1992, 1999) have used it in much more flexible ways. The term 'intercultural education' has been used more in continental European literature and is used, for example, in various Council of Europe projects (Perotti 1994). 'Intercultural education' is being used more widely now in the UK, partly under European influence and because it seems consistent with the idea that 'cultures' are not discrete but constantly interacting, and that people can draw on a variety of cultural resources in creating new culture.

2 Rattansi was writing against a background where there had been a virtual breakdown in communication between strident antiracists from the political left and more liberal writers and educators and where radical antiracists had been unable to negotiate within the institutional constraints of education and other public services. His term 'reflexive multicultural education' was intended to suggest dialogue, negotiation, self-awareness and flexibility in finding practical ways to effect reforms that could possibly lead to institutional change (Rattansi 1999).

3 General Certificate of Secondary Education examinations are taken at age 15–16.

4 In a letter written in 1988, Kenneth Baker, the Secretary of State for Education in England, instructed the National Curriculum Council, as it began work on the new National Curriculum, to 'take account of ethnic and cultural diversity and the importance of the curriculum in promoting equal opportunities for all pupils regardless of ethnic origin or gender' (DES 1988).

5 John Hull is one of the writers in religious education who works with sophisticated views of culture informed by the social sciences. For example, Hull's critique of 'religionism' attacks the simplistic view of 'Christian cultural heritage' suggested in DfE Circular 1/94: 'The United Kingdom belongs to all its people.

Every man, woman and child, whatever his or her religion, is part of the country's ongoing heritage' (Hull 1998: 126).

6 The formation of a youth shadow Standing Advisory Council for Religious Education (SACRE) in the city of Bradford, which gives responsibility to young people from different backgrounds to interact with one another in helping to plan and monitor religious education, is one positive response to such recommendations (Miller 2003).

References

Ball, S. (1990) *Politics and Policy Making in Education*, London: Routledge.

Baumann, G. (1996) *Contesting Culture: Discourses of Identity in Multi-Ethnic London*, Cambridge: Cambridge University Press.

—— (1999) *The Multicultural Riddle: Rethinking National, Ethnic and Religious Identities*, London: Routledge.

Cole, W.O. (1972) *Religion in the Multifaith School* (1st edn), Yorkshire Committee for Community Relations.

DES (1977) *Education in Schools: a consultative document*, London: HMSO.

—— (1988) Letter to National Curriculum Council from Kenneth Baker, Secretary of State for Education, York: NCC.

DfEE/QCA (1999a) *The National Curriculum for England: Citizenship*, London: Department for Education and Employment and Qualifications and Curriculum Authority.

—— (1999b) *The National Curriculum for England: Non-statutory Frameworks for Personal, Social and Health Education and Citizenship at Key Stages 1 & 2; Personal, Social and Health Education at Key Stages 3 & 4*, London: Department for Education and Employment and Qualifications and Curriculum Authority.

Gearon, L. (2002) 'Religious education and human rights: some postcolonial perspectives', *British Journal of Religious Education*, 24(2): 140–51.

Graham, D. (1993) *A Lesson for Us All: The Making of the National Curriculum*, London: Routledge.

Home Office (2001a) *Building Cohesive Communities: A Report of the Ministerial Group on Public Order and Community Cohesion*, December, London: Home Office.

—— (2001b) *Community Cohesion: A Report of the Independent Review Team chaired by Ted Cantle*, December, London: Home Office.

Hull, J.M. (1998) *Utopian Whispers: Moral, Religious and Spiritual Values in Schools*, London: RMEP.

Ipgrave, J. (2001) *Pupil to Pupil Dialogue in the Classroom as a Tool for Religious Education*, Warwick Religions and Education Research Unit Occasional Papers II, University of Warwick, Institute of Education.

—— (2002) *Inter faith encounter and religious understanding in an inner city primary school*, unpublished Ph.D. thesis, University of Warwick.

—— (2003) 'Dialogue, citizenship and religious education', in R. Jackson (ed.) *International Perspectives on Citizenship, Education and Religious Diversity*, London: RoutledgeFalmer, 147–68.

Jackson, R. (1997) *Religious Education: An Interpretive Approach*, London: Hodder and Stoughton.

—— (2002) *Intercultural Education and the Challenge of Religious Diversity and Dialogue: A Response*, unpublished Report for Head of Educational Policies and

European Dimension Division in the Directorate of School, Out of School and Higher Education, Strasbourg: Council of Europe.

Jackson, R. (ed.) (2003) *International Perspectives on Citizenship, Education and Religious Diversity*, London: RoutledgeFalmer.

Jackson, R. (2004) *Rethinking Religious Education and Plurality: Issues in Diversity and Pedagogy*, London: RoutledgeFalmer.

Krisman, A. (1997) *Speak from the Heart: Exploring and Responding to RE in the Special School*, Oxford: Farmington Institute for Christian Studies. Available online: http://www.farmington.ac.uk/documents/reports/framed/teaching_training.html (accessed June 2003).

Larsen, L. and Plesner, I.T. (eds) (2002) *Teaching for Tolerance and Freedom of Religion or Belief*, Oslo: The Oslo Coalition on Freedom of Religion and Belief, University of Oslo.

Leganger-Krogstad, H. (2000) 'Developing a contextual theory and practice of religious education', *Panorama: International Journal of Comparative Religious Education and Values*, 12(1): 94–104.

—— (2001) 'Religious education in a global perspective: a contextual approach', in H-G. Heimbrock, P. Schreiner and C. Sheilke (eds) *Towards Religious Competence: Diversity as a Challenge for Education in Europe*, Hamburg: Lit Verlag, 53–73.

Leicester, M. (1992) 'Antiracism versus the new multiculturalism: moving beyond the interminable debate', in J. Lynch, C. Modgil and S. Modgil (eds) *Cultural Diversity and the schools: Equity or Excellence? Education and Cultural Reproduction*, London: Falmer Press.

McIntyre, J. (1978) *Multi-Culture and Multifaith Societies: Some Examinable Assumptions*, Occasional Papers, Oxford: Farmington Institute for Christian Studies.

McRoy, A. (2001) 'BNP's anti-Muslim Crusade' *Q News – The Muslim Magazine*: 18–19.

May, S. (ed.) (1999) *Critical Multiculturalism: Rethinking Multicultural and Antiracist Education*, London: Falmer Press.

Meijer, W.A.J. (1995) 'The plural self: a hermeneutical view on identity and plurality', *British Journal of Religious Education*, 17(2): 92–9.

Miller, J. (2003) 'Faith and belonging in Bradford', *RE Today* 20(3): 34.

Modood, T. (1992) 'On not being white in Britain: discrimination, diversity and commonality', in M. Leicester and M. Taylor (eds) *Ethics, Ethnicity and Education*, London: Kogan Page, 72–87.

—— (1997) '"Difference", cultural racism and antiracism', in P. Werbner and T. Modood (eds) *Debating Cultural Hybridity*, London: Zed Books, 154–72.

Mullard, C. (1984) *Anti-Racist Education: The Three O's*, Cardiff: National Association for Multiracial Education.

O'Grady, K. (2003) 'Motivation in religious education: a collaborative investigation with year eight students', *British Journal of Religious Education*, 25(3): 214–25.

Ouseley, H. (ed.) (2001) *Community Pride Not Prejudice: Making Diversity Work in Bradford*, Bradford: Bradford Vision.

Perotti, A. (1994) *The Case for Intercultural Education*, Strasbourg: Council of Europe.

QCA (1998) *Education for Citizenship and the Teaching of Democracy in Schools, Final Report of the Advisory Group on Citizenship*, London: Qualifications and Curriculum Authority.

Rattansi, A. (1992) 'Changing the subject: racism, culture and education', in

J. Donald and A. Rattansi (eds) *Race Culture and Difference*, London: Sage in association with The Open University, 11–48.

—— (1999) 'Racism, postmodernism and reflexive multiculturalism', in S. May (ed.) *Critical Multiculturalism: Rethinking Multicultural and Antiracist Education*, London: Falmer Press.

Runnymede Trust (2000) *The Future of Multi-Ethnic Britain: The Parekh Report*, London: Profile Books.

Schools Council (1971) *Religious Education in Secondary Schools*, Schools Council Working Paper 36, London: Evans/Methuen.

Skeie, Geir (1995) 'Plurality and pluralism: a challenge for religious education', *British Journal of Religious Education*, 25(1): 47–59.

—— (2002) 'The concept of plurality and its meaning for religious education', *British Journal of Religious Education*, 25(2): 47–59.

Tomlinson, S. and Craft, M. (eds) (1995) *Ethnic Relations and Schooling: Policy and Practice in the 1990s*, London: The Athlone Press.

Troyna, B. (1983) 'Multiracial education: just another brick in the wall?' *New Community*, 10: 424–8.

Troyna, B. (1995) 'The Local Management of Schools and Racial Equality', in S. Tomlinson and M. Craft (eds) *Ethnic Relations and Schooling: Policy and Practice in the 1990s*, London: The Athlone Press, 140–54.

Weisse, Wolfram (1996a) 'Approaches to religious education in the multicultural city of Hamburg', in W. Weisse (ed.) *Interreligious and Intercultural Education: Methodologies, Conceptions and Pilot Projects in South Africa, Namibia, Great Britain, the Netherlands and Germany*, Münster: Comenius Institut, 83–93.

—— (1996b) 'Christianity and its neighbour-religions: a question of tolerance?', *Scriptura: International Journal of Bible, Religion and Theology*, 55(4): 263–76.

—— (2003) 'Difference without discrimination: religious education as a field of learning for social understanding?', in R. Jackson (ed.) *International Perspectives on Citizenship, Education and Religious Diversity*, London: RoutledgeFalmer, 191–208.

Wright, A. (1993) *Religious Education in the Secondary School: Prospects for Religious Literacy*, London: David Fulton.

—— (1999) *Discerning the Spirit*, Abingdon: Culham College Institute.

—— (2003) 'The contours of critical religious education: knowledge, wisdom, truth', *British Journal of Religious Education*, 25(4): 279–91.

3 The contribution of the philosophy of religion to religious education

John Hick

Unlike other contributors to this volume I am not an authority on religious education in schools. I write as a friend of John Hull's over many years who wants to join in celebrating his enormous professional and personal achievements. At the same time however, my own field, the philosophy of religion, is relevant to religious education in schools, particularly in the way in which it opens up multi-faith issues in a non-confessional manner. The basic principle that the proper function of religious education in schools is not to induct students into any one particular form of religion, or indeed into the more basic acceptance of a religious as opposed to a naturalistic faith, was established in this country in the 1960s and 70s.

John Hull played a major part in that all-important transition and, as all of us who were concerned with him at that time in creating the then new multi-faith Birmingham Agreed Syllabus remember, the transition was not an easy and uncontested development. Now, syllabuses which are to varying extents multi-faith are virtually universal in British schools. However, whilst in practice a variety of approaches and methods are in use, a widespread assumption seems to have formed that the only alternative to the old, rejected, confessional stance is a purely phenomenological treatment of the material. In practice this has often been interpreted as meaning the study of religions in isolation, learning about their origin, history, scriptures, practices, etc. However this, by itself, teaches only the external phenomena of religion. Fortunately this is often enriched and enlivened, at least in multi-faith areas, by contributions from adherents of the faith currently being taught and by visits, again in areas where this is possible, to one of its places of worship, giving the students some sense of what it means to be a Muslim, or a Christian, or a Hindu, or Sikh, or Buddhist, etc. When this happens, an important further dimension is added to the phenomenological approach.

The philosophy of religion adds yet another dimension. Its basic first question is 'What is religion?' This may look at first like a straightforward question to be answered by consulting a dictionary; but when we do so, we are likely to find that the definitions provided presuppose long-established western conceptions which have the unintended effect of excluding most forms of Buddhism, Jainism, Taoism and Confucianism. Thus, central to the

Oxford English Dictionary (OED 1971) definitions is the idea of 'a divine ruling power' or 'some higher unseen power ("especially of a personal God or gods" Concise Oxford Dictionary 6th edn 1976) as having control of [mankind's] destiny and as being entitled to obedience, reverence, and worship'. The OED also offers the broader definition, 'a particular system of faith and worship'; but Buddhism does not affirm a higher controlling power, specifically not a personal God, and accordingly does not involve worship – although it does involve reverence for the Buddha(s). It also refers to innumerable *devas*, who are gods with a small 'g', perhaps comparable with angels in the Judaeo-Christian-Islamic traditions, but these are not ruling powers who control our destiny. It might perhaps be said that for Buddhism the unseen power of *karma* controls our destiny, but this is not so much a distinct power as a law of nature.

Some, following Ninian Smart and others, prefer the term 'world-view' to 'religion' because it includes not only the non-theistic faiths of Buddhism, Taoism, etc., but also the secular faiths of Marxism and Humanism. Others however want to maintain a clear distinction between religious and secular world-views, the former hinging on some conception of an ultimate reality transcending the material universe whilst the secular faiths deny any such transcendence.

Yet another approach seems to some of us to be even more useful. This is suggested by Wittgenstein's notion of family-resemblance (or cluster) concepts, his well-known example being the concept of a game. Activities which we identify as games are enormously varied and have no common essence. Some are competitive, being played between teams or individuals, whilst others are solitary and non-competitive; some are played with balls of different sizes and shapes, some with cards, some with sticks, darts, etc.; some depend on skill, others on chance; some are played for fun, some for a prize or a monetary reward . . . There is no one feature that they all have in common; but what makes us apply the name 'game' to this wide variety of activities, from football to chess, and from a child playing with her doll to the Olympic Games, is that each has features in common with some others of the family, though not in all respects with any or in any respect with all. We see, says Wittgenstein, 'a complicated network of similarities overlapping and criss-crosssing' like 'the various resemblances between members of a family: build, features, colour of eyes, gait, temperament, etc. etc. overlap and criss-cross in the same way – and, I shall say: "games" form a family' (Wittgenstein 1953: 31–2).

I suggest that 'religion' is another example of a family-resemblance concept, as suggested at one time by Ninian Smart (Smart 1986: 46–7). It has no common essence, but links together a wide range of different phenomena, including communal and solitary worship, a sense of the numinous or holy, animal and human sacrifices, singing, preaching, meditating, praying, obeying commandments, fasts, penances, pilgrimages, propitiating unseen powers, revering paradigm figures, rites of passage, sanctifying marriages, solemnising the disposal of the dead, validating rulers, class structures, wars ... The network can be stretched more widely or less widely. More widely it includes Soviet Marxism, which had its revered paradigm figure in Lenin, its validation of the 'powers that be', its solemn ceremonies, its power to bind a community together, although rejecting belief in God. Used more compactly 'religion' requires some kind of belief in a transcendent supra-natural reality. The wider and narrower clusters are relevant to different interests. From the point of view of sociology the more far flung net is more useful. From the point of view of the 'great world faiths' some transcendental belief is central. The situation is not that one usage is correct and the other wrong, but that they serve different legitimate purposes.

Wilfred Cantwell Smith, who founded and directed the Center for the Study of World Religions at Harvard, has distinguished the two concerns in a very helpful way. In *The Meaning and End of Religion* (1962), a classic of modern religious studies, he distinguished between the cumulative traditions and what he called faith. The cumulative traditions are historical phenomena, integral to different cultures and civilisations and interacting with all the other forces that go to make up human history. Within them, influencing and being influenced by them, there occurs the life of faith, by which he meant the individual's inner spiritual response to what is believed to be the Divine, variously conceived and experienced in both personal and transpersonal ways. The term 'faith' for this inner side of religion is not ideal because it is so often used to mean something quite different, namely belief in propositions which cannot be proved. Unfortunately I cannot think, any more than he could – it was an issue that we discussed on several occasions – of a better term for what Cantwell Smith is referring to. 'Spirituality' is another possibility, but it too has developed misleading connotations in many peoples' minds.

For the purposes of the philosophy, as distinguished from the sociology and the phenomenology, of religion, interest centres on faith (in Cantwell Smith's sense) rather than on the cumulative traditions; but of course it is not a given that faith has any object or that its supposed objects are not creations of the human imagination. A central topic in the philosophy of religion component of religious education, therefore, has always been the arguments for the existence of God – or more broadly for the existence of an ultimate transcendent reality, whether or not personal. Among the traditional 'theistic proofs' – none of which succeed, in the view of most philosophers today – the most pedagogically rewarding is the ontological argument. This is the most subtle of the arguments, involving the concepts of existence, attributes, perfection, and introduces the student to several major thinkers – Anselm, Descartes, Kant, Bertrand Russell. On the other hand, the design argument which is the most readily accessible and introduces the student to Thomas Aquinas and David Hume, has the added interest that it takes new forms today based on the remarkable 'fine tuning'

– an example of a philosophical 'spin' term – in virtue of which the Big Bang has produced galaxies of stars, planets, life, and intelligence. It thus connects with the current science–religion debate, which is both intrinsically important and also of immediate interest to many students.

On the other side of the ledger the most formidable anti-religious argument is, of course, the problem of evil: if the world is created and ruled by an omnipotent loving God, or if the ultimate nature of the universe is benign, how can there be so much human and animal suffering and wickedness in it? Here the student learns to grapple with 'the free will defence' built into the Augustinian and the Irenaean types of theodicy, and the alternative ideas of a finite deity and of a 'God of good and evil', each approach having its own strengths and weaknesses. Arguing about the problem of evil seems to be of natural interest to students. The outcome of the whole debate about what we may infer from the data of human life and the world is, for many of us, an acceptance of the ambiguity of the universe. That is to say, it is possible, at least in principle, to offer both a complete and consistent naturalistic and a complete and consistent religious account of the universe, each including an explanation of the other.

However another approach altogether has now for many people superseded the attempts to prove or disprove the existence of God, or to show that this is more probable than improbable, or vice versa. The traditional arguments continue to be excellent teaching material to stretch students' minds, and should continue to be taught, but they probably nevertheless constitute a philosophical cul-de-sac. The new approach centres on religious experience (e.g. Hick 1988; Alston 1991). It is not however the traditional argument from this to God as its cause. That suffers from the same defect as all other arguments which seek to infer God, whether as first cause, creator, designer etc. from evidences in the world, including religious experience. Instead of arguing *from* some aspect of our experience *to* God, the new approach claims that we experience God or the Transcendent – though not, as we shall see, in a direct and unmediated way. Experience *of* that which impinges on us occurs most obviously in sense experience. When I am looking at, say, a tree I do not infer its existence from my apparent perception of it. If I did, the inference would, as Hume showed, be very insecure. I cannot even *prove* that anything exists beyond the contents of my own present consciousness; but in fact, instead of inferring that there is a tree there, I simply see the tree ('simply' needs to be qualified presently). In ordinary life we take sense perception as the paradigm of reliable cognition.

More precisely, the principle on which we operate – which is almost a definition of sanity – is that it is rational to believe that what appears to exist does indeed exist, *except* when we have reason to doubt it. For we have discovered from experience that there are illusions, hallucinations, mirages as well as veridical perceptions. In what we know to be a hall of distorting mirrors, we do not believe that we are as fat or as thin as we appear in the mirrors to be; but it would be irrational to distrust appearances when we have no reason at all to be suspicious of them. Put positively, it is rational to trust our cognitive experience – i.e. experience that is apparently experience *of* something – except when we have reason not to. Richard Swinburne has called this the principle of credulity (Swinburne 1979: 254), or as I would rather say, the principle of rational credulity. An even better term has recently been introduced: 'critical trust' (Kwan 2003 no. 2).

The big question is whether we can properly apply this principle to religious as well as to sense experience. 'Religious experience', however, has an enormously broad reference stretching from the sublime to the ridiculous. If we define it as forms of experience that are described in terms of religious concepts, it will include at one end of the scale such different experiences as the theistic 'sense of the presence of God' and the non-theistic awareness of being integral to a totality which transcends the physical universe and is 'friendly' or benign in relation to we humans; and at the other end of the scale to such experiences as hearing a divine voice tipping you to bet on a certain horse or select a certain lottery number or commanding you to murder your neighbour.

Clearly, from a religious point of view, some criterion is needed to distinguish between genuine and false forms of religious experience – religious in the formal sense defined above. For just as there are errors and hallucinations in sensory experience, it is to be expected that there should be errors and hallucinations in religious experience. Such a criterion has always operated within the great world faiths, and it is the long-term moral and spiritual effects of the experience in the experiencer's life. The medieval Christian mystics, for example, were acutely conscious that not every vision and voice comes from God. They generally thought of what we call self-delusion as being deceived by the devil. For them the test (apart from the tradition-specific test of doctrinal orthodoxy) lay in the fruits of the experience in one's life. For example, St Teresa of Avila was acutely conscious of the danger of deception and was persuaded of the genuineness of her own visions by their effects in her life, which were evident to everyone. She used the analogy of someone who encounters a stranger who leaves her a gift of jewels. If someone later suggested that the stranger had been a mere apparition, the jewels left in her hand would prove otherwise; and in the case of her visions:

> I could show [any doubters] these jewels – for all who knew me were well aware how my soul had changed: my confessor himself testified to this, for the difference was very great in every respect, and no fancy, but such as all could clearly see ... I concluded, I could not believe that, if the devil were doing this to delude me and drag me down to hell, he would make use of means which so completely defeated their own ends by taking away my vices and making me virtuous and strong; for it was quite clear to me that these experiences had immediately made me a different person.
>
> (Teresa of Avila 1960: 238–9)

In general, among the mystics of each of the great traditions, the difference between delusion and reality is shown by the presence or absence of a transforming effect in the individual's personality and life.

I mentioned earlier that our accepted paradigm of authentic cognitive experience is sense perception; and the main argument for religious experience as delusion lies in its two obvious differences from sense perception. First, sense experience is universal among humans, whereas religious experience apparently, is not. Some indication of the latter's extent in the contemporary western world is given by a survey by National Opinion Polls in 1978, finding that some 66 per cent of adults in Britain report some kind of experience that they regard as religious (Hay 1990: 79). Second, sense experience is uniform around the world (with relatively slight cultural differences which we can overlook for our present purpose) whereas religious experience takes markedly different forms within the different religions. Further, these differences are clearly correlated with the different teachings and practices of the religious traditions. Christians may see visions of Jesus, whereas Vaishnavite Hindus may see visions of Krishna, and Jews of neither; and whereas theists experience the divine as personal, Buddhists have quite different forms of religious experience. Do not these manifest differences between sensory and religious experience make it proper to trust the one but distrust the other?

These arguments *against* trusting religious experience cohere with the pervasive naturalistic assumption of our culture and do not need further elaboration; but the argument *for* trusting it needs to be made out. The key is the profound differences between the two objects of putative experience. The physical world of which we are part has conditioned us to experience it correctly, that is, in the way appropriate to animals of our size in our biological niche. If humanity had not long since learned by experience that we cannot breathe under water, or walk with impunity into a rock face, or jump off a high cliff without being injured or killed, *homo sapiens* would not have survived. Indeed all this must already have been learned much further back in the evolutionary process. A correct perception of our physical environment is compulsory; we obey the teachings of nature on pain of death. However whilst this massively intrusive givenness of the material world constitutes the situation within which we exercise our moral freedom, it does not undermine that freedom. It restricts our freedom of physical movement but not our moral freedom within the given world.

This is significantly in contrast to our putative experience of the divine. Suppose that, interpenetrating and transcending our material or natural environment there is a supra-natural environment. This is variously known, by Jews and Christians, as the universal presence of God, who is 'God in heaven above and on earth beneath' (Joshua, 2: 11, Revised Standard Version 2nd ed. 1971); by Muslims, as being under the eye of Allah, for 'To God belong the East and the West. Wherever you turn the face of God is everywhere: all pervading and He is all-knowing' (Qur'an, 2: 115 – Ali: 1988);

by Buddhists, as the Dharma or the universal Buddha nature; by Hindus, as the ultimate ineffable reality of Brahman, revealed in many forms, including Vishnu who declares, 'I pervade the world. All beings have their being in me' (Bhagavad Gita, 9: 4 – Bolle 1979); and in a range of other terms within these and other religions.

Now whereas our natural environment forces itself upon our attention, our supra-natural environment does not. If we were compelled to be conscious of it, we would lack the inner freedom in virtue of which we are moral and spiritual persons rather then creaturely puppets. In theistic terms, if we existed from the beginning in the immediate presence of the omnipotent and omniscient God, so that it was impossible not to be conscious of being under God's all-seeing eye, the idea of a free response to God would never arise. According to Christianity, even God incarnate did not force himself upon the world but appealed for a free response of faith; and so it is appropriate, indeed necessary, that as finite, free beings we exist at an epistemic distance from the divine reality. God has to be *deus absconditus*, the hidden God, whom we come to know through a venture of trust. Likewise, to realise our union with Brahman, or to realise the universal Buddha nature within us, we have deliberately to open ourselves to that higher, and also deeper, reality.

According to each of the great traditions, this is possible because there is already an aspect of our being which naturally responds to the divine reality – the image of God, Allah being 'immanent ... in human souls (*anfus*)' (Yaran 2004: 5), the *atman*, the Buddha nature deep within us, the divine spark, 'that of God in every man', so that in St Augustine's words, 'our hearts are restless until they rest in thee' (Augustine 1945: 1). This capacity for religious response, however, exists in tension with our natural animal self-centredness, deriving from the instinctive desire to survive. We live in the freedom and responsibility created by the opposition between these two poles of our nature.

To be liberated from, or to grow out of, the dominance of the ego, which sees and judges everything as it affects oneself, is to become open to others in compassion (feeling with and for others) and love, to be unthreatened by the otherness of others, to be a creator of peace and justice in a violent and unjust world. From a religious point of view, this is a response to the divine reality, made possible by our inner openness to it; but we are all aware today that such a response, in its varying degrees, does not *have* to be conceptualised in religious terms, or indeed in any specific terms. In the past, and still in many parts of the world today, it has normally been thought of in explicitly religious terms; but because those terms have generally failed to develop with the development of human knowledge and thought they have been increasingly jettisoned by modern secular society. So as well as both genuine and illusory religious experience, in the sense of experience structured by religious concepts, there is also awareness of the divine which is not formed in terms of religious concepts at all but more often in moral and political terms – or indeed often without systematic conceptuality of any kind.

What, however, about the other obvious difference from sense experience, namely the latter's (virtual) uniformity throughout the world in contrast to the immense variety of forms of religious experience and belief within the different religious traditions? It seems obvious that these differences are correlated with differences in the human cultures within which they arise. For example, historians of religion have pointed out that ancient nomadic herd-keeping societies of the Middle East, where herding was mainly a male activity, tended to think of the divine in male terms, whilst the ancient settled agricultural societies of north India, sustained by mother earth, tended to worship female gods. But if we can explain the distinctive nature of the different religions in such purely mundane terms, why not see religion as a whole as a human creation? Why not add to the cultural formation of the traditions either the suggestion of Freud that God is a projection of the infant's early memory of the omnipotent parent, or Marx's theory that it is an instrument of social control by the ruling class, or Durkheim's proposal that the gods are representations of society as a greater reality than the individual, or the contemporary assumption that religion is a form of wish fulfilment in a precarious world?

At this point we have to turn to epistemology and within this to critical realism. This term was introduced by a group of American philosophers in the last century who were concerned with the problems of sense perception, though it is now also much used in the philosophy of science. The central idea, however, was familiar centuries earlier. Thomas Aquinas wrote that 'The thing known is in the knower according to the mode of the knower' (Aquinas 1945: 1057); and the critical realist principle is that we do not experience our environment as it is in itself, independently of the human observer, but as it appears to us with our distinctively human cognitive equipment. This is in distinction from both the non-realism which denies that there is anything 'out there' beyond our own consciousness (as argued by Berkeley, though qualified for him by the activity of God), and the naïve realism of ordinary life which assumes that we are directly perceiving the world as it is. In the case of the material world, our sensory faculties are extremely limited and selective, and our conceptual apparatus then further organises their reports into the three-dimensional world of solid objects in which we live. Immanuel Kant, with his distinction between noumenal and phenomenal reality, is of course much the greatest influence here. However, he did not apply his epistemology to religious awareness. If he had he would, I suggest, have concluded that, as in the case of sense perception, we experience the divine environment, not as it is in itself, independently of the structures of human awareness, but in the forms in which our religious conceptualities are able to receive it in our consciousness. Whereas, however, in sense perception the 'mode of the knower' is substantially constant throughout the human race, in religious awareness it is deeply influenced by the different cultures, including their differing religious thought systems.

Thus, in religion, naïve realism is the assumption of many 'ordinary believers' that the divine reality is in itself just as conceived and experienced within the believer's particular tradition or sub-tradition. In sharp contrast to this, non-realism is the rejection of any transcendent divine reality, however conceived. Within the Christian world the classical statement is that of Ludwig Feuerbach in the early nineteenth century, particularly in *The Essence of Christianity* (1841). Today, its leading exponent in Britain is Don Cupitt, particularly in his writings of about twenty years ago, such as *Taking Leave of God* (1980). Critical realism is the middle position – that there is a transcendent divine reality, but that we can only be conscious of it in the various ways made possible by our different human religious conceptualities and spiritual practices – these being embodied in the different religious traditions. If this is indeed the case, it meets the objection that, in contrast to sense experience, religious experience takes such a wide variety of very different forms.

The discussion of such issues is open ended. Indeed this is why the philosophy of religion provides such ample material to provoke students to think for themselves – which is the primary aim of education.

References

Ali, A. (1988) *Al-Quran: a Contemporary Translation*, Princeton, NJ: Princeton University Press.

Alston, W. (1991) *Perceiving God*, Ithaca and London: Cornell University Press.

Aquinas, T. (1945) *Summa Theologica* II:II, Q. 1, art. 2, *Basic Writings of Saint Thomas Aquinas*, Vol. 2, A.C. Pegis (ed.), New York: Random House.

Augustine, St. (1945) *Confessions*, trans. F.J. Sheed, London: Sheed & Ward.

Bolle, K.E. (1979) *The Bhagavadgita: a New Translation*, Berkeley, Los Angeles, London: University of California Press.

Cupitt, D. (1980) *Taking Leave of God*, London: SCM Press.

Feuerbach, L. (1957) *The Essence of Christianity* 1841, trans. George Eliot, New York: Harper & Brothers.

Hay, D. (1990) *Religious Experience Today*, London: Mowbray.

Hick, J. (1988) *Faith and Knowledge*, 2nd edn, Ithaca: Cornell University Press, and London: Macmillan.

Kwan, K. (2003) 'Is the Critical Trust Approach to Religious Experience Incompatible with Religious Particularism?', *Faith and Philosophy*, 20: 2.

Smart, N. (1986) *Concept and Empathy*, Donald Wiebe (ed.), London: Macmillan.

Smith, W.C. (1962) *The Meaning and End of Religion*, Minneapolis: Fortress Press.

Swinburne, R. (1979) *The Existence of God*, Oxford: Clarendon Press.

Teresa of Avila (1960) *The Autobiography of St Teresa of Avila*, trans. E. Allison Peers, New York: Image Books.

Wittgenstein, L. (1953) *Philosophical Investigations*, trans. G.E.M. Anscombe, Oxford: Blackwell.

Yaran, C.S. (2004) *Muslim Religious Experience*, Lampeter: Religious Experience Research Centre.

4 The teaching of human rights in religious education

The case of genocide

Liam Gearon

Samantha Power's magisterial *A Problem from Hell: America and the Age of Genocide* is powerful testimony to horror in the twentieth century and to a crime terrible enough to need a new name: 'genocide' (Power 2003: 42). Raphael Lemkin's controversial hybrid word combined 'the Greek derivative of *geno* for "race" or "tribe" and the Latin derivative *cide* from *caedere* meaning "killing"' (ibid.). Covering a vast territory from the systematic slaughter and destruction of Armenians by Turks in the early part of the twentieth century through the Cambodia of Pol Pot in the 1970s to the Balkans and Kosovo in the 1990s – her Pulitzer Prize winning work *America and the Age of Genocide* is a tale of what in colonial days the writer Joseph Conrad defined as *The Heart of Darkness*.

The day before the UN General Assembly signed the 'Universal Declaration of Human Rights' on 10 December, it approved the 1948 Convention against Genocide, with its famous preamble:

> Having considered the declaration made by the General Assembly of the United Nations ... that genocide is a crime under international law, contrary to the spirit and aims of the United Nations and condemned by the civilized world, recognizing that at all periods of history genocide has inflicted great losses on humanity, and being convinced that, in order to liberate mankind from such an odious scourge, international co-operation is required.

In a world weary of two world wars and with a clear awareness of the systematic Nazi practices of mass-death, the Convention was born out of a 'never again' mentality.

Yet at the World Conference on Human Rights at Vienna in 1993, condemnation of 'massive violations of human rights especially in the form of genocide, ethnic cleansing and systematic rape of women in war situations' (Para 28) was notable amongst the laments of the gathered international community. The fact that such laments came close on the heels of the massive violence of the Balkans in the early 1990s and only two years before the numerically even more atrocious figures of mass death in Rwanda and neighbouring countries, is itself arguably indicative of a massive failure by the same international community to do anything but talk. The history of such apparent failure goes back much further than the 1990s.

Convention on the Prevention and Punishment of the Crime of Genocide 9 December 1948, entry into force 12 January 1951

Article 1 states that 'Genocide, whether committed in time of peace or in time of war, is a crime under international law' which the international community undertakes to prevent and to punish.

Article 2 states that 'In the present Convention, genocide means any of the following acts committed with intent to destroy, in whole or in part, a national, ethnical, racial or religious group, as such:

(a) Killing members of the group;
(b) Causing serious bodily or mental harm to members of the group;
(c) Deliberately inflicting on the group conditions of life calculated to bring about its physical destruction in whole or in part;
(d) Imposing measures intended to prevent births within the group;
(e) Forcibly transferring children of the group to another group.'

Article 3 states that the following acts shall be punishable:

'(a) Genocide;
(b) Conspiracy to commit genocide;
(c) Direct and public incitement to commit genocide;
(d) Attempt to commit genocide;
(e) Complicity in genocide.'

Article 4 states that 'Persons committing genocide or any of the other acts enumerated in article III shall be punished, whether they are constitutionally responsible rulers, public officials or private individuals.'

For the full text of the 19 articles and other international legal standards on genocide and human rights, follow links at www.unhchr.org.

Since 1948, genocide, defined here as the systematic and deliberate targeting for extinction of particular sections of a population, has happened repeatedly. Ryan's study of the United Nations (Ryan 2000) includes some depressing figures on its regularity not only decade-to-decade but within each decade since the late 1940s, and this is clearly illustrated here:

Mass Slaughter Since the 1948 Convention Against Genocide			
Date	State	Victims	Deaths
1943–57	USSR	Chechens, Ingushi, Karachai	230,000
1944–68	USSR	Crimean Tartars, Meskhetians	57,000–175,000
1955–77	China	Tibetans	Not available
1959–75	Iraq	Kurds	Not available
1962–72	Paraguay	Ache Indians	90,000
1963–64	Rwanda	Tutsis	5,000–14,000
1963	Laos	Meo Tribesmen	18,000–20,000
1965–66	Indonesia	Chinese	500,000–1 million
1965–73	Burundi	Hutus	103,000–205,000
1966	Nigeria	Ibos in North	9,000–30,000
1966–84	Guatemala	Indians	30,000–63,000
1968–85	Philippines	Moros	10,000–100,000
	Equatorial Guinea	Bubi Tribe	1,000–50,000
1971	Pakistan	Bengalis of Eastern Pakistan	1.25–3 million
1971–79	Uganda	Karamajong, Acholi, Lango	100,000–500,000
1975–79	Cambodia	Including Muslim Cham	2 million?
1975–98	Indonesia	East Timorese	60,000–200,000
1978 to present	Burma	Muslims in border regions	Not available
1979–86	Uganda	Karamanjong, Nilotic Tribes Bagandans	50,000–100,000
1981	Iran	Kurds, Bahais	10,000–20,000
1983–87	Sri Lanka	Tamils	2,000–10,000
1994	Rwanda	Tutsis	500,000–1 million
1992–95	Bosnia-Herzegovina	Mainly Bosnian Muslims	200,000

(Ryan, in Gearon 2002)

Since the failures of the 1948 Genocide Convention and related international standards to curtail effectively post-Holocaust instances of systematic and mass killing, the practice known as genocide and its punishment through international human rights law (Schabas 2000) become the source of serious academic study. Analyses vary from generic (Ball 1999; Kressel 2001), comparative (Chorbajian and Shirnian 1999; Hinton 2002; Lorey and Beezley

2002) and even encyclopaedic (Charny 1999) treatments to assessments of the regional and specific, from Armenia (Dadrian 1999), Cambodia (Chandler 2001) to Bosnia-Herzogovina (Weine 1999) and Rwanda (Gourevitch 1999). The defining genocide of the Holocaust remains an abiding academic interest for historians in ever-new guises and nuances such as a recent interpretation of the Nazi atrocities as an economic as well as ideological process (Allen 2002). The Holocaust also remains an official interest of government bodies overseeing education, at least in England and Wales (DfEE 2000).

Genocide in the twentieth century remains, then, our foundational guide to human rights discourse in the twenty-first: the historical path from the signing of the UN's 1948 Convention on the Prevention and Punishment of the Crime of Genocide to the evident failures in the international community to prevent further instances of genocide, ethnic cleansing and crimes against humanity in subsequent decades. The creation of a modern discourse of human rights, then, arises principally from the facts of mass death, from attempts of one party or another to end the discourse of another, usually the other. The most extreme form of this attempt to end discourse is genocide where the 'other' is defined most characteristically by diametric opposition to an ideological position identifiable often by religious, cultural or ethnic minority. The first dictatorial act of the Nazis in Berlin was the burning of books. The seventieth anniversary of this was commemorated in Berlin and other major German cities in 2003.

Since the contemporary manifestation of rights arises from the historical circumstances of genocide, there is a direct causal link between genocide and wider human rights as understood from the mid-twentieth century onwards. There is an integral connection between the form of words, then, that materialized in the United Nations Charter in 1945, the 'Universal Declaration of Human Rights' three years later, and the genocide which preceded these declarations. Genocide is the ultimate in terms of ending the cultural discourse of the other. In this regard, genocide is the ultimate attempt at human silence. It is from this silence – the silence of genocide – that the words of the UN, the UN itself, arose.

Teaching genocide through religious education

By contrast with such a frightening and fearsome global history, the theory and practice of religious education over recent decades has tended, at least within the UK, towards a benign neglect of the political, as a review of otherwise significant work here demonstrates (Grimmitt 2000). Whether or not this reflects the indifference of the young and their teachers to mainstream politics (Gearon 2003) this 'benign neglect of the political' arguably results from a pedagogy that consciously or otherwise engages with a study of religious culture and concepts without significant reference to the power structures that underpin these (Gearon 2001; cf. Hull 1999, 2001, 2001a; Jackson 2002).

The local and global circumstances from which such neglect has arisen highlights a crisis of isolation, and manifold examples can be cited. I present two, and arguably religious education was ready for neither of these local or global events. It was a lack of readiness that could have been predicted from the absence of a systematic response to politics in the broadest possible of senses. Local to England are the challenges brought to religious education by the introduction of Citizenship since September 2001 (Gearon 2003a, 2003b). With citizenship education increasingly an issue across Europe for religious educators (Jackson 2002), the devastating effects of 11 September have also brought a sense that curricula based on high-minded principles of tolerance, understanding and empathy, also need something of a more hard-edged engagement for times when there are clashes between supposedly *universal* values such as human rights and *culturally particular* religious beliefs and/or moral values (Ayton-Shenker 1995; Lerner 2000; Marshall 2000; Bloom, Martin and Proudfoot 2000; Gearon 2002).

With the prevalence of post-Holocaust instances of genocide and ethnic cleansing, there are studies that question its uniqueness (Rosenbaum 2001; Smith 2002; Waller 2002). Aside, however, from studies related to the role of nationalism and ethnicity (Haynes 2001), the role of religion in genocidal practices has received fairly scant attention, though there are some studies rectifying this (Bartov and Mack 2001). The 'suffering citizen' raises wider issues of moral responsibility as well as acute philosophical problems. This difficult territory presents challenges for teacher and student alike but now means that religious education needs to develop a more politically engaged pedagogy.

Tremendous possibilities exist here for widening and developing relationships between history, citizenship and religious education. For instance, history and religious education departments could explore possibilities for a joint visit to a war museum to explore the political as well as philosophical implications of religion and war, human rights and genocide. In England the notable example is the Imperial War Museum, particularly the Holocaust exhibition. The Imperial War Museum also contains a vast range of materials for religious educators to use in relation to ethical issues and moral dilemmas raised by war more generally, including the 'Just War', development issues and conflict, as well as terrorism. The museum contains two significant galleries of art from World War I and II.

For more advanced studies, the UN Research Institute for Social Development (UNRISD), based in Geneva, has for some time been developing a number of research programmes directed at religious, cultural and ethnic conflict. At the UNRISD website religious educators will find the following links helpful:

> The Search for Identity Ethnicity Religion and Political Violence;
> Ethnic Violence Conflict Resolution and Cultural Pluralism;
> Ethnic Diversity and Public Policy: An Overview.

One of the major international developments is the development of the International Criminal Court (ICC) that presents opportunities for those guilty of war crimes and crimes against humanity to be brought to justice.

Religious Education and Genocide: The International Criminal Court

UN International Criminal Court Site
http://www.un.org/law/icc
Council of Europe page on the International Criminal Court
http://www.legal.coe.int/criminal/icc
Amnesty International ICC Site
http://www.amnesty.org.uk/action/camp/icc
International Criminal Tribunal for Rwanda
http://www.un.org/ictr
International Criminal Tribunal for the Former Yugoslavia
http://www.un.org/icty

Genocide remains a central challenge to religious education especially where ethnic and cultural concerns are paramount. Ideals of tolerance and mutual understanding, dialogue and engagement are principles that most religious educators will recognize as integral to their pedagogical practice. The United Nations has only belatedly recognized here that issues of explicit religious belonging and identity cannot be ignored, and a mark of this is international declarations related directly to religion and belief.

The Universal Declaration of Human Rights includes a number of articles of relevance to freedom of religion and belief. These include Article 2 (forbidding prejudicial distinctions of any kind, including those related to religion), Article 26 (on the rights to a particular religious education) and Article 29 (on responsibilities and proscription against limitations of proclaimed rights). The foundation stone of freedom of religion and belief, though, is to be found in Article 18 of the 'Universal Declaration of Human Rights'. This states that, 'Everyone has the right to freedom of: thought, conscience and religion; this right includes freedom to change his/her religion or belief, and freedom, either alone or in community with others and in public or private, to manifest his/her religion or belief in teaching, practice, worship and observance.' Article 18 greatly influenced the texts incorporated in the 1966 Covenants, and was influential in regional treaties and the 1981 *Declaration on the Elimination of All Forms of Intolerance and Discrimination Based on Religion or Belief.*

International Legal Standard: Defending Freedom of Religion and Belief

Declaration on the Elimination of All Forms of Intolerance and of Discrimination based on Religion or Belief (25 November 1981)
Declaration on the Rights of Persons Belonging to National or Ethnic, Religious and Linguistic Minorities (18 December 1992)
Oslo Declaration on Freedom of Religion and Belief (1998)
World Conference against Racism, Xenophobia and Related Forms of Discrimination (September, 2002)

For a full text of the documents, follow links at www.unhcr.org.

The preamble to this Declaration restates the wider context of the Charter of the UN. Notably this reiterates the 'dignity and equality inherent in all human beings', international commitment on the promotion of universal human rights and fundamental freedoms for all, 'without distinction as to race, sex, language or religion' and the principles of 'non-discrimination and equality before the law and the right to freedom of thought, conscience, religion and belief'.

As with the Convention on the International Rights of Correction, the UN *Declaration on the Elimination of All Forms of Intolerance and Discrimination Based on Religion or Belief* also emphasizes the role of such freedoms in the maintenance of a stable international order:

> Considering that the disregard and infringement of human rights and fundamental freedoms, in particular of the right to freedom of thought, conscience, religion or whatever belief, have brought, directly or indirectly, wars and great suffering to mankind, especially where they serve as a means of foreign interference in the internal affairs of other States and amount to kindling hatred between peoples and nations.

Positively phrased, this might read: 'freedom of religion and belief should also contribute to the attainment of the goals of world peace, social justice and friendship among peoples and to the elimination of ideologies or practices of colonialism and racial discrimination'.

Yet it is not simply past ills that are the concern of the UN, for the 1981 Declaration is also concerned about 'manifestations of intolerance and by the existence of discrimination in matters of religion or belief still in evidence in some areas of the world'. The 1981 Declaration also offers a commitment to adopt 'all necessary measures for the speedy elimination of such intolerance in all its forms and manifestations and to prevent and combat discrimination on the ground of religion or belief'.

There are two important contexts, both US-based, where religion and rights are seen as a barometer of wider democratic freedoms and indicative of an increasing importance of religious and cultural factors in international relations: the United States legislature and a Non-Government Organization (NGO) called Freedom House. First, the 1998 International Religious Freedom Act made it a requirement for the US Secretary of State to publish an Annual Report on religious freedom worldwide. Published each September, the Annual Report is submitted to the Committee on International Relations at the US House of Representatives and the Committee on Foreign Relations of the US Senate by the Department of State. The Report is extensive and provides country-by-country accounts of religious freedoms, the infringements of and improvements in relation to such rights to belief. It is available at http://www.house.gov/international_relations/ and http://www.state.gov/g/drl/rls/inf/2001/ (or whichever date the Report refers to). The Report contains an extremely useful executive summary – the 2001 Report was close to 700 pages. Fundamentally, the US Department of State clearly links freedom of religion and the likelihood that countries that preserve this will respect other fundamental rights. It goes on to reiterate how, in the international domain, 'Freedom of religion and conscience is one of the foundational rights in the post-War system of human rights instruments.' It again makes explicit how in 'recent years, the international commitment to religious freedom has increased'.

Second, the world's foremost independent NGO concerned with issues of religious freedom is Freedom House. A major achievement of Freedom House has been the publication of its highly accessible *Religious Freedom in the World* (Marshall 2000). Marshall's survey interestingly overlaps with developments in the US Department of State and its Report on International Religious Freedom, a document that Marshall welcomes but with reservations. Marshall's comment is that the US Department of State Report can lessen criticism of states that happen to be key allies at a particular time in history. Human Rights Watch similarly claim that the 'War on Terror' has lessened US Department of State criticisms of certain countries – especially in the 2001 Report where the United States required strategic allies. The Freedom House global survey reviewed the state of religious freedom in the majority of the world's countries, providing useful snapshot insights into the political context of religious life in each. The survey criteria were developed from the UN *Declaration on the Elimination of All Forms of Intolerance and of Discrimination Based on Religion or Belief*, and related UN instruments.

A number of broad trends can be identified here, all of which impinge upon any teaching about genocide understood as the targeting of particular segments of a national population:

First, after a long neglect (or low-level treatment) of religion explicitly, since the late 1970s and early 1980s, global politics and the UN system in particular have begun to recognize the international significance of religion for a stable world order. Thus, during the 1990s, religion emerges explicitly in numerous international statements, gaining new and unprecedented prominence. For instance, there were the *Cairo Declaration on Human Rights in Islam* (1990), the *Fundamental Agreement between the Holy See and the State of Israel* (1993), *The Vienna Declaration and Plan of Action* (1993) and the follow-up to the World Conference on Human Rights – the Report of the UN High Commissioner for Human Rights (1998) also gave some prominence to religion, important in the light of their respective post-Yugoslavia and post-Rwanda contexts (especially paragraphs 34–9). The new prominence given to religion culminated in the *Oslo Declaration on Freedom of Religion and Belief* (1998).

Second, and indicated by both the 1981 Declaration and the 1998 Oslo Declaration, the notion of freedom of religion was itself extended to freedom of religion and belief to allow for a wider interpretation of worldviews (Lerner 2000; UN 2002a, 2002b, 2002c).

Third, this has in turn had the effect of linking in a fairly direct way the fundamental first and second generation rights of 'freedom of thought, conscience and religion' to third generation rights of human solidarity, most notable in the linking of religious intolerance to the ending of racism, xenophobia and discrimination more broadly. For example, we might note the 1981 *Declaration on the Elimination of All Forms of Intolerance and of Discrimination Based on Religion or Belief* was followed just over a decade later by the UN *Declaration on the Rights of Persons Belonging to National or Ethnic, Religious, and Linguistic Minorities* (1992), and the theme of unifying religious freedom with other forms of discrimination was highlighted by the World Conference Against Racism (2001) (cf. Marshall, 2000). The conclusion of this event immediately before the events of 11 September in the US powerfully underlines the complexities and heightened importance of religious, cultural and political difference to the curriculum.

Religion, culture and crimes against humanity

It is self-evident that the twentieth century witnessed death on a mass, almost industrial, scale, often consciously directed at specific ethnic, cultural and religious elements of national populations. These 'crimes against humanity' were of a kind that required a new name: 'genocide'. It was genocide that was on the mind of the newly formed United Nations when it made its Universal Declaration of Human Rights in the form of 30 articles on 10 December 1948. The late twentieth century was witness to massive failure by the international community in preventing repetition of these historical scars. These failures present historical truths as urgent questions for teachers of religious education. Can any ultimate good come out of cultural violence and intolerance, 'ethnic cleansing' and genocide? What does violence on a systematic scale directed at religious or ethnic minorities do to change our understanding of citizenship? Is there ever justice for crimes against humanity? Does genocide make notions such as civilization and citizenship a veneer, and the hopes of religion a matter of wishful thinking?

Here, not all religions have a good record on human rights – issues as broad as gender equality, or freedom of expression, or even freedom of religion and belief. Religious fanaticism and democracy do not often go easily hand in hand. Ironically or not, in England, the Qualifications and Curriculum Authority (QCA) unit (13) on 'Citizenship and Religious Education' (www.qca.gov.org.uk) also focuses explicitly on 'Conflict', heightening the historical and contemporary political arenas where religion remains a source of war and violence. The risk here is of another stereotype, that religion *per se* is the source of too much fighting and too many of the world's wars. This negative image problem has been exacerbated since 11 September 2001. By an odd twist of fate the UN's 'World Conference against Racism, Racial Discrimination, Xenophobia and Related Intolerance' had just concluded in South Africa days earlier – on 8 September 2001 – and on a supposedly optimistic note. Ugly debates about the clash of civilizations soon re-emerged.

Religious education runs two risks: either it represents religion as inoffensive, or it confirms what media stereotypes too often repeat, that religion remains a major source of conflict in the modern world. What teachers of religious education possess is the expert knowledge of religious traditions that can provide informed, balanced and engaging perspectives on real and important matters of belief and values, belonging and identity – and what happens when these clash.

Questions of belonging, belief and identity contain the potential for conflict. At the extreme, and with an inflammatory political context, violently contended concepts of what it means to be a citizen can become crimes against humanity. Without religious education all of those involving questions of belonging, belief and identity are likely to be ill informed.

Genocide is a warning of the risk of accepting what I have designated a 'violent silence', and in education this 'accepting' can mean the most benign form of simply 'not teaching about'. Systems intolerant of cultural and religious expression can easily transform into mass death. Sometimes, sadly, religious and cultural difference is part of the problem. Pedagogical neglect of the controversial, public, political face of religious traditions will solve nothing; pedagogical engagement between religious and political education will not resolve the world's problems, but it is now unavoidable.

Conclusion

Genocide is a vacuum into which all notions of human goodness, all thought of rights, all optimism, can sink without trace. What this chapter is an attempt to do is to provide some brief space for the religious educator to reflect – on the fact that genocide fundamentally challenges all notions of civilization, culture, social and political order. A space to reflect on the fact that, of all species that have ever existed, only human beings do this to each other. Genocide is an amoral vacuum, a black hole into which all social and political order is sucked until the point of singularity, nothingness. Yet history has recorded its aftermath. As we look back from the twenty-first century, the trace of this history still blazes across the decades, every decade, of the twentieth.

If there was any justification for religious education making a contribution to citizenship, especially the complexities of religious and cultural difference here, it is to learn the lessons about human nature and human history that genocide teaches: its origins, the horror of its enactment, its punishment and its prevention.

References

Ayton-Shenker, D. (1995) *The Challenge of Human Rights and Cultural Diversity*, Geneva: United Nations Department of Public Information.

Allen, M.T. (2002) *The Business of Genocide: The SS, Slave Labour and the Concentration Camps*, Chapel Hill: University of North Carolina Press.

Ball, H. (1999) *Prosecuting War Crimes and Genocide: The Twentieth-Century Experience*, Lawrence: University Press of Kansas.

Bartov, O. and Mack, P. (eds) (2001) *In God's Name: Genocide and Religion in the Twentieth Century*, Oxford: Berghahn Books.

Bloom, I., Martin, J.P. and Proudfoot, W.L. (eds) (2000) *Religious Diversity and Human Rights*, New York: Columbia University Press.

Chandler, D.P. (2001) *Voices from S-21: Terror and History in Pol Pot's Secret Prison*, Berkeley: University of California Press.

Charny, I.W. (ed.) (1999) *Encyclopedia of Genocide*, forewords by Desmond M. Tutu and Simon Weisenthal, Santa Barbara, CA: ABC-CLIO.

Chorbajian, L. and Shirnian, G. (eds) (1999) *Studies in Comparative Genocide*, Basingstoke: Macmillan.

Dadrian, V.N. (1999) *Warrant for Genocide: Key Elements of Turko-Armenian Conflict*, New Brunswick, NJ: Transaction Publishers.

DFEE (2000) *Holocaust Memorial Day: Remembering Genocides, Lessons for the Future Education Pack*, London: DfEE.

Gearon, L. (ed.) (2001) 'The Imagined Other: Postcolonial Theory and Religious Education', *British Journal of Religious Education*, 23: 98–106.

—— (2002a) 'Human Rights and Religious Education: Some Postcolonial Perspectives', *British Journal of Religious Education*, 24: 140–50.

—— (2002) *Human Rights and Religion: A Reader*, Brighton and Portland: Sussex Academic Press.

—— (2003) *How Do We Become Good Citizens: A Review of Citizenship Education Research for the British Educational Research Association*, London: BERA.

—— (2003a) *Citizenship through Religious Education*, London: Routledge.

—— (2003b) *Learning to Teach Citizenship in the Secondary School*, London: Routledge.

Gourevitch, P. (1999) *We Wish to Inform You That Tomorrow We Will Be Killed With Our Families: Stories from Rwanda*, London: Picador.

Grimmitt, M. (2000) *Pedagogies of Religious Education*, Great Wakering: McCrimmons.

Haynes, J. (1998) *Religion in Global Politics*, Harlow: Longman.

Hinton, A.L. (ed.) (2002) *Genocide: An Anthropological Reader*, Malden: Blackwell.

Hull, J. (1999) 'Bargaining with God: Religious Development and Economic Socialization, *Journal of Psychology and Theology*, 27: 241–9.

—— (2001) 'The Contribution of Religious Education to Religious Freedom: A Global Perspective', in Zarín T. Caldwell (ed.) *Religious Education in Schools: Ideas and Experiences from around the World*, Oxford: International Association for Religious Freedom.

—— (2001a) 'Competition and Spiritual Development', *International Journal of Children's Spirituality*, 6(3): 263–75.

Jackson, R. (2003) *International Perspectives on Citizenship, Education and Religious Diversity*, London: Routledge.

—— (2004) *Rethinking Religious Education and Plurality: Issues in Diversity and Plurality*, London: Routledge.

Kressel, N.J. (2001) *Mass Hate: The Global Rise of Genocide and Terror*, Cambridge, MA: Westview.

Lerner, N. (2000) *Religion, Beliefs, and Human Rights*, Maryknoll, NY: Orbis.

Lorey, D.E. and Beezley, W.H. (eds) (2002) *Genocide, Collective Violence and Popular Memory: The Politics of Remembrance in the Twentieth Century*, Wilmington, DE: SR Books.

Marshall, P. (ed.) (2000) *Religious Freedom in the World: A Global Report on Freedom and Persecution*, London: Broadman and Holman.

Power, S. (2003) *A Problem from Hell: America and the Age of Genocide*, London: Flamingo.

Rosenbaum, A.S. (ed.) (2001) *Is the Holocaust Unique?: Perspectives on Comparative Genocide*, Oxford: Westview Press.

Ryan, S. (2000) *The United Nations and International Politics*, London: Macmillan.

—— (2002) in L. Gearon (ed.) *Human Rights and Religion: A Reader*, Brighton and Portland: Sussex Academic Press.

Schabas, W. (2000) *Genocide in International Law: The Crime of Crimes*, Cambridge: Cambridge University Press.

Smith, H.W. (ed.) (2002) *The Holocaust and Other Genocides: History, Representation, Ethics*, Nashville, TN: Vanderbilt University Press.

United Nations (1998a) *Report of the UN High Commissioner for Human Rights*, Geneva: United Nations.

—— (1998b) *The UN Decade for Human Rights Education 1995–2004*, (New York: United Nations.

—— (2002a) *Extrajudicial, Summary or Arbitrary Executions Fact Sheet 11*, New York: United Nations.

—— (2002b) *Elimination of All Forms of Intolerance and Discrimination based on Religion or Belief*, Human Rights Study Series, No. 2, New York: United Nations.

—— (2002c) *Study on the Rights of Persons belonging to Ethnic, Religious or Linguistic Minorities*, Human Rights Study Series, No. 5, New York: United Nations.

Waller, J. (2002) *Becoming Evil: How Ordinary People Commit Genocide and Mass Killing*, Oxford: Oxford University Press.

Weine, S.M. (1999) *When History is a Nightmare: Lives and Memories of Ethnic Cleansing in Bosnia-Herzogovina*, New Brunswick, NJ: Rutgers University Press.

5   Open minds, ongoing heritage, open future

The educational theology of John Hull

Wilna Meijer

In 1982 a volume on religious education appeared in the 'New Directions Series', a series of readers having 'the purpose of indicating the state of thought, research and enquiry into specific areas within the study of education', as the blurb explains. John Hull was the editor of this volume. He had compiled a selection of articles from the *British Journal of Religious Education* and its predecessor *Learning for Living* in the 1970s, the decade in which religious education in Britain was 'emerging as virtually a new subject' (Hull 1982: xiv). The Birmingham Agreed Syllabus of 1975, to the development of which Hull himself had been a key contributor, can be regarded as a milestone in that history. In this decade an agreement had developed that religious education 'could not continue as the attempt to foster Christian faith', or indeed any particular religion, but that it should rather 'promote a sympathetic but critical understanding of religions' (ibid.).

Hull mentions two aspects of the context relevant to this new course: the increased plurality and secularity of British society and 'the rise of a new view of education which seeks to foster a more critical and more autonomous individual' (ibid. xiii). I take it that the latter refers to the concept of education as explicated in the philosophy of education of Dearden, Hirst and Peters, that also had its heyday in the 1970s (cf. their famous three volume *Education and the Development of Reason* (1972)). These three philosophers of education, sometimes called *the trinity*, were highly influential. The involved concept of education was explained in terms of 'the development of states of a person that involve knowledge and understanding in depth and breadth', as the formulation in Hirst and Peters's classic *The Logic of Education* (1970) goes. The newly developed phenomenological approach to world religions in religious education was in harmony with this educational concept.

In his introduction to the *New Directions* volume of 1982, Hull, overseeing the developments, emphasises the merits of the new approach, but also discerns its imminent danger:

> The best was the ideal of a truly educational enterprise, appropriate to the common schools of a pluralist and freedom loving democracy in which a wide variety of beliefs and values exist, a religious education

which would not seek to mould the mind along sectarian lines or even in conformity with the wishes of a powerful majority, but would be informative and rational, enabling pupils to express and defend their positions, making them 'worth attending to' and thus raising the level of general intelligent participation in matters which are controversial precisely because they are so important. The worst was a religious education which was afraid of controversy, one which sought in fact to avoid the direct teaching of religion, one which was insufficiently vibrant, consisting of inert facts unrelated to pupils' lives, one which became falsely academic instead of truly liberating, and which failed to confront pupils with the rich religious experience of humanity.

(Hull 1982: xiii)

Although it was quite understandable that teachers, coming from the 'faith-fostering period' and now facing the job of teaching the new religious education, were apprehensive of possible unconscious tendencies to convert pupils and would therefore emphasise factual knowledge and try to present it objectively and impartially; the stakes of the new approach were higher.

So it was right from the start that Hull identified the Achilles heel of the world faiths approach of RE. I would like to draw attention to the fact that he emphasises educational reasons in his critique of 'arid factuality': 'Pupils are not being stimulated to think' when 'too much religious education teaching remains at the level of information giving' (ibid. 157). That is remarkable – against the background of the recurring debate on the role of commitment in religious education in Great Britain as much as in other multicultural and multireligious societies of Western Europe. I myself have been involved in this debate in the Netherlands in the 1980s and have often experienced discussions having the following course.

Contributing to the debate as a philosopher of education I was identified – and identified myself – as a non-religious person, interested in religious education in common schools from an educational perspective. The non-confessional type of religious education that I advocated (I thought we could learn and profit from the British experience with the world religions approach in the Netherlands) was often criticised for its assumed purely informative, factual, external, arid, superficial character – and for that very reason missing out on the essential, inward, warm, living, real, authentic and so on true nature of religion, which was then identified with the commitment of religious believers. The immediate effect of this argument is that non-religious persons are 'excommunicated', shut out from the debate as outsiders. Relevant considerations can only come from the insiders of religion because their religious commitment is made into the prerequisite for understanding what religion is about. In a discussion thus polarised (cf. Meijer 1998), educational considerations and religious or theological considerations as to the subject of religious education have fallen apart.

One of John Hull's great merits is that he has quite successfully brought the two perspectives together in conceiving of religious education. I know of no other thinker who has so uncompromisingly developed a theology of education by taking the modern concept of education – often labelled 'liberal humanist' or 'secular humanist' and as such opposed to religion – as a new challenge to ongoing, open-ended theological reflection. I think he has set an example for educationists as well as theologians. The present philosophy of education in Britain seems to have lost touch with the tradition of the 'liberal philosophy of education' of Dearden, Hirst and Peters to the extent that it has regained interest in religion. In a recent discussion in the *Journal of Philosophy of Education* (JOPE), John White, heir to that tradition, draws our attention to this intriguing connection. White observes that '[t]here has been a notable increase since the 1980s in the number of JOPE articles written from a religious perspective. From 1966 until 1979 there were three; from 1980 until 1988 nine; from 1989 until 2001 nineteen' (White 2003: 159) – mark the somewhat peculiar division in periods. The turn away from the concept of education of Peters *et al.* occurred in the context of the liberalism-communitarianism debate that is also the locus of the recurrence of the religious perspective. The involved educational concept had indeed been labelled *'liberal* education',[1] but one could question whether that in itself justifies identifying it with the liberalist position in the recent political philosophical debate. Anyway, as White observes:

> [w]riters advocating communitarian perspectives, often explicitly in opposition to liberalism . . . overlap significantly with . . . defenders of religious views writing on matters to do with the nature of education, moral education, religious education in schools, separate religious schools, the rights of religious parents to bring their children up in their own religion.
>
> (ibid. 159)

Hirst's contribution to the debate on Christian theology and educational theory (Hirst 1974a) may well have contributed to the continuing partition in British philosophy of education into 'the religious' on the one hand and 'modern, liberal education' on the other. The philosophers of education have clearly missed the opportunity to learn from John Hull's remarkable endeavour to work out fruitful connections and instead have become resigned to a presumed invincible dichotomy. Hull's discussion with Hirst can be seen as part of his preparing the ground for a theology of education (in Hull 1984, 229–47 (originally from 1976); cf. Bates 2002: 11–12 and this volume, 7–11; Nipkow 2002: 45).

> There are forms of Christian theology in which critical enquiry and controversial examination flow directly and necessarily from the values and beliefs to which the theology is committed . . . An alliance . . . between

such theology and such education, far from hindering the critical freedom of education, might do a little to enhance and support it.

(Hull 1984: 241)

I will now turn to the educational cum theological line of thought that Hull developed from this point. Special attention will be given to the idea of *divergence*.

In 1975, the reader *New Movements in Religious Education*, edited by Ninian Smart and Donald Horder, appeared. John Hull contributed the article 'Agreed syllabuses, past, present and future' (reprinted in Hull 1984: 73–92). It must have been written while the heated political and public debate of 1974 on the new Birmingham Agreed Syllabus was in progress. That debate delayed publication of the syllabus and companion handbook, which had been agreed upon in 1973, until 1975. The syllabus included various other religions besides Christianity, but what really sparked off the debate was the inclusion of communism with humanism as one of the 'non-religious stances for living'. Hull's article, amongst other things, reviews the debate and points out the misunderstanding shared by the critics of the syllabus:

> The politicians assume that if a teacher teaches about Christianity, it is because he is a Christian and wants others to share his view. Similarly, they assume that if a teacher wants to teach about communism, it is because he is a communist and wants others to share his views. Just as the clergy used to interpret trends in religious education in terms of the pulpit so now politicians are interpreting them in terms of the hustings. It seems difficult for them to understand that the teacher is neither an evangelist nor a propagandist but an educator.
>
> (Hull 1984: 90)

Obviously, the oppositional language of the debate flows into the characterisation of the new type of religious education in this article. Take, for example, the negative characterisations that explain the idea of religious education as an intrinsically valid educational activity: it is *not* propaganda or evangelisation; the teacher is asked to teach things which he does *not* believe and to *refrain from* commending the things he does believe (ibid. 84, 88, 90). Soon, however, Hull develops more positive characterisations. In a journal article of 1978, 'From Christian Nurture to Religious Education: The British Experience' (reprinted in Hull 1984: 27–44), he explains why it is not right to describe the Birmingham Syllabus as being *neutral* (in the sense of '*not* committed'). 'The Syllabus is certainly impartial between the religions. . . . But this impartiality is itself an expression of values, and springs from commitment' (ibid. 33). This way Hull escapes the dichotomy of religious commitment versus factual objectivity that has haunted so many discussions on 'multireligious' education for so many years. The question mark in the title of his article 'Open Minds and Empty Hearts?' (in Jackson 1982; reprinted in Hull 1984: 175–85) is essential: the implied opposition is indeed questioned, and rejected. The idea of divergence, that had already been introduced in 1981, is essential in that connection ('The divergent teacher', also in Hull 1984: 187–95). It replaces false and misleading claims as to the neutrality of the new religious education: 'divergence is itself a value, or a bundle of values' (Hull 1984: 181).

Certainly, the idea of divergence can itself be explained again negatively: 'Education does *not* seek or assume convergence' (ibid. 179, italics added) – convergence, that is, of the commitment of the teacher, the content of the teaching, and the commitment or desired commitment of the pupils. But the essentially positive characterisations of the values of divergent teaching follow in a section with the significant title 'Education and passion' (ibid. 181ff.): it is directed to all pupils whatever their religious or non-religious background, it seeks to teach them to think for themselves, and, therefore, questions and inquiry are central to it – indeed quite a contrast to the 'arid factuality' touched upon above. Education requires questioning and inquiring and thus *open minds* – which again implies an *open future*:

> [T]he teacher as educator seeks to make his pupils critical of the content of his lessons. He asks many questions. It is not true that he gives no answers; he gives many answers, and more questions spring from any answer. There is no end to this process; indeed, one of the purposes of this teacher is that his pupils shall not cease their education simply because their schooling is over. They are to go on asking questions and finding answers which lead to more questions all their lives.
>
> (ibid. 182–3)

The future is open because of the permanence of the inquiring, questioning attitude; and, related to this, the future is open for the future adults to make up their own minds. Elsewhere, Hull has indeed emphasised that the rights of present adults have to be balanced against the rights of children 'to their own time'.[2] Therefore, the future is also open in the sense that education 'is able to tolerate and even to promote a variety of religious and secular outcomes' (ibid. 189). It should, in other words, 'include and promote pluralism' (ibid. 188) or indeed, divergence. It is this educational commitment to divergence, to cultivating an open mind for an open future, that results in a question for theology: what can be the significance of the values of divergence in a theological perspective? 'Are the ideas of learning, autonomy and inquiry actually an integral part of my theological system?' (ibid. 184).

The sought-after connection is found in 'New Testament Christianity' (ibid. 194), in the 'critical attitude of the New Testament Church', demanded because 'there was a pluralism *within* Christianity' (ibid. 191). The article 'The Divergent Teacher' that we have followed in the last paragraphs continues with a collection of scriptural passages from the New

Testament (ibid. 191–4) that demonstrate this spirit. Indeed, the open mind and the open future once again go hand in hand:

> This enquiring spirit of the early church may be called eschatological criticism. It springs from the knowledge that the goal has not yet been grasped (Phil. 3: 122). The future not yet known (1 John 3: 2), the true and false grow side by side (Matt. 13: 30). Everything therefore was to be tested.
>
> (ibid. 193)

A well-known verse about 'being like a child' is, I would say, read from an essentially educational understanding of the child.[3]

Any child or young person growing up into this kingdom would have to grow up into that spirit of testing criticism, being examined and learning to examine. This was however an easy task because of the curious critical nature of the child himself, and because of the very nature of the kingdom. For unless the kingdom was received as a little child, it could not be entered (Mark 10: 15). For the child, such learning is natural, and it is the nature of the kingdom to consist of such critical, curious learners (ibid. 194).

Hull's book of 1984, in which the articles that I have referred to so far are collected together, culminates in his theology of education: Part V: Christian Theology and Educational Theory (ibid. 227ff.). We have followed the course of his line of thought: how the 'virtually new' religious education demanded new theological reflection, for 'In a changing world an unchanging theology soon becomes irrelevant' (ibid. 208). As uncompromisingly clear as these are the final words before Part V starts: it is 'difficult to see how Christian faith can avoid becoming invisible' if it would not try to cope with the 'problems raised by Christian presence within secular and pluralistic culture' (ibid. 224).

In one of the articles in Part V, namely, 'What is Theology of Education?' (ibid. 249–72), Hull explains that this discipline is, like, for example, theology of history or theology of the arts, directed at an area '*beyond* the community of faith' (ibid. 255). The comparison between theology of the sacraments and theology of education is elucidating: 'the former deals with concepts which are themselves already part of the theological sphere, whereas the latter is seeking to comprehend, from within that sphere, concepts which lie beyond it. Theology of education is a frontier discipline in that it seeks to extend the theological system' (ibid. 259). In trying to apply its concepts to new areas – such as modern education – theology is also necessarily engaged in self-reflection and self-criticism: 'Indeed the dominant mood of all these interpretative theological disciplines is that of a dialogue in which theology is also seeking to appraise itself and to reformulate itself' (ibid. 257).

Dialogue or interaction is indeed characteristic of all interpretative reflection. The hermeneutical philosophy of Gadamer and Ricoeur is helpful in

understanding the characteristic reflexivity of processes of reading and interpreting texts as much as other cultural and historical human phenomena.
According to Ricoeur, it is a process of *recontextualisation*: reading is essentially an interaction between the world of the text and the world of the
reader (cf. Meijer 2002). A text speaks in a different voice to people who
come to it with different expectations and different questions. This holds
certainly for biblical texts, that have been read over and over again by so
many generations. 'Old-time classics' come with their 'history of effects'
(that is Gadamer's concept of *Wirkungsgeschichte*), with a transmitted horizon
of expectation. Readers come to it with expectations: they already know
what they will find there. Defamiliarisation of the work, its escaping from
the given expectations, and thus *negativity* in the reception of the work, is
crucial in that case. The primordial closure of the work as understood from a
transmitted horizon of expectation makes room for a reflective openness of
questioning. The point, according to Gadamer, is to discover the questions
to which the work responded in the transmitted familiar reading, and then
to find new questions to which it may respond, in other words: to find new
readings (cf. Meijer 2004).

I think that John Hull's re-reading of New Testament passages from the
modern understanding of education could count as an example here. Besides
reminding me of Gadamer's and Ricoeur's hermeneutics, it reminded me of
Calvino's brilliant little essay 'Why Read the Classics?' It is perfectly possible for old-time classics to speak to today's readers, because reading is an
interaction between two worlds:

> To be able to read the classics, you have to know 'from where' you are
> reading them; otherwise both the book and the reader will be lost in a
> timeless cloud. This, then, is the reason why the greatest 'yield' from
> reading the classics will be obtained by someone who knows how to
> alternate them with the proper dose of current affairs.
>
> (Calvino 1997: 131–2)

So Calvino gives a very clear idea about reading as recontextualisation – to
use Ricoeur's term. The work speaks to me, as a reader, in my present
context. I experience its significance and vitality in what it has to say to me,
here and now. That very experience revivifies the work's significance, which
is therefore yet again lasting. The meaning and truth of works of art are a
historical matter – the classics are no exception. The interaction of two
worlds, the world of the reader and the world of the text, is essential.
Perhaps inter*play* is the better word, because of the back and forth movement that hints at the endlessness of reading and rereading.

Hull is quite explicit as to the position of the Christian theology of education: it is not 'intellectually imperialistic', it has no pretension to being
the necessary basis for the new pluralistic religious education. That can, on
the contrary, be justified in the entirely secular terms of philosophy of

education. But what Hull has shown is that a theological justification *is possible*. Thus, he has defeated the often assumed dichotomy of religion and education. This is 'relevant in the first place to those who are religious and wish to articulate their participation in education in terms of their religious consciousness' (Hull 1984: 262). It is a matter of personal integrity, of making sense of their work in terms of their 'outlook on life' (ibid. 261).

What is at present urgently needed for (religious) education in our pluralist societies is an *Islamic* theology of education after the fashion of John Hull's Christian theology of education. Here, as in the discussion on religious education in the 1970s and the 1980s that was reviewed above, dichotomies reign that need to be surmounted. To paraphrase Hull: Islam has to try to cope with the problems raised by Islamic presence within secular and pluralistic culture. Being neither a Muslim nor a theologian, I am not the person for the job; but from previous research I do expect there to exist a hopeful perspective for Islam and modern education, as I will try to explain in closing.

In my work on Islamic and western perspectives on education I ran up against a persistent dichotomy. On various related topics, such as the aims of education and of literary education in particular, the image of the human being, and conceptions of tradition, history and change, essentially the same dichotomy would appear time and time again (cf. Meijer 1999, 2000). The dichotomy 'Islam versus the West' can be found both in the work of Islamic educationists and in that of non-Islamic western authors. When elaborated in some detail, the opposition of 'Islam versus the West' has interesting aspects to it. For example, I was fascinated by the different time-orientation in education, depending on whether the past or rather the future is faced, so to speak. In characterising tradition and cultural transmission – certainly a main theme in any educational theory – Muslim thinkers emphasise authority by comparing educators to prophets. The legitimacy of authority lies in chains of transmission ending up with the prophet Muhammad.

This orientation toward a fixed past forms a perfect contrast with the orientation toward an open, unknown future with which I was familiar from a western educational point of view. Of course, there is tradition and intergenerational transmission, but initiation into traditions and learning to participate within them is essentially about 'testing, expanding, and altering them for the better' (as Scheffler put it, cf. Meijer 2000: 437). By this token, the teacher's authority is relatively limited and provisional; ultimately he is just as much a learner as his students are. A community of learners thriving on criticism and discussion is emphasised as opposed to authority and obedience.

Although intrigued by the very detail of this opposition, I wasn't satisfied. The dichotomy of Islam versus the West can hardly be considered a fruitful option for present multicultural societies. Meanwhile, I had been arguing the option of open pluralism which was quite incompatible with this dichotomy. This pluralistic option combines two tenets: 1. Cultural diversity is accepted: in a multicultural society cultural difference is here to stay; 2. In a multicultural society confronting cultural difference is unavoidable: members of such a society shouldn't shy away from it but face it head on, having the nerve to engage in genuine intercultural interaction. It is this second tenet that turns the pluralism of the first tenet into *open* pluralism – as opposed to a closed or insular pluralism or cultural apartheid (cf. Meijer 1999a).

In line with this idea of open pluralism I continued trying to further the educational exchange between Muslim and western perspectives. I turned, amongst other things, to historical studies on Islamic education, hoping to find the detail and nuance that are blotted out where the dichotomy reigns. Indeed, stepping back and making detours may constitute a sound procedure for dislodging and furthering a dialogue stuck in polarising dichotomies. Assumptions and prejudices as to the characteristics of Islamic education underlying the dichotomy give way, first, to the detail and nuance of a particular historical case, but will, I hope, eventually lead on to a revised understanding of the relation between the East and the West in education.

In the light of this search I find the historical work of Makdisi on 'classical Islam' (1981, 1990, 1997) quite interesting. In a way, I can see a parallel between John Hull's going back to New Testament Christianity in order to find meaningful links with the critical, open divergence of modern education and Makdisi's enterprise, although the latter is historical rather than theological in nature. In his study on the coming into being of madrasas in early medieval Baghdad, Makdisi is likewise turning to an era in which divergence was real because 'orthodoxy' was not yet instituted. Perhaps one could say that he is turning to a divergence that is more original than Islamic convergence or consensus.[4]

I cannot, in the present context, go into the detail of Makdisi's study on the madrasa in eleventh century Baghdad and its development during the centuries preceding (Makdisi 1981) but I do want to draw attention to the distinction between *riwaya* and *diraya* that I found there. It is a remarkable distinction for someone like me, coming from the present debate on the dichotomy of Islam and the West in which Islamic education is as a rule identified with the transmission of a purely closed, dogmatic, reproductive type. The distinction between *riwaya* and *diraya* developed, according to Makdisi, when classes in law were differentiated from classes in hadith. Mere memorisation of traditions and keeping them in store is contrasted with the higher ability of understanding and making use of them in juridical argument. 'The truly learned man was able not only to *carry, transmit* (riwaya, from rawa) the hadith, but also to understand it and make intelligent use of it (diraya, from dara), which was tantamount to fiqh, jurisprudence' (Makdisi 1981: 144). The contrast between classes of hadith and classes of law is, in my opinion, educationally significant. It boils down to the distinction between a *closed fist* versus an *open hand* pedagogy that Hamilton (1990) identified as essential in the shift from medieval western education to modern western education. It is the difference between tradition being handed down as a closed text, literally, word for word, versus a situation in which the role assigned to debate suggests a concept of tradition as an open-ended process in which change and progress are an integral part.

In the concluding section of his book on the madrasa, Makdisi ties the *diraya* of classes of law to the idea of academic freedom. He demonstrates that the intellectual culture of classical Islam originated with the madrasa and, hence, that intellectual and pedagogical culture are closely interwoven. Early medieval Muslim (advanced) education in the madrasa, with its pivotal role assigned to dialectic and disputation, originated in the second half of the third century AH (ninth century AD). In earlier days the Alpha and Omega of Muslim education had consisted entirely of dictation, copying and memorising. The dynamic of education comes with the practice of disputation and that again is related to academic freedom 'as embodied in the practice of ijtihad' (Makdisi 1981: 285; cf. note 4). The shift from the cumulative 'hadith' phase to the later 'fiqh' phase is connected to the crucial idea of agreement or *ijma*:

> Because of the nature of [the] process of determining orthodoxy, derived from a consensus based on the interplay of the legal opinions of jurisconsults, Muslim educational methods shifted early in the history of Muslim education from a cumulative phase to one of critical under-standing and creative inquiry.
>
> (ibid. 284)

Makdisi subsequently points out the parallel in the scholastic method of the medieval Christian West, suggesting an historical influence in this respect from East to West (cf. ibid. 285–9).

Maybe Makdisi is slightly overstating his case. His later book on the rise of humanism starts out with an even more outspoken formulation of the same idea:

> Classical Islam produced an intellectual culture that influenced the Christian West in university scholarship. It furnished the factor which gave rise to the university, namely the scholastic method, with its con-comitants the doctorate and academic freedom. This freedom can only have existed in an intellectual culture in which all the 'teachers' involved were considered equal in their authority or right to teach.... In modern university scholarship, as in the religious scholarship of clas-sical Islam, orthodoxy is consensual; that is to say that the 'orthodoxy', so to speak, of the results of scholarly research is judged by the eventual consensus of the community of scholars themselves. Dissent plays a vital role in these two intellectual cultures.
>
> (Makdisi 1990: 37)

One could as well argue that the factor shared by East and West is of ancient Greek origin, namely, the Aristotelian heritage of dialectic and disputation. Whatever the factual truth of Makdisi's claim about the origin of academic freedom,[5] the importance of freedom as a characteristic of intellectual cum educational culture can be endorsed. In closing, I would like to emphasise the interrelatedness of the educational and intellectual aspect. The academic freedom of the Islamic intellectual, the doctor of law, lies according to Makdisi in the practice of ijtihad, that is, the individual forming his own judgement. The educational side of academic freedom is the student's freedom to learn. Although it is only mentioned in a footnote, to me this is one of the essential educational conclusions of Makdisi's enterprise: 'In its original meaning, the student's freedom to learn meant the exercise of his own judgement regarding the opinions of the professors' (ibid. 45); and although only the higher educated, intellectual elite is involved in Makdisi's historical case, nevertheless the values of divergence as advocated by John Hull are at issue here: students learn to think for themselves in a questioning, inquiring atmosphere and the outcome of the inquiry is genuinely open.

Notes

1 For example, in Hirst's famous article 'Liberal education and the nature of knowledge', in Archambault 1965. It was reprinted many times (e.g., in the third volume of Dearden, Hirst and Peters 1972 and in Hirst 1974), but Hirst never developed a fully fledged theory of the forms of knowledge from this promising but rather sketchy piece. Eventually, he even rejected the whole conception of liberal education that he had helped to develop, surprisingly in the article that concludes the volume of essays in his honour (Barrow and White 1993, cf. Meijer 1995).

2 'The right of the parent to control the future by child upbringing must be limited by the right of a child to his own time. Time is the crux of the nurture/education distinction as it bears on human rights. Who has the right to withhold the past by denying nurture or to diminish the future by imposing nurture? Only a religion which is free concerning its own future can offer freedom to its young people' (in the 1978 journal article 'From Christian Nurture to Religious Education: The British Experience', also in Hull 1984: 42). In the last sentence the third element of the title of the present contribution is at issue: *ongoing heritage*.

3 Herbart (1835), one of the founders of the discipline of education, developed the idea of 'Bildsamkeit', i.e. the given that children *can learn*, as the foundational concept, the sine qua non, of education.

4 It concerns the period before the thirteenth century closing of 'the gates of ijtihad' in (Sunni) Islam. The relation between ijtihad and the consensus among the mujtahids is essential: 'Idjma' (literally 'agreeing upon') is one of the four [principles] from which the Muslim faith is derived and is defined as the agreement of the mudjtahid's of the people (i.e. those who have a right, in virtue of knowledge, to form a judgement of their own: idjtihad) after the death of Muhammad, in any age, on any matter of the faith. As this agreement is not fixed by council or synod but is reached instinctively and automatically, its existence on any point is perceived only on looking back and seeing that such an agreement has actually been attained; it is then consciously accepted and called an *idjma'*.

Thus the agreement gradually fixed points which had been in dispute, and each point, when thus fixed, became an essential part of the faith' (Gibb and Kramers 1995: 156–7).

5 One could further doubt whether it should be called *academic freedom*. Cf., for example, Magee (2003), according to whom it is the *rationality* that distinguished the philosophy of the Presocratics from previous 'magic' or 'religious' ways of grasping being. Interestingly, Magee also draws attention to the educational aspect of this transition to rationality: the first philosophers were the first teachers who did not intend to transmit knowledge as intact as possible, but who stimulated students to think for themselves, to develop their own ideas and thoughts and to join in the debate (Magee 2003: 12).

References

Archambault, R.D. (1965) *Philosophical Analysis and Education*, London: Routledge & Kegan Paul.

Barrow, R. and White, P. (eds) (1993) *Beyond Liberal Education. Essays in honour of Paul H. Hirst*, London: Routledge.

Bates, D. (2002) 'In Celebration of Professor John Hull: Christian Theologian and Educationist', *Panorama: International Journal of Comparative Education and Values*, 14: 9–19 (the introductory chapter of this volume is a revised and extended version of this article – eds).

Calvino, I. (1997) *The Literature Machine*, London: Vintage.

Dearden, R.F., Hirst, P.H. and Peters, R.S. (eds) (1972) *Education and the Development of Reason* (3 vols), London: Routledge & Kegan Paul.

Gibb, H.A.R. and Kramers, J.H. (eds) (1995) *Shorter Encyclopaedia of Islam* (edited on behalf of the Royal Netherlands Academy), Leiden, New York, Köln: Brill.

Hamilton, D. (1990) *Learning about Education*, Milton Keynes, Philadelphia: Open University Press.

Herbart, J.F. (1835) Umriß pädagogischer Vorlesungen.

Hirst, P.H. (1974) *Knowledge and the Curriculum*, London: Routledge & Kegan Paul.

—— (1974a) *Moral Education in a Secular Society*, London: University of London Press.

Hirst, P.H. and Peters, R.S. (1970) *The Logic of Education*, London: Routledge & Kegan Paul.

Hull, J.M. (ed.) (1982) *New Directions in Religious Education*, Lewes, Sussex: Falmer Press.

—— (1984) *Studies in Religion and Education*, Lewes, Sussex: Falmer Press.

Jackson, R. (ed.) (1982) *Approaching World Religions*, London: John Murray.

Magee, B. (2003) *Het Verhaal van de Filosofie*, Antwerpen, Utrecht: Standaard Het Spectrum (translation of *The Story of Philosophy*, 1998)

Makdisi, G. (1981) *The Rise of Colleges. Institutions of Learning in Islam and the West*, Edinburgh: Edinburgh University Press.

—— (1990) *The Rise of Humanism in Classical Islam and the Christian West*, Edinburgh: Edinburgh University Press.

—— (1997) *Ibn 'Aqil: Religion and Culture in Classical Islam*, Edinburgh: Edinburgh University Press.

Meijer, W.A.J. (1995) 'Beter bekeerd dan ten halve gekeerd?' (review article of R.

Barrow and P. White (eds) *Beyond Liberal Education. Essays in Honour of Paul H. Hirst*, London: Routledge 1993), *Comenius* 15: 64–77.

—— (1998) 'Innen und Außen. Weltreligionen in der allgemeinen Bildung', in H-G. Heimbrock (ed.) *Religionspädagogik und Phänomenologie*, Weinheim: Deutscher Studienverlag.

—— (1999) 'Islam versus Modernity: a contrast in educational thought', *British Journal of Religious Education*, 21: 158–66.

—— (1999a) 'General Education for an Open Pluralist Society', *Canadian and International Education (Éducation canadienne et internationale)*, 28: 181–202.

—— (2000) 'The Image of the Human Being in Islamic and "Secular Humanistic" Educational Thought', *Religious Education*, 95: 424–41.

—— (2002) 'On the Relevance of Literature to Life: The Significance of the Act of Reading', *The European Legacy*, 7: 567–77.

—— (2004) 'Tradition and Reflexivity in Religious Education', in H. Lombaerts and D. Pollefeyt (eds) *Hermeneutics and Religious Education*, Leuven: BETL

Nipkow, K-E. (2002) 'Importance of Personal Bridges', *Panorama. International Journal of Comparative Education and Values*, 14: 45–8.

Smart, N. and Horder, D. (eds) (1975) *New Movements in Religious Education*, London: Temple Smith.

White, J. (2003) 'Five Critical Stances Towards Liberal Philosophy of Education in Britain. With responses by Wilfred Carr, Richard Smith, Paul Standish and Terence H McLaughlin', *Journal of Philosophy of Education*, 37: 147–84.

Part 2

Current issues in Christian education and practical theology

Introduction

Dennis Bates

Part 2 consists of six essays in practical theology reflecting John Hull's theological interest in religious education, self deception and disability. The first three consider important issues relating to Christian education, namely the issue of indoctrination in relation to RE in German state schools; the problem of race in Christian education; and the pivotal role of relationships in religious education. The second three essays focus on self deception in pastoral and teaching relationships; social exclusion in Christian and Shi'a Muslim perspective; and the role of the Bible in Christian life for disabled people, particularly the profoundly deaf.

Karl Ernst Nipkow's essay (Chapter 6) defends the continued confessional basis of German state school religious education ('initiation into a special confession/religion by authentic representatives') against the charge of indoctrination. Opposing the 'ahistorical character of [the] concept analysis' which characterized the British rationalistic analytical philosophy of education of the 1960s and 70s, the proponents of which often levelled the charge of indoctrination at religious education, he argues for a greater recognition of historical and cultural context. In Germany, the experience of Nazi political indoctrination and, in the GDR, indoctrination into atheistic state socialism together with the recognition that the religious communities were major centres of resistance, have been formative factors on educational thought. This and the very different German philosophical tradition of critical theory and ideology critique of the Frankfurt School made German postwar religious education aware of the need for critical perspectives to be built into religious education. The critical initiation into Protestant or Catholic Christianity which resulted, Nipkow argues, coupled with the current availability of intercultural and inter-religious education, provides for initiation into children's traditional religious culture (potentially including Islam) and safeguards against indoctrination. Whilst John Hull's concept of 'critical openness' is warmly embraced, the English model of multi-faith religious education is seen as a less popular option in the German context.

Anthony Reddie's essay (Chapter 7) addresses the need for Christian education to confront the problem of the 'color line' identified by the early twentieth century Black American sociologist W.E.B. Dubois as a key future problem. Black people have become accustomed to a 'double consciousness' in which their own positive perceptions of themselves clash with the rejective, racist attitudes they encounter in dominantly white cultures, often leading to negative self images and mental ill health. Such racist attitudes have long been present in the Christian churches and Christian theology. Reacting to this, many cultural, political, religious and theological movements have appeared, asserting pride in Black identity. Reddie utilizes one of Black American culture's greatest creations, Jazz, as a 'trope' – a symbol – for the development of an anti-racist approach to Christian education in multicultural contexts. Jazz's combination of improvization and individualism with disciplined group music making, and its constant reworking of established melodies to create something new, symbolize the creative activity of the spirit of God prompting people to move away from the stereotyping fixed identities underlying racial prejudice. The 'new story' is a Christian theology and education which rejects the oppression and marginalization of minority groups and 'challenges the reality of the colour line'.

The central importance of relationship between pupil and teacher in the educational process has long been stressed by progressive educationists such as Rousseau and Pestalozzi and early twentieth century philosophers such as Buber, Nohl and Korczak. Reinhold Boschki (Chapter 8), building upon this foundation and upon contemporary interdisciplinary research highlighting the importance of the network of relationships for the development of the personalities of young people, relates these research findings to the process of religious education. He contends that 'since relationship is a basic concept in religion and in the lifeworld of people, it should also be a basic formative concept in religious education'. The importance of relationship with God and fellow human beings is constantly apparent in the Bible and is also found in other faiths. Relationships between teacher and pupil in the learning process should be based on an 'absolute respect' for the pupils and sensitivity towards their ideas and feelings. Developmental psychology identifies relationship with self, others and the social and historical context in which young people live as crucial for their healthy development. Adopting this for the process of religious education, Boschki adds relationship with 'God and the Ultimate'. This dimension, which should also pervade the other dimensions, is what makes 'education' religious and is best realized by personal encounter with other religious persons.

Charles Melchert's essay (Chapter 9), raises fundamental theological questions about the nature of Christianity and how this should be reflected in the attitudes underpinning relationships between Christians. It is based on a case study – a conversation recorded by a church pastor with a member of his congregation about her unwillingness to accept his interpretation of a text in Ephesians about a wife's duty to submit to her husband. Seeing her objection as a challenge to his authority, the pastor sets out to justify his interpretation of the text without paying proper heed to what she was saying. In a detailed and perceptive analysis and discussion of the case, Melchert sees in the pastor's attitude an example of 'self deception' – deriving from the influence on him of traditional notions of the church as being concerned with doctrinal orthodoxy, hierarchy and institutional power. Such notions were far removed from the humility and loving concern exemplified in Jesus's life and in the 'mutual submission' also advocated by Paul in Ephesians. With reference to John Hull's thought and Panikar's notion of 'Christian-ness', Melchert concludes 'Learning to be a citizen in the kingdom of God means becoming more and more like the King: that is, humble, just and loving'.

Mary Beasley (Chapter 10), as a disabled person, has encountered the insensitivity of the churches to the needs of the disabled as William Booth did with the marginalized people with whom he worked. She has spent her working life as a social worker in the city of Birmingham, UK, dealing much of her time with the homeless and other socially marginalized groups. Her essay explores Christian and Islamic perspectives on such people, utilizing in particular the thought of René Girard, James Alison, Mahmoud Ayoub and Husayn Nasr. She contends that images of social exclusion are also used of spiritual enlightenment. Following Victor Turner, she argues that every person needs the wilderness experience of marginalization, the 'stripping of the self' to realize their 'shared humanity' and thereby to overcome the social rivalries of wealth and status which often lead to violence and cruelty and the scapegoating of the weak. Both Christian spirituality and the Islamic 'greater jihad' provide for this. The crucifixion of Christ in Christianity and the martyrdom of Imam Husayn in Shi'a Islam are models of the self giving love and identification with the weak and the marginalized which both faiths see as being ultimately manifested in the coming inclusive 'new Israel' [kingdom of God] and the God ruled society inaugurated at the coming of the Mahdi. She concludes that for both faiths, 'it is in God that they find their common humanity'.

Wayne Morris's essay (Chapter 11) gives further valuable insight into the consciousness of the disabled. It is with the inaccessibility of the Bible to various groups and in particular the profoundly deaf that Morris is concerned, especially in relation to what he sees as the growing emphasis in the churches on the importance of reading the Bible 'as the benchmark for how to live and what to believe'. Members of the Deaf Community regard (unwritten) British Sign Language as their first language and cannot access the Bible by that means. Although not denying that the Bible has a special role as the record of salvation history and a source for 'our incomplete knowledge of God', he wonders whether it is really as important for Christian faith and life as some would contend. For the greater part of Christian history, the illiterate majority of Christians were not able to access the Bible by themselves. Orally delivered story, art and statuary were the more usual media. It is only since the nineteenth century that literacy has become widespread in industrialized western countries; and in Africa, illiteracy is still common. He questions whether literate Christians are necessarily any closer to God than illiterate ones and contends that God has many ways of communicating with people (e.g. through music, art, dance) other than through the written word. He concludes with an example of the religious sensitivity of a deaf and blind young woman to illustrate his point and urges the churches to reconsider the role of the Bible in Christian life and experience and in particular in the lives of the disabled.

6 Christian education and the charge of indoctrination

A German perspective

Karl Ernst Nipkow

Critical openness is a discipline which the Christian follows not in spite of his faith but because of it.

(Hull 1984: 220)

Section 1: indoctrination: a comparative contextual introduction

Since the 1960s and 70s, the heyday in the UK of analytical philosophy of education, 'one of the central objections against religious instruction as it occurs in the home, in the church, and in church-related schools and colleges is that such instruction often, and even necessarily, involves indoctrination' (Thiessen 1993: 3). The argument is directed in particular against 'Christian nurture' and a 'confessional' approach in schools. It is not being argued 'that we should not teach the young *about* the various religions, the various perspectives they provide on life, their histories and their influence on various cultures' (Kazepides 1991: 12). This latter objective, multi-faith approach is represented as resting on educational grounds whereas the confessional approach is rejected since many writers assume that even in its modern forms this approach is dominated by theology and that Christian education can only be practised in this way. For Paul Hirst, closed-mindedness is a necessary characteristic of 'separate schools for particular religious groups' which 'necessarily encourage social fragmentation in the society along religious lines' (Hirst 1985: 16).

Having been introduced to this debate by John Hull in the late nineteen seventies, this German observer found it both highly fascinating but also odd and disappointing. Some years before, Hirst's classical article 'Christian education: a contradiction in terms?' (1972, see also in Astley and Francis 1994) had distinguished between two different views of education. The first of these concepts he had called the 'primitive' concept, for it clearly expresses the view of education a primitive tribe might have when it seeks to 'pass on to the next generation its rituals, its ways of farming and so on, according to its own customs and beliefs' (Hirst 1994: 308). The second concept had been called a 'much more sophisticated' one. According to this, education is essentially bound to the task of critically assessing whatever might be taught. The second view:

> is thus concerned with passing on beliefs and practices according to, and together with, their objective status. It is dominated by a concern for knowledge, for truth, for reasons, distinguishing these clearly from mere belief, conjecture and subjective preference, *even when the latter happen to be justifiable.*

> (ibid.)

'In so far as any form of religious education goes beyond this concern for objectivity and reason, Hirst declares himself "against it" ' (Astley in his summary in Astley and Francis 1994: 303).

John Hull forcefully responded to Hirst's argument in his article entitled 'Christian theology and educational theory: can there be connections?' (1976; in Astley and Francis 1994). He uncovered the inconsistencies in Hirst's argument and found them 'unconvincing' (Astley and Francis 1994: 329). What I welcomed very much was that John Hull focussed on the understanding of the academic disciplines involved – 'theology' and 'educational theory'; both then and now, one of my own central concerns has been to demonstrate the rational, self-reflexive, critical status of theology which enables one to speak of an academic partnership between theology and educational theory.

In the 1980s the 'multi-faith approach' in England and Wales seems to have satisfied the opponents of Christian nurture in county schools and the debate about indoctrination became less intense. The widely adopted phenomenological approach appeared to be immune to the charge of indoctrination. The focus of my article is not this development in the United Kingdom, but the likelihood that, for many British observers, indoctrination might (or even must) still be perceived as existing in Germany and other European countries which have maintained the so-called 'confessional' approach. Is this approach in its present theory and practice indoctrinating? Are the epistemological underpinnings and methodological roads of Protestant and Roman-Catholic religious education in state schools and therefore the theological faculties at German state universities places of brooding, indoctrinating forms of Christian education and theological training?

Interestingly the debate was not to cease in Great Britain and North America as more recent publications show (Spiecker and Straughan 1991; Thiessen 1993; Francis and Thatcher 1990: Chapter 8; Astley and Francis 1994: Chapter 8; for the earlier phase of the debate see Snook 1972a, 1972b). The charge of indoctrination is an enduring issue with regard to church schools and Christian education in the home and in the congregation. Even more, it is a fundamental and general issue that cannot be restricted to religion alone, although it is puzzling how advocates of a non-indoctrinatory education are permanently singling out the Christian religion and in particular the Catholic Church.

My historical experiences as a German theologian and educationist differ from those impressions which have been attracting attention to the topic in Great Britain and North America. The debate in these regions suffers from a certain geographical narrowness. Important differences in political, cultural, legal and religious history and experience between the UK and continental Europe are neglected. The same is true about the relative philosophical backgrounds – in England the monopolizing position held by a rationalistic analytic philosophy of education; in Germany, a broad 'hermeneutical' philosophical tradition and the 'critical theory' of the Frankfurt School with its emphasis on 'ideology critique'. Twenty years ago there was the feeling in the British debate that the concept of indoctrination had been 'analyzed to death' (Laura 1983: 43; cf. Thiessen 1993: 20). This was partly due to the focus of Anglo-Saxon analytic philosophy on 'concepts' rather than on educational theory-building. History served as a field for selecting specific examples that seemed to fit in with the isolated hypotheses of scientific evidence and objectivity.

In Germany the restorative ideological dreams in education of the first post-war period were gradually replaced by a critical approach to education. The churches were impelled to follow the process of belated democratization in our society with a thoroughgoing revision of their educational commitments in schools. It is interesting that this self-critical evaluation and transformation could draw on developments within theology itself. During the 1950s, Protestant German RE in schools opened itself to the powerful rise of historical-critical exegesis. In the 1960s, Catholic catechetical thinking was prompted to a gradual transformation in the light of the Second Vatican Council. In connection with this, an intriguing broader change took place, the construction of a rejuvenated positive view of the European Enlightenment.

Another most important factor refers to aspects of twentieth century German history – to the Nazi-regime, the aggressive wars against other nations, the Holocaust, and – in shameful retrospect – the weakness of the German educated elite's resistance. It would be highly inappropriate for German educationists and theologians ever to forget this. Indoctrination had been a terrible reality which surpassed the criticism against the churches. On the contrary, they had partly belonged to the few sources of resistance against state indoctrination. This was also the case when for about forty years, the East German population was indoctrinated by the atheistic state socialism of the German Democratic Republic. Christian parents, at least a minority, let their children experience alternative life forms in the name of independent Christian faith. Congregational Christian nurture established a miniature counter-culture. It is these historical processes which form the concrete context of the issue of indoctrination in Germany and demand a history-bound treatment.

In my own recent research on the issues of warfare and peace education (Nipkow 2003), data from evolutionary psychology (Shaw and Wong 1989; Eibl-Eibesfeldt and Salter 1998) have led me to become aware of the vulnerability of human beings to indoctrination by political persuasion, mass media and advertising. Today much of this occurs under the pressure of the interests of neo-liberal economy (see John Hull's justified criticism of the 'money-culture' (Hull 1997)). All of these factors led to my approach to the issue of indoctrination becoming broader in content and more interdisciplinary in methodology.

The historical events in both parts of Germany, now re-united since 1990, have transformed Christian education in theory and practice to an extent that would render it difficult to label it as indoctrination. It might be surprising that in the German debate about Christian education, regardless of context (home, church, school), the explicit charge of indoctrination is completely lacking despite the voicing of quite a few objections to confessional religious education. However, a growing number of studies on the issue of pluralism by Catholic and Protestant educators (Hans-Georg Ziebertz; Friedrich Schweitzer; Karl Ernst Nipkow), and the interest of leading philosophers of education in the role of religion in education, (Jürgen Oelkers, Dietrich Benner), make it even more difficult to speak bluntly of indoctrination. The future is open although the issue of indoctrination is by no means satisfactorily settled. The present state of academic studies on the topic in Germany is seriously deficient (Nipkow 2004) and a more intensive discussion is necessary. The German discussion can learn a lot from the elaborated Anglo-Saxon debate (Spiecker and Straughan 1991; Thiessen 1993), while the Anglo-Saxon controversies might gain new insights by presenting the German approach to Christian education (see below).

Elmar J. Thiessen has uncovered a host of inconsistencies in the way in which the notion of indoctrination is understood and applied, particularly in Great Britain. He is one of the first to draw upon a wider context. In opposition to the dominating ahistorical character of a 'concept analysis' he rightly sees that 'concepts do not float in mid-air. To understand them we need to look at historical, cultural, and political contexts' (Thiessen 1993: 33–4). He contends that the European Enlightenment ideal of 'liberal education' is behind the charge of indoctrination. The bulk of his monograph is dedicated to the factors which the opponents to 'Christian nurture' have tried to brand as the constitutive elements of indoctrination. They are: 'content' – 'doctrines' as the expression of 'unshakeable beliefs'; 'methods' – indoctrinatory teaching methods like the transmission of a religious tradition by 'socialization' understood as involuntary initiation into religious rituals and customs, instilling doctrines by evangelistic zeal and catechetical memorization, methods which are all accused of being 'non-rational'; 'intention' – the intentional inculcation of beliefs regardless of evidence and without presenting alternative thought-patterns; 'consequences' – closed-mindedness, intolerance; and, added by Thiessen, 'institutional indoctrination' – for example, in church schools.

Thiessen wants to defend Christian nurture and prove that every education will share the problems which are unwarrantedly applied to religion only. Together with a new clarification of the understanding of 'indoctrination', it is recommended that hasty generalizations should be avoided and more caution shown in labelling Christian nurture as indoctrinatory. Where there are negative traits in Christian education, they ought to be identified and avoided; but, he argues, 'Christian nurture therefore does not necessarily entail indoctrination' (ibid. 242). Although exploring new ground, Thiessen's critique still largely assumes the rationalistic context outlined above. He does not enter the field of concrete Christian educational traditions and their present character; neither does he draw upon any other European developments beside those in Great Britain.

Section 2: educational and theological responses to indoctrination

Education as cultural initiation and self-forming: the perspective of German philosophy of education

In his essay 'Freedom and Learning: Some Thoughts on Liberal and Progressive Education', the German philosopher of education Jürgen Oelkers, living in Switzerland, quotes Immanuel Kant's question 'how can freedom be cultivated if constraints cannot be avoided?' (Oelkers 1991: 70; cf. Kant 1964: 711: 'Wie kultiviere ich die Freiheit bei dem Zwang').

> Education *as* indoctrination would be *not* legitimate, but liberal education pretends to *form* the mind and it looks as if this must be called 'indoctrination' too. The mind cannot resist the forming when the process of education takes place, and it must take place because human learning is related to human culture. At least in some aspects culture represents authority for the learner; at the beginning of education the learner has no choice, he cannot decide *against* education which, on the other hand, strongly influences him. So how can we defend this and not call it 'indoctrination'? If we abandon all connotations of 'natural education', that is, the development of germs in what Froebel called the garden of education, then we have only *one* criterion for whether education is indoctrination or not, the criterion of *understanding*.
>
> (Oelkers 1991: 80)

Before turning to Christian education, this lengthy passage clarifies some basic general characteristics of education. Kant's question has many aspects, one being the anthropological difference between adults and children. Given the consensus that to become educated is a human right and governments which do not sufficiently provide for education for all violate this right and prevent people from discovering and displaying their individual possi-bilities, this self-discovery and self-development *necessarily* takes place *within* a culture into which it is necessary to initiate children.

The process takes place in three basic forms: (1) as 'intentional' education (as a planned influence, e.g. in schools); (2) as 'unintentional' education (as 'functional' or 'structural' 'socialization' into social life); and (3) in a form which has been called 'extensional' (Treml 2000: 74–81) in which one element of the first form and one of the second are combined. Due to its intensive holistic 'functional' effects upon the whole person, an educational 'environment' is purposefully ('intentionally') arranged (see already in Rousseau's 'Emile', cf. also the attractive educational equipment of a room designed to invite and motivate children to play with the objects and to learn in interaction with them and with other children). The latter method seems to be particularly 'child-centered', but as a matter of fact none of these three ways of influencing the child is a 'natural education', which is an illu-sion. Each generation of adults wants to shape the younger generation, not only (1) by curriculum-bound schooling, but also, and even much more per-vasively, (2) by allowing the societal structures to exert their power and (3) by subtly steering the children's attention in the arbitrary ways a 'kinder-garten', a school, and so on can be equipped (the hidden curriculum). In all cases adults are aware of what they are doing to children. The relation between them and the young is an asymmetrical relation of power.

Thus education and learning necessarily express and use authority, 'not necessarily that of teachers but that of traditions' (Oelkers 1991: 79), a fact that has recently been underscored by Dietrich Benner (2003a), another leading philosopher of education. 'The learner can alter traditions but only *after* he becomes initiated into them. He can also ignore traditions but then he must consider himself as not competent' (Oelkers 1991: 79). By looking at the anthropological situation of children, the first response to Kant's 'paradox', that is to prevent the unavoidable legitimate constraints from becoming illegitimate means of indoctrination, leads to a developmental perspective. We find it already with some authors. They distinguish between a justified '"initiation into forms of life", "training" and "socializa-tion" and "indoctrination"' (Spiecker 1991: 22; see also R.S. Peters' (1965) positive notion of 'education as initiation').

For Thiessen 'the curtailment of a person's growth towards normal ratio-nal autonomy' is the 'core idea of indoctrination' (Thiessen 1993: 233). I do not completely agree, however, with his 'two-phase approach' (ibid. 225) – first 'the initiation or nurture phase' (ibid. 236), then 'a gradual opening-up phase' where the children 'are exposed to other influences, other beliefs, though still from the vantage point of the tradition into which they were first initiated' (ibid.). Only 'at a final stage vigorous critically reflective skills are developed' (ibid.). In modern plural societies children observe cultural differences, including religious ones, at a very early age, not to speak of different moral standpoints. Therefore 'initiation' and reflection on 'difference' are factually intertwined and have correspondingly to be dealt with together early on in life. 'Educational' learning ('bildendes' Lernen) as opposed to 'indoctrinatory' learning, is a way that will constantly lead through tensions that are generated by the familiar and the still unfamiliar, by different inter-pretations of situations, by negative or positive comments on action and behaviour already within one and the same family, by encounters with chil-dren of different social background, ethnic origin and religious upbringing including non-religious backgrounds (e.g. atheist, secularist, indifferent).

A second response comes into sight when we comment on Oelkers' hint at 'understanding' by which he points to the structure of the human learn-ing process. Alongside what has just been explicated and following a famous classical analysis (F. Schleiermacher 1799; cf. Nipkow 2004) as well as modern neurobiological findings, the human mind is evolving in a process that, on the one hand, needs to be initiated into something that is culturally given, whilst on the other hand, must involve a process of self-organization ('autopoiesis'), 'a mental "growing in" that includes biological processes but cannot be reduced to them' (Oelkers 1991: 78; Treml 2000: 23, 235). Thus 'knowledge can be altered by further learning; indoctrinated beliefs can be corrected, at least in most cases' (Oelkers 1991: 81). The 'child's mind is not a map of reasoning but a map-in-being' (ibid.). If so, education, in whatever form, can contribute to the development of the mind, 'but basically it is a process of self-promotion that can or must be helped by education' (ibid.). To conclude: 'there is no *contradiction* between "freedom" and "education" because education will not necessarily lead to *indoctrination*'. Nor can, on the other hand, 'education produce "freedom"' (ibid.).

In the light of this, the understanding of education in the meaning of the German word 'Bildung' can be mistaken twice, either by misunderstanding education as 'organic natural growth' or as the 'mechanical production' of mental states of the inner mind. In both cases education and with it the way towards freedom can easily become subject to deterministic thinking, either to natural laws or to the rules of technological production. Indoctrination attempts to take a firm grip on human persons in the second way; the popu-lation of a nation or the membership of a religious organization become instruments to be shaped in outer behaviour and inner attitudes.

This is possible since the human capacity for education necessarily implies also an openness to indoctrination. In evolutionary perspectives both sides, the genetically acquired positive pro-social, affiliative feelings with the readiness of bonding within one's own group (in-group-amity) and the simultaneously acquired negative predisposition to shrink back and separate from others (out-group-enmity) are 'whispering within' humans (Barash 1979), ready to be misused. Ideologies can 'key in' or 'hook into' these pre-dispositions so that people fall prey to propaganda and persuasion (Eibl-Eibesfeldt and Salter 1998). Indoctrination can be explained as the *systematic* attempt to exploit that readiness.

In recent German history not only political doctrines, the nationalism and racism of the 'Third Reich' (1933–45) and the ideology of Marxism-Leninism in the German Democratic Republic (1949–89), but also charismatic political 'leaders' (Adolf Hitler as the 'Führer') succeeded in indoctrinating the German population. Merely to look at 'doctrines' is too narrow (Kapezides 1991). No country is immune to indoctrination which is a sad fact and has also been identified in democracies, for example the USA. Studies on the 'rally round the flag effect' reveal how ideological and attitudinal homogeneity in the population can deliberately be produced by presidential speeches, whereby in particular the role of sex and emotional response has been exploited (Schubert 1998). Consequently, education has to promote 'intellectual virtues *and* rational emotions' (Spiecker 1991: 18–20).

Christian faith as a critical challenge to indoctrination: the perspective of German Protestant theology and education

In Germany the understanding of Christian education in present Protestantism shares the above principles of the general theory of education that dialectically relates tradition and self-development and is keen on protecting the outer and inner freedom of persons. As the two most important recent statements of the Evangelische Kirche in Deutschland (EKD) show, on Religious Education (RE) in plural societies (EKD 1994) and on education in a 'learning society' in general (EKD 2003), this is an official consensus.

(1)   In the Protestant view, Christian faith is based not on 'doctrines', but on faith experiences which make doctrines the debatable expression of them, not unshakeable dogma. Change of experiences leads to a changed meaning of theological notions and new language. Nothing follows for a living religion and its future from 'doctrines' per se; everything depends on experiential religious evidence.

(2)   Regardless of the place where it occurs, Protestant Christian education tries to pursue the tasks of initiation *and* reflection (including assessment) as *equally* important, complementary tasks. The axiom reads:

> Curriculum contents with their claims are not allowed to determine the student; 'educational' teaching (according to the category of 'Bildung') will have to deal with them in a way which at once allows for the development of critical reason which, at least potentially, can oppose the contents.
>
> (Blankertz 1969: 41; cf. Hirst's second type of education)

In Protestant RE, the assessment of Biblical texts along the lines of historical-critical exegesis was introduced as early as the 1950s. In the 1960s a 'thematic and problem-orientated approach' with conflict-laden issues helped to make RE become an even more attractive, open-minded enterprise.

(3)   As to the educational guidelines, we see no difference between Christian 'education' and Christian 'nurture'. In German terminology there is no equivalent to 'nurture'; the term 'catechesis' has been dropped. Therefore, since the 1960s both in school and congregation, teaching in Christian education has become a task of 'interpretation'. It aims at the promotion of 'understanding' ('Verstehen', see Oelkers), not 'proclamation' ('Verkündigung'). Understanding occurs in the dialectic of understanding and non-understanding, of varying interpretations, of pros and cons in valuing, altogether in a reasonable way open to everyone's knowledge and free opinion, not fixed at 'mere' belief (Hirst 1994: 308). In its best moments a lesson is propelled by 'negations' (Benner 2003b) of what at first sight seemed to be certain propositions or claims, thus creating a 'discourse' (a term used in our Tübingen research).

(4)   The classes of Protestant RE are open to all with voluntary attendance; the subject 'Moral Education' (ME) can be chosen as an alternative option. In many schools, Muslim students attend RE. In the East German regions of the former German Democratic Republic, considerable numbers (between 20 and 60 per cent) of non-Christian students prefer the Protestant RE to ME. Research data (1993/1994) on motives are conclusive; the students are 'curious' about religion (1st rank), they want to hear about 'God' (2nd), and they appreciate the 'atmosphere' of RE as an 'open-minded exchange'. In Germany, modern RE is widely working in a plural context constructively coping with 'diversity' 1) by dealing with several denominations and religions in the classroom and 2) by co-operation between the classes. Christian education is challenged by, and shaped by, learning 'through difference' (see above).

(5)   Protestant as well as Catholic religious educators are going to consider children as 'philosophers' and 'theologians' of their own (see F. Schweitzer, Chapter 12 in this volume). The child learns in a process of self-organization (autopoiesis) (see above) with remarkable discoveries (Hull 1991). The discoveries are made within the above circle of initiation and reflection.

(6)   Protestantism stresses the personal character of faith which has to be respected, be it the faith of the students or the teachers. The inner person's religious convictions are to be protected against all interventions from outside, the official church included. According to a representative survey, Protestant religious teachers are neither blindly serving the official church bodies' interests nor wanting to separate themselves from church and theology. The relationship has been called a 'critical-symbiotic' one (Feige *et al.* 2000).

(7)   The teachers are critically sensitive to tutelage from any standpoint including a 'neutral' attitude to religions(s) which is also rejected. One does not want to teach against one's own convictions under the umbrella of neutralism, objectivism and rationalism as a new secular 'doctrine'. In German pedagogy, a positivist view of education has never had a strong hold. One does not believe in disciplines without predispositions. Hirst's view of

education as 'critically assessing whatever might be taught' presupposes that something is taught. Education can never be nothing but 'assessment'.

(8)   The German constitution (1949) regards the existence of a confessional RE in state schools as the expression of 'positive religious freedom', as the right of corporate religious self-interpretation and individual religious self-orientation. This view has become a central guideline for the Protestant churches since the early 1970s. It implies that Muslims are entitled to an Islamic RE of their own. This is supported by all churches.

(9)   Faith in God as 'the Lord' with Jesus Christ as his 'son' (in the language of the Bible) makes possible a fundamental critique of all other 'lords' who attempt to suppress human beings. The danger of becoming systematically indoctrinated in our societies by open or hidden persuasions is great. A Christian education that locates the issue of God at its centre confronts young people with the diversity of truth-claims and invites them to learn to distinguish between what destroys or promotes freedom and reconciliation. In this light, 'confessional' RE can become, and does indeed exist already as, a place of open-minded critical illumination, 'not in spite of faith but because of it' (Hull 1984: 220).

(10)   A Religious Studies approach to religions (in the plural) is a necessary task in order to deepen the teachers' knowledge. German religious educators take it, however, as one source among others. They appreciate data about Islam and other non-Christian religions *within* a frame of reference which consists of *theological* and *educational* criteria.

(11)   Learning by comparing belongs to any (religious) instruction. It presupposes a solid initiation into a specific field as one half of the task. Protestant RE is interested in examining how each religion is able to allow for a critical assessment of itself and other worldviews ('Weltanschauungen'). In the light of our history, we feel the need for such critical assessment. In order to find out and promote the ability of informed and fair valuing, dialogue is needed in the forms of inter-cultural and inter-religious education which is provided for in the curricula.

(12)   The most effective critical response to indoctrination will and ought to come from the centre of each faith itself (see this chapter's epigraph). This is being practised in German schools, first, through initiation into a specific confession/religion by authentic representatives and, second, by starting, where possible, a systematic co-operation between Protestant and Catholic RE as well as Protestant RE and the subject Moral Education (ME).

Conclusion

In comparing the situation in Germany with the situation in England and Wales some concluding remarks might be useful on the relative status of Christianity in English and Welsh county (now 'community') schools. I should like to avoid giving the impression that Christianity has been severely downgraded and that all of the major world religions are given equal weighting in RE. It should be remembered that daily school worship has been legally obligatory since 1944 and that the Christian character and content of RE and daily worship has been re-emphasized in the 1988 Education Reform Act.

This situation, however, remains controversial. John Hull's rejection of worship in county schools on 'educational' grounds in his book *School Worship: an Obituary* (1975) has not been realized in practice. Together with many others he also disagreed with the neo-conservative tendencies in the 1988 Act. The teachers of RE and the leading advocates of a multi-faith approach in RE on the one hand, and governmental policy including much public opinion on the other hand, do not seem to share the same expectations.

In Germany there is no compulsory daily school worship and the teachers as well as the advocates of an open-ended confessional approach to RE fully agree with this. Thus, the state school system as a whole is much less permeated by Christianity, whereas RE is given its profile by approaches on 'educational' *and* 'theological' grounds; the Religious Studies approach is far less influential. Generally, Christian theology is supposed to form one side of the whole without leading to a one-sided religious education.

References

Astley, J. and Francis, L.J. (eds) (1994) *Critical Perspectives on Christian Education*, Leominster: Fowler Wright Books.

Barash, D. (1979) *The Whisperings Within*, New York: Harvard Row.

Benner, D. (2003a) 'Kritik und Negativität', *Zeitschrift für Pädagogik* 49, suppl. 46: 96–110.

—— (2003b) *Erziehung und Tradierung*, unpublished manuscript.

Blankertz, H. (1969) *Theorien und Modelle der Didaktik*, München: Juventa.

Eibl-Eibesfeldt, I. and Salter, F.K. (eds) (1998) *Indoctrinability, Ideology and Warfare: Evolutionary Perspectives*, New York and Oxford: Berghahn Books.

EKD (Evangelische Kirche in Deutschland) (1994) *Identität und Verständigung. Standort und Perspektive- des Religionsunterrichts. Eine Denkschrift*, Güters-loh: Gütersloher Verlagshaus.

—— (2003) *Maße des Menschlichen. Evangelische Perspektiven zur Bildung in einer Wissens- und Lengesellschaft. Eine Denkschrift*, Güters-loh: Gütersloher Verlagshaus.

Feige, A., Dressler, B., Lukatis, W. and Schöll, A. (2000) *'Religion' bei ReligionslehrerInnen*, Comenius-Institut *et al.*, Münster: LIT.

Francis, L.J. and Thatcher, A. (eds) (1990) *Christian Perspectives for Education*, Leominster: Gracewing.

Hirst, P.H. (1972) 'Christian Education: a contradiction in terms?', *Learning for Living*, 11: 6–11 (reprinted in Astley and Francis 1994: 305–13).

—— (1985) 'Education and Diversity of Belief', in M.C. Felderhof (ed.) *Religious Education in a Pluralistic Society*, London: Hodder & Stoughton.

Hull, J.M. (1975) *School Worship: An Obituary*, London: SCM Press.

—— (1976) 'Christian Theology and Educational Theory: can there be connections?', *British Journal of Educational Studies*, 24: 127–43 (reprinted in Astley and Francis 1994).

—— (1984) *Studies in Religion and Education*, Lewes, Sussex: Falmer Press.

—— (1991) *God-Talk With Young Children: Notes for Parents and Teachers*, Derby: CEM.

—— (1997) 'Karl Marx on Capital: Some Implications for Christian Adult Education', *Modern Believing*, 38: 22–31

Kant, I. (1964) *Über Pädagogik: Werke*, W. Weischedel (ed.) Vol. XII, Frankfurt: Insel.

Kapezides, T. (1991) 'Religious Indoctrination and Freedom', in B. Spiecker and R. Straughan (eds) *Freedom and Indoctrination in Education: International Perspectives*, London: Cassell.

Laura, R.S. (1983) 'To Educate or to Indoctrinate: That is still the Question', *Educational Philosophy and Theory*, 15: 43–55.

Nipkow, K.E. (2003) *God, Human Nature and Education for Peace: New Approaches to Moral and Religious Maturity*, Aldershot: Ashgate.

—— (2004) 'Bildung und Indoktrination – Bildsamkeit und Indoktrinierbarkeit', in B. Hadinger (ed.) *Die Bestimmung des Menschen: Der Mensch zwischen Verbiegung und Erfüllung*, Tübingen: Verlag Lebenskunst.

Oelkers, J. (1991) 'Freedom and Learning: Some Thoughts on Liberal and Progressive Education', in B. Spiecker and R. Straughan (eds) *Freedom and Indoctrination in Education: International Perspectives*, London: Cassell.

Peters, R.S. (1965) 'Education as Initiation', in R.D. Archambault (ed.) *Philosophical Analysis and Education*, London: Routledge & Kegan Paul.

Schleiermacher, F. (1799) *Reden über die Religion*, Berlin: J.F. Unger.

Schubert, J.N. (1998) 'The Role of Sex and Emotional Response in Indoctrinability', in I. Eibl-Eibesfeldt and F.K. Salter (eds) *Indoctrinability, Ideology, and Warfare: Evolutionary Perspectives*, New York and Oxford: Berghahn Books.

Shaw, R.P. and Wong, Y. (1989) *Genetic Seeds of Warfare: Evolution, Nationalism, and Patriotism*, Boston: Unwin Hyman.

Snook, I.A. (1972a) *Indoctrination and Education*, London: Routledge and Kegan Paul.

—— (ed.) (1972b) *Concepts of Indoctrination: Philosophical Essays*, London: Routledge and Kegan Paul.

Spiecker, B. (1991) 'Indoctrination: The Suppression of Critical Dispositions', in B. Spiecker and R. Straughan (eds) *Freedom and Indoctrination in Education: International Perspectives*, London: Cassell.

Spiecker, B. and Straughan, R. (eds) (1991) *Freedom and Indoctrination in Education: International Perspectives*, London: Cassell.

Thiessen, E.J. (1993) *Teaching for Commitment: Liberal Education, Indoctrination and Christian Nurture*, Leominster: Gracewing.

Treml, A.K. (2000) *Allgemeine Pädagogik*, Stuttgart: Kohlhammer.

7 Telling a new story

Reconfiguring Christian education for the challenges of the twenty-first century

Anthony Reddie

One of my most significant memories of growing up in a migrant African Caribbean family in Bradford, West Yorkshire, was my first day at school. I arrived at the gates of an infant school in September 1969, the first child of Noel and Lucille Reddie. I was five years old and the first British born Black child to enter an English school in my family. I remember being placed in a long line of young children, and standing as the teachers discussed what should be done with the 'odd' child towards the end of the line. Instinct told me that I was the subject of the heated conversations. I was the only Black person in that room. The conversation continued as I stood in the line. Gesticulating hands and furrowed brows indicated a deep sense of unease and confusion in the minds of the education officials and teachers.

After what seemed like an interminable delay, two teachers approached me and began speaking about me, but never to me. They wondered if I could cope in a class of White children? Could I speak English? Would my presence be conducive to the well-being of the class? Would I affect the education of the others? What struck me at the time was the strange sense of detachment I felt. I was the subject of the conversation but no one seemed interested in what I had to say. I was an object, not a subject. I knew I could speak perfectly good West Yorkshire influenced English because I did it everyday with my parents but my internalised sense of self was negated by an externalised force that had possessed little awareness of my subjective reality.

The upshot of the conversation was that I should be sent to an 'Immigration Centre' that lay adjacent to my primary school. This centre catered for the growing influx of children from the 'New Commonwealth' and was a crude attempt at the socialisation and acculturation of South Asian and Caribbean children into the 'British way of life'. For the first and the only time to date, I was a genius; for in the three days I attended this centre my teachers were amazed at my proficiency and eloquence for one so recently introduced to the English language. It took them three days to deduce that I was in fact born in Bradford, and English was my only tongue (as it was for my parents). What lay most stark in my recollections of that event all those years ago, was the sense of a dichotomy of experience that pervaded my life. For a brief second, as the teachers discussed my situation, I began to question my own reality. Could I really speak English? Was I so different and alarming, given that hitherto, I had always felt myself to be normal? There is a strange disjunction between these competing forms of reality. Which was true? Was there more truth in their accounts of me than in my own subjective understanding? (Reddie 1998b: 153–60).

Dubois and 'Double Consciousness'

The notion of competing realities is not a new phenomenon for Black people. This was first detailed by the great W.E.B. Dubois in his now classic text *The Souls of Black Folk* first published in 1903. Dubois detailed a phenomenon he termed 'Double Consciousness'. In using this term, Dubois was speaking of the struggle evinced within African American people to reconcile two opposing realities at war within the Black psyche (Dubois 1989: 3). This dialectical struggle was one between competing notions of truth, whether determined by a self affirming internalised form of subjectivity, what Pinn calls the quest for 'complex subjectivity' (Pinn, A.B. 2003: 82–107), or an all-embracing externalised form of negation and objectification. Dubois' most memorable comment in this book that has to a great extent helped to define Black Diasporan discourse over the course of the last century, was that the 'the problem of the 20th century is the problem of the color line' (Dubois 1989: xxxi). In the first instance there is the internal vision of a self that is positive and clothed in the garment of belonging and self-affirmation. This internalised vision is juxtaposed alongside the external world of White hegemony in which that same Black self is denigrated, demonised and disparaged. These two 'unreconciled strivings' (Dubois 1989: 3) have continued to fight their tumultuous struggle within the battlefield of the Black mind.

Jocelyn Maxime, in an address given to young Black Methodists at the 1990 Connexional conference for Black young people, details the importance of 'Racial Identity' as the central core in the formation of the personal identity of Black people (Maxime 1990: 3). Individuals unable to construct a positive racial identity will invariably harbour within their cognitive framework negative self-images of their race and concomitant cultures. This line of thinking owes its development to the pioneering work of Dubois. There are several substantive issues relating to notions of identity that affect children of the African diaspora. For example, there are questions related to the sense of dislocation felt by many African Caribbean children in Britain. This sense of dislocation is manifested in both psychological and physical terms. The forebears of these children were plucked from the ancestral cradle of Africa and transplanted to the Caribbean and the Americas. In the light of the rupture and breach in African diasporan history, the past five centuries have been a perpetual and substantive struggle for self-definition – a search for a sense of identity that has not been dictated and imposed by White hegemony (Woodson 1990).

Dubois understood the complexity of this dangerous ontological duality within Black people of African descent. The struggle to accommodate internalised subjectivity and external objectification carried within it the calamitous seeds for ongoing mental ill health and widespread pathology. Dubois understood the potency of tendentious racialised doctrines that asserted the sub-human character of the 'negro'. The struggle to resist the pernicious nature of this assault upon Black personhood has become the dominant motif in Black religio-cultural discourse since the epoch of slavery. Dubois writing in 1946 stated:

> The experience through which our ancestors have gone for four hundred years is part of our bone and sinew whether we know it or not. The methods which we evolved for opposing slavery and fighting prejudice are not to be forgotten, but learned for our own and others' instruction. . . . The problem of our children is distinctive: when shall a colored child learn the color line? At home, at school or suddenly in the street? What shall we do in art and literature? Shall we seek to ignore our background and graft on a culture which does not wholly admit us, or build anew on that marvellous African . . . heritage?
>
> (Dubois 1973: 144)

Dubois was chiefly a social scientist, and his early scholarly pursuits following his doctoral studies at Harvard University in 1895 were mainly concerned with using the insights of academics such as Max Weber to rebut the post Enlightenment social scientific basis of racial theory (Eze 1997). Dubois soon realised that empirical social science could not bear the burden of responding to the ongoing negation and oppression of Black people.

The response of Black religionists

Pre-dating Dubois' attempts to respond to the plight of Black people, activists such as Richard Allen and Edward Blyden (Blyden 1993: 109–21) had used Christian teachings and a nascent Black theology as their means of responding to the need for Black subjectivity. Richard Allen, a former slave, became the founder of the African American Episcopal Church (A.M.E.), which seceded from the American Episcopal Church due to the endemic racism of the latter ecclesial body (Pinn and Pinn 2002: 32–43). Henry McNeal Turner, a descendant of Allen in the A.M.E church, began to construct an explicit African centred conception of the Christian faith, arguing that an alignment with Africa should became a primary goal for Black Americans. This focus upon African ancestry would enable subjugated objects of Euro-American racism to find a suitable terrain for the subversive activism that would ultimately lead to liberation (Pinn, A.B. 2003: 90–3). Pinn acknowledges the link between the African centred strictures of the A.M.E. church and the later Black nationalism of Marcus Garvey and the

Black Star Line 'Back-to-Africa' movement of the early twentieth century (ibid. 93).

Edward Blyden, an African centred scholar of the late 19th century, put the case for an awareness and appreciation of the African roots of Black culture and identity as a means of asserting the selfhood of people of African descent. Blyden amplified this thesis by arguing that Africa's service to the world, and to Christendom in particular, laid siege to any fallacious doctrine enshrining the inferiority of Black people (Blyden 1993: 109–21). Blyden writes:

> To any one who has travelled in Africa, especially in the portion north of the equator, extending from the West Coast of Abyssinia, Nubia, and Egypt, and embracing what is known as the Nigritian and Soudanic countries, there cannot be the slightest doubt as to the country and the people to whom the terms Ethiopia and Ethiopian, as used in the Bible and the classical writer, were applied ... Africans were not unknown, therefore, to the writers of the Bible. Their peculiarities of complexion and hair were as well known to the ancient Greeks and Hebrews, as they are to the American people today. And when they spoke of the Ethiopians, they meant the ancestors of the black-skinned and woolly-haired people, who, for two hundred and fifty years, have been known as labourers on the plantations in the South.
>
> (Blyden 1993: 109–10)

Responding to the ongoing threat of non-being so eloquently detailed by Dubois has been one of the central aims of Black religionists. Harold Dean Trulear writing on the importance of Black Christian religious education says:

> Rather it (religious education) has carried upon its broad shoulders the heavy responsibility of helping African Americans find answers for the following question: What does it mean to be Black and Christian in a society where many people are hostile to the former while claiming allegiance to the latter?
>
> (Trulear 1997: 162)

Dubois' notion of 'Double Consciousness' has remained highly influential amongst African Diasporan scholars across a range of disciplines. In the area of cultural studies, for example, Susan Searls has investigated the notion of 'Double Consciousness' in terms of the literary output and socio-political positioning of Pulitzer prize winning writer Toni Morrison (Searls 1997: 153–76). Searls argues that Morrison, far from being a disinterested trans-racial universalist, is in actual fact a direct inheritor of Dubois' radical stance on acknowledging and chronicling the subtle and not so oblique concerns of racial categorisation (Searls 1997: 154). Searls writes:

Of course, the assertion of black inferiority and the retreat into color blindness both function to preserve white hegemony. Accommodating a different strategy for perpetuating racial exclusion, Morrison's project extends beyond Du Boisan preoccupation with the real contribution of black Americans to their country by engaging the degree to which 'white Americanism' is dependent upon a silent and abiding African presence.

(Searls 1997: 154)

During the course of my doctoral research I was concerned with how one represented the central tenets of double consciousness to Black children and young people within the context of an African centred Christian education curriculum (Reddie 2000). How could one assist these youngsters to gain some sense of the dynamics of internalised selfhood that is in conflict with an externalised form of objectification and negation? In order to delineate the dynamics of this phenomenon in a helpful manner, I devised an experiential exercise that sought to combine the insights of Dubois with the liberative formational concepts of Black Theology (Reddie 1998a: 29–32).

For this exercise, I used thin strips of paper on which were written short statements such as 'This person is stupid' or 'This person is poor' and many other statements of a similar ilk. Some of the statements were positive. Each young person was assigned a statement by the leader. This was done by means of the young person simply choosing a statement at random from some container holding all the strips and then the leader affixing it on the back of the young person. The aim of the exercise was for each young person to attempt to discover their identity by engaging with other young people in the group. No one person could see the strip or label that was placed on their back. In order to discover what kind of person they were (as detailed on the strip of paper), the other young people in the group would talk to them as if they were the person detailed on the label.

After some twenty minutes of playing this game, the young people soon discovered an undeniable truth. How you are treated (and spoken to) by others is very much dependent upon who you are and the status or the 'label' society places upon you. Those who are labelled in negative terms will be treated in a manner that accords with the value which the greater, corporate whole places upon them. On every occasion that I have used this exercise since it was first devised in the mid 1990s, I have yet to witness one situation when a young person could not guess what kind of person they were (according to the label or strip on their back) based solely on how others spoke to and engaged with them. As one youth memorably stated: 'Just because people don't call you stupid to your face, doesn't mean that they ain't treating you like there's something seriously wrong with you'. The resulting learning from this exercise is then juxtaposed with some Black Theology based on Matthew's gospel, in order to demonstrate the central importance of subjectivity and internalised self-generated personhood for Black people (Reddie 1998a: 29–32).

Robert Beckford, writing within the British context, has argued that one form of an objectified, externalised negation can be found in the repressed and submerged anger of Black people who suffer from a malaise he describes as 'low level rage' (Beckford 2001: 37–9). Beckford defines the latter as 'related to internalised rage in that it is experienced in mind and body. It is manifested in anger, depression and anxiety' (Beckford 2001: 38). The high incidence of anger, rage and pathological behaviour is a product of a system in which the Black self is constantly assaulted by externalised, racialised pressures (Carrington 2000: 133–56). Beckford proceeds to outline an approach to tackling 'low level rage' by means of an updated and revisited Black theological engagement with the radical ideal that is the realised eschatology of the Kingdom of God. This schema is one in which the concept of redemptive vengeance is harnessed in order to challenge the casual incidences of individual and institutional racism that afflict Black people in post colonial Britain (Beckford 2001: 29–65).

More recently, Anthony Pinn has adopted a multi-disciplinary approach to charting the negative effects of double consciousness upon African Americans (Pinn, A.B. 2003). Pinn argues that Black religion (not just Christianity) emerged as an attempt to counteract the worst excesses of Black dehumanisation (Pinn, A.B. 1998: 88–132). Reflecting upon the development of Black Church practices, as a response to racialised terror, Pinn writes:

> The liberative agenda has been played out in the very worship of black Christians. The Black Church as a manifestation of religion responds to terror by seeking to establish blacks as agents of will; Christian gatherings orchestrated by churches served as a ritual of 'exocosm' in that they fostered a break with status as will-less objects and encouraged new forms of relationship and interaction premised upon black intentionality.
>
> (Pinn, A.B. 2003: 99)

Pinn distils the nature of Black religion to the quest for 'complex subjectivity' (ibid. 177) – the desire to be more than the simplistic, racialised construct White supremacist enlightened thought deems one to be (Eze 1997: 29–94).

Utilising a jazz hermeneutic for an anti-racist approach to Christian education

Given the ways in which Black theological discourse has used Black (popular) culture as a resource for undertaking God-talk (see the likes of James Cone, Dwight Hopkins and Robert Beckford), utilising the aesthetics of jazz within the context of Christian education seems utterly timely and natural. My primary resource for analysing the claims of jazz music as a metaphor and heuristic for Christian education comes from Geoffrey C. Ward's and Ken Burn's book, *Jazz: A History of America's Music* (2001). The tendency of cultural commentators to assign generic, even universal status to White Euro-American forms of cultural production coupled with the insistence that Black forms be relegated to contextual, parochial positioning, is challenged by the author's declaration that this African American dominated practice is indeed the music of the whole nation, indeed the whole world.

From its earliest years in the highly syncretised and plural world of New Orleans through to the eclectic developments of urbanised New York in the 1940s and 50s, jazz has been an important chronicler of the Black experience. In an early section of the book Duke Ellington states:

> Put it this way. Jazz is a good barometer of freedom. . . . In its beginnings, the United States of America spawned certain ideals of freedom and independence through which, eventually jazz evolved, and the music is so free that many people say it is the only unhampered, unhindered expression of complete freedom yet produced in this country.
>
> (Ward and Burns 2001: vii)

Musicologists, cultural critics and historians have long been aware of the inextricable relationship between art, the artist and the environment that gives birth to that ongoing dynamic. Jazz was born in the flux of social advantage and repression, and human reward and pitiless indignity. The great modern icon, the trumpeter Wynton Marsalis (who acts as creative consultant on the project) states that:

> Jazz music celebrates life – human life. The range of it. The absurdity of it. The ignorance of it. The greatness of it. The intelligence of it. The sexuality of it. The profundity of it. And it deals with it in all of its . . . it deals with it.
>
> (Ward and Burns 2001: vii)

Jazz is not a form of music for faint hearts. I was once told by a music teacher that playing great jazz music was akin to standing on a high-backed chair and pushing that object onto two legs and seeing how far one could push and retain balance before you lost control and fell to the floor. Quite naturally, there are innumerable analogies one could invoke in an attempt to capture the sheer verve and nerve that is part of the emotional and technical repertoire of the jazz musician.

Jazz musicians are constantly re-working an established melody in order to create something new and spontaneous for that split moment in time in mid performance. Duke Ellington once remarked that there has never existed a jazz musician who did not have some inclination of what he or she was going to play before they walked onto the stage (ibid. 290–1). One's improvisation is never totally created or made up on the spot; one does not create new art in a vacuum. All jazz improvisation is a negotiation between what has been conceived previously and what emerges in that specific moment, either on stage or in the recording studio. All great jazz has its antecedents. To quote my musician friend, 'it all comes from someplace, it isn't entirely yours to make it up as you like, you have a responsibility for this stuff.'

Jazz is an important resource for all people engaged in Black theological discourse of whatever kind, from those in systematics through to religious educators such as myself. I make this claim with one principal thought in mind – namely, that jazz music represents both the best and worst in human nature. It straddles the contradictions between a group of intensely fierce individuals who come together to join forces to make music. This is a voluntary engagement, for jazz is a form that eschews rigid conventions or categorisations. It demands mutuality and community, and yet it has, since the early 1920s, been built around the searing geniuses and contradictions of brilliant soloists. It is free form and yet demands certain rules and conventions working alongside and with others – those with whom one might not possess any sense of empathy or love, save for the act of making music in that split moment of time.

Jazz represents the tension between time and eternity; between immanence and transcendence; between the sense that art is created within and through context, and yet appears to carry within it the traces of inspiration and magic that come from another space and time. When theologians investigate the contradictions of individuality and community, between being bound by conventions and yet being compelled to go beyond all that is known and accepted as given, one is dealing with the most fundamental of existential concerns. The questions jazz poses are concerns for Christian faith and for all humanity. What does it mean to improvise on a given melody? How far can one go before what you are creating is no longer faithful to the melody and sources that inspired the artist in the first instance? How inclusive can we be? Ward and Burns show that jazz music is not just an inconsequential art form; rather, it is a depiction of the most central concerns of human identity and existence in the twentieth century. Jazz music is part of a rich musical heritage. Older traditions, like the blues, spirituals, hymnals and gospel music, have offered us a rich tapestry of cultural production with which the theological can engage in order to discern the liberative impulse of God. Jazz music has become an integral part of this crucial matrix.

Juxtaposing the dichotomies of 'Double Consciousness' and jazz music for an anti racist approach to Christian education

Central to the practise of jazz music is the notion of alternative truths. Jazz is built upon improvisation, but it also demands particular and precise rules of engagement. The notion of dealing with the dichotomies or otherness of reality is not a new theme or form of heuristic for Christian education. Charles Foster, for example, is aware of the subtle issues of power and legitimation that often promote notions of exclusivity and superiority within seemingly homogeneous faith groupings. Foster warns against communities of faith perceiving their corporate life as being normative. The corollary of this normative belief is the objectifying of different ethnic and cultural groups as being 'other' (Foster 1987a: 467). Foster argues that faith communities need to engage with issues of multiculturalism and differing perspectives within their Christian religious education programmes. This alternative focus is crucial, for it offers opportunities to develop a growing appreciation of the importance of inclusivity and the valuing of people from different ethnic backgrounds. Foster stresses that Churches within multicultural societies must adopt a 'Double Consciousness' approach, one that enables people to recognise different perspectives and traditions, whilst valuing and affirming their own particularity (Foster 1991: 153–4). Foster continues by claiming that:

> A primary context for the Religious education of persons in multicultural contexts occurs not in isolation of their cultural experiences in teaching learning activities or in the imposition of one cultural perspective over another, but at the intersection of their encounters with each other.
>
> (ibid. 155)

Marina Herrera articulates her essential belief in the mutuality between people of different traditions and cultures in dialogue with the Christian Gospel. Herrera asserts that Christian religious education is a process that transforms and binds the individual to God (within the context of a wider family of faith), the wider community and ultimately, the whole world (Herrera 1992: 177). Charles Foster attempts to articulate the seeming tension inherent within many faith communities; the necessity, in the first instance, to move beyond endemic insularity and exclusivity. The alternative perspective in this dialectic is the attempt to unite people of all ages within that community of faith into an effective appropriation of the stories and traditions that are a part of any corporate group of people. The second half of this dialectic, asserts Foster, remains a primary task of every church. He writes:

> One of the most critical tasks facing the church, then, has to do with the effectiveness with which each successive generation appropriates the story of its heritage and internalises the promises inherent in the story.
>
> (Foster 1987b: 23)

Jane Hilyard locates the dichotomies and otherness of Christian education within the context of an all-encompassing, inter-generational process for

Christian education, located within an all-age faith community. Hilyard asserts that a corporate, inter-generational Christian education programme should include the specific intention of enabling children and young people to appropriate the family narrative, and consequently gain a positive affirmation of self (Hilyard 1979: 106). I have attempted to incorporate aspects of this approach in some of my previous work, with particular reference to an inter-generational approach to Christian education and practical theology (Reddie 2001a). This approach to Christian education – telling a new story in reconfiguring this discipline for this century – is predicated on a number of assumptions, some of which I will outline in brief as I conclude this essay.

First, that notions of fixed identity and fixity are anathema to the dynamic spirit of God. God is constantly breathing new life and creating fresh vistas that overturn and often mock existing truths as we have known them (Reddie 2001b: 27–42). Attempts to reify Christian culture and learning lead, almost axiomatically, to the exclusion, marginalisation and oppression of others (Byron 2002). When we insist on parading human constructions as metaphysical, essentialised truth, we often run the risk of reifying the aesthetics and conventions of the powerful, whilst marginalising and oppressing those outside the traditional hegemonies that govern many societies (Hope and Timmel 1999: 76–185). The latter tendency can be seen in the seemingly rigid determination of mainstream Christian thought to cling onto patriarchal, Judaic cultic beliefs and doctrines such as our often violent, blood-thirsty doctrines of atonement. The corollary of this for Christian education has been the reification of suffering, mutilation and servitude for Black women and those groups whose existential experiences would seem to suggest such eventualities as being their normative lot in life (Terrell 1998: 99–119). As A.B. Pinn reminds us, for Black African Diasporan people, the threat of 'fixed identity' has been the principal, real and pernicious threat of the last four centuries (Pinn, A.B. 2003: 52–77).

Black religio-cultural scholars have long assessed the many and creative ways in which Black people have used subterfuge, disguise and conceits and deceits of language in order to develop a bi-cultural means of dealing with reality and the oppressive nature of White hegemony (Reddie 2001a: 107–9). The travails of Black life, particularly the ongoing struggle with double consciousness, has required Black people to develop a complex repertoire of strategies, tools and performative skills to traverse the chasm that exists between the exhilaration of complex subjectivity and the absurd nothingness of objectification. In spirituals and the blues (Cone 1972), newer forms of Black cultural expression such as 'dub' (Beckford 2002: 67–82) and in my case, jazz music, Black people have constructed innovative and ingenious ways of constructing a improvisational approach to life in order to defy the terror of being located in a fixed identity – the fate of being an object (Gates 1988).

By utilising the improvisational qualities of jazz, one can begin to develop more conscious and explicit strategies for enabling Christian learning to be freed from the tyranny of conventional structures that insist upon single trajectory truths – such axiomatic truths that asserted that Black people could not be compared with Whites in terms of ontology (Hopkins 2000: 26–42) or that they were deprived of rational or cognitive abilities (Eze 1997: 42–64). Telling a new story – re-configuring Christian education for the challenges of the twenty-first century – is to acknowledge the deeply ambivalent role Christianity has played in the affairs of Diasporan Africans over the past five centuries (Gossai and Murrell 2000). It is to acknowledge that the Christian faith stands culpable and condemned for colluding in the oppression of 'others', both within and beyond its so-called boundaries (Reddie 2001a: 27–42 and Byron 2002); but thankfully, there is another story to be told. It is one of subversion, liberation and an alternative version of the truth. It is a story of another way of seeing the world, indeed another way of viewing the human-divine encounter at the heart of Christian theology (Grant 1989: 212–22). Jacquelyn Grant argues that Black women, in the light of their unique experiences of subjugation and oppression, have viewed the person of Jesus very differently from White feminists (Grant 1989: 177–94).

Telling a new story – reconfiguring Christian education for the challenges of the twenty-first century – is to conceive of the Christian project as a broad, inclusive terrain that contains many tributaries and possible ways of advancement. The task of Christian education, utilising the trope of jazz music, allied to a double consciousness sensibility, is to enable people to enhance their human subjectivity, and become imaginative and improvisatory players in the pluralistic, post modern game of the twenty-first century. This task constantly asks the question 'Who is being disadvantaged by this?', 'Who is being left behind?', 'Who will be marginalised or oppressed if we assert this?' These are questions Christian education has rarely asked in the last century. Perhaps Christian education can play its part in answering the challenging question W.E.B. Dubois posed at the beginning of the last century – will we finally gain the courage and nerve to challenge the reality of the colour line? To tell a new story is to gain the necessary strength to assert that very reality as the vision for this century.

References

Beckford, R. (1998) *Jesus is Dread*, London: Darton, Longman and Todd.
—— (2001) *God of the Rahtid: Redeeming Rage*, London: Darton, Longman and Todd.
—— (2002) 'Prophet of Dub: Dub as a heuristic for Theological Reflection', *Black Theology: an International Journal*, 1: 67–82.
Blyden, E.W. (1993) 'Africa's Service to the World: Discourse Delivered before the American Colonization Society, May 1880. The Scope and Meaning of "Ethiopia"', in Cain Hope Felder (ed.) *The Original African Heritage Study Bible*, Nashville, Tennessee: The James C. Winston Publishing Company.
Byron, G.L. (2002) *Symbolic Blackness and Ethnic Difference in Early Christian Literature*, New York: Routledge.

Carrington, B. (2000) 'Double Consciousness and the Black Athlete', in K. Owuso (ed.) *Black British Society: a Text Reader*, London: Routledge.

Cone, J.H. (1972) *The Spirituals and the Blues*, New York: Seabury Press.

Dubois, W.E.B. (1973) *The Education of Black People: Ten Critiques, 1905–1960* H. Aptheker (ed.), New York: Monthly Press.

—— (1989) *The Souls of Black Folk*, New York: Bantam Books. (First published in 1903.)

Eze, E.C. (1997) *Race and the Enlightenment*, Massachusetts: Blackwell.

Foster, C.R. (1987a) 'Double Messages: Ethnocentrism in Church Education', *Religious Education*, 82: 447–67.

—— (1987b) 'The Pastor: Agent of Vision in the Education of a Community of faith', in R.L. Browning (ed.) *The Pastor as Religious educator*, Birmingham Alabama: Religious Education Press.

—— (1991) 'Imperialism in the Religious Education of Cultural Minorities', *Religious Education*, 86: 143–55.

Gates, H.L. (1988) *The Signifying Monkey: a Theory of African American Literary Criticism*, Oxford: Oxford University Press.

Gossai, H. and Murrell, N. (eds) (2000) *Religion, Culture and Tradition in the Caribbean*, London: Macmillan.

Grant, J. (1989) *White Women's Christ and Black Women's Jesus: Feminist Christology and Womanist Response*, Atlanta, Georgia: Scholars Press.

Herrera, M. (1992) 'Meeting Cultures at the Well', *Religious Education* 87: 173–217.

Hope, A. and Timmel, S. (1999) *Training for Transformation: A Handbook for Community Workers: Book 4*, London: Intermediate Technology Publications.

Hopkins, D.N. (2000) *Down, Up and Over: Slave religion and Black Theology*, Philadelphia: Fortress Press.

Hilyard, J. (1979) 'Family and Intergenerational Education', in D.W. Perry (ed.) *Homegrown Christian Education*, New York: Seabury Press.

Maxime, J. (1990) 'The Importance of Racial Identity for the Psychological well being of Black Children and Young Black People', *To Overcome is to Undertake: First Connexional Conference of Young Black Methodists*, London: The Methodist Church.

Pinn, A.B. (1998) *Varieties of African American Religious Experience*, Minneapolis: Fortress Press.

—— (2003) *Terror and Triumph: the Nature of Black religion*, Minneapolis: Fortress Press.

Pinn, A.H. and Pinn, A.B. (2002) *Introduction to Black Church History*, Minneapolis: Fortress Press.

Reddie, A.G. (1998a) 'Advent Week 1 – Older', in *Growing into Hope Vol. 1: Believing and Expecting – Christian Education in Multi-ethnic Churches*, Peterborough: The Methodist Publishing House.

—— (1998b) 'An Unbroken Thread of experience', in J. King (ed.) *Family and all that Stuff*, Birmingham, UK: NCEC.

—— (2000) 'The Christian Education of African Caribbean Children in Birmingham: Creating a New Paradigm Through Developing Better Practice', unpublished Ph.D. thesis, University of Birmingham.

—— (2001a) *Faith, Stories and the Experience of Black Elders: Singing the Lord's Song in a Strange Land*, London: Jessica Kingsley.

—— (2001b) 'Pentecost, Dreams and Visions', in M. Edwards (ed.) *Discovering Christ: Ascension and Pentecost*, Birmingham, UK: IBRA.

Searls, S. (1997) 'Race, schooling and Double Consciousness: The Politics of Pedagogy in Toni Morrison's Fiction', in H.A. Giroux and P. Shannon (eds) *Education and Cultural Studies: Towards a Performative Practice*, New York: Routledge.

Terrell, J.M. (1998) *Power in the Blood?: The Cross in the African American Experience*, Maryknoll, New York: Orbis Books.

Trulear, H.D. (1997) 'African American Religious Education', in B. Wilkerson (ed.) *Multicultural Religious Education*, Birmingham, Alabama: Religious Education Press.

Ward, G.C. and Burns, K. (2001) *Jazz: a History of America's Music*, London: Pimlico.

Woodson, C.G. (1990) *The Miseducation of the Negro*, Trenton, New Jersey: Africa World Press. (First published in 1933.)

8 The concept of relationship and its centrality to religious education

Reinhold Boschki

In modern western societies a strange development is taking place; on the one hand we are all connected with one another – more than ever before – the Internet, mass communications, email and the mobile phone are putting almost everybody into contact with almost everybody else – provided that she or he has the possibility of getting trained and can afford the technical equipment to get access to it. On the other hand the quest, the yearning for personal relationships is stronger than in former ages where family and clan relationships used to be stable and lifelong. Today we know and feel that personal relationships are always fragile. Young people grow up experiencing the fact that there are no guarantees in personal relationships. Relationships can weaken, fail, break, or be destroyed.

This ambiguous development seems to have its roots in the same social processes that sociologists call the individualisation and pluralisation of modern society. If individualisation means by definition (Beck, Beck-Gernsheim 1994) that each individual must be the architect as well as the builder of his or her own biography, we are alone with ourselves as regards the crucial decisions of our life. Each person has to look after himself or herself. We feel terribly alone, lost in a world that offers all imaginable and unimaginable possibility, but not the security of permanent personal relationships.

But what exactly are personal relationships? How can they be defined and qualified in psychological, psycho-social, and sociological terms? What meaning do they have for each individual, especially for young people? Thinking in educational terms, the questions that present themselves are: does the concept of relationship have something to do with education and formation?; which are the dimensions of relationship that are involved in the process of education?; and, more specifically, do personal relationships have any influence on religious education; and if so, how do they affect religious development?

The remainder of this paper is devoted to dealing with these questions and to answering at least some of them. Everything that follows is dedicated to a friend and colleague whose life and work is in a very special way connected with the concept and reality of personal relationship: John M. Hull is forever bringing people together and strengthening the bonds between them

– colleagues from different nations, cultures and traditions such as in the ISREV (International Seminar on Religious Education and Values) community; persons from different religious backgrounds such as Christians, Hindus and Muslims who are searching for appropriate ways of giving religious education in Britain; parents and children asking about and seeking for God (Hull 1991) etc. My own thinking has benefited immensely from John Hull's work and message and above all from the privilege of being in personal relationship with him myself.

Dimensions of personal relationships

It is nearly three decades since personal relationships became a special focus of empirical investigations. The field of research in 'personal relationships', 'social relationships', 'close relationships', 'human relationships' and so on has expanded at an almost incredible rate (for an overview on the research field see Duck 1996). In various disciplines, research programmes are being carried out from different perspectives such as psychoanalytic or cognitive approaches, evolutionary psychological theory, attachment or equity theory, network approaches and so on. Only in the last few years have efforts been made to integrate the various branches of research on personal relationships (see the *Handbook of Personal Relationships* (Duck 1996) or the journals *Personal Relationships* and *Journal of Social and Personal Relationships;* in German speaking literature see Asendorpf, Banse 2000; Auhagen, Salisch 1993). One reason for the lack of integration can be found in the traditional single-subject paradigm in psychology, and even in social psychology as William Ickes and Steve Duck have pointed out:

> It is therefore ironic, and perhaps even paradoxical, that the social psychology of the past 50 years has relied primarily on single-participant research paradigms in which individuals are asked to report their own subjective reactions to normally 'social' stimuli or 'social' situations.
>
> (Ickes, Duck 2000: 2)

The gap between psychological and social theory approaches is still responsible for extreme differences in both presuppositions and methodology. It is only in the past decade that research on personal relationships has increasingly put the stress on the social aspect of relationships instead of focussing only on individuals (see the 2nd edition of the *Handbook* quoted above compared to its 1st edition (1988); see also Ickes, Duck 2000; Duck 1993). Meanwhile we know that external influences have an immense impact on the form that relationships take and how they are enacted. Place and situation, even the wider social context affect the ways interactions take place.

A second reason for the difficulties in constructing a common theory of personal relationship lies in the great variety of types of relationship – relationships among adults, romantic relationships, relationships between adults and children, between siblings, friends, colleagues, and neighbours, homosexual or heterosexual relationships, interracial, intercultural, and interreligious relationships and so on. The research on each of these forms of relationship needs a different theoretical and methodological framework, and it is very difficult if not impossible to bring these various perspectives together. I shall therefore focus in the following sections on the various personal relationships of children and young people. I do so also because of the chapter's special interest in educational issues. By studying at least some aspects of the broad research on personal relationship one can discern some basic elements of the concept of relationship (for detailed investigations see Boschki 2003).

From a psychological viewpoint, personal relationships can be defined as emotionally significant ties or connections between two or more individuals, comprising frequent and interdependent action sequences that occur across diverse settings and tasks. Here we have some of the most important elements of relationship. Relationship is rooted in emotional grounds. The difference between mere interaction and the reality of personal relationship consists above all in the affective dimension of relationship. 'Interaction' can be any human act that involves other people. The encounter with the cashier in a supermarket is a classical form of interaction, more exactly of a series of interactions: saying 'hello', presenting the goods, handing over cash or credit cards, getting the change back, receiving the receipt, saying 'goodbye'. I may meet the same cashier several times – it is and it remains an interaction, unless an emotional dimension deepens the interaction and pushes it forward towards a relationship. I could fall in love with the girl at the cash desk or become a friend, meeting her after work. The emotional dimension is particularly important in children's relationships; positive growing up needs positive emotional bonds.

The intensity of relationships can be measured by the frequency and diversity of action sequences. The broader the range of actions with another person, the more intense are the ties between the individuals. Thinking once more of the example of the cashier, it is clear that the 'relationship' is not very deep if I only happen to meet him or her while doing my shopping. If the variety of interaction increases (for example if we meet for lunch or go to the cinema together) the intensity of our relationship increases as well. The same thing happens in the relationship between parents and children – and of course also, as we will see later, in the relationship between teachers and pupils or students. Furthermore, children's and young people's relationships have some special characteristics as developmental psychology, socialisation theory and empirical research into childhood and youth have pointed out in recent decades (e.g. Krüger, Grunert 2002; Montemayor, Adams, Gullotta 1994). The importance of the experience of equality and reciprocity in relationships among siblings and peers can hardly be overestimated. Children need to experience non-dependent relations and communications with human beings who are not or who do not feel permanently superior to themselves.

Developmental psychology discovered that young people have three essential 'developmental tasks' during the time of puberty and adolescence (Fend 2000): (1) to find a new relationship with themselves; (2) to build new relational bonds with other people (especially peers and parents); (3) to construct a (new) relationship to the social and historical context in which they live (neighbourhood, township, city, society, and history). The first task is usually called the search for identity. In the years from twelve to eighteen young people have to find at least some aspects that bring them closer to a concept of their own identity: Who am I? What are my strengths and weaknesses? What are my goals in life? etc. Meanwhile we know that identity is not a static concept that comes to an end at a certain point in life. The questions raised are only partially answerable, and even when we are old we will not be able to answer them in all their dimensions. The relationship approach is more restrained than the identity approach; to find a new relationship with oneself does not mean to find a full answer to the question of identity. It is clear that the second task is as important as the first. The relationship to peers can become even more important than family relationships. Everything has to be renewed: our relations with our own and with the other sex, our relations with friends and 'enemies', our relations with 'significant adults' such as parents, relatives, and teachers. The main question being tackled here is: Where do I belong?

The third developmental task is perhaps the one that is still least investigated. The life-world of young people does not consist only of family, school, and peer groups but also of the social, political, and historical background. Young people have to find a relationship with their wider surroundings which have an essential impact on their biographies, their chances, and possibilities in life (e.g. via mass communication). The basic questions are in this case: Where do I come from? Where is my place within the greater setting? It is only in the past couple of years that research programmes have begun to be conducted into the historical consciousness of young people with respect to the societal context in which they live (e.g. Rüsen 2001).

These three developmental tasks can be understood as three dimensions of relationship: the relationship with oneself, with others, and with the social context. Such an understanding goes along with a social-ecological view on the life world of everybody, especially of children and young people. Urie Bronfenbrenner developed a social theory of understanding individuals within their social context in different social systems: the micro system (face to face relationships), the meso system (institutional level such as neighbourhoods, schools, and jobs) and the macro system (political and social situation as represented in mass media, for example in television and in the Internet). Later Bronfenbrenner added a fourth: the chrono system (biography and history) (Bronfenbrenner, Morris 1998; Bronfenbrenner 1979). All these systems represent special levels of social activities and all of them must be taken into account to understand and interpret the life of individuals.

Dimensions of educational relationships

The relationship approach with its various dimensions of personal relationship is especially helpful in describing and understanding educational relationships. Personal relationship is a basic concept in any educational process. Educational theory since Jean Jacques Rousseau and Johann Heinrich Pestalozzi has stressed the importance of the pedagogical relationship. At the beginning of the twentieth century the reflections on education of Martin Buber, Herman Nohl and Janusz Korczak made a special contribution to our understanding of the relationship between educator and student. But how can we define this relationship, and what is its significance for religious education?

Martin Buber stood for consequent, dialogical thinking in philosophy, philosophy of religion and education. It was he who introduced the concepts of encounter and relationship to modern philosophy, defining them as basic principles of all human life: 'I require a You to become; becoming I, I say You. All actual life is encounter.' (Buber [1923] 1984: 15) Even more: 'In the beginning is the relation' (ibid. 22). Relation appears as the principle of all being. Interestingly, Buber did not leave these insights to philosophy alone. In his speeches on education he points out that the same principle is valid for education as well, thus pushing educational theory forward to a deeper understanding of the process of education. He is convinced that the principle of education is always relation (Buber [1925] 1986: 30), a fundamental relation between educator and child. The real encounter with a concrete person, the educator, has its special significance for the child. It is for him and for her a basic experience, an 'elemental experience' (ibid. 36) that constitutes the educational process and stimulates development and maturity.

A similar educational thought is expressed in the work of Herman Nohl, one of the most important thinkers in educational theory in the last century. Nohl draws his ideas from the so-called 'reform pedagogy' movement, a fresh and powerful current in educational theory and practice at the end of the nineteenth and the beginning of the twentieth century. Like Buber, Nohl focuses on the relationship of the educator and the 'educandus'. He defines the educational relationship as a 'passionate relationship between a mature human being and a becoming human being' (Nohl [1933, 1935] 1988: 169). But despite the fact that both thinkers underline the importance of reciprocity in the practice of education, their concepts remain mainly one sided: the relationship between educator ('maturity') and educandus ('immaturity') always remains an unequal one.

In opposition to such an asymmetrical understanding of the educational relationship, Janusz Korczak, the so called 'Pestalozzi of Warsaw', came from his specific background to more radical conclusions for the theory and practice of education. He derives his ideas from his own phenomenological approach to the life world of children. Devoting his whole life to children –

even his death in the Nazi gas chambers of Treblinka where he was murdered in 1942 together with more than 200 of 'his' Jewish orphans – his educational work became even more powerful and significant than the writings of his above-mentioned contemporaries. Korczak abandons all asymmetrical thinking about education. Sharing the children's and young people's life day and night in the orphanages founded and headed by himself, he was convinced that the relationship between adults and young people must be an equal one – otherwise it would be inhuman and destructive. Teachers and children must live and learn together on the same level, not with teachers seeing themselves at a superior level. Korczak thus creates a pedagogy of radical 'respect for the child' (Korczak 1996ff.).

At the end of the twentieth century all three of these thinkers were rediscovered and their thoughts have been 'reconstructed' and revised in relation to the challenges of today's society. The basic insights of Buber, Nohl and Korczak have proved tremendously modern: education cannot be understood as a technical process in which persons are involved and where the younger one learns automatically from the older one. No, education in a broad and integral sense implies personal relationship! If education means not only cognitive training and instruction but extensive personal development, it is linked to personal bonds between educator and educandus.

As the twenty-first century begins, educational theory is being enriched by the above-mentioned interdisciplinary research on personal relationship. We have learned that relationship is constitutive for the life world of every individual, and especially of young people. For this reason it is possible to integrate the elements of personal relationship into a relation-based theory of education. The educational process occurs within different dimensions of relationship: relationship with oneself, with the educator(s), and with the social context. All these insights may have a great impact on a new and fresh understanding of religious education.

Towards a theological hermeneutics of relationship

Religious educational theory and practice need to be aware of the results of research in the social sciences as well as in education theory; but, as I see it, this is only one half of the task before us. The theory of religious education, as Friedrich Schweitzer points out, is an educational discipline (linked with all the other social sciences such as psychology, sociology, theory of socialisation etc.), and at the same time it is a theological one (Schweitzer 1995). Theology tries to understand religion from within. As regards the topic of personal relationships it is obvious that in Christian theology the concept of relationship is a very important biblical and theological idea. This can be illustrated with examples from contemporary biblical theology, feminist theology, and the most recent approaches to systematic theology.

'Personal relationship' is a modern concept based on notions of person, identity and individual that were unknown in the ancient and medieval world. This is the reason for the lack of Hebrew and Greek expressions for 'relationship' in the Bible; but although the term is missing, the reality of relationship can be found on every page of Holy Scripture. The overall biblical message that God is in personal relationship with God's creation, with people and with mankind as a whole is a fundamental theological idea that is constitutive of Jewish and Christian belief. God in the Bible is a 'God in search of mankind' (Heschel 1955), and human existence in the Bible is always understood from the standpoint of its 'Quest for God' (Heschel 1954).

Both conceptions come close together in biblical anthropology and biblical theology. All biblical characters are in a close personal relationship with God, be it Abraham, Isaac, Jacob or their descendants, be it in the prayers of the psalmists or the prophets. Their relationship with God changes their relationship to themselves (they change their lives), to other people (ethical dimension of belief), and to the world in which they live (new understanding of world and cosmos). The same is true for the New Testament. The life of Jesus is a 'life in relationship'. All dimensions of personal relationships can be found in his life, suffering, and death: the close relationship with his Father in Heaven is the cause of an intense relationship with himself (e.g. in his private prayers in loneliness), of a liberating and healing relationship with the people around him, and of a free and fearless relationship with the religious and political authorities of his time.

For these reasons 'relationship' can be used as a fundamental hermeneutics of biblical theology – and, as we will see in what follows, of systematic theology as well. Feminist theological studies were the first to introduce the relationship approach into actual theological discussions – in most cases starting with biblical investigations (e.g. Heyward 1982: Chapter II: 'Re-imaging Jesus: Power in relation', 25ff.). As late as the 1990s, feminist theologians found enough evidence to complain that relationship was still a 'forgotten dimension' of theology, especially of Christology (Moltmann-Wendel 1991). A few years later important attempts were undertaken to elaborate a Christian theology of relationship that brought the impulses of feminist theology into the whole range of systematic theology (Sattler 1997). The most recent approaches to an extensive understanding of theology use the terminus relationship as a basic terminus for theological thinking: 'Only because God is in relationship with us, and only because He wants to be in communion and in communication with us, are we able to talk of God, to God, and about God.' (Scharer, Hilberath 2002: 77). God is not only in relationship with all beings, God *is* relationship (ibid. 25).

To sum up, we can say that from a theological perspective relationship is at least four-dimensional: Everybody is in relationship with himself or herself, in relationship with other people, in relationship with the social context, and in an extensive and encircling relationship with God. All these dimensions are intensely interconnected. Sensitivity to these dimensions can renew the theory and practice of religious education.

Consequences for the theory and practice of religious education

The principal goal of religious education is that persons who are religiously educated will have developed a special skill and a special competence – namely to be able to make their own decisions in religious affairs. This means that religious education enables persons to think in religious terms, to understand religious matters, to have (at least to some degree) experienced religious acts, and to know about the religious thinking and acting of others. Religious education is from one point of view an intellectual process: but the relationship approach stresses the fact that religion is always more than a mere cognitive and intellectual process. In its depths, religion always implies relationships. My thesis is that since relationship is a basic concept in religion and in the life world of people, it should also be a basic, formative concept in religious education. Whoever wants to be religiously educated must be involved in all dimensions of relationship.

Relationship is an old concept in religious education and religious nurture, and one that is deeply rooted in the various religious traditions. It is an implicit concept in all religious teaching and learning in the different religious cultures. The issue today is to discover the relationship concept anew so that it can be helpful for planning and acting out processes of religious education. In the last section of this chapter I shall throw some light on this thesis.

Given that research into relationship has shown that relationships are intentionally enduring, have an emotional aspect and depend on the frequency and diversity of action sequences (as shown above), religious education should be an enduring (not 'everlasting'!) process over at the very least a couple of years so that children and young people have enough opportunities to become acquainted with religious matters and, above all, to get impulses from it for the life decisions they may make some years later. This teaching and learning process should not be only an intellectual one. When Watzlawick, Beavin and Jackson noted that messages contain both content and relational themes, they were pointing to something that is essential for communication theory as well as for everyday communication (Watzlawick, Beavin, Jackson 1967). Especially in the field of religious education these insights are of great importance. Religious teaching that puts the stress only on information ('content') forgets about the relational and emotional aspect of religious learning.

Emotional impulses should be part of religious education courses. The very best way to include such affective impulses lies in encounter. Encounters with persons who live in a religious tradition can be a point of identity for those who are born into the same tradition. For others the encounter with them offers the possibility of learning authentically from a representative of another denomination or another religion how he or she understands and lives his or her own religious life. If these encounters happen in a non-competitive setting and on the same level, meaning not with persons seeing themselves at a superior level, they can be a starting-point for a positive personal relationship. This will enrich religious learning tremendously.

Religious learning in its depths, either in one's 'own' tradition or in exchanges with another religious tradition, happens in such personal relationships. They should be 'passionate relationships' (Nohl [1933, 1935] 1988: 169) between educator and pupils or students, and include an absolute respect for the child and sensitivity to his and her own religious ideas, questions, doubts, and fantasies, that is to the 'children's theology' (see Friedrich Schweitzer's chapter in this volume).

In an multi-dimensional relationship approach to religious education, derived from the findings of the social sciences as well as from theological reflections, the process of religious learning is connected with at least four dimensions:

1   Religious education gives impulses to help (young) people to be sensitive in their relationship with themselves. As mentioned above, all religions focus on that basic relationship that is central for one's own concept of identity. The way somebody sees himself or herself, the self-knowledge and self-confidence, the feeling of one's own value and the sensitivity for one's own strengths and weaknesses need a great deal of self-reflection and self-contemplation. Religions offer a forum where people may tackle some of these tasks. Therefore meditative elements, symbolic acts, and exercises in silence should be part of any religious education, be it in public schools or in parishes. All this may help people to become aware of their own relationship with themselves and hopefully to find a positive self-concept.

2   It is obvious that the process of religious learning and teaching must include the dimension of personal relationship with others. There is no religion without extensive ethical teaching and implications, no religion that would not focus on face to face relationships; but social learning and ethical learning are only possible 'by doing', that is in real interactions for example with classmates, with peers, with persons belonging to one's own and to other religious traditions. The greater the frequency and the diversity of such action sequences, the greater the impact on the (religious and ethical) learning of individuals.

3   Religion implies a special relationship to the world that surrounds us. Religious education must be aware of the wider setting, of the social and political context, and of the world as a whole. Therefore religious education helps people to become sensitive to their own relationship with the world and with history.

4   In all these dimensions the relationship with God is intertwined. Religious education must give impulses to think about and maybe find one's own relationship with God and the Ultimate respectively. If this dimension is lacking, education is anything you like, but it is not *religious* edu-

cation. Children and young people are asking the question about God (the Ultimate): Does God exist? If so, in what relationship does he stand to me, and I to him? Is he watching me? Can I count on him? Where is he when people suffer? Is he waiting for us after death? etc. etc. Many of these questions are not answerable in one sentence, and not even in lengthier teaching sessions. They are only answerable personally within a specific religious tradition. Young people learn to give their own answers to such questions by encountering persons who live (or at least try to live) a religious life. Encounter is more than information and less then indoctrination.

To paraphrase the words of Martin Buber quoted above (Buber [1923] 1984: 15, 22): I require a You to become a religiously educated person. Becoming a religious I, I need a religious You. All actual religious education is encounter. Even more: In the beginning of religious education is the relation.

References

Asendorpf, J.B. and Banse, R. (eds) (2000) *Psychologie der Beziehung*, Bern etc.: Verlag Hans Huber.

Auhagen, A.E. and Salisch, M. von (eds) (1993) *Zwischenmenschliche Beziehungen*, Göttingen: Hogrefe.

Beck, U. and Beck-Gernsheim, E. (1994) *Riskante Freiheiten*, Frankfurt/M.: Suhrkamp.

Boschki, R. (2003) *Beziehung als Leitbegriff der Religionspädagogik. Grundlegung einer dialogisch-kreativen Religionsdidaktik*, Ostfildern (Germany): Schwabenverlag.

Bronfenbrenner, U. (1979) *The Ecology of Human Development*, New York: Harvard University Press.

Bronfenbrenner, U. and Morris, P.A. (1998) *The Ecology of Developmental Processes*, in Lerner, R.M. (ed.) *Handbook of Child Psychology*, Vol. I, New York etc.: Wiley & Sons.

Buber, M. ([1923] 1984) *Ich und Du*, in *Das dialogische Prinzip* (5th edn), Heidelberg: Lambert Schneider.

—— ([1925] 1986) *Über das Erzieherische*, in *Reden über Erziehung* (7th edn), Heidelberg: Lambert Schneider.

Duck, S.W. (ed.) (1993) *Social Context and Relationships*, London: Sage Publications.

—— (1996) *Handbook of personal relationships* (2nd edn), New York etc.: Wiley & Sons.

Fend, H. (2000) *Entwicklungspsychologie des Jugendalters*, Opladen: Leske & Budrich.

Heschel, A.J. (1954) *Man's quest for God. Studies in prayer and symbolism*, New York: Charles Scribner's Sons.

—— (1955) *God in search of man. A philosophy of Judaism*, New York: Farrar, Straus & Giroux.

Heyward, C. (1982) *The redemption of God. A theology of mutual relation*, Washington: University Press of America.

Hull, J.M. (1991) *God-talk with young children: Notes for parents and teachers*, Derby: CEM.

Ickes, W. and Duck, S.W. (eds) (2000) *The Social Psychology of Personal Relationships*, New York etc.: Wiley & Sons.

Korczak, J. (1996ff.) *Sämtliche Werke* (16 volumes), Gütersloh: Gütersloher Verlagshaus.

Krüger, H-H. and Grunert, C. (eds) (2002) *Handbuch Kindheits- und Jugendforschung*, Opladen: Leske & Budrich.

Moltmann-Wendel, E. (1991) *Beziehung – die vergessene Dimension der Christologie. Neutestamentliche Ansatzpunkte feministischer Christologie*, in D. Strahm and R. Strobel (eds) *Vom Verlangen nach Heilwerden. Christologie in feministisch-theologischer Sicht*, Fribourg, Luzern: Edition Exodus.

Montemayor, R., Adams, G.R. and Gullotta, T.P. (eds) (1994) *Personal relationships during adolescence*, London: Sage Publications.

Nohl, H. ([1933, 1935] 1988) *Die Theorie der Bildung*, in *Die pädagogische Bewegung in Deutschland und ihre Theorie*, Frankfurt/M.: Klostermann.

Rüsen, J. (2001) (ed.) *Geschichtsbewusstsein. Psychologische Grundlagen, Entwicklungskonzepte, empirische Befunde*, Köln etc.: Böhlau-Verlag.

Sattler, D. (1997) *Beziehungsdenken in der Erlösungslehre. Bedeutung und Grenzen*, Freiburg: Herder.

Scharer, M. and Hilberath, B.J. (2000) *Kommunikative Theologie. Eine Grundlegung*, Mainz: Grünewald-Verlag.

Schweitzer, F. (1995) *Vor neuen Herausforderungen: Bilanz und Perspektiven von Religionspädagogik als Theorie*, in *Jahrbuch der Religionspädagogik* 12: 143–60.

Watzlawick, P. Beavin, J. and Jackson, D. (1967) *Pragmatics of human communication. A study of interactional patterns, pathologies and paradoxes*, New York: Norton.

I should like to thank David Kelly, a professional translator, for correcting my chapter carefully and giving me helpful advice with regard to the English language.

9 Perceiving self-deception in teaching and learning

Charles Melchert

Is self-deception really a fact of life in the ministry of the church? Here is a case study, written by a pastor, describing one of his experiences in ministry:

Edith: a case study

1 After morning worship, as she left the sanctuary, Edith said abruptly to me, 'I disagree with your sermon.' I sought her out in the fellowship hall later, but she told me she could not talk and would come to see me Tuesday morning. Since the sermon had dealt with the Ephesians 5: 22 passage
5 ('Wives, be subject to your husbands, as to the Lord.') I ventured a question to her, hoping she might give some idea of what we would talk about on Tuesday. It was as I had expected, the issue of wives submitting to husbands.

The lady in question was an important person in the women's power
10 structure of the church, so I was eager to meet with her. She was almost a charter member of this twenty-five year old church, the mother of three grown children, one still active in the church. She had kept her membership active even though she had long since moved to a more expensive and exclusive neighborhood. Her husband had been an elder in the
15 church but had become inactive in church life. She continued to be a Bible teacher in the women's group, and thus she had influence. This was a small congregation of less than 100 members, though once there had been over 500. Many of the members had retired from the military where they had held career blue-collar jobs. The average income was under
20 $25,000. The educational level of the congregation was predominantly high school. The congregation was a family church and filled a social need for its members. Females outnumbered males in the membership and on the church session.

My intentions, when we met, were to discuss the text for Sunday's
25 sermon, Ephesians 5: 21–33, focusing on the key verse and then show her how a difficult passage is handled. We met in my office, just off the sanctuary, for about two hours. We began with the usual pleasantries and then I asked her to tell me about what specifically in Sunday's sermon she objected

to. I wanted her to state the problem and then through discussion we would get to the concerns I expected to deal with.

My thoughts	Our conversation
Let's get started.	Me: What in Sunday's sermon did you disagree with?
I knew it! Let's see if I can impress her with my sensitivity.	Edith: I didn't like the part about submitting to husbands.
I need to get to the point of seeing the passage as a whole.	Me: I knew it! I thought while I was writing the sermon someone was not going to like that verse.
I am not unaware of the problems here, but I did warn against abuses.	Edith: I don't believe a wife has to submit to her husband especially if her husband doesn't go to church. There are things we agree on and things we disagree on, but when it comes to church matters, they don't fit in.
I've got to get her to see other statements from the text. (Showing her the biblical text.)	Me: Did you hear me say in the sermon that this was a problem passage? It was not the only thing I said about submission. I began by noting verse 21, which speaks of mutual submission, and then pointed out the series of situations Paul gave about submission, but the bulk of the sermon dealt with mutual submission in the Lord.
	Edith: Yes, I know, but all I heard was the part about wives submitting to husbands and I just don't like it.
	Me: I know it's a tough statement given the women's movement, equal opportunity, and the obvious abuses of the statement. And I did tell the men in the congregation that this was not permission for them to be bossy or rude. I gave illustrations that worked out the dynamics in terms of responsibility in everyday situations. Mutuality was the pattern of decision making. Only on

70 Now we are at the real point. She
doesn't know how to properly
interpret scripture.

the rarest of occasions did it come
down to the husband having to say
the last word.

Edith: Yes, I know, but we don't
75　have it that way. You just gave men
permission to do what they want to
do and I will not accept it.

Me: Did you notice that I tried to
put the particular verse in the
context of the entire passage? Look,
80　here's the passage – and note all the
other examples of areas where
mutual submission is possible.

Agree here to get my point across.
Scripture is a whole and must be
85　read as such.

Edith: I see that verse but I just
don't accept it. I don't accept a lot
of what Paul says.

Me: Why accept any then? Are we
to pick and choose our favourite
Bible passages and then ignore the
rest? We have it as a whole and
90　that's how we must deal with the
Bible.

Edith: I just don't think Jesus said
what Paul said about women. Paul
did not like women. He was a
95　chauvinist and this is one of those
areas he just said what he thought
and not what Jesus said.

Me: Yes, in some areas Paul did say
that; for instance, in the I
100　Corinthians passage dealing with
marriage, Paul said, 'This is my
thought and not the Lord's but I
think I have the mind of the Lord.'
So you see this is not one of those
105　situations. The passage before us
doesn't say that, so we have to
struggle with its meaning. That's
what I tried to do. What do you
think we should do with the
110　passage?

Edith: I would ignore it. I'd just say Paul is wrong and it was just one of those things he got away with back then, but we don't think that way now.

Me: Yes, the role of women in society is different today but I don't think this is one of the culturally relative passages. There are certain texts we know come out of a particular cultural situation and they are dealt with differently than this passage.

She's on the point, now let me make it clear to her again.

Edith: If that is so, then why doesn't this one fit?

Me: We look for specific situations in the context of the passage that limit the meaning of the text to a specific situation. Remember in Timothy where Paul is speaking about women speaking in church? That was written for the city of Ephesus where the church was closely watched for order and keeping the order of worship was important.

Edith: Then why not in this text? It was the same city, wasn't it?

Me: Yes, but the context of the particular passage in Ephesians 5 doesn't make it pertain to the worship practices of the church, but to the more general situation of mutual submission to the Lord.

145 After this, Edith attended church less frequently. She continued in the women's group, contributed to the church and participated in some church projects. During an illness, I visited her in the hospital, but after her recovery she continued to attend infrequently. On reflection, my definition of the problem with the passage was not the same as her definition. She certainly 150 had her point of view, but, more important were her feelings about her husband and the trust present in their relationship. I think my educational assumptions dealt with the issues of power, control and authority. Moreover,

I did not do what I preached about and recommended in the sermon, which was to mutually submit to each other.

[******]

Can this be described as an example of self-deception?

What is so striking about self-deception is that to succeed in lying to ourselves, we must know both the truth and the lie for what they are – and yet also not know that we know. This avoidance is very intelligent. We have to know what is threatening to know exactly where not to look, lest we see it. But this means that somehow, we know what we don't know, what we refuse to notice. We have to have noticed once, so we can avoid noticing again and again.

A woman described her alcoholic family of origin thus: 'In our family there were two very clear rules: the first was that there is nothing wrong here, and the second was, don't tell anyone' (Goleman 1985: 17). Similarly, it is not uncommon for children of abusive parents to re-describe the abuse by saying things like, 'Oh, my parents were very strict.' Sometimes we even create a 'cover story' to enable us not to have to face the real story all the time (Via 1990: 13–17). Such 're-description' plays an important function in enabling such children to cope with their everyday reality. Using the language of 'strict discipline' to 'cover' over the reality of abuse is very useful, and not always reprehensible. If your father beats you unpredictably, lying may both reduce the internal pain, enhance surviving physically and also help protect whatever self-esteem remains. Goleman argues that we all, at times, in the interest of 'coping', find lying and self-deception necessary. It is what he (following Ibsen) calls the 'vital lie' (Goleman 1985: 16–22, 244–51). Sometimes that vital lie is, simultaneously, a source of destruction only cured by facing painful truth. At other times, it begins as a conscious (even public) manipulative strategy, and gradually the lie comes to be believed by the perpetrator, aided by those who collude with the lie.

One other aspect of self-deception must be noted. When we lie to ourselves, we not only believe mutually contradictory beliefs, but one belief is the 'causal condition' of its opposite: 'It is possible to believe each of two statements without believing the conjunction of the two' (Davidson 1985: 138–9). Sometimes we separate contradictory beliefs by isolating them one from another. For example, one can believe Jesus' sayings 'love one another' and 'love our enemies' yet also believe that we should vilify political opponents. We can do this by affirming that 'religion and politics don't mix.' As Davidson has shown, there is nothing irrational about holding divergent beliefs, for there may be supporting evidence for each. The irrationality emerges in constructing a boundary to keep them apart, which prevents 'noticing' or recognizing the contradiction and which thereby also prevents learning and growth (ibid. 147–8). Thus self-deception is both normal and even necessary under certain circumstances for some period of time – it may enable one to cope; but it is also dangerous if it persists and becomes a permanent way of life. Truth is essential for personal and social well-being in both religious traditions and human communities. Can we grow beyond self-deception?

The pastor described what he intended as he thought ahead about his conversation with Edith. He will first ask 'her to state the problem', that is, 'what specifically in Sunday's sermon she objected to' (lines 28–9), and then they can 'discuss the text' and he would 'show her' how to 'handle' it (25–6). Note, he does not seek to understand 'her' problem (39–41), but only the 'problem passage' (lines 47–8). He has already diagnosed the 'problematic' as her 'objecting' and his need to 'show her how a difficult passage is handled' (26) presumes that her 'objection' was misguided. Thus he hoped (my inference) that, as a result of his 'teaching', she would end up agreeing with his interpretation – and thus no longer 'object' to the sermon; and his strategy was to use discussion to bring her around to his viewpoint. This would benefit her and others as well, because as a Bible teacher in the women's group, she needs to understand better how to handle difficult texts.

Note that he has implicitly defined the roles in this interchange very carefully: he sees himself in the role of the teacher, that is, the one who explains. She is the learner, that is, the one who doesn't see clearly and thus needs explanations. When Edith first describes her 'objection' she says she doesn't like what the text says (34, 58) and won't accept it (76), while the pastor insists that 'liking or not liking' is an inadequate way to 'properly interpret scripture' (86–8). It is easy to notice (given the distance of a reader or observer) that the pastor was not hearing Edith fully, for he does not acknowledge the concerns Edith raises about her feelings and her relation with her own husband until later reflection (lines 42–5 and 150–1). But he might well doubt that such personal or private concerns have little to do with valid interpretation and public exposition of the biblical text.

It is possible that this is not so much an instance of self-deception, but rather an all-too-familiar conflict between two sets of pastoral responsibilities. On the one hand, a pastor should encourage sound interpretation and use of scripture, but on the other, a pastor ought also to respond to the needs parishioners bring. This pastor was clear about his pastoral responsibility for sound biblical interpretation, yet he also noticed that he and Edith defined the problem differently. He saw it as a matter of proper hermeneutics, but he noted that Edith did not. Rather 'more important were her feelings about her husband and the trust present in their relationship' (150–1). That he took note of her understanding of the problem may well indicate that he felt he had missed a pastoral opportunity with Edith.

These conflicting responsibilities call for a judgment related to how he sees himself as minister. In ministering with Edith, which understanding of 'the problem' takes priority? Is the interpretive problem hers or his? This is a familiar issue in teaching-learning interactions – who decides what are the salient 'problems'? The final sentence of this case suggests that, 'on reflection', the pastor noticed a new truth: he became aware of a contradiction between his espoused (verbalized) beliefs (reflected in his sermon) and the beliefs embedded in and expressed by his actions with Edith (151–3). Does that mean he really *didn't* believe what he preached? Or is it more accurate to see him holding two (or more) sets of beliefs – each of which might be internally consistent, but which were not congruent one with another – perhaps not even in conversation with one another?

For example, in this instance he espoused one set of beliefs expressed verbally (about Paul and historical-critical interpretation of texts) and yet seems to have acted out another set of beliefs (about power and control between pastor and lay person). Each set of beliefs may be legitimate. On the one hand, one's beliefs garnered from the Bible could affect one's way of relating with others. On the other hand, a pastor should also be concerned with pastoral authority and with sound interpretation of biblical texts. What would happen if these two sets of beliefs were allowed to be in conversation with one another? He himself seems to begin to wonder whether pastoral authority would look different if shaped by a concern for 'mutual submission.'

Even as Edith's pastor sought to increase Edith's learning about scriptural interpretation, he was also undermining her trust in him, which may have inhibited her further learning, and which may have led Edith to attend church less frequently (45). How often do students find themselves 'turned off' from education because they observe the self-contradictions in those who teach? Can we learn to detect and correct such forms of self-deception? Self-deception is an issue for individuals, yet there is a corresponding claim: If the corporate body encourages individuals to behave as they do, does that body not share responsibility? In what follows, I shall claim that self-deception can operate on both levels, and if present, must be addressed accordingly. Still, at the corporate level, as also for the individual, it is sometimes difficult to distinguish between corporate cover-up and corporate self-deception.

We observed a pastor focusing his attention on correct reading of the Ephesians text, on historical settings and original meanings, and ultimately on 'correct ideas.' As he did so, his attention was directed away from his own concurrent <u>actions</u>, so that only later did he notice that his actions had contradicted his words. One reason the pastor offered for 'not noticing' had to do with his notions about authority, power and control – which he demonstrated in his interactions with Edith. In so doing, the pastor behaved in a manner quite familiar from church history. All through history the church has struggled with issues of power, control and authority, first as a small minority movement struggling to survive, and later as an established power, aligned with state and military power, control and authority. At various points in this journey, historians and theologians alike have claimed occasionally that the church has not always chosen to follow the Pauline recognition that God's power is known in weakness and that Christian authority often looks like foolishness or vulnerability (I Corinthians 1).

Indeed, historians have often described the power struggles among theologians, rulers, bishops, popes and reformers seeking to use theological ideas for clerical authority or for extending political and social control of people. Such descriptions resemble aspects of the conversation above. Like the pastor's coercive teaching with Edith, the church's ministry has often been shaped by a concern with getting the doctrines 'right.' Theological controversies fuelled ecclesiastical councils, fused with political interests and eventually split East and West. The doctrinal wars of the Reformation and Counter-Reformation further fuelled these controversies, ensuring a widespread awareness that getting the doctrine right was not only a spiritual matter but often a matter of physical life or death. The religious wars which followed were bloody and long. They continue to this day in the Middle East and Northern Ireland, not to mention the various theological, ideological and cultural conflicts surrounding idea-battles over abortion, fundamentalism, conservative versus liberal, Christian versus Muslim, et cetera, ad nauseam.

There is an irony in these patterns of behaviour in that they seek to bring about unity among believers by coercing and enforcing a unity in doctrine, in theological ideas, and they do this as a way of serving Jesus, who reportedly refused the use of force even to avoid being taken prisoner. The remaining textual evidence suggests Jesus neither taught in abstractions, nor followed a systematic pattern in teaching, nor did he seek to coerce theological or interpretive unity. If Jesus' use of parables is taken to be something like his 'signature' mode of teaching, he rarely (if ever), offered definitive interpretations of those parables. Rather, Jesus reportedly concluded his parables with 'Let anyone with ear to hear, listen,' saying, in effect, 'What do you make of that?' He invited the hearer-learner to interpret, in their own way at their own pace, rather than dictating an authoritative interpretation. To be clear, this does not amount to an argument that we should do things as Jesus did – but it does raise provocative questions about possible approaches.

There have long been two incompatible underlying assumptions in approaches to teaching. One approach assumes: right ideas give rise to right behavior. Another approach assumes: behavior gives rise to (or calls forth) ideas which make sense of the behavior, and then those ideas can be used to enhance, assess, critique and even improve the behavior itself. The first approach typically starts by trying to get the ideas correct, and then we can infer correct actions from them. If the ideas are inadequate, so will the actions be. The second approach insists, especially in the realm of moral and religious behaviour, that one learns to behave correctly by 'being shown,' and trying things out, forming habits and eventually thinking more critically and systematically about what one has learned. This will come about naturally, if the inevitable conflicts which arise, interrupting the flow of our desires and actions, are dealt with openly and critically. Those conflicts not only bring to the surface conflicting ideas but also arouse conflicting emotions and reveal conflicting attitudes to others, to the world in which we live, and to the values expressed in our actions.

The texts we have from the Biblical sages (Proverbs, Job, Ecclesiastes, Sirach and the gospels as well) often seek to enlist readers in the process of becoming more wise in living life as God created it. In doing so, they rarely offered abstract, doctrinal explanations, based in authoritative revelation, but consistently relied upon the metaphorical and parabolic in narratives, proverbs, aphorisms – and focused upon actions, feelings and conflicts arising in everyday living (Melchert 1998). From those texts, later theologians forged systematic, logically coherent doctrinal explanations to make more ordered sense of them.

In the older period, wisdom was closely related to the events of concrete, everyday life, to civic and political activity, and one became wise by reflecting upon one's own and other people's experiences, trials and histories – that is, reflection upon the traditions of life in the mundane, material world and in the community's traditions. This hardly implies there was no controversy. Indeed, the sages who wrote Job and Ecclesiastes sharply contested the most basic convictions of Israelite religion, just as Jesus contested the conventions of his day. But they contested by raising doubts and posing questions rooted in coping with daily living more than arguing alternative abstract doctrinal explanations (ibid.).

From the third century on, early Christians were increasingly schooled in Greek, neo-Platonic abstract and formal ways of thinking, rather than in the concreteness of Hebraic mentality. In the process, 'wisdom' came to be seen less as reflection upon experience in the mundane, material world, and more as spiritual knowledge of divine things, granted to humans as a gift of grace, whose crowning achievement was a penultimate abstraction, beatific contemplation of the divine. Wisdom was identified with the second person of the Trinity, or the *Logos* of John, and the path to that Wisdom was the path of orthodox piety. This not only altered wisdom, it also helped shift the locus of theology away from clarifying Christian practices and away from theological convictions implicitly embedded (or incarnated) in creation and in everyday lived experience, toward intellectual practices which formulated and systematized abstract doctrines.

Why did this shift take place? Christian faith emerged into the public domain by distinguishing itself from the practices of Judaism and also from Graeco-Roman religions and philosophies. Because it was trying to make sense of its stories and its experience of a dying and risen God who is both three and one, conceptual matters were very important, and the best conceptual tools available to many were Greek and Latin philosophies. The church used these philosophies to find support for its views, to explain its experiences more completely, to justify and certify its experiences to those who did not share them – or, sometimes, to deny that non-Christian philosophers had any legitimate right to speak critically of the faith traditions at all.

In that process, however, theology itself changed considerably, and the church did not always recognize that. This became even more true in both Protestant and Catholic theologies from the Reformation on, especially under the influence of Enlightenment rationality (Placher 1996). Too often, in my view, those conceptual approaches didn't just interpret, clarify and support faithful practices, but actually <u>replaced</u> the traditional attention to practices of living faithfully, truthfully, lovingly and communally. When that happens, without clear awareness, I suggest, we can find ourselves deceived. Might these two differing approaches help illumine the conversation we have observed between the pastor and Edith?

Edith's pastor does 'care', but he has taken a disciplined, intellectual and abstracted approach to defining the problem. He did not notice, perhaps he was trained (in school? church? seminary?) not to notice, that the very language of 'submission' is not only relational but highly physical. To submit, whether mutual or not, is to lower oneself, put oneself under or below someone else. Thus, use of that language evokes a conceptual framework we have come to call 'hierarchy,' which has been built into church and culture for centuries. Until very recently, that concept was seldom discussed mutually by all participants. Rather it is embedded in how things work, it is 'embodied' in behavior, attitudes and structures, lines of authority and governance, even in physical spaces so arranged as to show who was 'higher' and who 'lower.'

This raises questions. Is hierarchy embodied in this local congregation and does it shape how pastor and Edith relate? Do they meet in the pastor's office, surrounded by his books and other reminders of his clerical authority? Did he sit behind his desk? Did he have his Bible before him or did they share her Bible? Can we infer from what he does that he believes that he is in 'control' (to use his own word), or is in a superior position relative to Edith, having the right and duty to instruct her in procedures of biblical interpretation? Does he expect to receive valid instruction from her on this subject? Can we infer that he believes that he is the teacher or master and she the disciple? Does he expect her to submit to him? If not, how else can we account for the fact that he treats his interpretation of the passage as authoritative and hopes to bring her to agreement with him. Is he following the model of his seminary professors? Can we safely imagine that his 'superior authority' has already been demonstrated <u>bodily</u> on the previous Sunday with the congregation seated, the pastor standing in the pulpit, 'four feet above contradiction' (Paul 1965), all the while urging mutual submission?

We can only guess about many aspects of this case, but what could we surmise about what Edith brings to the conversation? The pastor sees it as a contest of ideas – they 'disagree' (33). Edith, on the other hand, sees it more as a matter of 'liking' (35, 58), and what she has an aversion to is the need to 'submit' (35, 40, 57) and she 'will not accept it' (76, 84, 111–13). Following the insights of Cavell and Arcilla, Edith is expressing a feeling that something isn't right about this expected submission, as she understands it, and perhaps as she experiences it with her husband (34–5, 39–41). This is not so much the conclusion to an argument which she has reasoned out, as a feeling of injustice, a lack of mutuality, perhaps a sense of self in relation which does not contribute to an 'abundant life.' Something is clearly 'not good.' Were the pastor not so locked into his pre-definition of 'the problem' and his need to affirm his ideas, he might better trust and even affirm her feelings. She is hinting at or reporting a sense of self having to be given up – a demand upon her which is not reciprocal or mutual – and she rejects that feeling – as the pastor also rejects that as an idea (Cavell 1984: 98–105; Arcilla 1995: 136–48).

Edith is, in effect, pleading with her pastor to join with her in a hope for some better good. To do that, the pastor must put his own understanding at risk, back away from his notion of this as a 'contest,' and join her in a mutual pursuit toward the good. Indeed, that is what he says he wants, and yet in his self-deception, he can only see her as an adversary, not one who shares the journey. What is Edith seeking? Someone she can trust? Perhaps an authority other than her husband who has her best interests at heart? Her pastor has shown her that he cares about his ideas but does he want to encourage her (and open himself) to new learning? Perhaps she wants him to use his power and Biblical expertise to help her cope with her visceral feelings of conflict and non-trusting relations with her husband – and her visceral feelings arise because of actions and feelings which do not express mutual submission. Perhaps she is looking not for prophetic pronouncements about what it is right to think but wise counsel about what she can do that would make sense and positive use of what she experiences as a conflict between her marital relations and her faith.

Surely these are not just private or individual feelings and issues. Other women have similar concerns. Might others in the congregation share Edith's experience and feelings? Could a few persons explore together how mutual submission might be more fully enfleshed within the congregation and within the wider relationships of members in the congregation and community? The sage insists that knowledge is important, but important for what? John Hull has insisted that it is no longer adequate to consider oneself part of a triumphalist Christendom. Nor is it sufficient to be a faithful member of an exclusive and superior Christian religion. These modes of Christian participation are too heavily motivated by a need for control and power over others – whether political, cultural or educational. Both flourish best with heavy doses of self-deception. Rather what is needed is what Hull calls 'Christian-ness,' a term borrowed from Pannikar, which requires a life transformed, not just inwardly, but in self-critical mutuality and public sharing (Hull 1997: 41–3, 1999: 295).

An educator concerned with 'Christian-ness' may want people to know about the different kinds of love there are in the Bible, and it may help to learn how Hosea and God spoke about his love life. Or it may help to critically examine whether the love command was just one of the things Jesus taught or whether it was near the heart of his message. But learning and studying such material 'about' love is not nearly enough. Rather, Christian adults need to become lovers. Knowing this or that and 'knowing how' are important but the most important things are practised and lived into being until they become part of who we are and not just furnishings in our disembodied minds. This is actually a very old recognition – already we find it in Socrates, Plato and Aristotle as well as in Hebraic and other ancient religious traditions. It is not enough to know what justice is, how to define it, or even to learn how it could be practised; people need to learn to be just.

How does one learn something like justice or love? Is it enough to read a book, or study biblical ideas of love and justice? No, one must practise – try it out – experience what love and justice feel like – and their opposites. We must, by practising and critiquing ourselves, learn how they can be practised better – more fully, more deeply, more widely, more holistically, more fully in the public arena, less egoistically and more for the glory of God (Melchert 1998: 278–304). Insofar as these realities can be said, they often can best be said, as Jesus did, evocatively or indirectly, in parables or expressed in one's actions. More often it means learning to be like someone who lives that way. Learning to be a citizen in the kingdom of God means becoming more and more like the King: that is, humble, just and loving. We can use our people's trust of us and our own heart-felt commitments to help evoke their imagination, create an open space where they can explore or inquire, where their questions are valued and probed, where all are trusted and cared for, and where they may find a community sharing the joy of 'abundant' living.

References

Arcilla, R. (1995) *For the Love of Perfection: Richard Rorty and Liberal Education*, New York: Routledge.

Cavell, S. (1984) *Themes Out of School: Effects and Causes*, Chicago, IL: University of Chicago Press.

Davidson, D. (1985) 'Deception and Division', in E. LePore and B. McLaughlin (eds) *Actions and Events: Perspectives in the Philosophy of Donald Davidson*, Oxford: Blackwell.

Goleman, D. (1985) *Vital Lies, Simple Truths: The Psychology of Self-Deception*, New York: Simon & Schuster.

Hull, J. (1997) 'The Sufficiency of Christian Education', *Epworth Review*, 24: 40–8.

—— (1999) 'Spiritual Education, Religion and the Money Culture', in J. Conroy (ed.) *Catholic Education Inside-Out/Outside-In*, Dublin: Veritas.

Lash, N. (1996) *The Beginning and the End of 'Religion'*, Cambridge, UK: Cambridge University Press.

Melchert, C.F. (1998) *Wise Teaching: Biblical Wisdom and Educational Ministry*, Harrisburg, PA: Trinity Press International.

Paul, R. (1965) *Ministry*, Grand Rapids: Eerdmans.

Placher, W. (1996) *The Domestication of Transcendence: How Modern Thinking about God Went Wrong*, Louisville: Westminster John Knox.

Via, D. (1990) *Self-Deception and Wholeness in Paul and Matthew*, Minneapolis: Fortress Press.

10 From conflict to community

Mary Beasley

'Outsiders Need Not Apply' was a heading in the *Tablet* which highlighted the experience of marginalisation. It was about people who wanted to join the Roman Catholic Church but found they were unable to do so because their lifestyle, such as that of a single parent, made it difficult for them to fulfil the requirements of regular attendance at classes and Sunday Mass (Faucher 1992). I had both my own experience as a wheelchair user and that of the homeless people among whom I worked. As far as the former was concerned, before the Disability Discrimination Act came into effect, I was told by one church which I found to be inaccessible, that it would 'spoil the ambience of the building' to have wheelchair access but that if I wanted to attend church they had special services for people with disabilities every few months. There was a parallel with the experience of homeless people; the churches were prepared to 'do good' to them, but not to have them as part of their community.

William Booth, the Founder of the Salvation Army, had not set out with the intention of founding an organisation outside of the existing churches but once he began working with people on the streets he found that the two did not mix. According to one account he

> deeply offended the respectable members of the Wesleyan Chapel which he attended by invading their comfortable sanctimony with a crowd of roughs from the slums of Nottingham whom he marched into the chapel on a Sunday and placed in conspicuous pews. The deacons, whose noses had been offended as deeply as their sense of decorum, rebuked the young enthusiast, who declined to promise not to bring his band of roughs into select company again and would agree only to pass them through the back door and to seat them in less conspicuous pews.
>
> (Ervine 1934: 38)

There appeared to be a mental block inhibiting people from relating to, or hearing from, people on the margins. That this applied to people who were 'different' in such varied ways, suggested that the underlying problem went deeper than discomfort with those who have a different lifestyle (cf. Beasley

1997: 64–5). Since the term 'urban jungle' is used for the more disrupted areas of cities, the significance of the forest in symbolism and mythology is the starting point for an exploration of this.

Desert

The forest represents the unknown and contrasts to settled habitations; it symbolises a marginal state. Linked with the forest is the wilderness. In its primitive sense, 'forest' meant wilderness or an uncultivated tract of country. The term 'wilderness' is also interchangeable with 'desert', particularly when used in a Middle Eastern context. This raises the question as to whether there might be a link between the involuntarily marginalised inhabitants of the urban jungle, and the voluntarily marginalised monks of the desert, who had played such an important role in the early days of Christianity (Beasley 1997: 64ff.). The forest was seen as a place which harbours all kinds of dangers and demons, enemies and diseases. Such fears associated with the forest begin to explain the reactions of people in the churches to those on the streets; but the converse is that it can be a place of enlightenment, of discovery. It represents 'a condition of solitude in which the soul is freed from illusions and the lower attractions' (Gaskell 1988: 288). Therefore the place of coming face to face with reality is also a place of liberation – from false realities within, and oppressive social structures without. This suggests a possible link between freedom and marginality.

The work of Victor Turner is significant in that it demonstrates the essential function of marginality in human experience in general; it is not confined to the realm of Christian spirituality. In *The Ritual Process* he suggests that a state where people can stand apart temporarily from the social structures, in which they are stripped of status and property, and have an egalitarian relationship irrespective of status in the formal social structures, is essential. Turner uses the term liminality to describe the situation of 'threshold people' who are betwixt and between the positions assigned by law, custom, convention and ceremonial, which he also likens to the wilderness (Turner 1969: 95–6). One purpose of this liminal state is to ensure that relationships are based on shared humanity rather than on people's roles in the social structure. It thus acts as a safeguard for what occurs in the latter; since all, irrespective of status, have shared this formative experience, there is less likelihood that those in leadership positions will lose contact with the 'grassroots'.

Jihad al-nafs

This place of stripping the self has a parallel in Islamic spirituality. The term 'jihad' has become associated in Western minds with Islamic militancy and 'holy war' but its meaning is struggle. Whilst there is the concept of an outward struggle against the enemies of Islam, the 'greater jihad' is the inner struggle against one's lower self or the jihad al-nafs. Whilst much has been written on the jihad al-nafs, the writings of Seyyed Hossein Nasr provide one of the clearest expositions of the concept. Nasr demonstrates how all the 'pillars' of Islam can be seen as being related to jihad. The fundamental witnesses, 'There is no divinity but Allah' and 'Muhammad is the Messenger of Allah', through the utterance of which a person becomes a Muslim, are not only statements about the truth as seen from the Islamic perspective but also weapons for the practice of inner jihad. The very form of the first witness (*La ilaha illa' Lla-h* in Arabic) Nasr describes as being like a bent sword when written in Arabic calligraphy; with it, all otherness is removed from the Supreme Reality while all that is positive in manifestation is returned to that Reality.

The second witness is the blinding assertion of the powerful and majestic descent of all that constitutes in a positive manner the cosmos, man and revelation from that Supreme Reality. To invoke the two witnesses in the form of the sacred language in which they were revealed, Nasr says, is to practise the inner jihad and to bring about awareness of who we are, whence we come and where is our ultimate abode. He says that the daily prayers which lie at the heart of the Islamic rites are a continuous jihad which punctuate human existence in a continuous rhythm in conformity with the rhythm of the cosmos. To perform the prayers regularly and with concentration requires the constant exertion of the will and an unending struggle against forgetfulness, dissipation and laziness. Nasr suggests that it is itself a form of spiritual warfare. He points to the fast of Ramadan as being a period during which pilgrims wear the armour of inner purity and detachment against the passions and temptations of the outside world; this needs an asceticism and inner discipline which cannot come about except through an inner struggle.

Nasr also points to the hajj as entailing preparation, effort and the endurance of hardship. 'Like the knight in quest of the Holy Grail, the pilgrim to the house of the Beloved must engage in a spiritual warfare whose end makes all sacrifice and all hardship pale into insignificance'; he suggests that the pilgrimage to the House of God implies for the person who practises the inner jihad an encounter with the Master of the House 'who also resides at the centre of that other Ka'bah which is the heart' (Nasr). Although Nasr doesn't mention it, the uniform plain garment worn by pilgrims making the hajj symbolises their equal status. The giving of zakat or religious tax is also described as a form of jihad. This is not only because of the fight against covetousness when one has to give, but also because the way in which this tax is used furthers the cause of economic justice in human society.

While jihad is not itself one of the 'pillars of Islam', Nasr suggests it is at the heart of the other 'pillars'. He says that from the angle of spirituality all of the 'pillars' can be seen in the light of 'an inner jihad which is essential to the life of man from the Islamic point of view and which does not oppose but complements contemplativity and the peace which result from the contemplation of the One' (Nasr). What was described in *Mission on the Margins* (Beasley 1997) as being a stripping of self bears a resemblance to Nasr's concluding remarks about the jihad al-nafs:

> To melt the hardened heart into a flowing stream of love which would embrace the whole of creation in virtue of the love for God is to perform the alchemical process of *solve et coagula* inwardly through a 'work' which is none other than an inner struggle and battle against what the soul has become in order to transform it into that which it 'is' and has never ceased to be if only it were to become aware of its own nature.
>
> (Nasr ibid.)

Girard and scapegoating

The desert and the jihad al nafs may provide some response to social exclusion, but the work done by René Girard on scapegoating goes further into factors underlying inter-group violence and exclusion (see Girard 1977, 1986; cf. Williams 1996). Girard's academic career began in the literary world. Through this, he became aware of a pattern of mimetic rivalry: human beings imitate one another; then, as they find themselves competing for the same object, they become rivals, often leading to violence. Following the conflict, a scapegoat is found who is blamed for this. From a biblical viewpoint the goat who symbolically had the sins of the community placed on it on the Day of Atonement and was then sent out into the wilderness is an archetype of the scapegoat. Additionally, there is the tradition of the pharmakos in ancient Greece. The root pharm relates to medicine, and pharmakos may be translated as one who brings healing. Various 'marginal' people were rounded up; the essence appears to have been to find people who were not full members of the community, yet bore resemblance to them. On a designated day they were paraded around the outskirts of the city. People cursed them, thus symbolically placing the conflicts and problems of the community on to them; they were then taken away, killed and burned. The ashes were thrown in a river or the sea. The implication is that people who are peripheral to a community are in a position to take its conflicts away, in the same way as did the scapegoat described in Leviticus (Burkert 1985: 82–4).

Having recognised the pattern of mimetic rivalry in ancient literature and mythology, Girard also saw the same pattern in the Judaeo-Christian scriptures. However, there was a difference here in that God can be seen to be on the side of the 'victim', as opposed to being on the side of those who exclude marginal people. The significance of this is summed up by Giles Fraser:

> Jesus preaches about, and opens up the possibility of, the kingdom of God – a kingdom which is not built upon the violence and vanity of

human nature, but initiates a 'new creation'. Matthew 5: 38–48, and all
the emphasis on forgiving another and not returning violence for violence, is about not being trapped by a mimesis of the violent other. For-
giveness is, on one level, a refusal to imitate the violence of others and
thus begins the reconciliation of all humanity offered by the kingdom of
God.

(Fraser 2001: 28)

According to Fraser, Girard sees the significance of the cross as being that
the world is characterised by violence, that is ruled over by Satan. In contrast, Jesus' nature is defined by the love of God. His message to love one's
enemies strikes at the heart of mimetic violence. Therefore Jesus stands
against 'the world', exposing its violent constitution by speaking out against
it. James Alison describes this as being Jesus' recognition that the Jewish
texts, starting with Cain and Abel, gradually dissociate the divinity from
having any part in the violence. By the New Testament, God is entirely dis-
sociated from participation in our violence and is revealed

not as the one who expels us, but the One whom we expel, and who
allowed himself to be expelled so as to make of his expulsion a revelation of what he is really like, and of what we really, typically do to each
other, so that we can begin to learn to get beyond this.

(Alison 1996: 848)

Alison's description of the founding of the 'new Israel' shows how Jesus
recasts the passover meal as having the same function in the new Israel as
did the original passover for Israel – that is the founding of the nation. The
new Israel was to be founded on his lynch-expulsion as was Israel on the
expulsion from Egypt (Alison 1993: 68–70). Thus membership involves a
new way of relating to the victim and having to unlearn behaviour which
depended upon victims. Alison says that

it involves learning how to relate to and stand up for those who are
excluded, and of living for others in a way which runs the risk of being
excluded oneself, rather than basing security on expelling and excluding
victims.

(ibid. 72)

The desert, as discussed in *Mission on the Margins*, is more of an anthropological model for social inclusion; some references point the way to a Christ-
centred approach but the overall material is predominantly anthropological
in orientation. Alison, on the other hand, has a clearly Christ-centred model
in the new Israel. The task then is to examine how one progresses from the
desert to the new Israel; the paradigm is crossing the river Jordan. Crossing
the Jordan – God being on the side of victims suggests that solidarity with

victims is the way to meet God. One example of this is the grassroots experience of those who have worked with marginal people, another is the work of Aloysius Pieris SJ. David Rhodes gives the example of a church member's encounter with a homeless man who makes the statement 'Most of us on the streets believe in God. . . . We've got no one else to cry to in the night' (Rhodes 1996: 7). A recurring theme is how the words of life are often spoken by people on the margins of society. Later, Rhodes speaks of the Exodus and the formation of the community. He poses the question as to what was the one encounter with God that seemed to be the community's reference point of reality. He states that it was the Exodus that was

> the event by which the community, which had been captured and taken into slavery in Egypt, was delivered and led out into new life. The Exodus was the event by which God created that community out of nothing. God took a people who owned nothing but a few sheep, who were suffering crushing failure and gifted them with promise and life. The primal event for that people . . . was God's creative love and mercy. And that love came into play at the time they were at their weakest.
>
> (Rhodes 1996: 65)

Again there is the emphasis on the key role played by victims. This is moving in the direction of James Alison's account of the founding of the 'new Israel' as a 'society where widows and orphans, exiles, sojourners, escaped slaves, would be able to live, that is to say, a society whose sense of values derived from its memory of slavery in Egypt, and its own escape from that society' (Alison 1993: 65). The key role of the poor is also highlighted by Aloysius Pieris in a talk to religious in Ireland:

> The magisterium of bishops and theologians is impotent because they are not in touch with Yahweh's teaching authority which he has given to the poor of Yahweh. These poor people have nothing else to rely on except God, so God becomes a real experience and so they turn to God for everything because there is no-one else around, unlike us, we have gods with us already – other gods who give us comfort, who give us security, and even our fight for survival is based upon these other gods upon whom we depend.
>
> (Pieris)

Two relevant incidents struck this writer in relation to the above. The first was the reaction of a student who was part of a group of volunteers running a soup kitchen for the homeless. Meeting people whose worldly possessions were carried in two plastic bags made her think about the dependence most of us have on possessions. Again, an incident involving the writer occurred when having a late night sandwich with some homeless men who were taking shelter in a corner of the bus depot. Although the group was in a corner well away from anyone else, and therefore not in anyone's way, a security officer came at the group shouting at them, including the writer, in a way which most middle class, public school, university graduates would not expect. That provoked some thought on the subject of our dependence on our status. It could be seen in terms of the 'stripping' associated with the desert; it could also be seen as an encounter with the naked, insulted and crucified Victim while crossing the Jordan.

An Islamic perspective

Alison's article (1996) suggests an exclusive claim for Christianity. I felt that this needed to be at least examined, if not challenged, partly on its own merits and partly because I live in, and am deeply involved in, a community which is about eighty per cent Muslim. I therefore wanted to look at the faith dimension of inclusivity from an Islamic perspective. The martyrdom of Imam Husayn is a focal point of Shi'a Islam which has more points of similarity with Christianity than does Sunni Islam. Imitating Husayn is central to Shi'ite spirituality, as is imitation of the self-giving victim central to the Girard-Alison analysis of scapegoating.

Imitating Husayn

The background to the martyrdom of Imam Husayn lies in the conflict over the leadership of the Muslim community which arose during the caliphate of Uthman. Following Uthman's murder, the people of Medina acclaimed Ali, son-in-law and cousin of the Prophet Muhammed and therefore a member of the Hashim clan, as caliph. This was opposed by kinsmen of Uthman of the Umayyad clan, led by Mu'awiya, described by Ayoub as an 'old enemy of Ali' (Ayoub 1978: 88). The dispute lay in whether the leadership should come from the direct descendants of the Prophet Muhammad, or whether the leader should be chosen by the community as a whole. Ali was assassinated by a member of a group who thought that his willingness to accept an arbiter to settle the difference with Mu'awiya indicated a lack of trust in God to render a just verdict on the battlefield. The majority of believers then accepted Mu'awiya as caliph, though Fred M. Donner (1999: 16) suggests that this may have been more from a desire for stability than because they considered him the ideal ruler, and relates that he kept the discontented Shi'ite supporters of Ali's family under control. On his death, violence once again erupted; his son, Yazid, who had assumed the caliphate, was opposed by Husayn, the younger of Ali's two sons, on the basis that he was compromising the true values of Islam. In the course of the conflict Husayn was massacred with his entire family at Karbala.

S.H.M. Jafri, a modern Shi'a historian, has expressed disappointment that Western scholarship on Islam has concentrated on the external aspects of Karbala without attempting to look at the inside story, particularly the conflict in Husayn's mind. He suggests that such a study would reveal that right from the start Husayn was planning a revolution in Muslim religious consciousness. He also suggests that Husayn was aware that victory through military might would inevitably be temporary because of the possibility of a stronger power emerging subsequently; whereas victory achieved through suffering and sacrifice is everlasting and leaves permanent imprints on man's consciousness (Jafri 2000: 7).

The issue of suffering and sacrifice in the face of oppression opens up the question of solidarity with victims in Islamic thought. Esack writes: 'Given the Qur'an's own option for "the people" in general and for the oppressed in particular, in a context of oppression the highest form of righteousness is praxis in the service of the wronged and exploited' (Esack 1997: 193). This principle of active and organised solidarity with the oppressed received expression in Muhammad's life long before his prophethood, according to Esack. He cites an incident when some local people in Mecca had failed to pay a visiting Yemini merchant for goods supplied. This resulted in the formation of an alliance for the furtherance of justice and the protection of the weak; there was a meeting to sign a pact to this effect, at which Muhammad was present and emphasised his support for the pact (ibid.).

Ayoub describes Husayn's attitude to the poor and destitute by relating how Muawiyah sent him and his brother Hasan rich gifts of clothes, musk and other valuable goods with the comment that Hasan would give a good share of these to his wives and other women while Husayn would give them to the widows and orphans of the men killed in his father's wars. Another story related by Ayoub is how when Husayn had been martyred, people asked about the black scars on his back. His son explained that these were the result of carrying sacks of provisions on his back to the homes of widows and orphans. He had to do this at night in order to hide his good deeds from other men (Ayoub 1978: 88ff.).

The Iranian Islamic Revolution has been a landmark in the development of thought regarding imitating Husayn. Mary Hegland, who undertook research in an Iranian village, suggests that prior to the revolution there was a struggle between the adherents of two opposing ideologies (1983: 218ff.). The first model was of Husayn as intercessor which was related to the political stance of accommodation. In this, the believer is primarily concerned with the hierarchical relationship between himself and the imam Husayn; his conduct, accomplishments, ideals and values are less important than his connection with God and the resulting power. The preferred political action in this model is to connect with the powerful in order that they might help when the need arises. The overall attitude is one of accommodation, not active resistance. The second model was that of Husayn as example. The villagers in the study continued to accept the intercessor ideology as long as nothing economic or political contradicted it. But in the months leading up to the revolution, the ideology of accommodation was called into question on both economic and ideological grounds.

Husayn and his martyrdom are the central paradigm of Shi'a Islam and in that view of Islam, all human history is seen as a continuous struggle between the forces of evil and the forces of good. The believer becomes close to Husayn by emulating him, to the point of death. Hence the emphasis on a relationship with a powerful figure changes to one of communal co-operation in working towards a goal that will benefit humanity as a whole. An interesting question would be the way in which this move towards the model of Husayn as example has influenced the imitation of his solidarity with the oppressed.

The coming of the Mahdi

Ayoub has described the imams as being collectively like Christ for the Shi'i community, with each embodying one or more aspects of this quasi-Christological personality. Husayn represents the betrayed and suffering martyr, so mirroring the suffering Christ. The twelfth imam, the Mahdi, represents the judging and victorious Christ who is to come on the clouds of glory. The Mahdi disappeared from view, has remained concealed, but is expected to reappear to 'avenge the blood and wrongs of all those who were martyred or persecuted in the way of God from the beginning of the world' (Ayoub 1978: 18).

Ayatollah Ibrahim Amini describes it as a time when:

> There will be no more fighting among the people, since the justice of God will rule and will remove any reason for conflict and warfare. This will be the golden age of peace and harmony, under the government of God.
>
> (Amini)

It is possible to see a similarity between the coming of the Mahdi and the new Israel in that both are looking forward to an inclusive society. There seems to be some question as to whether the coming of the Mahdi is the cause or the effect of human beings treating one another as equals. According to Amini:

> When human beings begin to think in terms of their interconnectedness and when a brown or white or black person begins to think in terms of the common humanity that he or she shares with others, then it will be time for the final revolution to occur.
>
> (ibid.)

It needs to be remembered however, that Islamic thought is dependent upon a number of different 'traditions' in the teachings of imams and other leaders. There is therefore no one clear statement of doctrine other than what is set down in the Qur'an. In the writings of Ayoub, the coming of the

Mahdi is related to the end times and is linked with the return of Husayn in many traditions, unlike the new Israel which is a present possibility. Ayoub concludes the section with:

> We began with a pure and holy creation, a creation which has been confronted with a choice between judgment or salvation. History is the stage on which this choice is painfully and dramatically worked out. When the process is completed, creation will return to its original purity and 'the earth shall be changed to other than the earth. All dominion will belong to God.
>
> (Ayoub 1978: 229)

Conclusion

A key issue is the potential for defusing violence. The Girard-Alison analysis proposes that the irruption of God into human affairs has provided just that potential by breaking the cycle of mimetic rivalry. The question is whether this is matched by the effects of the martyrdom of Husayn. Ayoub has intimated that Husayn, as well as Jesus, may be part of the 'Suffering Servant' tradition to be found in religions in the Mesopotamian region (Ayoub 1978: 231–2). There is indeed the death of an innocent victim in answer to oppression suffered by followers but the question is whether the death of Husayn represented the scapegoat theme as did that of Jesus. The big difference is that one involved God incarnate, while the imams, although holding a special position between God and human kind, are distinct from any notion of being God incarnate. Then there is the solidarity with the oppressed. Here there is a convergence of the two faith traditions, since both are rooted in the Exodus paradigm, and each came into existence in a climate of confronting the ruling elite. However, there is also the development brought about by the relationship between Shi'a thinking and the Iranian Revolution; a comparison between this and the relationship between Latin American styled basic Christian communities and certain dictatorships would be of interest.

Lastly, in both Christianity and Shi'ism, the foundation of an inclusive community is a return to the roots of the religious tradition. The factors which have led to conflict have been those where the interests of the individual have come before those of the community. A humanist might suggest that this could be reversed without the intervention of religion. However, for Christians and Shi'ites there is the essential motivation of the link between one's relationship with God and acceptance of one's neighbour. For them, it is in God that they find their common humanity.

References

Alison, J. (1993) *Knowing Jesus*, London: SPCK.

—— (1996) 'Girard's Breakthrough', *The Tablet*, 29 June.

Amini, Ayatollah Ibrahim, *Al-Imam Al-Mahdi: The Just Leader of Humanity*, Ahlul Bayt Digital Library Project (online publication).

Ayoub, M. (1978) *Redemptive Suffering in Islam: A Study of the Devotional Aspects of Ashura in Twelver Shi'ism*, The Hague: Mouton.

Beasley, M. (1997) *Mission on the Margins*, Cambridge, UK: Lutterworth.

Burkert, W. (1985) *Greek Religion*, Cambridge, Mass.: Harvard University Press.

Donner, F.M. (1999) 'Muhammad and the Caliphate', in J.L. Esposito (ed.) *The Oxford History of Islam*, Oxford: Oxford University Press.

Ervine, St John (1934) *God's Soldier: General William Booth*, London: Heinemann.

Esack, F. (1997) *Qur'an, Liberation & Pluralism: An Islamic Perspective of Interreligious Solidarity against Oppression*, Oxford: Oneworld.

Faucher, T. (1992) 'Outsiders Need Not Apply', *The Tablet*, 12 December.

Fraser, G. (2001) *Christianity and Violence*, London: Darton, Longman and Todd.

Gaskell, G.A. (1988) *Dictionary of Scripture and Myth*, New York: Dorset Press.

Girard, R. (1977) *Violence and the Sacred*, Baltimore: Johns Hopkins University Press.

—— (1986) *The Scapegoat*, Baltimore: Johns Hopkins University Press.

Hegland, M. (1983) 'Two Images of Husain: Accommodation and Revolution in an Iranian Village', in N.R. Keddie (ed.) *Religion and Politics in Iran*, New Haven, Conn.: Yale University Press.

Jafri, S.H.M. (2000) *The Origins and Early Development of Shi'a Islam*, Qum, Iran: Ansariyan Publications.

Nasr, S.H. (no date) *The Spiritual Significance of Jihad*, Al-Serat Vol. IX. No. 1 (online publication).

Pieris, Aloysius SJ, an unpublished transcript of a talk given to religious in Ireland.

Rhodes, D. (1996) *Faith in Dark Places*, London: SPCK.

Turner, V.W. (1969) *The Ritual Process*, London: RKP.

Williams, J.G. (ed.) (1996) *The Girard Reader*, New York: Crossroad.

11 Does the Church need the Bible?

Reflections on the experiences of disabled people

Wayne Morris

When the Bible is read, there are many reasons why we might feel a sense of alienation from it. The New Testament texts were written nearly two thousand years ago and the majority of the books of the Christian Bible were written even earlier. The Bible emerged out of many cultures and experiences and makes use of a whole range of language, metaphor and idioms that a twenty-first century person is unlikely to fully understand. For example, the concept of atonement and the offering of sacrifices in the Temple provides the basis for much of the imagery in the New Testament, but the images do not speak to us with the same meaning and poignancy that they did to people of the first century because such practices have disappeared in Western Christianity. Feminist writers have brought to the attention of their fellow theologians and the wider church the way in which the Bible can and does alienate women, through, for example, the way some Pauline and pseudo-Pauline texts define the role of women (e.g. Schüssler Fiorenza 1993: 14ff.). Reflections from churches and theologians in non-western traditions similarly have illustrated the problematic nature of the Bible for people whose culture is not informed by, or akin to, that of the Bible (e.g. Kwok Pui-Lan 1995; Sugirtharajah 2001).

Some people will argue that they do not feel alienated by the Bible at all, particularly, I presume, if they happen to be a non-disabled male brought up in the Christian tradition. The Bible and its interpretation has so informed and shaped western traditions throughout the ages that its language and imagery are, as John Hull argues, thought to be the 'norm' (Hull 2001: 3). However, we cannot ignore the reality that many people do feel alienated from the Bible and the Christian faith, and feel pain because of that. A number of reasons have been offered by Hull to explain his particular sense of alienation. For example, Hull discusses a Gospel text about adultery: Jesus says, 'if your right eye causes you to sin, tear it out and throw it away; it is better for you to lose one of your members than for your whole body to be thrown into hell' (Matthew 5: 29). Hull argues that this is 'obviously a sighted person's view of sexual desire, and the comment about plucking your eye out should 'it cause you to sin' suggests that blind people are incapable of sexual sin, or are at least protected by blindness against this particular kind of visual offence' (Hull 2001: 151). Such Biblical texts reinforce the false stereotypes that disabled people do not have a sexuality, reflected in the way society often views the sexuality of disabled people as a taboo subject (Blackburn 2002: 1ff.; Johnstone 2001: 81–2). Elsewhere, Hull has lamented the way that each time Jesus encounters a blind person, he instantly turns them into a sighted person (Hull 1999/2000: 4–5). The Bible presents many problems for Hull, therefore, and no doubt for many other blind people who will share his sense of alienation.

This alienation from the Bible is shared by people with some other types of disability, though not necessarily for all the same reasons. Each time Jesus meets a person with any kind of disability, be it blindness, deafness, paralysis, his immediate response is to rid that person of their disability. This does not fit easily with many disabled people's view that they are quite comfortable in their disabled condition and do not particularly want to become non-disabled (McCloughry and Morris 2002: 102f.). The seeming connection that Jesus makes between disability and sin when he 'heals' disabled people (e.g. Mark 2: 9; Luke 5: 20), though not in every instance (e.g. John 9: 3; Luke 8: 43ff.), only serves to make the disabled person feel less adequate than non-disabled people and feel further alienated from the Bible.

Hull is not entirely negative about the Bible and its perspectives on blind people but also shows that the Biblical narratives can be used as a resource that is potentially liberating for blind people. One way that Hull demonstrates this is by identifying key Biblical figures who became supremely important characters in the Judeo-Christian tradition (Hull 2001: 5–33). Both Isaac and Jacob have sight impairments along with Samson, Eli, Ahijah, Zedekiah and Tobit. Although these characters live with a visual impairment, they play important roles in the outworking of God's purpose in history. There are fewer such characters in the New Testament and while Hull convincingly conjectures that Paul may never have fully recovered his sight after his conversion experience (Hull 2001: 84–91), this is not made explicit in the pages of the New Testament. Interestingly, as Jesus is blindfolded and mocked when he is before Pilate, Hull suggests that for the first time, Jesus experiences something of what it means to be blind and this experience is what enables him to say to Thomas, 'Blessed are those who have not seen and yet have come to believe' (John 19: 29b). Such significant figures in the Bible are liberating because they reflect the reality that disabled people can be and have been significant contributors to society and history. Jesus's blessing of blind people at the end of John's Gospel is further affirmation of people who are blind.

However, people with some types of disability may feel alienation from the Bible not simply because of the way disabled people are treated or because it uses language and imagery that is offensive but because the Bible is a written text. The text itself, the written word, can be largely inaccessible to people with certain types of disability such as dyslexia, profoundly Deaf people, people who are blind, and people who have some severe learning difficulties. Such people may not feel alienated so much by what is contained in the Bible but because they are excluded from accessing its contents due to the medium through which the Bible is expressed. This matter becomes significant in the light of growing movements in many parts of the world that use and interpret the Bible as the ultimate revelation of God to humanity that has direct Divine authority (e.g. at its extreme, fundamentalism, though the regard for the Bible as the ultimate revelation of God for today and as the primary or only source of Divine authority is much more widespread).

It is with these perspectives on the Bible that this paper is concerned and it attempts to engage with them as their influence grows in the churches in the UK. Even in more mainstream churches in the UK, many clergy and lay people suggest that the primary way to grow as a Christian person is by reading the Bible. You do not have to go far to hear the laments of preachers and members of Bible Study groups that 'people don't know their Bibles'. While I think this perspective on the Bible and its interpretation is almost certainly a relatively recent development in the churches' histories, as I will argue later, many people at least in the UK seem uncritically to assume that reading and understanding the Bible has been for all time the way to grow as followers of Christ. The experiences of disabled people have important contributions to make to theological understandings of the role of the Bible in contemporary society.

The written text and disability: further explorations

It is important not to make sweeping generalisations about disabled people because people with disabilities rarely if ever live with exactly the same sort of impairment and its consequences. Levels of exclusion or inclusion into a whole variety of aspects of living are influenced by such factors as the impairment with which a disabled person lives, their personality, their education, family, local, national, international, social, economic, cultural, religious and ethnic backgrounds as well as their gender and sexual orientation. However, there are many different groups of people with disabilities who, for varying reasons, find accessing the written text difficult if not impossible because of the nature of their impairment.

Members of the Deaf Community often have difficulties in gaining access to the written text. When I refer to the Deaf Community or Deaf People, I mean those people who use British Sign Language (BSL) as their first or preferred language (see Alker 2000: 24ff.; Ladd 2003: 32–3). This Community usually includes members who are born or become profoundly Deaf before acquiring language. It is generally acknowledged that Deaf children acquire English much more slowly than their hearing peers. Drawing on research from Gregory and Mogford (1981), Kyle and Woll argue that a Deaf child on average learns approximately one hundred English words by the age of thirty-four months, while a hearing child has acquired the same amount in just twenty months (Kyle and Woll 1985: 63). Woll has demonstrated in more recent research that Deaf infants can acquire British Sign Language at the same rate as hearing children acquire English (Woll 1998: 58–68) and so he, with many other Deaf people, argues that the first language of the Deaf Community should be British Sign Language and that English should only be used as a second language.

Lewis explains, 'Varied research evidence from Pintner and Paterson in 1916 to Conrad in 1979, confirms what for many teachers of hearing-impaired children is the reality of the classroom, i.e. that large numbers of hearing impaired children have left school without achieving functional literacy' (Lewis 1998: 101). Many more recent books and journals on Deaf education are devoted to techniques in teaching Deaf children how to learn English both spoken and written as though learning English was the sole purpose of education (e.g. any edition of *Journal of Deaf Studies and Deaf Education*). In March 2003, the British Government recognised in law that BSL was a language in its own right and now acknowledges it as an official minority community language (Department of Work and Pensions 2003). BSL is a language that cannot be written down and so Deaf people, using their first and natural language, have limited access to the written text (see Brennan 1992: 1–133). Attempts to translate the Bible into BSL and publish it on video and CD-ROM are hugely expensive and time-consuming exercises; since Deaf people have difficulties in acquiring English and their natural language cannot be written down, it is inevitable that they will be excluded from the Bible.

There are other groups of people who are not able to access the text of the Bible either, such as people who are blind. Many blind people make use of Braille or Moon scripts which make English more accessible in a script format, but not all blind people make use of them. Braille texts are also bulky and take up far more space than written English books, not to mention how much they cost to produce. For example, someone at the Royal National Institute for the Blind informed me that one translation of the Bible in Braille takes up 48 large volumes. Increasingly, technology is overcoming such barriers to the written text for Blind people. Computer software can be purchased which has the full text of the Bible on it which the computer can read audibly. Other software for scanning the written text can be obtained which transforms the script into audible words. Such technology will, as it becomes more widely available, enable visually impaired people, along with people with reading disabilities such as dyslexia, to have easier access to the text of the Bible.

Many children and adults with severe learning difficulties, whether or not they learn to speak, do not develop the ability to read English. Telling the story of her severely disabled son, Arthur, Young explains that 'some of the children at Arthur's school are capable of simple reading, but for most of them it is education into socially acceptable behaviour and self-help that is most important' (Young 1990: 18). Many people like Arthur with such severe learning impairments will never be able to read – despite the determination of educationists – and are thus excluded from access to the text of the Bible.

Deaf people, people with severe learning disabilities and, for now, many people with visual or reading impairments cannot easily access the pages of the Bible independently. Throughout the history of the churches, the Bible has been important, but its role and significance is changing and is increasingly perceived by many ordinary Christians as the benchmark for how to live and what to believe. In Protestantism, the Bible has always been understood as a part of the 'Word of God' (see Barth 1956 and 1975, for example), while in Roman Catholic Liturgy, the role of the Liturgy of the Word has increased in significance since Vatican II (Wainwright 1992: 328–38), giving scripture and its interpretation a more prominent place in Catholic worship.

This development in the role of the Bible is, to my mind, only possible because Western society has become more literate. You would be hard-pushed to find such a conservative understanding of the Bible as that developed by certain American and European evangelicals among groups in Africa where most people in society are not literate – hence the development and staggering growth of the African Indigenous Churches such as Simon Kimbangu and Johane Masowe (Mukonyora 1998: 191–207). It is important to acknowledge that in Western nations for centuries, the majority of people were not literate and relied on the paintings on walls of churches and the stories conveyed in stained glass to learn the Biblical narratives. Does this mean that Christians today, because they read the Bible more often, are better Christians or more developed Christians than our Western ancestors or many non-Western contemporaries? Or are Western Christians today fooling themselves by thinking that a thorough knowledge of the Bible is at all necessary to develop faith and follow the way of Christ? Is Christianity an exclusive religion that has no place for people who cannot read and maybe never will be able to read? Put simply: Does the Church *need* the Bible?

The Bible in history: the need for scripture?

The Early Church: forming a Canon

It is widely agreed by New Testament Scholarship that there was a gap of about 20 years between the death of Christ and the writing of the first texts which are now included in the New Testament Canon (see for example, Du Toit 1993: 98–104; Evans 1999: 2). Further, the Canon of the Christian Bible as we have it today did not have ecclesiastical status until the end of the fourth century and whilst various 'canons' were developing and being used in various parts of the Church much earlier (e.g. that of Marcion), for four centuries a common universal Christian canon did not exist (Barton 1997: 1–34). In fact, a *universal* canon of scripture has never existed and still does not today as is evidenced by, for example, the difference between

Roman Catholic and Protestant versions of the Bible and the place of the deutero-canonical (apocryphal) texts. For two decades, therefore, the only 'Bible' Christians had was the Hebrew Bible and for nearly four centuries, while New Testament texts were spreading across the Roman Empire and beyond, there was no shared fixed New Testament Canon by which Christians lived and developed their faith.

The Middle Ages: levels of literacy

Throughout most of the Church's history, the majority of Christian people had no access to the pages of the Bible. During the early years of the Church, it is generally accepted that the texts which form the New Testament Canon were not read by but to congregations and so the texts acted in support of an oral culture. In such a context, an ordinary blind person would have no less access to the Bible because of their visual impairment than most other people. Following the church's growth and the translation of the Bible into Latin, the Bible became even more esoteric and was accessible only to scholars and clerics. The narratives and characters were made available to others through artwork, wall paintings, carved wood and stone and stained glass windows. In this sense, the Bible was accessed through a visual means – a means accessible to Deaf people. In the churches of the Early and Medieval eras most people could only access the texts that literate people would share with them. Not until the work of figures such as William Morgan and Thomas Cranmer at the end of the Middle Ages did the Bible begin to be more widely accessible. However, a Bible that could be read by most people was not really achieved until the growth of the education system during the nineteenth century.

Were people any less Christian during the preceding 1900 years of the Church's history because they had limited access to the Bible? Was their faith any less meaningful? It seems hard to imagine and arrogant of a twenty-first century Christian to answer either of those questions in the affirmative; but the growing emphasis on the place and authority of the Bible, and the need to 'know' it in Western ecclesiastical contexts implies that we are better and closer to God than any of our Christian predecessors despite the fact that, at least in the UK, the Church probably has a lower percentage of followers today per head of population than it has had for over 1000 years. This decline cannot be blamed on people 'not reading their Bibles' because the decline of the churches in the UK has coincided with the growth of a nation that is educated and literate.

Access to the written word has many positive dimensions that I would not want to discount. The growth of education in the West and other parts of the world has enabled many more people from a variety of social, gender and ethnic backgrounds to aspire to and achieve an improved socio-economic status. Literacy provides access to knowledge and, as the saying goes, 'knowledge gives power' and the opportunity to 'progress'; but for those who cannot access the text, knowledge is held back and remains inaccessible and so to some degree, Deaf people and people with visual and other impairments find working towards an equal place in society more difficult. Liberation theologians have argued that God is alongside people who are forced to remain on the margins of society (e.g. Gutierrez 1988) and in one of the most significant liturgical texts of the New Testament, Luke 1: 46–55, Mary warns 'He has shown strength with his arm; he has scattered the proud in the thoughts of their hearts. He has brought down the powerful from their thrones, and lifted up the lowly' (1: 51–2).

In situations other than the West such as in parts of the world where economic resources are more limited, restricted access to education and thus to literacy skills is prevalent. Patrick Kalilombe provides an example from Malawi. He argues that, 'It is important to remember that, in general, Africa is largely non-literate' (Kalilombe 1995: 423). In the light of this, he nevertheless affirms the Ecumenical Association of African Theologians' statement that includes the phrase 'No theology can retain its identity apart from Scripture' (see Kalilombe 1995: 421); but what about the beliefs and experience of God among people who are not literate? Does that make such experiences and beliefs non-Christian? He suggests that in non-literate contexts like Malawi, the Bible could be read out loud – reflecting early church practices – and on hearing the narratives, those who do not read can use and interpret the texts they hear in ways appropriate to their culture. Even if these ideas are followed, however, access to the Bible is controlled by literate people who can exercise power over the access non-literate people have to knowledge and understanding of the Bible. Does God really need to rely on the powerful to engage with and relate to the powerless of the world?

God and the text

Writing is a human creation. Human beings do not instinctively know how to read and write down the language they speak, but rather they have to spend many years learning the skills necessary to have access to the text. Anyone who has spent time at school learning to read and write will verify this point. Many societies, both historically and today – including those of our European ancestors – did not rely on the text and need it to live their lives and develop a faith. However, we have no reason to assume that their faith, relationship with and understanding of God was any less adequate than that of Christians today. Literacy is an acquired skill developed through education. However, evidence from the field of linguistics suggests that the ability to acquire language itself, either spoken or sign language, the capacity for human beings to communicate with each other, is more akin to an instinct than an acquired skill.

Drawing on the work of Noam Chomsky, Pinker uses evidence from various cultures and peoples to argue that while the particular language we all learn is dependent on where we are born or who our parents are and that we need some input to be able to learn a language, our actual ability to acquire language and develop our understanding and use of grammar happens instinctively. That is not to say that people's abilities with language do not develop differently because of both genetic and social factors, but that the basic ability to learn language itself is an instinct present in virtually all of us.

Using an example from among Deaf people in Nicaragua, Pinker explains that prior to the opening of a school for Deaf children, Deaf people tended to live in relative isolation developing basic gestural systems for communicating with members of their family. Once the school opened, a common method of communication was needed by which the children could express themselves to one another. The research in this school showed that, without any formal tuition, within a generation as younger Deaf children became exposed to the various signing systems, a common communication system developed employing rules of grammar. Within that short space of time, therefore, the human instinct to communicate with other humans produced an entirely new language with a structure, grammar, and vocabulary of its own (Pinker 1994: 36–7).

A second example drawn from Pinker involves the study of infants and their developing use of language. He explains that children are able to recognise instinctively and without instruction that sentences are not individual words strung together. Rather, he continues, the algorithms in the brain 'groups words into phrases, and phrases into even bigger phrases, and give each one a mental label, like "subject noun phrase" or "verb phrase"' (Pinker 1994: 41). When, therefore, it comes to constructing sentences, children instinctively know where to put parts of a sentence in order for it to make sense. Pinker summarises an experiment by Crain and Nakayama on three to five year olds which demonstrates this point:

> One of the experimenters controlled a doll of Jabba the Hutt of *Star Wars* fame. The other coaxed the child to ask a set of questions, by saying, for example, 'Ask Jabba if the boy who is unhappy is watching Mickey Mouse'. Jabba would inspect a picture and answer yes or no, but it was really the child who was being tested not Jabba. The children cheerfully provided the appropriate questions, and, as Chomsky would have predicted, not a single one of them came up with an ungrammatical string like *Is the boy who unhappy is watching Mickey Mouse?*
>
> (Pinker 1994: 42)

Further studies on children also show that they instinctively know when to make verbs agree with nouns and pronouns such as adding the necessary 's' onto the end of a verb in such sentences as 'I know what a big chicken *looks* like' and 'Anybody *knows* how to scribble' (Pinker 1994: 44–5). Children do not memorise such agreements for each verb individually and neither are they formally taught that sentences work like this by parents, teachers or anyone else (Pinker 1994: 25–54).

The written text, I have argued, is a human invention only accessible to the majority of people in the West over the past 150 years or so. At the same time, however, the instinct to communicate with other humans, through spoken or signed language is a universal quality. Would God restrict himself to a human invention as a means of communicating with his creation or can we dare to think that God is free of human invention and the restrictions we put on to him to communicate and relate with human beings in whatever way he chooses – irrespective of the Bible?

What role for the Bible?

> Christian theology, for all its indebtedness to Platonic ideas of Being, eternity, completeness and perfection, cannot eschew the reality of Becoming, of human incompleteness and progress through discipline and experience, response and relationship. So it is that 'testimony' belongs at the heart of Christianity, and the most effective theology is 'incarnated' in the story.
>
> (Young 1990: 2)

In what I have argued above, I am by no means suggesting that God would not or could not use human inventions as a means of revelation. The experience of Christians throughout history and today suggests that God makes himself known and then more clearly known through the pages of the Bible, other texts, music, art, dance and so on. This is the ongoing story of the Christian Church in history but our knowledge of God remains incomplete despite the Bible and we only learn more and deepen our understanding through our experience of and relationship with God. I am certainly not suggesting that the Bible does not have a special role to play in the Christian faith as the record of salvation history for the Church as something that helps to inform our incomplete knowledge of God. My primary objection is the way that the Bible is so often seen by many Christians, at least with whom I come into contact, as the primary, indeed sometimes the only, source of Divine revelation to humanity today and that any other claims about God must be measured against that collection of texts.

It also seems erroneous to suggest that knowledge of the Bible is the only means by which you can become a better or more mature person of faith when most Christians throughout the ages have had such restricted access to the Bible. I do believe that the significance of the Bible and its authority for Christian living has only really developed as a result of events following the industrial revolution and the growth of capitalism where education and literacy have become key to economic and social success. I do not believe that God is closer to humans or that humans are better because they can access a written text and that God is therefore further away from those who live on the margins of national and global society because access to education and in particular literacy is not possible.

Some years ago I had a job working with Deaf-blind adults with multiple learning difficulties that involved being alongside these people, meeting their needs in terms of their general care, welfare and education. Part of this role included supporting those with whom I was working to develop and fulfil their 'spiritual' needs. On one occasion I recall taking Joanne into a church as her family was Christian and they wanted her to share in their tradition. Joanne had an unusual tendency to chew wood as soon as she came into contact with it. In her home, she had chewed the doors and furniture and a selection of pieces of wood had been given to her to fulfil what she so obviously enjoyed doing. She also did not like to sit down. She would not sit down during the day and would stand up all night if she could and fall asleep wherever she stood.

The church into which I took her contained, as many churches do, a lot of wood – doors, the floor, pews and so on. For some strange reason, however, her behaviour generally, as well as in terms of her love for wood, was markedly different. She showed no inclination to chew and sat down without any difficulty for quite a long period of time. What can the explanation for such a radical change in behaviour be? Psychologists may have some answers; I have no expertise to comment on such a perspective. It could just be coincidence. It may be that the church's wood was of an inferior quality. Could it be, however, that somehow, Joanne felt something of the presence of the Divine in that place and she responded to it? Such a possibility can never be studied scientifically, but this experience has suggested to me for many years now, that God does not need the Bible or the Church or anything else to engage with the people he loves and to make himself known to them but can reveal himself in ways different individuals can relate to. Joanne's story was and is part of the continuing narrative of the churches' 'becoming', of which the Bible is an important part. At the same time, her experiences and insights into the Divine, along with Deaf people's, blind people's and people with severe learning difficulties' should not be ignored.

References

Alker, D. (2000) *Really Not Interested in the Deaf?*, Darwen: Doug Alker.

Banana, C.S. (1995) 'The Case for a New Bible', in R.S. Sugirtharajah (ed.) *Voices from the Margin: Interpreting the Bible in the Third World*, London: SPCK.

Barth, K. (1956) *Church Dogmatics* Vol. I. ii: *The Doctrine of the Word of God*, Edinburgh: T. and T. Clark.

—— (1975) *Church Dogmatics* Vol. I. i: *The Doctrine of the Word of God*, Edinburgh: T. and T. Clark.

Barton, J. (1997) *The Spirit and The Letter: Studies in the Biblical Canon*, London: SPCK.

Blackburn, M. (2002) *Sexuality & Disability*, Oxford: Butterworth-Heineman.

Brennan, M. (1992) 'The Visual World of British Sign Language: An Introduction', in D. Brien (ed.) *Dictionary of British Sign Language/English*, London: Faber & Faber.

Department of Work and Pensions (2003) 'Joint Statement', in *British Deaf News*, (April) London: British Deaf Association.

Du Toit, A.B. (1993) 'Canon', in B.M. Metzger and M.D. Coogan (eds) *The Oxford Companion to the Bible*, New York: Oxford University Press.

Evans, R. (1999) *Using the Bible: Studying the Text*, London: Darton, Longman & Todd.

Gregory, S. and Mogford, K. (1981) 'Early Language Development in Deaf Children', in B. Woll, J.G. Kyle and M. Deuchar (eds) *Perspectives on BSL and Deafness*, London: Croom Helm.

Gutierrez, G. (1988) *A Theology of Liberation*, London: SCM Press.

Hull, J.M. (1997) *On Sight and Insight: A Journey into the World of Blindness*, Oxford: Oneworld Publications.

—— (1999/2000) 'Could a blind person have been a disciple?', in *Viewpoints* 7: 4–5.

—— (2001) *In the Beginning There was Darkness*, London: SCM Press.

Johnstone, D. (2001) *An Introduction to Disability Studies*, 2nd edn, London: David Fulton Publishers.

Journal of Deaf Studies and Deaf Education, 1996–2003 Vols 1–8, Oxford: Oxford University Press.

Kalilombe, P.A. (1995) 'A Malawian Example: The Bible and Non-Literate Communities', in R.S. Sugirtharajah (ed.) *Voices from the Margin: Interpreting the Bible in the Third World*, London: SPCK.

Kwok Pui-Lan (1995) *Discovering the Bible in the Non-Biblical World*, Maryknoll, New York: Orbis Books.

Kyle, J.G. and Woll, B. (1985) *Sign Language: The Study of Deaf People and their Language*, Cambridge: Cambridge University Press.

Ladd, P. (2003) *Understanding Deaf Culture: In Search of Deafhood*, Clevedon: Multilingual Matters.

Lewis, S. (1998) 'Reading and writing within an oral/aural approach', in S. Gregory, P. Knight, W. McCracken, S. Powers and L. Watson (eds) *Issues in Deaf Education*, London: David Fulton Publishing.

McCloughry, R. and Morris, W. (2002) *Making a World of Difference: Christian Reflections on Disability*, London: SPCK.

Mukonyora, I. (1998) 'The Dramatization of Life and Death by Johane Masowe', *The Journal of Humanities of the University of Zimbabwe*, Vol. XXV (ii): 191–207.

Mukonyora, I., Cox, J.L. and Verstraelen, F.J. (1993) *'Re-writing' the Bible: the real issues*, Gweru: Mambo Press.

Pinker, S. (1994) *The Language Instinct*, London: Penguin.

Schüssler Fiorenza, E. (1993) 'Transforming the Legacy of *The Woman's Bible*', in E. Schüssler Fiorenza (ed.) *Searching the Scriptures: A Feminist Introduction*, London: SCM Press.

Sugirtharajah, R.S. (2001) *The Bible and the Third World: Precolonial, Colonial and Postcolonial Encounters*, Cambridge: Cambridge University Press.

Wainwright, G. (1992) 'Recent Eucharistic Revision', in C. Jones, G. Wainwright, E. Yarnold and P. Bradshaw (eds) *The Study of Liturgy*, London: SPCK.

Woll, B. (1998) 'Development of signed and spoken languages', in S. Gregory *et al.* (eds) *Issues in Deaf Education*, London: David Fulton Publishing.

Young, F.M. (1990) *Face to Face: A Narrative Essay in the Theology of Suffering*, Edinburgh: T. and T. Clark.

All Biblical quotations are taken from *Holy Bible: New Revised Standard Version*, Oxford: Oxford University Press, 1989.

Part 3

Religious education

Theory and practice

Introduction

Dennis Bates

The essays in Part 3 explore developments in the theory and practice of religious education in Germany, the USA, Russia and Norway. Although the character and context of the subject in these countries varies, a recurring theme is the growing recognition of the rights, experience and creative contribution of children and young people in RE. Clear evidence of this is the growth of interest in the use of dialogue between teacher and pupils and also between children as a learning method (cf. Robert Jackson's discussion in Chapter 2 above). The influence of John Hull's *God-talk with Young Children* is apparent in two of the essays, one treating the subject of 'children's theology' (Chapter 12) and the other, spiritual dialogue between teacher and young person (Chapter 15). There are also essays on a creative approach to Christian education based on the Montessori method (Chapter 14) and a classroom evaluation of the 'Birmingham team's' *Gift to the Child* project methodology (Chapter 13). The complex life-world of young people coping with their identity problems and the pluralistic, relativistic, postmodern cultural ethos of Norway and Russia is the focus of Chapters 15 and 16; whilst in Chapter 17 a prominent psychologist and educationist writes on the value and relevance of psychology for religious education with young people. Evidence of the influence of the thinking of the 'Birmingham team' is often apparent.

Friedrich Schweitzer's essay (Chapter 12) is set in the context of the Christian nurturing approach to religious education typical of most German state schools; he emphasizes both the right of children to religious education and the need to encourage them to think in their own terms about religious and theological issues – to do 'children's theology'. He distinguishes this from what he calls 'miniature theology' – simplified adult theology adapted for children; and adopts a broad, functional definition of religion to make room for what he calls their 'big questions'. Taking John Hull's conversations with his children as a model, he sees the role of adults as to provide in dialogue, 'impulses' for children's thinking and only exceptionally correctives; he also sees developmental theory not as undermining the notion of a 'children's theology' but as providing valuable guidelines for how to understand children's theologizing at different stages. Schweitzer adopts the same child centred approach to 'inter-religious education' between Protestant and Roman Catholic children, stressing the educational value of allowing the children to work out differences and similarities for themselves in dialogue with each other.

Heinz Streib's essay (Chapter 13) explores children's reactions to experiences of strangeness in the context of religious education in two German schools and with reference to an evaluation of lessons on 'Angels' and 'the Call to Prayer' from the *Gift to the Child* project materials. In the first part of the article, he surveys research on strangeness, identifying various versions of strangeness and reactions thereto. He formulates a schema of reactions to the strange and a table of types of familiarity and strangeness associated with the *Gift to the Child* project. One of the schools used in the research was predominantly middle class native German in the socio-economic profile of the children's families, with some Muslim children; the other had a working class constituency which included 50 per cent mainly Turkish Muslim children. The 'Angels' topic used in the first school was uncontroversial but the 'Call to Prayer' topic used in the second caused controversy. Streib's discussion of this, whilst appreciative and supportive of the methodology of the *Gift* project, raises important questions about the complexities of inter-religious education, in particular when the sensitivities of minority groups are affected by what may be spontaneous and unintentionally offensive reactions to the 'strange'.

Jerome Berryman (Chapter 14) outlines an approach to religious education which he has developed in the USA and has entitled 'Godly Play'. The approach is based upon the educational philosophy and methods of the late nineteenth/early twentieth century Italian medical doctor and educationist, Maria Montessori, who created an educational environment in which children could learn through play, utilizing the apparatus which she designed. The teacher supervised what was essentially a creative self-teaching method. 'Godly Play' utilizes story, ritual and play and has won many admirers in the USA and other countries. Berryman contends that his method neither indoctrinates nor leaves children religiously rudderless but enables them to use their creativity in learning. For him, religion helps people to cope with what he calls 'trouble' – the problems of life – and he feels that his teaching methodology and the material and spiritual environment which it creates, supports children and young people in doing this. In the early part of his essay, Berryman outlines the sources of his theory of creativity and utilizes James Fowler's stage theory of faith development. He finds a more modern theoretical foundation for his Montessorian method in Jerome Bruner's work and in his concluding section gives an outline of the key features of 'Godly Play' utilizing the 'spiral curriculum'. Although related to Christian religious education, Berryman contends that his methods could be applied by other faiths in their own religious education programmes.

In the aftermath of the demise of the communist regime, the Russian education system is still in process of reorganization and the issue of the place, if any, of religious education in the school curriculum is still contro-versial and unresolved. There is, however, growing support for the non-con-fessional teaching of religion based on the principle of 'enculturation' which would, for most Russian children, focus on the study of Christian Orthodox culture but also include other world religions.[1] In Chapter 15, Fedor Kozyrev argues for an approach which he designates 'humanitarian religious education'. Within the framework of the humanities he contends, children and young people have the opportunity to express their natural religious insight and to explore the heart of religion which is 'creative experience'. In the postmodern situation with its fragmentation and breakdown of old cer-tainties dialogue between individuals assumes great importance. Referring to the work of several western proponents of dialogic methodology and uti-lizing the thought of the Russian existentialist philosopher Mikhail Bakhtin for whom 'to be is to communicate dialogically', Kozyrev argues that the school should take over from the church the role of spiritual guidance. There can be no return to the old, church provided, confessional, juridical approach to RE; the 'paradigm of modernity' requires an approach to 'spiritual psy-chotherapy' which recognizes that teacher and pupil approach these issues on an equal footing. Students are active participants not passive objects, being prepared for life in a 'society of peers'. Kozyrev's essay cites a wide range of Russian thinkers and educationists in support of his case and includes an interesting historical survey of aspects of Russian educational history.

Norway, a dominantly Lutheran country in which 85 per cent of the population are church members and which has only a small religio-ethnic minority, adopted a multifaith syllabus in 1997 which also includes the study of secular humanism. Despite the high level of church membership, there is concern at young people's so-called 'drift away from the church', a phenomenon common in many European countries. It is against this back-cloth that Geir Skeie discusses (Chapter 16) the 'complex' concept of 'youth', inter-generational tensions, the attitudes of young people towards religion and how religious education might relate to them. He places his discussion of the latter issues in the context of a consideration of the merits of student centred and content centred approaches to RE. Whilst being sympathetic to the youth culture approach, he argues that it is important to relate RE to the broader aims of the curriculum which he defines as knowledge, identity and competence. A balanced approach to RE has to take account of all three but it is important that young people be 'taken seriously in their own right' and that the plurality of their life-world is recognized. Flexibility is required to allow adequate expression for religion, spirituality and values as young people perceive them and to consider a variety of discourses about religion including the formation of their own. They should be 'allowed into the workshop of the teacher and encouraged to take more responsibility for their own learning'.

Helmut Reich's essay (Chapter 17) explores the contribution which psy-chology can make to religious education, considering the relation between pedagogy and psychology, the life-world of young people and the psychological dimensions of personal religion. He sees the first role of psychology as to furnish theories usable by educationists and illustrates this by the contribution of developmental psychology to stage development theory in RE and other areas through the work of Piaget, Fowler, Kohlberg, Oser and others. His section on the life-worlds of young people complements the previous two essays; although each child lives in an important sense in their own life-world, they all share the same 'zeitgeist' and all have to face the same religio-philosophical questions. Reich views the influence of the Freudian psychology of the 1960s and 70s critically for its excessive anti-authoritarianism. Whilst its emphasis on personal rights and entitlements has had wholesome effects, it has arguably been at the expense of a sense of duty and 'engagement for the common good'. He contends that the five dimensions of personal religiosity – ritual, doctrine, religious experience, knowledge and ethics – identified by psychology of religion, all have a contribution to make to a balanced religious education and offers suggestions as to how each can make that contribution. The wide range of recent research publications cited in this essay will make it particularly valuable for those wishing to explore this important subject.

Note

1 Cf. Fedor Kozyrev's paper 'The Current Situation of Religious Education in Russian Schools' delivered at the conference of 'The Oslo Coalition on Freedom of Religion or Belief' September 2–5 2004 and accessible, together with other papers on religious education in countries worldwide through the website: www.folk.uio.no.leirvik/OsloCoalition/CountriesRegions.htm.

12 Children as theologians

God-talk with children, developmental psychology, and inter-religious education

Friedrich Schweitzer

Some years ago I wrote a preface to the German edition of John Hull's *God-talk with Young Children* (Hull 1997). I ventured to introduce the book to German readers as a piece of 'children's theology' which, at that time, sounded quite daring and innovative. It was one of the first times that someone had used the phrase in Germany and perhaps in other countries as well. In the meantime, children's theology has become quite well known so that in 2002 a German publisher was prepared to start a yearbook for this topic (Bucher *et al.* 2002, 2003). It is probably safe to assume that the interest in this kind of theology parallels the new interest in children's spirituality, in children's rights in general and in children's spiritual rights in particular (cf. Hull 1998: 59). Slowly but surely western culture seems to be warming up to the idea that children should not only be objects of education but that their own voice should be respected.

Although the interest in children's theology is growing, it is not particularly clear what different authors and educators mean when they refer to this theology. Many will think of children's *philosophy* which sounds like a close parallel to the theology of children. Is it the same? Why then use a second term? And if it is not the same, what is the difference? Others may think of developmental psychology and of studies like Ronald Goldman's early investigations into children's thinking (Goldman 1964) or of James Fowler's *Stages of Faith* (1981). If we want to speak of children's theology we must first become clear about its relationship to both children's philosophy and developmental psychology; and if we want to use it as an approach within the field of religious education, we must also be clear about its practical advantages.

The present article will discuss all three questions with a special focus on the following aspects:

1   What exactly is children's theology? How does it differ from the more well-known approaches of philosophy for children, the child as a philosopher, etc.? Is there a need to speak of children's theology?

2   How is children's theology related to developmental psychology? Is it true that a children's theology approach should take over from

psychological approaches because they tend to treat the child as an object of study rather than doing justice to the child's philosophical or theological potentialities?

3   Concerning practical implications for RE, I want to examine how the need for inter-religious education and respecting the child as a theologian can be combined. Drawing on our Tübingen study on cooperative RE, I will suggest ways in which children's views of other religions can be taken more seriously.

I will take up these questions mainly against the background of the growing discussion of children's theology but also with special reference to John Hull's *God-talk with Young Children* (1990).

What is children's theology?

The driving force behind children's theology is the wish to take children more seriously and to do justice to the power of their thinking or, more broadly, of their imagination. This wish is part of the more comprehensive democratic tendencies operative in western societies which aim at overcoming former authoritarian structures and giving a voice to those who were thought to be dependent on others to speak in their place – women, the handicapped, the sick and now children as well. This more general background explains the moral impetus sometimes connected to approaches like children's theology and it may also indicate why viewing the child as a theologian in his or her own right is important. Yet it does not make clear what exactly is meant by this new phrase.

While some authors are eager to maintain a very broad understanding so that children's theology would include everything religious on a child's mind, I consider it important to have a definition which may be more limited but which is clear and which really justifies speaking of children's theology rather than of children's religious thinking (cf. the discussion between Bucher 2002 and Schweitzer 2003). To claim that something like children's theology really exists means that we consider children capable of some kind of self-reflexive religious thinking. In other words, children do not only have their own images or understandings, for example, of God, but they are also quite capable of reflecting upon such images and understandings and, in doing this, of producing their own answers. This indicates that we could also call the object of reflection in children's theology spiritual rather than religious (in a number of languages like German the two terms are much closer in their meaning than in English). As I will argue below it is not the content as defined, for example, by a traditional catechism which is decisive for children's theology; it is reflective thinking about one's own religious ideas. Clearly the relationship between religious thinking and children's theology is a continuum. Yet only if we take the self-reflexive nature of this kind of theology seriously will we be able to do justice to it.

It is even more difficult to draw a line between the philosophy and the theology of children. Philosophers working with children often rely upon topics which are as much religious or theological as philosophical. Eva Zoller, a Swiss philosopher, mentions questions like the following (Zoller 1995: 102):

- Does God live in heaven?
- Is grandma an angel now?
- What will happen to my guinea pig after she dies?
- Do angels go on vacation?
- If God sees everything why does he not help the hungry children?

These are indeed questions which I would like to see addressed by children's theology, not only by philosophy. This does not mean that theology should claim any exclusive right to particular questions; but it is important to make it clear to religious educators as well as to the wider public that children do not only have philosophical interests. Since western societies are mostly driven by an economic interest in science and technology, they tend to neglect what appears to be a private and only church-related interest in religious issues. This is why children's right to religion (Schweitzer 2000) has to be defended and why it should be emphasized that there is a need for both children's philosophy and children's theology.

The difference between a philosophy and a theology of children will become clearer as we consider three possible meanings of children's theology: (1)   Just like the philosophy of children, children's theology is subject to the misunderstanding that such approaches should aim at introducing children to academic philosophy or theology. If this were true, the objective would be to design simplified versions of theological theories so that children can grasp them. Traditional children's Bibles tend to work like that – with simple sentences, simple images and with something like an abbreviated creed and so on. Often such materials are based on the expectation that children should internalize a set of contents and ultimately a predefined credal system.

It is important to note that the endeavour of creating a 'miniature theology' for children is not identical with children's theology. Miniature theology means transmitting given theological views to children – children's theology means being open to children's creative ideas. Miniature theology tries to simplify and to reduce adult thinking – children's theology welcomes the fascinating power of children's imagination and of their questions which even academic theologians cannot really answer, for example: '*Why doesn't God help children in need?*' To take this question seriously has little to do with simplified textbook answers or with adapting adult notions to the grasp of the child. This is why children's theology should be seen as a theology *of* children – as a theology not produced for them but produced by the children themselves.

It is at this point that some educators and theologians raise the question as to whether it really makes sense to speak of children's theology. It is certainly true that academic theology and children's thinking about religious ideas are two different things which should not be confused. The problem of miniature theology arises when people assume that children's needs can be fulfilled by giving them a smaller version of (adult) theology which is different from this theology only in scale but which otherwise is identical with it, that is, has the same content, is based on the same internal order and presents the same answers to the same questions. Children's theology has to avoid the temptation of just reducing the size of adult thinking. Yet in spite of possible misunderstandings, the phrase children's *theology* is indispensable. Only by learning to see children as theologians will we become able to take them seriously and to understand that they have important things to say about God, Christ, Christian ethics and so on; and only if we are willing to dignify their ideas by accepting their theological character will we move beyond the traditional assumption that religious education means to hand on predefined religious knowledge.

Another important question concerns the definition of religion which a theology of children should presuppose. Drawing on the categories of the social scientific study of religion we can distinguish between substantive and functional definitions. Substantive definitions tend to identify religion through reference to specific religious concepts and topics like 'God', 'redemption', 'sin' and so on. Functional definitions focus on what convictions, rites, liturgies and so on mean for the person, for example, in terms of 'functions' like meaning making, creating world order and so on. Some authors argue that children's theology should limit itself to substantive religious ideas (Bucher 2002: 14) because otherwise it would become too vague. Others like myself (Schweitzer 2003) argue that the definition of religion used in the context of children's theology must be in line with children's right to religion and should therefore focus on what sometimes is called their 'big questions'. In my own work (Schweitzer 2000: 27), five such questions have come to play a dominant role and can also serve as a starting point in the present context. In part, it is the children themselves who ask these questions. In part these questions arise for the adults in their living and working with children:

- Who am I, and who am I allowed to be?
- Why do you have to die?
- Where do I find protection and safety?
- Why should I treat others fairly?
- Why do some children believe in a different god?

As far as the religious dimension of these questions is taken up (and children strongly tend to focus on this dimension), they refer to substantive as well as to functional aspects of religion which speaks against a narrow definition of religion in children's theology.

(2)   That children should be allowed to produce their own ideas and that educators should not interfere with them is a conviction which many associate with Jean-Jacques Rousseau's so-called negative education. Experience shows, however, that children do not consider theological questions as something to be pursued in solitude. They probably are thinking about these questions by themselves but they also like to confront adults with them (often to their parents' surprise who 'all of the sudden' are supposed to say what comes after death while standing in line at the cashier in a local supermarket with everybody listening quite intently, until they decide that this is a topic for 'later on'). Children want to share their views and they are curious about what others are thinking about death and dying, about God and the world. This is why we should not only speak of a theology of children but also of a theology *with* children.

Again, the philosophy of children offers a good parallel (cf. Martens 1999). Children's philosophy often refers to the praxis of doing philosophical thinking together with children. In a similar way, theology with children refers to the exchanges between children and adults or with other children concerning theological topics. In its refined forms, this kind of praxis is a real art. It presupposes listening to children in the broad sense of also having an ear for what is not said; and it means finding a balance between not ending conversations prematurely by, on the one hand, offering final answers and, on the other, not conveying or creating enough interest by refusing to answer.

It is certainly too early to offer guidelines for how children's theology should be conducted. We do not have empirical studies on which such recommendations could be based (for beginnings see Erricker *et al.* 1997; Schweitzer *et al.* 1995, 2002); but we do have convincing examples which indicate that the most important step towards children's theology is taking children's views, understandings, and arguments seriously. John Hull, for example, does not correct the children and he is also not interested in teaching them something in the traditional sense. Rather, he points out counter arguments, observations and insights which are accessible to the children themselves and which allow them to proceed to their own theological insights. Consider the following dialogue between John Hull and his child:

CHILD (aged 3.10): Who wins all the battles?
PARENT: Nobody wins all the battles. You win some, and you lose some.
CHILD: God wins all the battles.
PARENT: Well (*hesitation*) perhaps he does in the end, but he loses some along the way.
CHILD: How does God fight? He's in the sky.
PARENT: Maybe he fights by helping people.

So far, this is a fairly typical conversation between a child and a parent who is desperately looking for answers that will make sense to the child while also being acceptable to the adult. The next statement, however, constitutes something like a turn-around which demarcates the transition into children's theology:

PARENT: If God's in the sky why doesn't he fall down?
CHILD: (*Laughs*) Because he's magic. (*Pause*) And because he lives ... in a little cottage.
PARENT: Why doesn't the little cottage fall down?

(Hull 1990: 19)

Now the parent is asking the questions, and these questions provoke the child to think about his own ideas. In this sense we can call this an example of thinking about religious thinking or of the self-reflexive characteristic of children's theology.

(3)   It is at this point that a theology with children leads back to the question of what kind of theology adults should offer to children. True conversation cannot be unilateral. Dialogue always means a give and take. Inevitably there will be an input from the adults as well as from the children. The idea of children's theology is no romanticism which expects everything from the so-called natural and undisturbed development of the child. We should not forget that what children say, for example, about how God 'spies' on people in order to punish them, is far from being helpful or healthy. Children's theology does not mean that there is no need for offering impulses to the child which may operate as a corrective to unhealthy images of God.

Since this sounds close to more traditional understandings of religious education, some readers may think that I want to return to miniature theology; but this is not the case. I am speaking of theological impulses which adults can give to the child, not about a theological system which the child is supposed to internalize. Such impulses are part of any true conversation and their influence should not be denied in order to have a 'pure' theology of children. Reality is not so simple. Children's theological reflections will often be about something that comes from adults – artefacts, stories, questions and so on. The point is not to deprive them of all of this but to allow for their own ways of making sense of it.

If we again take John Hull's conversations with children as an example, it is easy to see that they do not only stand for a theology with children but that they also contain a theology *for* children. Moreover, these conversations show that such a theology does not contradict the approach of children's theology. When the child asks 'Is God the air?' the parent responds 'No, God's not the air but he's a bit like the air', thus introducing, without leaving the child's way of thinking, a theology of metaphor. In the end the parent suggests 'God is a bit like a very big idea' (Hull 1990: 21f.) – an understanding which (as John Hull certainly knows) is not without its own difficulties in that it implies an idealistic theology.

As is the case with frightening images of God which can be overcome through the introduction of biblical understandings of God, insights of academic theology can also be helpful for children in other cases. A historical-critical reading of how the Israelites crossed the sea in Exodus 14 can help in dealing with doubt in late childhood or adolescence. The basic impulses of a theology of liberation or of justification by faith can also be important for children. This is why I consider a theology for children legitimate. Rather than falling back upon the approach of miniature theology this theology means that we must ask ourselves what theological impulses we should offer to the child in dialogue. The notion of dialogue implies that we should not expect the child to just take in whatever theology we are presenting. The child remains the active centre of experience, with a theology *for* children no less than with a theology *of* children and a theology *with* children.

Children's theology and developmental psychology: contradiction or cooperation?

Philosophers working with children often believe that their views contradict developmental psychology (for an influential example cf. Matthews 1994). According to them, the concept of stage development prevents adults from appreciating children's true power of thinking. They fear that the notion of stages implies looking down upon children in a condescending manner, stressing what children allegedly are *not yet* able to understand rather than being open to what they might grasp more accurately than adults. This is why John Hull emphasizes what he calls the 'power of a concrete theology' and the 'versatility of the concrete thinker' (Hull 1990: 7, 9):

> We should not only be challenging children so that their readiness for abstract thinking will be enhanced, but we should be encouraging them to think imaginatively within their immediate experience and in concrete terms.
>
> (ibid. 13)

A similar but more educational critique of developmental psychology refers to its potential abuse by educators whose dominating styles of treating children are further strengthened by the insights of developmental psychology. According to this view, this kind of psychology seems to empower the adult but not the child (Hull 1991).

These are some of the reasons why there appears to be more contradiction than cooperation between children's theology and developmental psychology. In my own work with children and with children's religion or spirituality, however, I have come to a different conclusion (Schweitzer 2000). In my understanding, we actually need developmental insights in order to become able to enter into true dialogue with children. Adults do by no means automatically possess the ability to understand children's worldviews, and rarely are they willing to let themselves be truly challenged by understandings which contradict their own. When we make use of developmental psychology as a tool which can teach us to listen to the child and to carefully reconstruct their understandings by taking their point of view, this psychology can become an important partner for children's theology.

Let me come back to the example given above in which John Hull asks the child why God does not fall down if God is in the sky:

CHILD: . . . because he lives . . . in a little cottage.

PARENT: Why doesn't the little cottage fall down?

CHILD: *(Merry with laughter)* Because it's on the clouds *(pause)* and because God makes it not fall down *(pause, sucks fingers noisily)* because God's got his servants who make it not fall down *(pause)* it's on bricks. *(With more confidence and animation)* It's on very big, heavy bricks. They hold it up.

PARENT: What? On the clouds?

CHILD: No. There on the earth.

PARENT: But I thought you said God's cottage was on the clouds.

CHILD: Well, it goes up in *(emphatically)* the clouds, but it stands on the earth. Yes, *(with growing confidence)* it starts on earth but goes up into the clouds . . .

(Hull 1990: 19)

For the adult, there is a clear alternative – in the sky *or* on the earth. This is why this parent keeps trying to make the child aware of the contradiction in his answers. An understanding which is informed by developmental psychology suggests a different reading of the child's attempt of making sense of why God does not fall down. First, the passage quoted clearly shows how the child becomes more and more 'confident'. The child tries out a number of different understandings, discarding most of them in order to stay with the image of a cottage standing on earth and reaching 'into the clouds'. In my reading, this description of the child's behaviour seems to imply that the child has actually reached a convincing solution – exactly in the sense of children's theology, by trying to make sense of his ideas. Second, the cottage which reaches 'into the clouds' is quite consonant with children's worldviews which tend to be based on a layerlike sequence of earth and sky so that buildings or other entities can clearly stand on the surface of the earth while reaching into the next layer, that is, into the sky, because they are 'so high'.

Including this developmental perspective clearly allows for a more sensitive and appreciative response. Developmental insights can support the approach of taking the child seriously in dialogue because such insights can help the adult in overcoming the limitation to an adult view of the world. This example suggests that there must be no contradiction between children's theology and developmental psychology. Developmentalists like Jean Piaget or Lawrence Kohlberg repeatedly speak of 'children's philosophies' or of the child as a 'moral philosopher' (for references see Bucher 2002). If psychology is used to avoid taking the perspective of the child so that it explains rather than understands what the child is saying, it clearly contradicts the idea of children's theology. Yet when used appropriately and sensitively, developmental psychology can be enormously useful for children's theology.

Children's theology and inter-religious education: practical implications for religious education

In this last section of this chapter, I am interested in the practical implications of a children's theology approach, and this not only in terms of theological questions in the traditional sense but also with an eye on current issues in religious education. This is why I will consider the relationship between children's theology and inter-religious education.

It is probably fair to say that, until today, the relationship between children's theology and inter-religious education has not received much attention. The focus on children's religious ideas and imaginations seems to apply more to general concepts or conceptual questions referring to God, Christology (Büttner 2002), the world, creation, etc., and less to experiential issues arising in contemporary society. Some authors like David Elkind with his now classic study on children's conceptions of denominational (Protestant, Catholic, Jewish) affiliations (Elkind 1961–63) or Robert Jackson and Eleanor Nesbitt with their ethnographic studies of Hindu children in Britain (Jackson and Nesbitt 1993) have rightly pointed out the importance of including the children's views in inter-religious education. Yet on the whole their interest is not in children's theology, just as those interested in children's theology (or philosophy) tend to have their own conversations apart from the current discussion on the need for intercultural and inter-religious education. Sometimes an interest in theology seems to contradict the interest in a multifaith approach.

In a recent study on cooperative religious education conducted at Tübingen we have become aware of the need to take children's understandings of religious identities much more seriously. This study, which has been described in more detail elsewhere (Schweitzer *et al.* 2002; Schweitzer and Boschki 2004), was focused on Protestant and Catholic RE and on the possibilities of cooperation between different denominational groups in German schools. Whilst most of the more than 300 children interviewed in this study were Protestant or Catholic, some of them had no official religious affiliation or belonged to non-Christian religions (mostly Islam). The children were between six and ten years old. The interviews were conducted in small groups at the beginning and at the end of the school year. The semi-structured interviews focused on questions of denominational and religious identity.

One of the most striking results, which is of central importance for inter-religious education, refers to the children's understanding of being

Protestant or Catholic. When asked about the meaning of such terms, the children sometimes started arguing about the question as to whether these categories referred to something 'interior' or 'exterior'. They started asking questions: 'Does a Protestant think in different ways compared to a Catholic?' and 'How does one know that a child is Catholic rather than Protestant?' 'Are all children the same at birth in respect of religion?' 'Do children have certain characteristics which, over time, show up and indicate that a child is Catholic or Protestant?'

Similar questions referred to the more institutional level of the rites or processes through which a child comes to belong to a religious denomination. The children formulated fascinating ideas about what is happening at baptism. Whilst many agreed that it is baptism on which being Protestant or Catholic depends, this did not mean that the children just reproduced the churches' understanding of the sacrament. Some assumed that the minister announces sometime during the process as to which denomination the child will belong. Others suggested that it might be written on the baptismal font, while one child said that it will not be known before much later when the child gets older.

It is easy to see that such questions are of a theological and philosophical nature. They again indicate that children not only have their own religious ideas but that they are also trying to make sense of their ideas by asking how different ideas fit together. In our own study with its focus on Christian RE, this understanding has led us to the conclusion that ecumenical education should not be seen as introducing children to predefined notions of ecumenism. Rather, it must mean starting with the children's own views and with their ways of making sense of denominational differences. In other words, ecumenical or inter-religious education has much to learn from children's theology.

Let me take up one last example from John Hull's conversations with children:

PARENT: How many gods are there?
CHILD: I don't know.
PARENT: Lots?
CHILD: Lots, hundreds...
PARENT: Or just one?
CHILD: Four, I think.
PARENT: Four?
CHILD: Odin, Loki, Thor and Freie.
PARENT: Yes. They're the Nordic gods, aren't they?
CHILD: Yes.
PARENT: Can you think of any Greek gods?
CHILD: Have we got a Greek god?
PARENT: Not exactly.
CHILD: Is ours an English god?
PARENT: *(Laughs)* Yes, I suppose he is.

CHILD: How many gods in all the world?
PARENT: I don't know. Thousands, I suppose.
CHILD: Thousands, hundreds, millions, trillions, billions.
PARENT: Some people say there's only –
CHILD: Two, three *(laughs)*.
PARENT: Some people say there's only one.
CHILD: What's three and a hundred?
PARENT: One hundred and three.

(Hull 1990: 24)

John Hull himself does not seem to attribute much meaning to the details of this conversation. His own comment is short: 'God has many names, yet his names are one' (ibid. 25). From the perspective of children's theology there is much more to learn from this piece of dialogue. Quite obviously, the child is far away from the parent's clear-cut answer that there is oneness behind the different names. The child is trying to sort out a number of complex and surprising relationships, for example between God and nationality ('Have we got a Greek god? Is ours an English god?') and between different gods and the total number of gods in the world ('How many gods in all the world?'). These questions are quite close to the issues debated in a theology of religions. They cannot be answered by drawing on predefined or consensual teachings; rather, they refer to lasting challenges of religious faith in a multi-religious world which does not allow for confining oneself to one's own beliefs by denying the possible truth of other beliefs. The conversation quoted above shows that children can experience something of this fascination early on.

So far our empirical research has mostly been geared to children with a broadly Christian background (a limitation which is the result of the absence of non-Christian RE in most parts of Germany). As far as children's constructions of religious identities can be interpreted in terms of developmental psychology it is at least very likely that children from non-Christian backgrounds will have similar questions and develop similar strategies in answering them.

This is not the place to spell out the consequences of a children's theology approach for inter-religious education in any detail. Yet it is easy to see from the examples described in this section that there must be no contradiction between an interest in (children's) theology and inter-religious education and that this kind of education could greatly profit from re-casting or re-framing it from the perspective of the children as true persons with a voice of their own, with a mind of their own, and with answers of their own.

References

Bucher, A.A. (2002) 'Kindertheologie: Provokation? Romantizismus? Neues Paradigma?', in A.A. Bucher, G. Büttner, P. Freudenberger-Lötz and M. Schreiner (eds) *'Mittendrin ist Gott'. Kinder denken nach über Gott, Leben und Tod*, Stuttgart: Calwer, 9–27.

Bucher, A.A., Büttner, G., Freudenberger-Lötz, P. and Schreiner, M. (eds) (2002) *'Mittendrin ist Gott'. Kinder denken nach über Gott, Leben und Tod*, Stuttgart: Calwer.

—— (2003) *'Im Himmelreich ist keiner sauer'. Kinder als Exegeten. Jahrbuch für Kindertheologie* Vol. 2, Stuttgart: Calwer.

Büttner, G. (2002) *'Jesus Hilft!' Untersuchungen zur Christologie von Schülerinnen und Schülern*, Stuttgart: Calwer.

Elkind, D. (1961–63) 'The child's conception of his religious denomination. I. The Jewish child. II. The Catholic child. III. The Protestant child', *Journal of Genetic Psychology*, 99: 209–25, 101: 185–93, 103: 291–304.

Erricker, C., Erricker, J., Ota, C., Sullivan, D. and Fletcher, M. (1997) *The Education of the Whole Child*, London: Cassell.

Fowler, J.W. (1981) *Stages of Faith: Human Development and the Quest for Meaning*, San Francisco, CA: Jossey Bass.

Goldman, R. (1964) *Religious Thinking from Childhood to Adolescence*, London: Routledge & Kegan Paul.

Hull, J.M. (1991) *God-talk with Young Children: Notes for Parents and Teachers*, Derby: Christian Education Movement.

—— (1991) 'Human Development and Capitalist Society', in J.W. Fowler, K.E. Nipkow and F. Schweitzer (eds) *Stages of Faith and Religious Development: Implications for Church, Education, and Society*, New York: Crossroad, 209–23.

—— (1997) *Wie Kinder über Gott reden. Ein Ratgeber für Eltern und Erziehende*, Gütersloh: Gütersloher Verlagshaus.

—— (1998) *Utopian Whispers: Moral, Religious and Spiritual Values in Schools*, London: RMEP.

Jackson, R. and Nesbitt, E. (1993) *Hindu Children in Britain*, Stoke-on-Trent: Trentham.

Martens, E. (1999) *Philosophieren mit Kindern. Eine Einführung in die Philosophie*, Stuttgart: P. Reclam.

Matthews, G.B. (1994) *The Philosophy of Childhood*, Cambridge MA and London: Harvard University Press.

Schweitzer, F. (2000) *Das Recht des Kindes auf Religion: Ermutigungen für Eltern und Erzieher*, Gütersloh: Gütersloher Verlagshaus.

—— (2003) 'Was ist und wozu Kindertheologie?', in A.A. Bucher, G. Büttner, P. Freudenberger-Lötz and M. Schreiner (eds) *Im Himmelreich ist keiner sauer: Kinder als Exegeten. Jahrbuch für Kindertheologie* Vol. 2, Stuttgart: Calwer, 9–18.

Schweitzer, F., Biesinger, A. in cooperation with Boschki, R., Schlenker, C., Edelbrock, A., Kliss, O. and Scheidler, M. (2002) *Gemeinsamkeiten stärken – Unterschieden gerecht werden: Erfahrungen und Perspektiven zum konfessionell-kooperativen Religionsunterricht*, Freiburg and Gütersloh: Herder Gütersloher Verlagshaus.

Schweitzer, F. and Boschki, R. (2004) 'What children need: cooperative religious education in German schools – results from an empirical study', *British Journal of Religious Education*, 26: 33–44.

Schweitzer, F., Nipkow, K-E., Faust-Siehl, G. and Krupka, B. (1995) *Religionsunterricht und Entwicklungspsychologie: Elementarisierung in der Praxis*, Gütersloh: Gütersloher Verlagshaus.

Zoller, E. (1995) *Die kleinen Philosophen: Vom Umgang mit schwierigen Kinderfragen*, Freiburg: Herder.

13 Strangeness in inter-religious classroom communication

Research on the *Gift-to-the-Child* material

Heinz Streib

The new, the unheard-of, the strange are stimuli for learning. There is no learning without response to experiences of strangeness. We thus have strong reason to focus attention on strangeness and its association with religion. We need, however, to distinguish here between the strangeness of a new and unheard-of aspect of the religion with which the child has some familiarity; and the strangeness of the symbols, practices or beliefs of a religion which is foreign to the child's experience. While the former rather concerns the learning process in religious education, which concentrates on the one tradition or denomination of the pupils, the latter is especially an issue in inter-religious education. Exploring the world of 'strange' religions involves more and rather 'pure' experiences of strangeness since there is no immediate and obvious relation to the child's previous experience and imagination. It is thus of special interest when analyzing and conceptualizing inter-religious learning that we pay attention to the ways in which pupils develop and deal with strangeness when they encounter an unknown aspect of religion.

We can deal with this question theoretically (and prescriptively) and engage in reflections about strangeness in religion(s), religious development and religious education; and we can take a closer look into the classroom and try to understand the reaction of the pupils (descriptively). This article does both: in the second section, it presents results from empirical classroom research in Germany focusing on the question of familiarity and strangeness. In the first section, theoretical considerations of strangeness provide the starting point for developmental and educational perspectives.

Section 1: theoretical perspectives on strangeness and religion

There is a plentitude of experiences – and they may have increased in present-day multi-cultural and multi-religious society – which we cannot integrate: experiences of the strange, of strange persons, strange habits, strange religious symbols which we cannot easily understand and which may even resist assimilation. They are unexpected and they do not fit. It may even not only be difficult or impossible to assimilate such experiences of strangeness; there may be reason to refrain from and prevent such assimilation of the strange.

Strangeness as challenge and demand, strangeness as gift

Philosophical reflection on strangeness warns against the assimilation and reduction of strangeness into a framework of one's own. The strange, to refer to Bernhard Waldenfels (1990, 1997a, 1997b), is a challenge, a 'goad' [*Stachel*], which does not conform to and confirm one's own identity, but triggers new insights and thus offers a surplus.

> The strange . . . brings itself to attention as surplus which precedes and exceeds every observation and treatment of the strange. Not only the reduction of the strange to one's own, but also the attempt of a synthesis between the two belongs to the violent acts which silence the demand of the strange.
>
> (Waldenfels 1999: 50, own translation)

The act of assimilating the strange is a violent act. In general agreement with Waldenfels, Yoshiro Nakamura (2000), in his study on *Xenosophy*, calls this assimilation of the strange *exoticism*, which he defines as 'replacement of the experienced strange with an orchestrated strange ['inszeniertes Fremdes'], replacement of strangeness with otherness' (Nakamura 2000: 72). This exposure and critique of such violent assimilation and reduction of strangeness opens a critical perspective on programmes such as Theo Sundermeier's (1996) which aim at an 'understanding of the strange' at the cost of the encounter with the 'unexpected strange'; it also allows for a clarifying reinterpretation and appraisal of Ortfried Schäfter's (1991) fourth modus of 'complementarity' which he correctly juxtaposes against the modi of understanding the strange as 'counter-image' to, as 'resonance corpus', or as 'enrichment' of one's own. Schäfter's fourth modus – as border experience – is intended to keep the possibility open for the experience of the unexpected strange which cannot be integrated and assimilated. In this radical or neo-phenomenological philosophical perspective, a conceptualization of the strange is suggested which we must explicate in terms of learning and development: the experience of the strange as a challenging, curiosity-eliciting and demanding resistance or obstacle.

If the experience of unexpected strangeness is a challenge and demand, and, by the same token, a gift which should not be destroyed by the violent act of assimilation and integration, a development of John Hull's talk about religion as 'a gift to the child' seems likely. Experiences of strangeness not only belong to the encounter with religion (of every provenance) from the very beginning of this encounter, but the unexpected experience of the strange needs to be preserved and protected against the collapse into assimilation. In my view, the *Gift-to-the-Child* material promises to manage such processes. Will it stand the test in the classroom? Before I go into greater detail, I should like to draw some implications of this phenomenological approach to strangeness for a perspective on learning, on inter-religious learning, and on development.

Styles of strangeness – a developmental perspective

From the philosophical perspective as outlined above, strangeness may appear as monolithic. On closer scrutiny, however, it becomes obvious that there are several varieties of strangeness. Strangeness can be coupled with anxiety or fear, with the desire to assimilate and abandon strangeness, with the attempt to grasp and understand it, with reflection, or with curiosity and an openness to its challenge, opposition and demand. Thus, strangeness occurs in a variety of styles. Figure 13.1 presents an account of the varieties of strangeness – with a clear developmental direction toward the more advanced style of dealing with the strange. This variety of styles of strangeness is embedded, on the one hand, in Robert Selman's (1980) framework of perspective taking and its further advancement into interpersonal negotiation styles (Selman and Schultz 1988) and, on the other hand, in the framework of inter-religious negotiation styles (Streib 2001b) which correspond to the religious styles (Streib 2001a).

The column 'Versions of Strangeness' lists variations which range from xenophobic anxiety and xeno-polemic fear, to convention-based dissonance and reflective understanding of the strange as the other (reducing strangeness to otherness) – both are forms of exoticism – and to the experience of the strange as challenging, curiosity-eliciting and demanding resistance.

This scale, of course, is derived from developmental theory; but, as I have made it clear for religious development (Streib 1997, 2001a, 2003a, 2003b, 2003c), I have come to question assumptions of a linear, unidirectional and unidimensional developmental progress through structural-holistic stages. Nevertheless, I claim that there is a hierarchical order of these styles: the styles of strangeness describe a movement of declining anxiety and increasing curiosity, a movement of increasing tolerance and appreciation of strangeness. This movement also describes a learning process: 'cultivating strangeness' could be the brief formula for the direction of this process. For the learning process with respect to the strange, this means developing and nurturing the ability to tolerate experiences of perplexity, it means strengthening frustration tolerance toward non-understanding – developing a non-hermeneutic, to refer to Nakamura (2000) – respecting the challenging and demanding resistance of the strange, and giving curiosity and openness for the surplus of the strange an increasingly greater chance.

Niveaus of Interpersonal Understanding and Negotiation (Selman 1980)	Action Choice in Inter-Religious Negotiation (H.S. with reference to Selman & Schultz 1988)	Inter-Religious Negotiation Styles (adapted from Streib 2001b)	Strangeness & Familiarity in Inter-Religious Encounter		Religious Styles (Streib 2001a)
			Versions of Strangeness	Versions of Familiarity	
Depth Psychological or Societal-Symbolic Coordination of Social Perspectives (CSP)	**Dialog** as appreciation of the other as a gift, as openness for self-critique and learning through the encounter with the other / the foreign	**Dialogical / Inter-Religious** (perspective change, accounting for the 'surplus' of the strange)	**Resistance / Demand** Strangeness as challenging, curiosity-eliciting and demanding resistance which offers a 'surplus'	**Selfhood** Familiarity as sense of oneself (one's own) as another	**Dialogical**
	Individuative Communication recognizing – with attention to emotions – inter-religious interdependence, but with preoccupation for guarding one's own intimacy and autonomy	**Reflective & Explicit / Multi-Religious** (pluralistic or identifying common ground)	**Otherness** Strangeness as reflective assimilation of the religion of the other	**Identity** Familiarity as (partial) conformity or identity of the other religion with one's own	**Individuative-Systemic**
Mutual / Third Person CSP	**Collaboration** with the other based on mutual interest in cross-religious consent and harmony	**Mutual & Implicit / Multi-Religious** (harmonizing or ignorant)	**Dissonance** Convention-based, implicit sense of strangeness toward the other religion; or ignoring the other by demarcation	**Resonance** Familiarity as resonance with the religion of the other; strong identification with one's own group	**Mutual**
Reciprocal / Self-reflective CSP	**Reciprocal interaction** in the service of the self's religious perspective	**Reciprocal-Imperial / Mono-Religious** (inclusive or exclusive)	**Xeno-Polemic Fear** Dominance of strangeness as xeno-polemic attitude toward the other religion	**Egocentric Suppression of Alternatives** Egocentric familiarity with one's own religion	**Instrumental-Reciprocal**
Subjective / Unilateral / One-Way CSP	**One Way Directives** or requests to consent to one's own religion	**Egocentric or Xenophobic / Mono-Religious**	**Xenophobic Anxiety** Strangeness as xenophobic attitude toward the other religion	**Egocentric Lack of Alternatives** 'Blind' egocentric familiarity with one's own religion	**Subjective**
Egocentric / Impulsive CSP	**Physical / Non-Verbal Methods** or force consent to one's own religion				

Figure 13.1 Styles of strangeness and familiarity within the framework of inter-religious negotiation and religious styles.

Pedagogical arrangement of encounter with the strange: a new introduction to the Gift-to-the-Child *material*

The *Gift-to-the-Child* approach (cf. Hull 1996, 2000; Grimmitt *et al.* 1991a) has been designed at the University of Birmingham as a method of introducing children to a variety of religions. It suggests initiating the religious learning process by introducing a – potentially unknown – aspect of religion which is called a 'numen'. Fourteen booklets have been designed for use by the pupils. It is the special merit of this approach that it not only introduces material from a broad variety of religions, but also engages in a decisive elementarization process. Such reduction and concentration of the material on a religious phenomenon, a numen, allows a sensitive, step-by-step, response-eliciting learning process.

The *Gift-to-the-Child* procedure is particularly interesting because of its intentionally playful arrangement of *approaching* and *distancing*, its working with *familiarity* as well as with *difference* and *strangeness* in a pedagogically productive method. The child has, Hull says, 'a spiritual right to come close to religion but also a spiritual right not to come too close' (Hull 1996: 178). In a particular sequence however, Hull notes that these phases include the chance of encountering the unfamiliar and strange, but especially after the distancing devices are employed intentionally. It is assumed that the pedagogical process with the *Gift-to-the-Child* material begins with closeness and finishes with strangeness.

On closer scrutiny, however, there are experiences of strangeness and experiences of familiarity right at the beginning of this encountering process; and at the end of this process, there is not only distance, but feelings of familiarity may also develop. Therefore, I have designed the following table (Figure 13.2) which I regard as accordant with the *Gift-to-the-Child* approach:

For an understanding of the processes of children's encounter with, and introduction to, religion, it is of particular interest to observe what happens right at the beginning of this encountering process; and here we should be open to, and expect, both familiarity and strangeness. Here several possibilities are open; it probably makes a significant difference whether the numen belongs to the children's own or to their families' system of religious symbols or to those of another religion. In the *Gift-to-the-Child* approach, this contrast has been termed the difference between the gift for the believing child and the gift to the unbelieving child. The distinction appears to be somewhat rough, but it indicates that socialization may be an important factor for whether familiarity or strangeness arises and prevails. But other possibilities exist below this rough distinction: the child may be well informed and knowledgeable about a religion which is foreign to his or her family; or some symbols such as angels or God may belong to a common ground of symbols which several religions share in the perspective of the children or which belongs to a rather invisible or implicit religious symbol

	Familiarity	Strangeness
Engagement and Exploration	Familiarity as spontaneous recognition and / or identification with the numen	Strangeness as perplexity and astonishment (because of an unfamiliarity with the numen)
Contextualization and Reflection	Familiarity as reflective identification	Strangeness as reflective distance

Figure 13.2 Strangeness and familiarity in the *Gift-to-the-Child* approach.

system. Thus, the initial situation may be even more open and undetermined.

Furthermore, it should be taken into account that experiences of familiarity and strangeness arise not only in regard to the numen with which the classical *Gift-to-the-Child* lesson starts. Familiarity and strangeness develop also towards the classmates' religious view. Since the child does not encounter the numen merely individually, the interaction with the contextual variety of the peer group also needs to be taken into account when the numen is introduced. Familiarity and strangeness also develop in the pupil-to-pupil interaction in the classroom. The children may very soon form coalitions; they identify with or they dissociate themselves from the feelings of familiarity or strangeness of their peers. Finally, it must be taken into account that both strangeness and familiarity are not monolithic experiences and feelings. They each exist in many varieties. Figure 13.2 contrasts a more spontaneous, mainly *pre-reflective* strangeness (and familiarity) with *reflective* strangeness (and familiarity). Figure 13.1 includes and accounts for an even more diverse variety of styles of strangeness.

In summary, the *Gift-to-the-Child* procedure is interesting because of its intentional playful arrangement of *approaching* and *distancing*, its working with *familiarity* and with *strangeness* in a potentially productive way. We may, however, encounter a factor field in classroom interaction which is far more complex than that envisioned in the *Gift-to-the-Child* approach. With this expectation in mind, we move on to the classroom research.

Section 2: classroom research on strangeness: the *Gift-to-the Child* material at work

Research design

Given the limited empirical results on inter-religious classroom communication available so far, and given the fact that the special focus on pupils' reactions to strangeness has not yet been taken up in research, our research breaks new ground. This concerns not only the field of research, but also the method used. In order to complete a careful analysis of the children's reactions, of dialogues between teacher and pupils and among the pupils themselves, the project design includes videotaping the first lessons in which the *Gift-to-the-Child* material is used. To document more thoroughly the feelings and thoughts which the pupils did not or could not express during the class period, 'simulated recall' interviews of approximately thirty minutes are scheduled immediately following the lesson in different rooms. Selected pupils, or pairs of pupils, are invited to watch the videotape of the lesson and comment upon it.

The videotapes of the lessons and the audio tapes of the simulated recall sessions, after transcription, are evaluated step by step (sequence analytical procedure) by interpretive methods. The visual documentation by video recording makes it possible to attend to the non-verbal expression. The main focus of evaluation is not on the structure and process of *teaching*, but on the *individual pupil reactions* to the stimuli provided by the teacher and by the comments of other pupils, which may be verbal or non-verbal. Through these instruments and evaluation procedures, a comprehensive portrait of the pupils' process of encounter with the religious phenomenon should be achieved.

Results

In the following, I present an analysis of two lessons documented during our research. They contrast in many regards, and this may inspire the direction of further research. A difference is obvious already in the demographics of the classes; the first lesson ('Angels') took place in a second-grade primary school class in which the pupils' parents are mostly members of either the Protestant or the Catholic Church, with only one exception – that of a Muslim child. This reflects the demographics of a middle class neighbourhood with a majority of indigenous families. The teacher has been class-teacher for this group for two years and has established clear and firm rules and arrangements in everyday classroom communication. The second lesson ('Call to Prayer'), in contrast, was recorded in a third-grade class of a school located in a neighbourhood of predominantly working class families with a significant percentage of Turkish immigrant families. Therefore, about half of the class are members of Muslim families, and the other half have mostly Protestant or Catholic parents. The teacher is relatively new to the class; she became their class-teacher half a year before the recording.

The lesson on 'Angels' (first recording)

Three large-size posters with pictures of angels – two of them were selected from the children's book on angels (Grimmitt *et al.* 1991b), a third one was an Islamic picture of an angel talking to Mohammed – were reproduced and hung on the blackboard, but covered with a white sheet. After inviting the children to come to the front of the classroom and form a 'cinema seating arrangement', the pictures are unveiled. The teacher very sensitively asks the children to take time to look and observe what the pictures show; she repeatedly reminds them to continue looking for special details. The children thus first concentrate mostly on details: the spear, looks like a devil, stairway, angels with wings, Arabic script, crown of an angel, a horse or centaur. Can we observe reactions of strangeness on the part of the children? Not at all, if we attend to their verbal contributions which demonstrate how the children connect their observations with familiar knowledge. The children even 'know' more and have more specific ideas about their observations than the teacher is willing to accept and integrate in the course of classroom communication. The only signs of strangeness are non-verbal: one girl obviously feels very uncomfortable – we can see it in her face – when her classmate interprets the angel with the spear as being the devil. Experiences of strangeness appear to be only marginal and temporary.

The teacher then opens up a second phase of reactions from the children with the question: 'What are angels, really?' This changes the perspective significantly and the teacher apparently has a very precise intention: to elicit the children's own inner pictures and interpretations of angels. This impulse distracts the children's attention from the pictures on the wall and directs their attention to their inner world of imagination and knowledge. The children respond with many different ideas: 'flying people', 'souls of people', 'flying spirits', 'people after their death', 'God's servants', 'guardian angels'.

This is the occasion for the teacher to reinforce this focus; she asks 'Have you ever met an angel?' Immediately, we see the children following this line of thought and turning their attention further away from the pictures on the wall towards their inner world of experience. 'In a dream', one child says and expresses what will guide the conversation to follow. The children are eager to recount that they have dreamed of angels; but, despite all encouragement from the teacher, most of them say that they cannot remember details from their dreams. It seems likely that the children indeed cannot remember precisely enough to tell even a brief story; so we hear only details. One child tells about a bad dream, when the angel 'wanted to push me down out of the clouds'. Another remembers a dream of a castle in front of which there were two servants. This remembrance of angel dreams is the perfect introduction to the next step in the lesson: the teacher asks the children to draw a picture of an angel and she specifies that it should be an angel the children have seen in their dreams or an angel that they wish to be there.

In this lesson, it can be concluded, a 'piece of religion' has been introduced which produced no reaction of strangeness in the sense of inter-religious encounter with a specific religion or religious symbol. It did not produce reactions of familiarity in the sense of identifying this aspect as belonging to one's own religious community over against the background of other religions. Rather, the symbolic representations of the angels on the wall elicit shared internal symbolic representations. Only some representational details produce some irritation and some temporary reactions of strangeness; and the more the attention is directed away from the posters on the wall and toward the inner representations of the children, the more we observe the prevalence of familiarity. The encounter with an angel in one's *dreams* is not an experience of pure familiarity. It is an experience of an internal realm below conscious reflection and control which gives rise to strange images, events and stories.

If we look for an explanation for this prevalence of familiarity, we may, in the first place, point to the specific character of the numen selected. Angels appear to belong to the kind of numena of which supposedly every child raised in the Christian and Islamic religious cultures has some more or less veiled, but familiar experience. The teacher apparently anticipates the prevalence of familiarity with angels and she functions as a catalyst for the children to express and communicate their internal experiences of familiarity and transitory strangeness.

The lesson 'Call to Prayer' (second recording).

The teacher begins by recalling the previous lesson in which, for preparation, various signal sounds were identified. Then the call to prayer sound is played as a kind of surprise, a kind of quiz game, to see if the children are able to identify the signal sound they hear from audio-tape. The children could not have anticipated that they would listen to a 'piece of religion'. Thus, the play of alternatives between strangeness and familiarity is wide open.

The children use their freedom of interpretation – at least in the beginning. Already after the first segment of the call, we hear a joyful outcry from many in the classroom: they have an idea what it is. After the second segment of the call, we hear the children laugh aloud. This laughter is an expression of strangeness – a strangeness which is probably due to the German children's unfamiliarity with Arabic language, especially with its guttural consonant sound, and due also to their unfamiliarity with the melody of the call. It is estrangement by the sound of a foreign language and the music of a public announcement, rather than the encounter with the foreign religion or belief system which elicits such reactions. Nevertheless, we observe an unconstrained expression of strangeness here. As far as we can interpret this non-verbal expression, no xenophobic or xeno-polemic strangeness is visible here, but rather a kind of exotic dissonance.

A few seconds later – it all happens within seconds – we notice a very rapid whispering communication among the children; a message spread out through the class. Also we notice that fewer children laugh after hearing the third segment of the call. This is surprising. Both observations are closely connected, as we later learn from children who confirm that the message went round that one ought not to laugh when the call to prayer sounds. We also hear from a group of girls that some of the Muslim boys frightened them by explaining that there will be punishment from the Almighty for all who laugh when the call sounds. In one of the simulated-recall interviews, three girls report (S., N. and L. speaking simultaneously):

> And then he just said that we will die at fifty 'cause and the other boys said that as well./Because we've been laughing/F. and J. [. . .] yes they always said they always said that we will die at fifty/because we've been laughing./Yes because we've been laughing/and he is laughing himself about it/And I also noticed that J. also sometimes made like this, that he was grinning/Then we can tell them that we have proof on video . . .

This may also be the reason why some of the children ask to hear the call to prayer a second time: they want to demonstrate, as reparation for their offence, that they are able to listen without laughing. After the lesson, in the schoolyard, the girls were taken to task and reproached by some Muslim boys. The girls reported also that the boys kicked and pushed them so that one girl fell down. Such verbally threatening and rude behaviour – the boys obviously felt entitled to actively anticipate a bit of the punishment of the Last Judgement – was directed especially against a Muslim girl whose family originated not from Turkey, but from Kosovo.

With the help of this background information which came to light in the simulated recall interviews, we can better understand what was going on in the classroom at that moment. The reason for this surprisingly sudden quietness and suppression of laughter are explicit and firm religious beliefs which have suddenly come on stage. However, these religious beliefs and the prohibition of laughing do not come as issues to think and talk about, but as unquestioned and unquestionable beliefs and norms reinforced by fear of punishment. In terms of our framework of strangeness and familiarity, we can say that suddenly a quite strong feeling of familiarity has entered the scene – a familiarity which is based on an egocentric perspective and which denies any alternative. We can conclude that this strong and dominating breaking-in of egocentric familiarity paired with xeno-polemical strangeness has taken over and interrupted the play of strangeness and familiarity toward the numen which the *Gift-to-the-Child* material is supposed to produce.

This interruption divides the class. Some of the children, especially the Muslim boys, establish their version of familiarity and strangeness. Other children who are not familiar with the call to prayer are no longer free to direct their curiosity toward the numen, they are no longer free to react with their own feelings of strangeness or familiarity, but find themselves in a position of forced reaction to the powerful communication of a specific Islamic theological interpretation of religious norms brought forth by their Muslim male classmates. We could understand this event in the classroom as an accident, as subversion or distortion of the ideal course of steps as proposed by the *Gift-to-the-Child* material; but this is real life in the classroom and we must reckon with such unexpected effects.

This division among the children pre-structures the next phase of the lesson; the Muslim boys – one of them became the real 'expert' – are called to come to the blackboard and explain to the rest of the class how Muslims pray and other details of Islamic praxis. The familiarity of these 'experts' with their religion stands in the foreground and is dominating. Even the teacher is less certain about some issues and submits to the authority of the student 'experts'. The boys' very active participation and relatively broad knowledge anticipates at least some of the contextualization stage planned for a later phase in this lesson with the pictures of *Yaseen's Book* (Grimmitt *et al.* 1991c).

What did the non-Islamic children do, how did they feel? We can observe that many, especially the girls, have their fingers on their lips or put them into their mouth; it looks as if some want to hide their faces. This could be a non-verbal sign indicating a feeling of estrangement about the issues talked about; it could also be some sign of frustration that the male 'experts' on Islam dominate the communicative situation. We don't know for sure. One boy, holding his open hands at his ears, asks 'Why do they do this?' His question was not answered. A girl wants to ask a question, but is ignored. Strangeness on the part of the non-Islamic children develops, but it comes to expression only at the margins. The feeling of familiarity of the Islamic boys dominates. Some girls get tired and lose interest. 'Impressive, what you already know', says the teacher – thinking only of the 'experts' in Islam.

Discussion and conclusions

Some conclusions can be drawn from our study: first, the factor field of inter-religious classroom communication appears to be far more complex than accounted for in the *Gift-to-the-Child* conception. Our research reveals that the classroom reality is not always the fulfilment of the curriculum designers' dreams. Granted, the interplay of entering ('coming in') and distancing ('coming out') is an ingenious and highly productive pedagogical idea which deserves further consideration, application and development; and the input of the material has proven to be productive in eliciting strangeness and familiarity. However, our classroom research indicates that strangeness and familiarity cannot easily be predicted and confined within a clear-cut curricular mechanism.

Second, the experiences of strangeness and familiarity are related to and recall 'lived religion', which may consist in a shared experience of the numen, for example in dreams and so on, but also may derive from a firm and sometimes narrow or even fundamentalist religious socialization. We may or may not like the kind of religiosity with which the Islamic boys confront the rest of the class, including the teacher – reflecting powerful elements from their religion, practised and passed on in their families and religious communities. If we appreciate the coming-into-play of lived religion in the classroom (which I do appreciate), we may also invite 'strange' beliefs such as the fear of hell, and proscriptions such as the prohibition of laughing. This has consequences for what to expect in further research, but also for teaching arrangements using this material.

Third, the difference between the reaction of the 'believing child' and the reaction of the 'unbelieving child', turns out to be more influential than we anticipated; it may even polarize a class. We observe a polarity here which needs to be considered when we start constructing a typology of classroom reactions to religious phenomena. On the other hand, as the 'Angels' lesson demonstrates, any clear-cut distinction between belief and unbelief may be challenged. 'Believing' and 'unbelieving' are used to refer to the child's religious belonging to, and socialization in, his or her family or religious community – or not so belonging etc. as the case may be; however, some experiences – in our case, of angels – may subvert this assumption of a clear-cut distinction. 'Lived religion', as a 'sense of the Holy' (Heimbrock 2004) must also be taken seriously as a precondition which pupils may bring with them into their religious education lessons. Another highly influential factor therefore is the *type* of numen with which the lesson starts. Does it elicit a clear reaction of beliefs and prescriptions by at least part of the class or does it elicit more or less latent experiences or feelings which the majority of children bring with them?

Fourth, teachers are a factor in the force field. They bring into play not only personal convictions and interpretations, but also their teaching styles; and it is possible that they may also experience estrangement, namely in face of an unexpectedly strange kind of religion, for example fundamentalist beliefs and prescriptions, or because of the children's innocent disregard for theological correctness.

Finally, one of the most significant observations is the dependency of the classroom reactions on the style of strangeness and familiarity (which may give some importance to the scales which I have presented in Figure 13.1). If curiosity develops and prevails, as in the angels lesson, the flow of interaction between strangeness and familiarity can take its course – allowing the children to express their feelings of unexpected strangeness, perplexity and inability to grasp it. This is a very productive situation developmentally and educationally. If, on the contrary, anxiety and fear enter the scene, styles of strangeness may dominate the interaction, arresting the flow of curiosity and impeding the potential for further development and learning.

As an outlook for further research, we admit that our conclusions are based on a small amount of empirical observation. More detailed accounts of the interplay of strangeness and familiarity in the classroom could be expected from a comparison of more and different classroom interactions not only in Germany, but also in the UK. This would also enable us to better account for the context of regional and national conditions for the children's inter-religious encounter.

References

Grimmitt, M., Grove, J., Hull, J.M. and Spencer, L. (1991a) *A Gift to the Child: Religious Education in the Primary School* (Teacher's Source Book), London: Simon & Schuster.

—— (1991b) *The Angels' Book* (Gift-to-the-Child Picture Book), London: Simon & Schuster.

—— (1991c) *Yaseen's Book* (Gift-to-the-Child Picture Book), London: Simon & Schuster.

Heimbrock, H.-G. (2004) 'Beyond Secularisation: Experiences of the Sacred in Childhood and Adolescence as a Challenge for RE Development Theory', paper presented at the International Seminar on Religious Education and Values in Kristiansand, 29 July 2002 and published in *British Journal of Religious Education*, 26: 119–31.

Hull, J.M. (1996) 'A Gift to the Child: A New Pedagogy For Teaching Religion To Young Children', *Religious Education*, 91: 172–90.

—— (2000) Religion in the Service of the Child Project: The Gift Approach to Religious Education, in M. Grimmitt (ed.) *Pedagogies of Religious Education. Case Studies in the Research and Development of Good Pedagogic Practice in RE*, Great Wakering, Essex: McCrimmons.

Nakamura, Y. (2000) *Xenosophie*, Darmstadt: Wissenschaftliche Buchgesellschaft.

Schäffter, O. (1991) 'Modi des Fremderlebens. Deutungsmuster im Umgang mit Fremdheit', in O. Schäffter (ed.) *Das Fremde. Erfahrungsmöglichkeiten zwischen Faszination und Bedrohung*, Opladen: Westdeutscher Verlag.

Selman, R.L. (1980) *The Growth of Personal Understanding: Developmental and Clinical Aspects*, New York: Academic Press.

Selman, R.L. and Schultz, L.H. (1988) 'Interpersonal thought and action in the case of a troubled early adolescent. Toward a developmental model of the gap', in S.R. Shirk (ed.) *Cognitive development and child Psychotherapy*, New York, London: Plenum Press.

Streib, H. (1997) 'Religion als Stilfrage. Zur Revision struktureller Differenzierung von Religion im Blick auf die Analyse der pluralistisch-religiösen Lage der Gegenwart', *Archiv für Religionspsychologie*, 22: 48–69.

—— (2001a). 'Faith Development Theory Revisited: The Religious Styles Perspective', *International Journal for the Psychology of Religion*, 11: 143–58.

—— (2001b) 'Inter-Religious Negotiations: Case Studies on Students' Perception of and Dealing With Religious Diversity', in H.-G. Heimbrock, C.T. Scheilke and P. Schreiner (eds) *Towards Religious Competence. Diversity as a Challenge for Education in Europe*, Münster: Comenius-Institut.

—— (2003a) 'Faith Development Research Revisited: Accounting for Diversity in Structure, Content, and Narrativity of Faith', *International Journal for the Psychology of Religion* (accepted for publication).

—— (2003b) 'Religion as a Question of Style: Revising the Structural Differentiation of Religion from the Perspective of the Analysis of the Contemporary Pluralistic-Religious Situation', *International Journal for Practical Theology*, 7: 1–22.

—— (2003c) 'Variety and complexity of religious development: perspectives for the 21st century', in P.H.M.P. Roelofsma, J.M.T. Corveleyn and J.W. Van Saane (eds) *One Hundred Years of Psychology of Religion: Issues and trends in a century long quest*, Amsterdam: Free University Press.

Sundermeier, T. (1996) *Den Fremden verstehen. Eine praktische Hermeneutik*, Göttingen: Vandenhoeck & Rupprecht.

Waldenfels, B. (1990) *Der Stachel des Fremden*, Frankfurt/M.: Suhrkamp.

—— (1997a) 'Phänomenologie des Eigenen und des Fremden', in H. Münkler (ed.) *Furcht und Faszination. Facetten der Fremdheit*, Berlin: Akad.-Verlag.

—— (1997b) *Topographie des Fremden*, Frankfurt/M.: Suhrkamp.

—— (1999) 'Der Anspruch des Fremden', in R. Breuninger (ed.) *Andersheit – Fremdheit – Toleranz*, Ulm: Humboldt-Studienzentrum.

14 Playful orthodoxy

Religious education's solution to pluralism

Jerome Berryman

Religious education appears to be caught in a dangerous dilemma. If one teaches for orthodoxy by memorization, other-directed activities, forming habits, serious initiation, single-minded duty and with an 'us' against 'them' mentality, then the result is a deeply centred and participatory practice. The danger that results from this approach is the formation of an orthodoxy that is rigid, close-minded, defensive and sometimes violent. The opposite extreme is also problematic. Teaching religion in a way that encourages creativity, self-direction, wonder, discovery and play to find a meaningful approach to life and death is also harmful. It can result in the ironic impossibility of being unorthodox because there is no identity or community to depart from. This approach can lead to insanity at worst and an inability to cope with life's complexities at best. This dilemma is false, however, because it is possible to teach religion in a way that is both deeply centring and participatory as well as open and flexible. This chapter will explain how and why this is possible as well as desirable.

We will begin by asking how creativity appears in human systems and what constitutes its process in the individual. Style and stage constraints on creativity will then be examined and related to teaching. Finally, a theory will be suggested to guide the method called Godly Play™. The principles of this method can be used by any of the world religions to create playful orthodoxy and restore religion to coping with trouble rather than causing it.

The where and what of creativity

Mihaly Csikszentmihalyi has spent about three decades studying creativity. He discovered that the experience of 'flow' which is related to 'deep play' (Csikszentmihalyi 1975: 74–5) is what makes creativity pleasurable and therefore self-reinforcing. The tendency to create new ideas and ways of solving problems, however, is not the only clue to our survival. We are programmed with 'two contradictory sets of instructions' (Csikszentmihalyi 1996: 11). Human survival is the result of the tendency to conserve as well as to create. Our instinct for self-preservation, self-aggrandizement and conservation of energy exists alongside our tendency to explore, enjoy novelty, and take risks. Religion has rarely been on the side of creativity, to say the least, but in our time this preference can no longer be a matter of mild curiosity or sardonic comment. It is too lethal, so it must be addressed.

We will begin by asking with Csikszentmihalyi 'where' creativity is located to better understand it. He proposed a systems model to define it within a network of relationships involving a domain, a field and a person. It takes place when any act, idea or product changes an existing domain or creates a new one (ibid. 28). A domain consists of a set of language rules, vocabulary and procedures. Mathematics is one example. Religion is another. The second component of creativity is the field. This is the group of people who act as gatekeepers to the domain. The third component of a creative system is the individual.

In *Godly Play* (Berryman 1991), individual creativity was described as a movement with an opening (exploring) and a closing (conserving) phase. The opening begins when an established meaning is broken by a crisis or dissolved by wonder. This forces the expending of energy to scan for a more adequate kind of coherence to heal the disruption. This second step might last for hours, days or years and be conscious or unconscious. The third step is insight. A new, more adequate pattern is formed and forces its way into consciousness by means of an image, a fragment of a song, a piece of poetry, a dream or by some other means. After the insight, the closing part of the process begins. This is when creativity might be used in the service of conservation. Up to now, the process has been largely non-verbal and outside the confines of customary thought. After the insight, the development of the idea begins as the fourth step in this process. It is worked about according to the rules of a particular domain. The fifth step is closure. The idea is considered by the creator to be fully worked out.

The whole loop of discovery is available to all of us, but individuals prefer different parts of the process. Some people love the free flowing spirit of scanning so much they don't want to interrupt it by an insight. That takes an effort of focused energy quite different from that used in scanning. Sometimes this shift is noticed before the insight is evident so that you are aware of 'having' an idea before you know what it is. Still other people are so delighted by having insights that they can endure long periods of what they might experience as the pain of lonely and chaotic scanning. Once the insight is experienced, however, they lose interest and do not develop it. Conserving people step in after the insight. They can't stand the loss of meaning by crisis and certainly don't want to participate in the potential chaos of wonder. They hate scanning and do not find the insight worth it. They don't even like to be around 'creative' people who enjoy such things.

At first one might think that conservative people are not creative but developing an idea requires intelligence, focus, talent and effort. The difference is that they often use only part of the process (steps four and five) and are likely to help maintain stability by trimming new ideas to fit what is accepted by the field. The people who step into the creative loop only at closure maintain the greatest control and avoid the most risk. They occupy only the executive, digital step of saying 'Yes' or 'No'. Children, stuck at various points in the five steps of the process, need to be encouraged and supported to move through the whole process. This will enable them to use religious language creatively as well as to conserve it.

A word of caution, however, must be firmly set in place before advancing to the next section. The creative loop can be used to accomplish destructive as well as constructive results. Sometimes an outcome is unknowable, so one goes forward with the process, betting that the outcome will be constructive. Destructive outcomes are, therefore, sometimes accidents. It is also true that one must tear down to build a new idea or structure. At other times, however, creativity is explicitly placed in the service of destruction. This is as true of the religious domain as any other, but in religion we expect more, because its origin was to cope with trouble, not create it. Religion, then, has both creating and conserving tendencies. The creative loop, however, joins them into one process of opening and closing. Two more features of creativity will now be examined, especially because of their bearing on teaching and learning religion in a way that supports playful orthodoxy.

Styles, stages, and the bridging of gaps between them

The styles and stages of creativity give further definition to the creative process. This discussion will be guided primarily by Howard Gardner's theory of 'multiple intelligences' (Gardner 1983) and James W. Fowler's theory of 'faith development' (Fowler 1981) and applied to the role of the teacher of religion. Gardner's *Frames of Mind: The Theory of Multiple Intelligences* was published in 1983. Ten years later he applied his theory to creativity in *Creating Minds* (Gardner 1993) which described what we are calling 'styles' of creativity. Although *Creating Minds* was published three years before Csikszentmihalyi's *Creativity*, Gardner still relied on Csikszentmihalyi's systems model, which had previously been a lively topic in their conversations. What Gardner contributed to this discussion was the variety of ways people create and his interest in the connection between the creativity of the child and that of the master, which we will save to comment on another time.

Einstein was Gardner's exemplar for logical-mathematical intelligence, Picasso was used to illustrate spatial knowing and Stravinsky represented the musical frame. T.S. Eliot shows how a particular linguistic sensitivity to words can shape one's creativity and Martha Graham was his example of bodily kinesthetic creating. Gandhi showed interpersonal creativity at work and Freud was his exemplar for a person tuned especially to the intrapersonal. The lesson religious educators can draw from this is that we need to be aware of our own style of creating so we will not project it on children. This is so that the children we work with can be supported in their religious journey in a way that is most appropriate for them. When a teacher unconsciously or consciously requires a style of creativity when teaching, then the child is placed at risk for developing frustration with religious meaning at least and a false religious self at most.

In *Intelligence Reframed: Multiple Intelligences for the 21st Century* (Gardner 1999) Gardner reported that he had found an additional frame of knowing to the first seven. It is the kind of person who is especially attracted to patterns in nature. He also discussed why existential, spiritual or moral sensitivities are important aspects of character, but do not qualify as one of his frames of knowing. They are different in kind. He also cautioned that his theory of multiple intelligences was not a recipe for education. To run children through all the ways of knowing for a particular lesson is a waste of the teacher's and children's time and energy. It is better to be aware of the multiple ways of knowing to understand when learning and communication difficulties arise (Gardner 1999: 89–92).

We turn now from creativity styles to the constraints that human development place on creating religious meaning. I have used Fowler's model, among others, since editing and contributing to *Life Maps: Conversations on the Journey of Faith* (Berryman 1978). One of the most powerful realizations one gains from several decades of such developmental interest is how religious people can share the same deep values but disagree violently within their own traditions and between religions because of logical misunderstandings related to stage development. When people are about two stages apart, the person at the less complex and flexible stage cannot understand the way the other person is speaking or writing. This creates so much static in the discourse that points of agreement are missed. My interest here is how to bridge the gap.

To discuss bridging stage gaps we need to say a few more words about non-verbal communication. This is because bridging stages is not only a matter of linguistic behaviour; it also involves our non-linguistic communication system. The repertoire of facial expressions, vocalizations, gestures, calls, grunts, social grooming, pointing and other such communication should not be considered as a 'simple language'. We are not 'bilingual' because we use both verbal and non-verbal communication. Instead there is a discontinuity between linguistic and non-linguistic behaviour and the two systems are not always aware of what the other is doing. These two systems evolved in a separate but parallel way and are produced by different regions of the brain (Deacon 1997: 54 and Chapters 8–10). We can, therefore, describe non-verbal communication with words, but it makes no sense to ask what kind of word a laugh or sob is expressive of. Furthermore, much of what we say, such as 'Good morning' needs non-verbal communication to correctly interpret it. Some people may wish you a 'Good morning' and mean to ruin your day.

Fowler's stages, then, can be interpreted as the tracing of the development of language about faith, although he would caution us to include feelings as well as culture within that linguistic net. The linguistic qualities most important for the teaching of religion begin to emerge at what he calls the 'Conjunctive Stage'. It is not necessary for a teacher of religion to actually 'dwell' in Fowler's fifth stage. What is important is to acquire as much of that stage's quality of communication as possible to use in one's role as a teacher. In other areas of life, apart from one's professional role, another stage might dominate. What is important about the linguistic communication that Fowler's fifth stage describes is that often non-verbal communication has begun again to be valued. This is because the exciting and useful developments of the preceding stage, such as the shift from narrative to concept, begins to be experienced as a dead end for religious knowing.

One cannot go back to the naivete-without-options of childhood, so the adult chooses to allow the non-verbal communication system to reassert itself for particular situations. An example from Christianity is participating in Holy Communion. One chooses not to think about the process like an anthropologist, a physicist, a physician or even a gossip while participating in it. In this way the non-linguistic meaning in the quality of relationships can be discovered. Both a commitment to participate and to recognize the unique quality of this kind of communication are required to participate in the kind of knowing available in the ritual. This was noticed by Ian T. Ramsey (1915–72) about the middle of the twentieth century, during the linguistic turn in philosophy. He was appointed the Nolloth Professor of the Philosophy of Christian Religion at Oxford in 1951, and became Bishop of Durham in 1966. He argued that there is an 'empirical placement of theological phrases' and that religious language is not a kind of emotional venting. Rather it is an 'odd discernment' (Ramsey 1957) requiring commitment to the linguistic domain to be made. A teacher, therefore, needs to develop 'a nose for odd language', as Ramsey put it and a non-linguistic involvement in such language, such as play, to teach it well.

The 'oddness' is more than religious language's difference from scientific language. It is, it seems to me, that religious language re-directs one back into the non-verbal communication system one began life with and where our spirituality is located (Berryman 2001). Ritual is an intermediate position between the two systems that is always 'ajar' for either. It both holds in an overlapping way and is open to moving into either communication system during participation. It is a place of structured safety and yet open to the possibility of playful day dreaming to stimulate the whole loop of creativity. Playful orthodoxy supports both the exploring and conserving tendencies of creativity.

Bridging faith development gaps, then, is not as simple as it is sometimes portrayed. Matching creativity styles is easier, because it is assumed that such styles are mostly non-verbal. Stages, however, are embedded in the verbal system. This means that a person at the more complex and flexible stage might be able to speak in a way that matches a 'lower' stage, but to the person at the lower stage it feels like being 'talked down to' and is resented. An extreme example is the patronizing, singsong voice some adults use when addressing children. Erik Erikson called those who take an interest in the coming generation 'generative'. In *The Life Cycle Completed*, written in his 80s, Erikson noted that when generativity fails 'regressing to earlier stages may occur either in the form of an obsessive need for pseudo-intimacy or of a compulsive kind of preoccupation with self-imagery – both with a pervading sense of stagnation' (E. and J. Erikson 1998: 67).

In *Toys and Reasons: Stages in the Ritualization of Experience*, Erikson defined ritual as 'an agreed upon interplay between at least two persons who repeat it at meaningful intervals and in recurring contexts' (Erikson 1977: 37). It is this interplay that can bridge the gap between childhood and adulthood and the repeated, meaningful intervals can be religion classes. For such interplay to take place, however, the adult needs to be comfortable with being 'a numinous model in the next generation's eyes' as well as a 'judge of evil and the transmitter of ideal values'. When the adult is not comfortable, then the ritual becomes ritualism and the mentoring authority of the adult degenerates into what Erikson called 'Authoritism' – the non-verbal communication of being self-important and judgemental.

The psycho-social crisis of 'Initiative versus Guilt' was negotiated during childhood during what Erikson called the 'Play Age'. Play, of course, does not go away as one continues to develop. It becomes critical however, when an adult turns toward the coming generation if the gap is to be bridged between them. One's turning toward children is largely non-verbal. When the teaching of religion teaches the conflict between the verbal and the non-verbal, as in angry demands for love or punishing for peace, verbal and non-verbal contradiction is established as normal for religious communication for children. This disjunction renders religion unable to help cope with troubles but only to cause them.

Romano Guardini (1885–1968), is an example from the Christian tradition of a generative teacher of ritual. He helped prepare the way for Vatican II as a liturgist by the 'content and form' of his writing (Krieg 1995: 26). He taught that worship is 'a kind of holy play in which the soul, with utter abandonment, learns how to waste time for the sake of God' (Guardini 1935a: 106). It is 'to play the divinely ordained game of the liturgy in liberty and beauty and holy joy before God' (ibid.). Our non-linguistic communication, especially the signalling of play, then, is critical for bridging both style and stage gaps for teaching the art of how to use religious language for coping with trouble. What is needed, therefore, is a method and foundational theory, which supports and creates an appropriate setting for such bridging. We turn to that discussion now.

A method in search of a theory

Maria Montessori (1870–1952) said that the educational method of the Roman Catholic Church was the mass. I trained as a Montessori teacher in Bergamo, Italy, in 1971–72. At that time I was a Presbyterian minister but when I became an Episcopal priest in 1984 I experienced what she meant. Between 1984 and 1994 I was Canon Educator at Christ Church Cathedral in downtown Houston. When I celebrated Holy Communion, I turned to the tabernacle behind me and took out the corporal. I then turned back to the altar and smoothed the calm folds of cloth upon the table's surface, like a Montessori underlay. I then placed the chalice, the paten and other objects upon the corporal, also like a Montessori lesson. Montessori must have watched this respectfully hundreds of times and knew that was how she was going to do her teaching. The spoken part of the experience that accompanied the ritual's gestures began with a story about a supper that took place a long time ago. Then step by step the story moved into the present and everyone present became part of it. When the experience ended people were sent forth into the future in a new or renewed way.

Godly Play™ is rooted in play, ritual and story but the method stems from Montessori. It need not be described here, since information about it is widely available. See, for example: *Godly Play* (Berryman 1991) *Teaching Godly Play* (Berryman 1995) and *The Complete Guide to Godly Play* (Berryman 2002, 2003). The history of this method's relation to Montessori education is traced in volume 1 of *The Complete Guide* (Berryman 2002). What does need to be discussed is the theory for this method. Montessori used to say that she had a method in search of a theory. Despite her disclaimer, she worked hard on her theory, which was based mostly on her medical training which was completed in 1896, and her training and experience in education. It cannot help but be dated, so the method, which is still powerful, is again in search of a theory.

Godly Play™ is based on play, ritual and story, as we said. Unfortunately, many children today do not have the ability to deeply play, participate in rituals or be active listeners to stories. The open classroom of the Montessori method is used to help children become more active and self-directed in their discovery of religious meaning by playing deeply with foundational rituals and narrative. The play of children is neither silly nor superficial. Adults confuse the entertainment of over-stimulation of children with play, so it is important to be clear about what play is. Catherine Garvey's description of 'play' is hard to improve on (Garvey 1977). First, play is pleasurable; that is why it is self-reinforcing. Second, it is done for itself without regard for a product. Third, play is voluntary; you can make people work but not play. Fourth, it involves deep concentration. Finally, play is connected to the learning of languages, creativity, problem solving and the learning of social roles. Godly Play™ incorporates all of these elements.

Ritual helped organize life for pre-linguistic people, as it does for us. Take for example, the small modern ritual of locating one's keys. It was the Cro-Magnon people, however, who linked language to play and ritual to cope with trouble and we still stand in their debt after about 40,000 years. In fact we have no choice, for we function with what is essentially the same brain that they had. It is the playful approach to ritual and storytelling that enables Godly Play™ to nourish a specific religious identity and stimulate new ways of coping with trouble and new stages in which that can be done. While this method is based on Montessori, the educational theory is based on the work of Jerome Bruner.

Jerome Bruner's theory took shape in *The Process of Education* (Bruner 1963) in which he develops his concept of the 'spiral curriculum' through which children's thinking and learning develops by means of the carefully planned revisiting of key material of increasing complexity at progressive developmental stages. By the time of his *The Culture of Education* in 1996 he had developed nine 'tenets' about how children make meaning (Bruner 1996: 13–43, 130–49). It is my view that his theory, Montessori's method, and the use of play, ritual and story in religious education can be integrated to explain why Godly Play™ is so useful and to provide ways to continue testing and developing its theory and practice.

Teaching playful orthodoxy

We human beings do not learn 'language in general'; we learn particular languages such as Arabic or Chinese and even within a particular language, such as English, we learn special languages such as medicine, law or religion, and each special language in turn has its own sub-functions. Similarly, we need to learn a particular religious language system well, such as Christianity, if we are going to be able to understand another religion such as Islam or make meaningful comments about religion in general. What follows is a description of a way to teach 'how to speak Christian' that is rooted in the whole of the creative process so it includes both the rooting of orthodoxy and the openness needed to meet new challenges.

Children are invited into a circle with a mentoring storyteller. The surrounding room is carefully laid out with sacred stories, parables and liturgical action materials. This makes most of the language system and the part-whole relationship clear to the children at the level of intuition from age two years onward. The complexity of the Christian system is not simplified but presented appropriately in this way so that the whole system is taught when any part of it is taught. There is playfulness, clarity about the rules of the game and safety in the atmosphere. A clear ritual defines the time spent as carefully as the space has been laid out.

The deep structure of the Holy Eucharist provides the rules for profoundly playing this orthodox, Christian language game. Children are invited to enter the teaching/learning time and space after they are 'ready' because this language does not work unless people can make the 'odd discernment' necessary for it to work. They bring their existential troubles with them to be juxtaposed with the power of religious language and God's presence. The lesson is then presented and in the wondering and expressive art that follows, these troubles can be creatively coped with. A feast and prayers are shared and respectful good-byes are said one by one with a sense of blessing and constructive closure.

The adult guides show, rather than talk about, how to use the language to make meaning. It takes being ready, wonder, and play. It is assumed that children naturally know God. What they lack is the language and a community in which to be at play with God, as creators created in God's image. Learning the art of how 'to speak Christian' in this way supplies what nature cannot provide for their spiritual maturity. The curriculum is an integrated spiral for children usually about two to twelve years of age. If adolescents have grown up in such classes many additional options for teaching are available, for the language is already creatively rooted. Adolescents who have not been raised this way can benefit by starting at the beginning with this approach, as can adults. The basic lessons are returned to year after year, so children can learn to find what is new for them, according to their expanding life experience and stage development, in each classical story, parable or rite. The content of this kind of language is never exhausted but it takes practice and creativity to find its hidden meanings and God's presence there.

On the other hand, the spiral of the curriculum adds complexity and additional lessons as the years go by. For example the lessons about 'The Creation' and 'The Faces of Christ' (the story of Jesus) are told as single lessons and then children are invited to formulate an incarnational theology by placing the tiles from the two lessons together, as they see fit, into an integrated whole. Later, about age ten or eleven years, 'The Creation', 'The Faces' and the lesson about Paul are joined with part of the lesson about Holy Baptism to create an experience of the Holy Trinity. This recapitulates the development from narrative to concept in the history of theology and parallels the stages of faith development children have the potential for at this time in their lives.

Conclusion

The quality of religious education is critical for the survival of the human species. This is because of the dangerous way pluralism is unfolding. To solve the problem of pluralism we need to join the opposite tendencies driving religious education to reach the goal of playful orthodoxy. What is proposed here has been developed from within the Christian tradition but it is intended to have general application to any of the world religions.

References

Berryman, J. (ed.) (1978) *Life Maps: Conversations on the Journey of Faith*, Waco, Texas: Word Inc.
—— (1991) *Godly Play*, San Francisco, California: HarperSanFrancisco.
—— (1995) *Teaching Godly Play*, Nashville, Tennessee: Abingdon.

—— (2001) 'The Nonverbal Nature of Spirituality and Religious Education', in J. Erricker, C. Ota and C. Erricker (eds) *Spiritual Education: Cultural, Religious and Social Differences*, Brighton: Sussex Academic Press.

—— (2002) *The Complete Guide To Godly Play*, vols 1–3, Denver, Colorado: Living the Good News.

—— (2003) *The Complete Guide To Godly Play*, Vol. 4, Denver, Colorado: Living the Good News.

Bruner, J. (1963) *The Process of Education*, Cambridge, Massachusetts: Harvard University Press.

—— (1996) *The Culture of Education*, Cambridge, Massachusetts: Harvard University Press.

Csikszentmihalyi, M. (1975) *Beyond Boredom and Anxiety: The Experience of Play in Work and Games*, San Francisco, California: Jossey-Bass Publishers.

—— (1996) *Creativity*, New York: HarperCollins.

Deacon, T. (1997) *The Symbolic Species: The Co-Evolution of Language and the Brain*, New York: W.W. Norton.

Erikson, E. (1977) *Toys and Reasons: Stages in the Ritualization of Experience*, New York: W.W. Norton.

Erikson, E. and J. (1998) *The Life Cycle Completed: Extended Version with New Chapters on the Ninth Stage of Development*, Norton paperback, New York: W.W. Norton.

Fowler, J. (1981) *Stages of Faith: The Psychology of Human Development and the Quest for Meaning*, San Francisco, California: HarperSanFrancisco.

Gardner, H. (1983) *Frames of Mind: The Theory of Multiple Intelligences*, New York: Basic Books.

—— (1993) *Creating Minds*, New York: Basic Books.

—— (1999) *Intelligence Reframed: Multiple Intelligences for the 21st Century*, New York: Basic Books.

Garvey, C. (1977) *Play*, Cambridge, Massachusetts: Harvard University Press.

Guardini, R. (1935a) *The Spirit of the Liturgy*, trans. Ada Lane from the German (1918), New York: Sheed and Ward.

—— (1935b) *The Church and the Catholic*, trans. Ada Lane from the German (1922), New York: Sheed and Ward.

Krieg, R. (1995) *Romano Guardini: Proclaiming the Sacred in a Modern World*, Chicago, Illinois: The Archdiocese of Chicago, Liturgy Training Publications.

Ramsey, I. (1957) *Religious Language*, London: SCM Press

(For further information, consult the Internet sites godlyplay.org and godlyplay.com.)

15 The roles of dialogue in religious education

A Russian perspective

Fedor Kozyrev

There are many papers dealing with the multifunction of dialogue in religious education. One recent example is a successful categorization used by Norwegian educators (Leganger-Krogstad 2003). It distinguishes three types of dialogue: *necessary*, *structured* and *spiritual*. The first is stipulated by the coexistence of different cultural representatives in the modern world. In school life it appears as a dialogue between classmates – neighbours in a class. The second usually takes the form of a planned talk by teachers to their pupils and structured and targeted towards advancing the students' understanding of the subject, examining their level of knowledge and correcting their educational progress accordingly. The third appears spontaneously and constitutes the climactic point of the pedagogical process – a moment disclosing the reality of the Other.

The categorization seems to be successful because it reflects the three main purposes of dialogue: to help to communicate, to facilitate progress in personal development and to provide an impulse for spiritual growth. In other words, education as an encounter with the surrounding world (society), education as a tool for self-understanding (focusing on 'self') and education as touching the great mystery of one's individuality being a part of the whole. This article does not pretend to offer a new systematic approach; it simply invites one more evaluation of the significance of dialogue, as it is seen through the history of the interaction of Russian and European pedagogical thought.

It is the second of the dialogical forms described that is the most obvious and also the most often experienced in pedagogics. Since the times of ancient Greek liberal education, 'Socratic talk' has occupied a prominent position among the classical forms of educational method. Even the medieval schools, never infatuated with active methods, used dialogue in theological debates for developing the art of argumentation. Education as an operational process is hardly possible at all without some such sort of dialogue, ensuring the existence of 'feedback' in the 'teacher-pupil' relationship and thus, management of the system. Of course, dialogue can be of very different kinds depending greatly upon the type of school subject. In the case of RE, it is important to choose which type of school subjects or activities are most similar to the study of religion: natural sciences or humanities, ideologies, ethics, law or arts.

The structural design of a subject, the correlation of its elements and its arrangement are different in specific cases; and forms of informational exchange in dialogue also differ. If we ask in geography or history classes, for example, 'In what country is Paris located?' or 'When did the Battle of Waterloo take place?', it is possible to expect only two types of answers: correct and incorrect. It is surely the same with the factual aspect present in religious education and the humanities; but the humanities deal also with moral and aesthetic evaluation, associations and insights, producing general visions, studying personal impressions, religious experience and so on. Since all of these qualities are relative, it means that the dialogue between teacher and pupil is essentially open, allowing the student to disagree with the teacher and still not to be wrong; the positions of the teacher and student at the final point of the dialogue remain unresolved. This characteristic distinguishes humanities from positive science as well as the new RE from the old confessional approach.

We use the term *humanitarian religious education* to describe this new, open and non-confessional approach to the study of religion at school. This term, corresponding to *learning from religion*, places stronger emphasis on treating religion as a part of humanities; it also emphasizes the priority of humanism among the values of the modern school. These two meanings have something in common – that is, a faith in personality, placing a high value on personal creative work and the cognitive efficiency of personal perception. How much can we rely upon our subjective impressions, insights and emotions when studying spiritual reality? The type of dialogue used in a classroom depends upon the answer to this question.

Appealing to religious feelings in dialogue as one of the creative forces opens new prospects in studying both religion as a phenomenon and human nature. It particularly helps us to discover that the striking sensitivity and receptivity children display towards religion is due not only to their naivety or primitive (mythological) mental processes, but also to some special non-rational insight which we lose with age and which is, as an Orthodox pedagogue Vasiliy Zenkovsky believed, a sign of a spirituality of children's life that is 'difficult for us to understand and to receive' (Zenkovsky 1996b: 110). We guess it intuitively and it touches us no less than their moral purity and innocence.

John Hull is among those modern teachers who understand this better than others. His 'God-talks' with young children (Hull 1991b) have seriously questioned earlier assumptions regarding children's religious receptivity and once again have reminded us of a gospel revelation about children which was in oblivion before Rousseau. Our own investigations confirm Hull's findings on a child's ability for deep and intelligent assimilation of complex religious concepts. For example, my nine year old son, several weeks after we had had a conversation on divine omnipresence asked: 'Pa, you said that God is everywhere. But then God is in sin too, is not that true?' Since there were no explicit reasons for such a question at that moment, this event appeared to be evidence of a child's ability for a long, productive and independent theological reflection.

The development of this kind of ability must surely be a topic for religious education. At the same time, the classical demand for focusing on the development of religious feeling via images and stories before theological formation must also not be neglected. This historically admitted priority of religious feeling over knowledge is one of the additional arguments for treating RE as a part of the humanities. Religion, either as literature, the arts, history and even philosophy appears within the *humanitarian* approach not as systematic knowledge but first of all as a resource of inspiration and creative experience. It is equally necessary to be shared for aesthetic and intellectual development, for an enlightened and enriching outlook, and thus for preparing a pupil to live in an open and tolerant society. This last mentioned task of socialization leads us to the second aspect of our topic.

According to one existing and well-argued point of view, postmodern society does not become increasingly atheistic; it simply practises new forms of religious life (Nipkow 1995). Radical pluralism, relativism and privatization of religious life on the one hand; and persistent searching for common spiritual ground with other religions on the other – all these features of new religious consciousness alarm modern teachers and compel them to look for new approaches; the old ones just do not work. 'The question whether we can prove the existence of God or not, is no longer important, if students maintain: God is just a feeling inside myself' (Gossmann 1997: 43). Our own survey conducted in the senior classes of St. Petersburg state schools in 2002 found a similar pattern (Kozyrev 2003). Teenagers do not tend to identify themselves with any one confession even if they have reasons to do so and do not regard commitment to religious traditions as a criterion for true faith.

As secularization spreads, religion progressively loses the potency to carry on its main function as described by Durkheim – the function of consolidation in which religion works as social cement. Postmodern society is less traditionally structured than earlier national, class (or caste) or confessional societies. The social environment in which we dwell today is more discrete than in earlier times. Atoms of individuals seem to pull towards them a significant part of their value and dignity from class, religious, tribal or some other kind of solidarity, and find themselves in rare space. Equal and open dialogue appears in this space to be the only means of communication. It becomes necessary both for ensuring social relationships and for enabling the individual's search for meaning in life. Dialogue, paving the way through the gap from one ontologically significant monad to another becomes something more than the transference of knowledge. It turns out to be a source of knowledge, a place where the meaning of the subject being studied, my relationship with it and my existence arise and reveal.

Mikhail Bakhtin is one of the best-known Russian theorists who made a substantial contribution to understanding dialogue in such a way. Today his idea of *polyphony* (Chidester 2001) or *heteroglossia* (Erricker 1999) is broadly used in RE in very different parts of the world, and there are good reasons for it. Focusing on the problem of knowing another self, as all disciples of the Kantian Professor Alexander Vvedensky did, Bakhtin managed not only to give a vivid interpretation of existentialism as a dominant mood of the present; he also showed a positive way to escape alienation and the self-isolation that accompanies it. This way, according to Bakhtin, is dialogue, and this belief of his withstood both the pessimistic Kantian conviction of the cognitive inaccessibility of the *other* shared by his teacher, and the optimistic ontology of the universal unity or class solidarity held by the majority of contemporary Russian religious or Marxist philosophers.

Bakhtin's outlook is often called the philosophy of dialogue and this is accurate since dialogue obtains ontological status in his constructions and turns out to be a *proto-matter* generating a world for divided individual consciousnesses to inhabit. According to Bakhtin 'to be is to communicate dialogically' and vice versa – not to communicate dialogically means not to be. 'When dialogue ends, everything ends' (Bakhtin 1979: 294) and an 'isolated individual', as Vvedensky used to say, proves to be a 'metaphysical spectre' (Vvedensky 1892: 117). It was while studying Dostoevsky's poetics that Bakhtin discovered this special vision similar to some interpretations of quantum physics, where reality appears in the course of contact with an observer (Bonetskaya 1993). This kind of poetics, when putting dialogue in the centre of a fictitious world – 'all is instrumental, dialogue is the aim' (Bakhtin ibid.) – creates a new and surprising image of reality as a product of interaction of autonomous spiritual atoms (internal worlds of characters) with energetic fields radiated by them in the spiritual vacuum, proposing the existence of God (creator of characters), but impervious to the divine will.

The world we live in becomes, with the destruction of traditional social links and the development of technical facilities ensuring greater individual autonomy, more and more reminiscent of that of Dostoevsky. There is a famous vision received by Versilov – a character from Dostoevsky's *The Adolescent*; it is about 'the last day of humanity' – a lull after the frantic war with 'the great idea of old', when:

> men suddenly understood that they were left quite alone, and at once felt terribly forlorn ... The great idea of immortality would have vanished, and they would have to fill its place; and all the wealth of love lavished of old upon Him who was immortal, would be turned upon the whole of nature, on the world, on men, on every blade of grass. They would inevitably grow to love the earth and life as they gradually became aware of their own transitory and finite nature, and with a special love, not as of old ... Oh, they would be in haste to love, to stifle

the great sorrow in their hearts. They would be proud and brave for themselves, but would grow timid for one another; every one would tremble for the life and for happiness of each. They would grow tender for one another, and would not be ashamed of it as now, and would be caressing as children.

(Dostoevsky 1916: 446)

Another Russian devotee of Dostoevsky, Nikolay Berdyaev regarded Versilov's fantasy as a revelation of the 'religious lie of humanism in its ultimate manifestations' by matching the religious idea of personality with the socialist idea of building the kingdom of God here on earth (Berdyaev 1990: 78). His disbelief in love without Christ proved dialectically that the inhabitants of this fantasy world were not non-believers at all. 'Such a love is never possible in atheistic mankind. . . . Atheistic mankind must come to cruelty, to killing each other' (Berdyaev 1968: 131).

This society described in Versilov's vision is undoubtedly more humane than societies centred around the interests of any kind of solidarity. It is as ethical as religious, but the religion and ethics of this society have specific and familiar features – that of postmodernism. The dialogical approach becomes in this world not one of several possibilities, but the only possible approach to religious education, since after society rejects the absolute value and truthfulness of religious ideas, traditions and other historical forms of consolidation, these values lose their primary position in individual ethics also. As the collective and continuous self dies off in the discrete postmodern world, an authoritarian education loses its power to make the individual a partaker of the commonwealth and common responsibility; it then becomes transformed into the imposition of the teacher's individual will, unfairly presented as being ethically and spiritually superior.

In Bakhtin's model, where communication is equal to existence, socialization gains religious meaning. Consequently the functions of 'necessary' and 'spiritual' dialogue coincide, both of them leading to depths of human self. When one unified system of criteria for the religious life is refused, every step towards another individual can prove to be like entering another co-ordinate system, opening up a new spiritual dimension. So besides connecting persons by 'horizontal' social links, dialogue sets 'verticals' connecting the empirical consciousness of students with the transcendence of the subconscious and supernatural. In the secular world, school takes over a function earlier regarded as a prerogative of the Church. It is a function of *ministry*, or *spiritual guidance*, of initiation of the *inward man* (2 Corinthians 4: 16), or, as Zenkovsky writes, 'the healing of spirituality itself within us' (ibid. 130).

When criticizing pragmatic American pedagogy, Zenkovsky argued that the main reason for life's failures sits not outside, but inside the person, and therefore superficial pedagogical realism does not protect children 'from tragedies, from cruel and hurting failures, from depression and even the senselessness of life'. That's why every school aiming towards the authentic realization of pedagogical goals cannot ignore religious depth within the individual, cannot but recognize that the success of education is acquired by 'setting up conditions of internal balance and the self-renewing of the soul' (ibid. 31).

To fulfil this task – to choose what is actually healthy for spiritual growth and what is harmful among the things a modern school offers – is difficult. The issue is especially crucial with RE insofar as religion can have both good and bad effects. If not necessarily going so far as to distinguish between true and false religion, as John Hull suggests (Hull 1991a: 16), we can at least distinguish between what profit and harm religion can bring to a person. The following anecdote was popular amongst intellectuals in Soviet Russia. A boy travelling with his father by bus sees on a wall a well-known Marxist slogan – 'religion is an opiate for the people'. He asks his father who is reading the newspaper: 'Pa, but what is an opiate?' – and father, not tearing away his eye from the newspaper, answers: 'Poison for fools, medicine for the clever'. We must not overlook the ability of religion not only to revive a person, but to become a source of spiritual falsehood and disease. This raises another function of dialogue – the *psychotherapeutic* one.

Freud was the first to try to show the connection – or bridge the gap – between religion and psychopathology practically; and up to the present, the construction of the bridge has been mainly from one side despite an alternative perspective having been outlined before Freud by William James. Although the idea of spiritual psychotherapy is popular in the Eastern Christian world (Hierotheos 1994), little research has been undertaken on whether schools might carry out this function. Theological and religious education obviously lacks both an empirical base for the systematic study of the psychological influence of religion on the person and a practical therapeutic strategy based on these studies. Frank dialogue between teacher and pupil, certain professional ethics being provided, could overcome both shortcomings and occupy a similar dominant position in the science of spiritual development as a dialogue between the physician and patient occupies in the practice of psychoanalysis. We may expect it to be even more fruitful since it is based upon the recognition of the freedom of the human spirit.

James wrote about the diseases of faith and defined them as consequences of wrong answers given by religions to personal religious inquiries (James 1904: 45). It is, however, the responsibility of the school to offer right answers to vital questions, and it is evidently impossible to fulfil this task outside dialogue. Of course the working situation of teachers in public schools does not make work with individuals easy, but it is quite suitable for group therapy in RE classes. Equal dialogue of peers on religious subjects opens up greater possibilities for reflection over their own religious insights and the search for 'right answers', thus correcting spiritual development and preventing 'diseases of faith' even without teacher interference.

The *ideological* dimension of the modern practice of 'spiritual dialogue' has also to be recognized. The big problems that traditional confessional approaches face today are caused largely by their incongruity with the general pedagogical paradigm of modernity. A *juridical* approach to religion would effectively be a relic of scholasticism in a school having stated its credo and shaped its ideals in opposition to scholasticism in education. One of the outstanding Russian teachers of the nineteenth century, Vladimir Stoyunin, gave an insightful and laconic description of the spirit of the old scholastic paradigm: science 'did not teach at that time, how to search for new truths ... it only taught how to invent thoughts, ... i.e. pointed to ready, general sources from which to take material' (Modzalevsky 2000 Part 1: 336). The *theocentric* frame of reference distinctive of medieval cultures identified the main goal of education as the *instilling* into persons of the fixed and elaborate system of relations with God, world and society. Dialogue appeared within this system mainly in the form of debates and had a competitive purpose rather than serving ideological pluralism.

Renaissance, Reformation, Humanism, Enlightenment – all these social and cultural movements which have opened up ground for changing the medieval paradigm, were inspired by a common faith in the spiritual receptivity, creative activity and legal autonomy of the individual. The emergence of a new theory of education was closely related to this change in the concept of the person as an object of education. In Fichte's words: 'the old education took care of the transfer of information only and was based on the fundamental, inborn depravity of human nature ... the religion of the new education must be a religion of spending our lives with God' (ibid. Part 2: 194). The anthropocentric trends of the new culture changed the priorities of education. It gave prominence to the task of developing the student's abilities to discern truths and to 'walk with God' (Genesis 5: 24) – that is, to make an independent, responsible choice of individual spiritual path. Dialogue becomes a sign of these new priorities. Are teachers ready to see their students not as passive subjects but as active participants in the educational process? Are they ready to organize this process as a continuing dialogue with an unpredictable outcome rather than as a programmed operational cycle? Their choice would disclose their devotion to one of two incompatible pedagogical frames of reference.

These conceptual changes have a social aspect. It is mainly in school that civil consciousness is shaped since that is the place where most young people find themselves members of a society for the first time. They often project this first social experience onto their adult life and social models of school life can easily become archetypes. Occasionally school was even considered as the main tool for social reforms (Dewey 1915), and this idea is not so fantastic if we take into account the power of early impressions to influence future individual perception and development. A teacher participating as an equal in dialogue with a pupil makes a major contribution towards preparing the pupil for life in a society of peers; and this ideological function of dialogue in education has turned the school into an arena of political struggle where dialogue has become a criterion not only for professional but also for political devotion, a sign of liberalism and progressive thought.

The history of the clash between two opposing approaches to the study of religion in Russian schools is highly dramatic. Until the revolution, a juridical study of Orthodoxy at 'God Law' classes was the norm in all Russian church-parochial schools, gymnasiums and universities. At least two attempts were made to reform the subject – giving it a more humanitarian character and placing the emphasis on 'inward Christianity' aiming at the awakening of religious and moral initiative within society. This first occurred during the reign of the emperor Alexander I. As a famous church historian Georges Florovsky affirms, it was in the Charter of the St. Petersburg Academy (1814), that the educational system was first 'established on an authentic pedagogical base' by the Metropolitan Filaret. It was noted in this that

> a good method of teaching is to promote students' own mental powers and activity; therefore, the verbosity of professors who try to show their wit instead of stimulating the wit of their listeners goes against such a method. For the same reason, dictating lessons in classes is also contrary to good method.
>
> (Florovsky 1937: 145)

It was at this time that the Russian Biblical Society – 'a kind of autonomous division' of the British and Foreign Bible Society, to use Florovsky's expression (ibid. 47), translated the Bible into Russian. Pedagogical purposes and ideas were surely behind this project; but in 1824, owing to Archimandrite Foty's and Admiral Shishkov's efforts, school reform stopped, translated Bible editions were burnt in the stoves of Nevsky laurel and the catechism by Filaret, written in Russian, was withdrawn from sale. There began, as Filaret expresses it, a 'reverse motion to the times of scholasticism' (ibid. 166).

The second attempt at change took place under Alexander II in the course of his liberating reforms in the 1860s. This time it was a powerful chief of synod, Konstantin Pobedonostsev, who led the opposition to the reforms by promoting the idea of education 'in the Orthodox spirit' with the purpose of keeping people 'in strict subservience to the order of public life' (Pinkevich 2001z: 70, 72). Curiously enough, an advocate of progressive pedagogy, Konstantin Ushinsky, was persecuted for coming out against cramming the very Filaret catechism that had been forbidden to be read forty years before. Parrying the accusation, Ushinsky said that cramming of any kind of a schoolbook may kill one's innate religious feeling: 'It produced a lot of harm and stopped the religious and moral development of many' (Vasilevskaya 1993: 185).

The fight for the new pedagogical paradigm was therefore lost by the progressive forces of Russia. The results of this loss were described in a note by the Alliance of Teachers in Secondary Schools (1905):

> We are witnesses of a portentous moment – the crashing of the secondary school. It was shielded from every aspect of life, but life burst into the school and threw the youth, mostly the boys, onto the streets under Cossack lashes. It imposed Orthodoxy but having brought it forth in heavy forms of government formalism, cultivated religious indifferentism.
>
> (Pinkevich ibid. 76)

Less than fifteen years after, there came into Russia a new and much less tolerant atheistic dogmatism requiring 'only the true' answers in history, literature and biology classes, and this was made possible largely due to the authoritarian mentality promoted by the Russian school. Attacks on civil liberties caused active protest and we see amongst Russian teachers, besides apologists of the authoritarian forms of education, a lot of carriers of opposite and often quite drastic views. It is enough to mention just one movement called 'Free Education'. Its founder, Lev Tolstoy, wrote not only world-famous novels but also a lot of pedagogical works developing the most radical ideas of Rousseau. He insisted that, before establishing schools, society must prove its right to mould children, and he denied this right in principle (Tolstoy 1880). The 'Free Education' group developed ideas very distant from traditional ones even in today's context. Its main theorist K.N. Ventzel wrote: 'For the sake of the development of creativity in a child we must use all our power to discredit any faith in absolute truth'. Applied to RE this meant that it 'must not aim to import any kind of orthodoxy, however perfect it be, into a child's life. It must help a child to gain his own religion in a creative way. Only personal religion ... can be called religion in the true sense of the word' (Zenkovsky 1996a: 133).

The main alternative to Tolstoy's moralistic approach to RE was formed within religious mysticism, ever popular in Russia. The second most popular Russian author of that time, Fedor Dostoevsky, inspired that sort of mystical pietism and romanticism which he may have caught himself from Chateaubriand's *The Genius of Christianity* (Jackson 1993). Some Russian philosophers opposed Dostoevsky's revealing 'abyss of spirit' and Tolstoy's poetizing 'abyss of flesh' (Merezhkovsky 1995). Avoiding such sharp contrapositions, it is probably better to notice that with regard to human being, Dostoevsky focused not on human nature as Tolstoy did, but on the spirit or, better, spirits inhabiting it. However high the position of personal liberty ranked in Tolstoy's system of values, the only way to a true existence and true reality went, for him, through the refusal of the illusion of self. The individualism of Dostoevsky and his followers, including Bakhtin, formed a polar opposite to this impersonalism of Tolstoy in the space of Russian culture.

Philosophers of the circle to which Bakhtin belonged put the problems of transpersonal communication into the centre of their interests; but Bakhtin himself did not systematically develop pedagogical aspects of the problem. This was done by Sergei Hessen in his fundamental work *Basics of Pedagogy: Introduction to Applied Philosophy* (1923). His three-level system of education is based on distinguishing three stages of personal ethical development: anomy, heteronomy and autonomy. Liberty is a central concept of the system. Treating it according to Rousseau as an 'obedience to the law given to self by self' (Hessen 1995: 60), Hessen however criticizes Rousseau for the false contraposition of liberty and enforcement. Following nature at the first *anomy* stage of spiritual development is not a liberty but submission to natural need. To overcome this lowest form of enforcement it is necessary 'to awaken the internal power of liberty' in a child; but this is possible only through 'the appointment of *super-personal* goals to a person', through acquaintance with the concept of *due*, of debt and right; by exposing the personality to 'external, public enforcement' at the *heteronomy* stage. Only when the individual is provided with internal discipline can he approach liberty as the task of his life, that is to enter the way of creative and endless progress as it is seen from the perspective of self-given tasks. Here he has reached the stage of ethical *autonomy*.

This system was in fact Hessen's answer to the problem of inaccessibility of another self. His pedagogical idealism overcame the existentialist outlook shared particularly by Bakhtin through the necessary tendency of a mature person to super-personal goals. Nevertheless he was not indifferent to the problem of alienation in general as well as to its special items concerning individual interaction with tradition and culture.

Julia Ipgrave recently used Bakhtin's notions of 'centrifugal' and 'centripetal' forces when applying them respectively to *diversity* and *collective identity* – two sides of citizenship produced by interaction of the individual and society (Ipgrave 2003: 151). Remarkably enough Hessen used the same imagery but in an opposite coordinate system, with its point of reference connected to personality, not to a group.

On account of relativity, the integrating social forces turn out to be in this case centrifugal with regard to personality. Hessen identifies this power with culture and as a result, culture becomes a factor of alienation. Paying attention to the *anti-cultural* pathos of Rousseau being the background of the new pedagogics, according to which the goal of education is 'not to do something with a pupil, but to protect a person from culture' (Hessen ibid. 47), Hessen turns again to the problem of the relation of personality to external culture: 'Which of the external cultural surroundings is most favorable for the development of individual liberty?' For Rousseau and Tolstoy these favourable conditions correspond to a minimum of cultural influence on the natural individual. Hessen thinks differently: 'The Rousseau protest against culture appears on closer examination to be a struggle for the ethical ideal of free and holistic personality' (ibid. 46). Repeatedly focusing on this point, Hessen nevertheless treats this protest as a justified reaction to 'historical violations', but not as a positive solution. From his standpoint, correctly delivered education is able to obtain an harmonic correlation of two powers so that the 'centrifugal power of external cultural contents', trying to get the person torn into pieces, will be balanced by the centripetal power of mature personality. When the correct correlation is reached, the person forces 'cultural contents' to revolve around itself, processing them into 'its own', and emerging as a maker of culture; and this is the ultimate goal of education.

Actually helpful in this reasoning is that it elucidates in an unusual way the most important and special task of pedagogy – to be a safeguard, an *attorney* of a child (Nipkow ibid. 81), warning about all of the hazards for the child's development, even if these hazards reside in the things normally perceived as good – for instance, in culture. Hessen's ideas highlight a further *protecting* function of dialogue. This ability of dialogue to protect internal personal unity and liberty is particularly obvious in the sphere of religion in which there is tension between cultural periphery and personal mystic experience in the centre of religious phenomena; and where contradictions between tradition and charisma, between priest and prophet are of such a vital importance. This brings us back to the psychotherapeutic function of dialogue.

When students get the opportunity to talk about their faith with a teacher instead of learning what kind of faith they ought to have, they get a better chance not to lose their *self* in the raging informational stream or under the pressure of religious authority. In some way this last function of dialogue is opposite to the first one which was mentioned at the beginning of this essay. It comprises the restriction of disproportionate influence of 'external contents', that is, somebody else's beliefs, impressions and life experiences, and the construction of a sort of isolating cover, activating an internal resource of development. A classroom dialogue dealing with religion should serve as a force for the sprouts of children's religious experience to break through the strata of religious culture, enriched but not smashed by its mass, having absorbed all its beneficial fluids without any shortfall of the power, hope and daring which make them active, assimilating human beings.

References

Bakhtin, M. (1979) *The Problems of Dostoevsky's Poetics*, 4th edn, Moscow: Sovetskaya Rossia (first published 1929). (R)

Berdyaev, N. (1968) *Dostoevskiy's Outlook*, London: YMCA Press (first published 1923).

—— (1990) 'The Spirit of the Russian Revolution', in *From the Depth: a Collection of Articles on the Russian Revolution*, Moscow: MGU Press (first published 1918). (R)

Bonetskaya, N.K. (1993) 'M.M. Bakhtin and the Traditions of Russian Philosophy', in *Voprosy Philosophii (Journal of Philosophy)*, 1: 83–93.

Chidester, D. (2001) 'Multiple Voices: Challenges Posed for Religious Education in South Africa', in *Religious Education in Schools: Ideas and Experiences from around the World* International Association for Religious Freedom, 2001 (papers for a UN conference held in Madrid 2001).

Dewey, J. (1915) *The School and Society*, revised edition, Chicago: University of Chicago Press (first published 1899).

Dostoevsky, F. (1916) *A Raw Youth* (translated from the Russian by Constance Garnett), London: William Heinemann (first published in Russian in 1875).

Erricker, J. (1999) 'Teachers Developing Spiritual and Moral Education', *Teacher Development* 3: 383–96.

Florovsky, G. (1937) *The Paths of Russian Theology*, Paris: (publisher unknown).

Gossmann, K. (1997) 'The Current Situation of Religious Education in Germany', in W. Sennhauser (ed.) *Religious Education in the Protestant and Anglican Traditions*, Berg: RE Network.

Hessen, S. (1995) *The Basics of Pedagogy: an Introduction to Applied Philosophy*, Moscow: Shkola Press (first published in 1923). (R)

Hierotheos, V. (1994) *Orthodox Psychotherapy: The Science of the Fathers*, Lavadia: Theotokos Monastery.

Hull, J. (1991a) *Religion, Education and Madness: a Modern Trinity* CREDAR lecture series No. 2, Birmingham: University of Birmingham.

—— (1991b) *God-talk with Young Children: Notes for Parents and Teachers*, Derby: CEM.

Ipgrave, J. (2003) 'Dialogue, Citizenship and Religious Education', in R. Jackson (ed.) *International Perspectives on Citizenship, Education, and Religious Diversity*, London and New York: RoutledgeFalmer.

Jackson, R.L. (1993) *Dialogues with Dostoevsky: the overwhelming questions*, Stanford, California: Stanford University Press.

James, W. (1904) *The Will to Believe and other Essays* (translated into Russian by S.I. Ceretelli), St. Petersburg: Pirozhkov.

Kozyrev, F. (2003) 'The Religious and Moral Beliefs of Adolescents in St. Petersburg', *Journal of Education and Christian Belief*, 7: 69–91.

Leganger-Krogstad, H. (2003) 'Dialogue among Young Citizens in a Pluralistic Religious Education Classroom', in R. Jackson (ed.) *International Perspectives on Citizenship, Education, and Religious Diversity*, London and New York: Routledge-Falmer.

Merezhkovsky, D.S. (1995) *Tolstoy and Dostoevsky: Perpetual Fellows*, Moscow: Respublika (first published 1900). (R)

Modzalevsky, L.N. (2000) *Essay on the History of Education and Didactics from Ancient Times until Today* (in 2 parts), St. Petersburg: Aleteya (first published in 1866). (R)

Nipkow, K-E. (1995) *Comenius Today* (translated into Russian by D.S. Bumazhnov), St. Petersburg: Glagol. (R)

Pinkevich, V.K. (2001) 'Church and State Politics in Education at the Beginning of the Twentieth Century', in *State, Religion, Church in Russia and Abroad*, Moscow: RUGS Press. (R)

Tolstoy, L. (1989) 'Formation and Education', in *Works by Count L.N. Tolstoy*, Moscow: Heirs of Brother Salaevy (first published in 1880). (R)

Vasilevskaya, V.J. (1993) 'Ushinsky's Theory of Education', in S. Kulomzina (ed.) *Our Church and Our Children*, Moscow: Martis (first published in 1979). (R)

Vvedensky, A. (1892) 'On Limits and Signs of Animation', *Zhurnal Ministerstva Narodnogo Prosveschinia (The Journal of the Ministry of Education)*, V: parts 5–6. (R)
Zenkovsky, V. (1996a) *Pedagogy*, Moscow: St. Tikhon Orthodox Theological Institute. (R)
—— (1996b) *Problems of Formation in the Light of Christian Anthropology*, Moscow: Shkola Press (first published in 1934). (R)

(R) These publications are only available in Russian and book, journal and/or article titles given in English are translations by the author of this chapter.

16 Is there a place for youth in religious education?

Geir Skeie

This essay is inspired by John Hull's will to critically 'unpack' concepts and rhetoric related to the relationship between politics, power, education and religion (Hull 1990, 1991, 1992, 2000a) and to take the perspective of children and youth as is reflected in his 'gift to the child' approach (Hull 2000b). In this spirit I will ask my own questions dealing with the understanding of youth, the relationship between youth and education in a society marked by modern plurality and, more particularly, to investigate the prospects of developing a religious education that is for and with young people.[1]

Young people are often considered to be society's pilots or scouts into the future. Such an attitude can be seen to reflect a sociocultural environment very different from the picture we have of a former, traditional society. Then, the older generation had the knowledge and experience necessary to navigate through the challenges of everyday life. They also had the wisdom needed in times of crisis or celebration. The socialisation of young people was aimed at internalising those norms and skills that were expressed and performed by the older generation. Even though the process of socialisation in the form of *transmission* probably never was a purely harmonious one it seems to have worked then. Social change has altered this dramatically, and in late modern society the diffusion of values and lifestyle is not constrained by geography. Still, however, memories of traditional socialisation are vivid, at least in Norway. These memories tend to colour the understanding of the present situation, partly by making it look more unusual than it probably is.

Today 'future' has lost its flavour of repeating the old and known, even if we keep memories of the past. Our memories seem more like museums of outdated artefacts. Future means to explore the new and unknown; stability has gone and has been replaced by change as the major value. Socialisation takes the form of *transformation*, more than transmission, and due to the lack of knowledge about the future this transformation is largely of an informal nature. The new and unknown may create fascination and curiosity, but it can also be a source of challenge and anxiety. To control the future means to have power; when young people show familiarity and competence in dealing with the new, this can be interpreted as a shift in power between the generations and cause the older generation to fear losing control. The rhetoric portraying young people as being 'pilots of the future' hides a strong ambiguity. One side of the coin shows a positive image of the future and consequently a positive image of young people. The other shows a negative picture of the future and also a more negative view of young people. They are seen as representatives or carriers of the disturbing tendencies that are coming up, like moral decay, lack of citizenship, individualism and violence.

In this way the discourse about youth is woven into the discourse about the future. It also conceals the fact that adults more than young people have the power to change the future, and that many adults are hiding from this responsibility and rather project it towards the young. Within this interplay between generations, religion also plays a part. Many religions are closely tied to old texts and inherited traditions with their roots deep down in a traditional society. This has given a superior position to adults, mostly to men, and probably influences the general attitudes of young people towards organised religion. Apart from the relatively small but significant proportion of young people who are religiously active within organised religion, many others see religion as something best suited for older people who are orientated more towards the past than towards the future. This diversity within the young population itself is a challenge for religious educators.

What is it like to be young?

It is a universal aspect of human life to pass through different phases with growing age, and for thousands of years people seem to have reflected on this, relating their experiences to the concepts at hand. In this sense 'generations' have always existed, but it does not mean that 'youth' or 'childhood' are universal concepts independent of time and place. Human beings understand life in the light of the knowledge they have access to, and often in opposition to other, different ways of understanding. Today it is possible to understand 'youth' as a conceptual signifier in public discourse. By using this word, people are referring to a certain age group as such, and at the same time they are presenting a certain interpretation or meaning attributed to this age group. There is hardly any mention of 'youth' without some sort of value judgement. This perspective-dependent interpretation of 'youth' is also reflected in research.

In Scandinavian youth research, the age span referred to as 'youth' is often sixteen to twenty year olds. A survey of youth research up to the late 1980s refers to three main trends in theories about youth (Stafseng and Frønes 1987). First, emphasis may be put on youth as the generation following other generations, but with particular generation-specific experiences influencing the rest of their life; second, emphasis may be put on youth as a certain age-related sociocultural context with strong impact on the socialisation of young people; third, some researchers underline youth as a distinct sub-culture more or less different from other age-groups of society. The three perspectives may be seen both as challenging each other and at the same time as being complementary. Together they also contribute to the deconstruction of 'youth' as a concept, challenging us to be critical towards any picture of young people presented to us.

The critical approach of research is particularly relevant because 'youth' has become such a central ideological issue in western culture. In many ways 'youth' seems to be stronger as a cult than religion is, at least if consumerism can be seen as part of a cult. It might be difficult for organisations to monopolise 'youth' in the way they have monopolised religion, but on the other hand 'youth' is everywhere an ideal, crossing political and economic borders. It is spreading towards all age-groups, loosening up its reference to sixteen to twenty year olds, because everybody wants to be 'young'. The positive values attributed to 'youth' and 'young' are exploited by those who seek power, whether it be in the market or in politics. Implicitly this leaves young people aside because it is their belonging to the category of 'youth' that is interesting, not themselves as persons.

It is this idealisation of 'youth' that puts pressure on young people to live up to ideal images of what it is to be young; but there is a 'double bind' here (Bateson 1972). If young people try to live up to the values attributed to youth, they may be accused of being victims of commercialisation or consumerism. If they reject these values or launch their own ideals, it is sometimes considered to be a sign of 'youth problems'. A third possibility is that young people's self-determined lifestyle is commercialised and returned to them as a market commodity. Attitudes towards young people from the adult part of society are in real life highly ambiguous. On the one hand, young people represent our common hope and future and on the other, they are seen as carriers of the threats to that very same hope and future. Youth has become something of a 'mysterium tremendum et fascinosum'.

To counter some of this mystification and ambiguity, it is imperative to employ a critique of ideology. It is possible, by means of sociological and cultural analysis, to question the type of consciousness that is taking the dominant discourse for granted. By combining a cultural and a social perspective it is easier to see the limitations of psychological theories with an emphasis on youth (adolescence) as a stage of development. Often these theories focus too much on young people representing a certain level of development. In order to understand young people it is just as important to understand the sociocultural context in which they operate and the content of their own constructions of meaning. Some of these constructions include religion.

Are young people religious?

When we deal with questions related to the religion of young people we should keep in mind both the rhetorical construction of public discourse about 'youth' and the analysis of how this age group is placed in the social dynamic. This is complicated enough in itself; the introduction of religion does not make it any easier. One very simple, but useful way to differentiate research perspectives on youth and religion is to separate a focus on the person from a focus on the social context (Birkedal 2001: 9–29). Both 'youth' and 'religion' are complex concepts, and this may also call for more subtle perspectives on both sides. Friedrich Schweitzer suggests a subtle and clarifying approach by distinguishing between five complementary perspectives in his approach to youth and religious education; psychological, sociological, historical, biographical and theological (Schweitzer 1996). Debates within sociology of religion about secularisation, privatisation, re-traditionalisation and new religious movements are often related to the way western religious traditions have developed and changed. In recent decades there has also been an increasing focus on the multi-ethnic and multi-religious society. Debates on these 'new' issues are often mixed with debates about 'youth'. One example is the widespread worry about young people 'drifting away' from the churches. In Norway the dominant Lutheran state church is presently launching a large and expensive national programme partly to counter this 'drifting away', and to nurture children and young people into the faith to which they 'belong'. The main reason why this issue is arising now is a recent change in religious education in Norwegian schools. Since 1997, religious education has consisted of a broad introduction to different faiths as well as secular humanism, and this explicitly excludes any normative privileges on the part of Christian faith within public schools (Haakedal 2001).[2] Similar initiatives can be seen within other religious groups.

Seen from the perspective of a religious organisation, the faith of young people is often measured by its closeness to or distance from official doctrines or practices. Much research within both sociology of religion and psychology of religion has a similar perspective while other approaches favour a more open concept of religion. If the concept of religion is opened up towards a life-world perspective, including values and spirituality, we come closer to the daily life of youth. A series of research surveys carried out by a Norwegian company undertaking market analysis are designed to draw a picture of what values different people pursue.[3] This company has been 'monitoring' Norwegian society since the mid-1980s, basing their analyses on theories about cultural typologies from Ronald Ingelhart and Scott Flanagan. One result is that in terms of values, age seems to be one of the most important dividing lines (Hellevik 2001). Young people are more drawn towards 'modern' and 'materialist' values, while older people prefer values that are 'traditional' and 'idealist'.[4] When it comes to the politically relevant 'conservative-radical dimension', the differences are less visible. A closer analysis seems to indicate that the most pronounced differences between young and older people are not mainly related to their different phase of life as such. What rather seems to be the case is that the sociocultural context of young people has some kind of lasting effect on their values and becomes 'typical' of their cohort. The older live within the same context, but do not experience it in the same way. The findings seem to support the 'generation' perspective in youth research mentioned above.

In terms of religion, this and other research indicates that young people as such are no less religious than any other age group. When it often appears to be so in surveys, this partly reflects the fact that youth are less involved in organised religion. It also suggests that their understanding of 'religion' might be different from that of those making the survey. The relevance of the conceptualisation of religion is particularly clear in the debate on 'drift away from the churches'. The expression itself seems to portray churches as being firmly located on solid rock, and young people as risking their lives on open sea. Of course, the metaphor may be critically reversed; the young are making their voyage through life, while the churches prefer to stay behind. One could argue that religious organisations are products of values cherished by older age cohorts and even partly based on their youthful experiences. When rapid sociocultural change occurs it is not easy for religious organisations to grasp the context and content of young people's philosophy of life (Engebretson 2003). Churches (and schools) are busy with institutional management, while young people are busy with identity management, and therefore they do not always have the same agenda.

Rapid social change can also have an opposite result when it comes to religion, as is the case with young immigrants. According to recent research, they show a higher commitment to religion than young people with a Norwegian ethnic background (Øia 1998). The religious institutions to which immigrant youth belong are often weak and this sometimes gives young people more space. At the same time, religion is used much more as a sign of identification in their context than in the lifeworld of secularised Norwegians. In Norwegian ethnic vocabulary words like 'Pakistani' and 'Muslim' are almost used as interchangeable terms, while hardly anyone would use 'Norwegian' and 'Christian' as synonymous. The situations where the latter happens are likely to be when ethnic Norwegians are advocating nationalist views, playing on the fact that about 85 per cent of the population are members of the same Lutheran church. Still, religion is much more relevant to young people with an immigrant background, and they need to deal with it as part of identity management.

In conclusion, empirical investigations do not solve our questions dealing with young people and religion. In general they tell us that the interest in religious issues as defined by religious organisations is declining among youth, and lower than in older age groups. Closer investigation shows that variations exist and that it is impossible to treat 'youth' as a homogenous group when it comes to religion. It also shows that these issues are highly context dependent. To ask questions about youth and religion reveals a specific interest and normative background knowledge as in the case of religious educators. This normative background fits only with some young people, and there may therefore be good reason for not starting with religion and ending with youth, but to reverse the order and start with the life-world of young people and look for something that resembles 'religion'. There are also sound educational reasons for this.

Youth culture and approaches to religious education

The concept of 'youth culture' takes its starting point in the life-world of young people and justifies itself by reference to empirical findings within this field. Even if the research tools may be academically sophisticated, the overall approach represents a bottom-up perspective. In terms of pedagogical theory, this often corresponds to pedagogies that are based on a student-orientated perspective towards learning (Illeris *et al.* 2002). In line with much pedagogical theory, it claims that the learning process starts with understanding the present knowledge of the learner. It also claims that the curriculum has to take the situation and knowledge of the learner into account.

This fits with a concept of 'culture' that is understood in terms of 'meaning' or 'values', but without introducing a normative hierarchy from outside. A radical version of this perspective would lead the teacher to start with a student perspective, encouraging students to define their own learning aims by formulating problems they want to investigate, taking full responsibility for their learning outcomes. The teacher is seen as a helper or tutor and the curriculum as something that is partly negotiated within the classroom. Learning may therefore be understood as a self-governed development that is part of youth culture itself. To some extent this blurs the difference between general socialisation and learning within institutions like schools; it also underlines the complexity of learning and acknowledges that learning may be located in many social arenas.

A second, different interest in 'youth culture' may come from educationists who want to complement the research findings of developmental psychology by including a sociocultural perspective. The basic pedagogical approach may be that the curriculum should be a product of tradition, not of a negotiation between teacher and learner. Its main content is drawn from the 'cultural heritage', and this heritage also includes critique of tradition. Even if this justifies the curriculum on a political level, it does not necessarily work with young people. In order to facilitate the learning process, the teacher therefore needs to know as much as possible about the mental capacities of the learners (developmental psychology) and their life-world (youth research). By means of such background knowledge, both teaching methods and learning results may be improved. Instead of underlining the fluid borders between learning arenas, this approach tries to establish some control over the communication process within the classroom whilst taking into account knowledge of youth culture.

The main difference between the student-centred and content-centred approaches is that the latter has a more instrumental interest in 'youth culture' whilst the former allows it to play a more central role in defining the learning content and outcome. This has consequences for the role of the teacher. If knowledge about young people mainly functions as background knowledge informing teaching strategies, it means that the teacher employs knowledge that is consciously hidden from the students. The type of knowledge that is hidden is not content-knowledge, but meta-knowledge or context-knowledge. In this situation, the teacher is in danger of violating the basic human relationship that should be part of learning in which the learner and the teacher are considered on an equal level in the sense that the student is not an object but a participating subject with responsibilities. The teacher-learner relationship is ethical, not instrumental.

The student-centred approach acknowledges this problem, thus involving the students both in the teaching and in the learning decisions and thereby becoming much more dependent on them. This radical student-orientated perspective is, however, only possible in radical educational institutions and hardly any politicians are willing to apply it in a public school system. This leaves teachers with the option of using modified versions of a student-centred approach, which runs the risk of putting up double standards. If this kind of teaching goes on in a school that is placed within the framework of a national system with extensive testing and evaluations, a student-centred approach might be seen to mislead the students, causing them to believe that what they are doing inside the classroom situation has a relevance for life in society at large. What happens is that student-centred approaches may be seen as compensatory in a competitive school and society, and sometimes RE as such is understood in this compensatory perspective. An emphasis on the student-centred approach in this kind of situation may be rejected by some of the students, causing disappointment and confusion in teachers who are full of good intentions. Other students may appreciate it as something 'different' from the rest of the school subjects.

In the case of RE it can be especially tempting to argue that a life-world approach would solve many of the problems teachers have making religion relevant to students. As noted above, there seems to be a certain gap between the content of much RE focusing on world religions and the way religion is part of, or not part of, 'youth culture'. In order to deal with this, one necessary, if not always sufficient, option is to open up the concept of 'religion' towards the life-world of young people using a 'philosophy of life' perspective as a starting point rather than emphasising 'religion'. An important advantage of this is that it respects and builds on knowledge that the students are willing to present in the classroom, acknowledging their competence of mastering the life-world of young people, instead of placing them from the very start in the position of a receiver of knowledge.

Among the Nordic countries, it is particularly in Sweden that the life-world approach has been commonly used. The method of starting with the students' 'questions of life' and then moving towards religions and belief systems dates back to the worries about the generation gap in the late 1960s and was inspired by people like Mathews, Loukes, Cox and Goldman in Britain (Hartman 1994). Hartman sums up the history of Swedish RE curriculae in four didactic categories, which, he also contends, follow each other more or less chronologically (see Figure 16.1).

This categorisation of didactic approaches can also be used more generally to map approaches to RE. What has been discussed above is mainly the difference between approaches 1 and 4. The non-instrumental perspective on youth culture suggests that a student-centred approach is necessary if not sufficient in order to make the teaching relevant for young people. One particular reason for this is the internal plurality within youth culture, which dissolves any essentialist notion of 'the' youth culture. This plurality includes traditional religious plurality, which calls for approaches that fall within category 2.

The above categorisation is clarifying for analytical purposes, mainly dealing with content and 'pedagogical strategies' (Grimmitt 2000: 18); it does not cover the 'why' of RE. Underlying the 'pedagogical strategies' we find 'pedagogical principles'. According to Grimmitt, these should be based on generic principles before expressing them in terms specific to RE. Such principles seem to cover the 'whys' as well as being close to the aims of education. In order to place RE within a more general framework of educational aims, I suggest a triangular model presenting three different, but interrelated perspectives (Stafseng 2001, 2002; see Figure 16.2).

The three perspectives represent both justifications and aims of education that can be paralleled with aims of religious education. While Grimmitt is mainly drawing upon the aims 'learning from' and 'learning about' religion, this can be complemented by introducing a third aim; learning to live together with people from different religions and cultures. By drawing on the triangular model of perspectives on education and three main aims of religious education as these have been summarised by Everington (2000) it is possible to visualise the basic principles (aims/justifications) of RE in a larger educational perspective:

The first perspective understands education mainly as a tool for improving economic growth, owing its importance to the change from agricultural to industrial society and later into an information- and knowledge-based

WHAT		HOW	
		Subject-matter-centred method	Child-centred method
	Religious documents and traditions	1	2
	Existential dimensions of religion	3	4

Figure 16.1 A categorisation of didactic approaches to religious education.

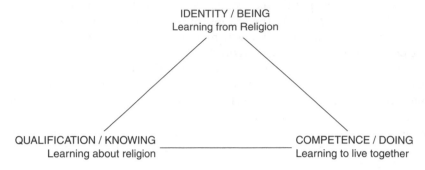

Figure 16.2 A model of educational perspectives and aims of religious education.

society. More generally, this perspective often focuses on 'skills' or competences suited to serve the needs of society. A second perspective sees the role of education mainly as transmission of knowledge in order to ensure that people have the qualifications necessary for certain jobs or for further education or research. Here, the focus is on acquiring a stock of established and developed, but also contested, knowledge. The third perspective puts emphasis on education as the transformation of persons, including questions of identity, connecting with the German idea of 'Bildung'.

If the three perspectives are seen as poles in a triangle with dialectical relationships between them, the possible positions towards education become somewhat more refined, doing justice to the different commitments. There are certainly tensions between the poles that may be fruitful, not only opposites challenging us to take sides. The axis between 'qualification' and 'competence' underlines the importance of education for society, for a profession and for performing certain skills. Here we find those who believe in 'learning by doing', while others speak about acquiring 'basic knowledge'. The axis between 'identity' and 'competence' focuses on education as a path to professional identity, and the importance of personal involvement in the way skills and competences are acquired. Finally, the axis between 'identity' and 'qualification' includes a tension between a perspective rooted in the 'Bildung' tradition and another with more emphasis on socialisation and informal learning.

Already E.H. Ericsson, writing under the influence of the post-war focus on youth, puts particular emphasis on the issue of identity for this age group. In spite of shortcomings it is still worth noting his focus on identity formation as a major challenge of the youth years. Today, questions of identity are discussed more than ever, and in view of the expansion of 'youth' towards other generations, questions of identity are relevant to any age group. In this respect it is interesting to note Erikson's judgement forty years ago: 'The study of identity, then, becomes as strategic in our time as the study of sexuality was in Freud's time' (Erikson 1963: 282).

In spite of the broad interest in questions of identity, it is vital to keep a focus on identity as an important part of young people's lives, as Erikson did. Since he formulated his theories, our picture of socialisation as well as identity has become even more complex. T. Ziehe has focused on 'new' ways of learning and learning arenas, and claimed that worries about narcissism should be re-examined (Ziehe 1989). K. Gergen argues from a social-constructionist point of view that identity is something 'between' people, more than something 'inside' them (Gergen 1991). A. Giddens has from another position seen identity as a reflexive process working with, and managing life within, a late modern society characterised by dissolution and fragmentation (Giddens 1991). In addition to this preoccupation with identity as part of 'modern plurality', the 1990s has also brought a stronger focus on questions of identity within 'traditional plurality' (Skeie 1995, 2002; Baumann 1996, 1999; Østberg 1998).

These new insights into sociocultural aspects of late modern society tell something about the life-world of young people being pluralised and contradictory and affects its relationship to questions of identity. RE should therefore always give attention to issues of identity or subjective relevance for the young student. In the triangular model this is visualised by the location of 'Identity' at the top corner or peak. Still this insight can also be exaggerated if the importance of religion for young people is seen only from the identity-perspective, especially if identity is interpreted mainly as personal, and the social context is neglected. The religion of the young person is hardly more inward looking than that of other phases of life. In some social environments, religious competence is called for, whether it be by the demands within a strong religious group or by the managerial skills needed in a multi-religious neighbourhood. Such competence is difficult to uphold without relating it to knowledge, whether provided through school or elsewhere. Research into 'integrated plural identity' is an indication of how important the interplay between identity, knowledge and competence is in religious socialisation (Østberg 1998).

Approaching youth and religion through religious education

Young people deal with religion in many ways and in many different contexts. In this they do not differ from other human beings, younger or older. It is possible to see religion as a complex cultural flow of meaning and part of this flow of meaning is an ongoing discourse about what 'religion' is (Hannertz 1992). In spite of fixed curriculae, there is no ready-made concept of religion suited for transmission through education. Instead we find discourses about religion that RE can choose to relate to. To speak of discourses rather than transmission of knowledge indicates that a basic precondition is to acknowledge differences. In a school system this constitutes a huge challenge. Traditionally school has been an institution designed for disciplining children and young people, forming them into groups and teaching them to adjust to the rules of the group. From an historical perspective, at least in Norway, religion used to be the core of the curriculum and the reference point for uniformity. This has changed dramatically through the years ending with the present curriculum. In spite of a lasting controversy about the curriculum, plurality now is part of religious education in Norway, and it is difficult to envisage this process being reversed. In today's Norway, modern plurality constitutes the sociocultural context of traditional plurality both for young and old. The curriculum has embraced this plurality on the level of principles, and the practise of religious education needs to be highly context-sensitive. To be able to include the plural life-world of young people it needs a cultural approach. This challenge is taken up by religious educators both in Norway and in other parts of Europe (Heimbrock *et al.* (eds) 2001; Jackson 2003).

In some countries, the main challenges may be related to the curriculum, but even with a well-balanced curriculum, and even more so then, the questions of choice are vital. There are approaches, aims and content to be chosen. A reason for advocating a cultural and contextual approach with focus on diversity is that young people deserve to be taken seriously in their own right, not the least when dealing with religion. In order to do so religious educators should open up the choices of teaching to young people, and one place to start is to open up the concept of religion by introducing young people to different discourses on religion and spirituality. On the basis of this they may be invited to form their own discourse in the class. The same applies to questions of priority within aims and content, and to the questions of approaches. This relieves teachers of some of the burden of choice, but challenges them to be 'fluent' in their knowledge of the discourses of pedagogy and subject matter within RE. Taking into account the differing and demanding aims of religious education, as well as the impossibility of reaching them all to the same extent, young people should be allowed into the workshop of the teacher and encouraged to take more responsibility for their own learning.

Notes

1 Some of the same issues are addressed in Skeie 2003.
2 Even if these questions are raised in other countries, not all suggest large-scale education programmes as the main solution (Engebretson 2003).
3 MMI, see http:/www.mmi.no/omni/English.htm.
4 Similar results from Germany can be found in the Shell Jugendstudie (Gensicke 2002).

References

Bateson, G. (1972) *Toward a Theory of Schizofrenia, Steps to an Ecology of Mind*, New York: Ballantine Books.

Baumann, G. (1996) *Contesting Culture: Discourses of Identity in Multi-Ethnic London*, Cambridge: Cambridge University Press.

—— (1999) *The Multicultural Riddle. Rethinking National, Ethnic and Religious Identities*, London: Routledge.

Birkedal, E. (2001) '*Noen ganger tror jeg på Gud, men. . .?*' *En undersøkelse av gudstro og erfaringer med religiøs praksis i tidlig ungdomsalder*, KIFO Perspektiv nr. 8, Trondheim: Tapir Forlag. ('An empirical investigation into religiosity and faith in God among 13-to-15-year-olds'. Ph.D. thesis, Norwegian University of Science and Technology.)

Engebretson, K. (2003) 'Young people, culture and spirituality: some implications for ministry', *Religious Education*, 98: 5–24.

Erikson, E.H. (1963) *Childhood and society*, New York: W.W. Norton.

Everington, J. (2000) 'Mission Impossible: Religious Education in the 1990s', in M. Leicester, C. Modgil and S. Modgil (eds) *Spiritual and Religious Education: Education, Culture and Values* Vol. V, London: Falmer Press, 183–97.

Gensicke, T. (2002) 'Individualität und Sicherheit in neuer Synthese? Wertorientierungen und gesellschaftliche Aktivität', in *Deutsche Shell*, Frankfurt am Main: Fisher Taschenbuch Verlag.

Gergen, K. (1991) *The Saturated Self. Dilemmas of Identity in Contemporary Life*, New York: Basic Books.

Giddens, A. (1991) *Modernity and Self-Identity. Self and Society in Late Modern Age*, Cambridge: Polity Press.

Grimmitt, M. (ed.) (2000) *Pedagogies of Religious Education. Case Studies in the Research and Development of Good Pedagogic Practice in RE*, Great Wakering, Essex: McCrimmons.

Haakedal, E. (2001) 'From Lutheran Cathechism to World Religions and Humanism: Dilemmas and Middle Ways through the Story of Norwegian Religious Education', *British Journal of Religious Education*, 23: 88–97.

Hannertz, U. (1992) *Cultural Complexity. Studies in the Social Organization of Meaning*, New York: Colombia University Press.

Hartman, S.G. (1994) 'Children's Personal Philosophy of Life as the Basis for Religious Education', *Panorama*, 6: 104–28.

Heimbrock, H-G., Scheilke, C. and Schreiner, P. (eds) (2001) *Towards Religious Competence. Diversity as a Challenge for Education in Europe*, Münster: LIT Verlag.

Hellevik, O. (2001) 'Ungdommens verdisyn – livsfase eller generasjonsbetinget?', *Tidsskrift for ungdomsforskning*, 1: 47–70.

Hull, J. (1990) 'Religious Education in the State Schools of Late Capitalist Society', *British Journal of Educational Studies*, 38: 335–48.

—— (1991) *Mishmash. Religious Education in Multi-Cultural Britain. A Study in Metaphor*, Derby: Christian Education Movement.

—— (1992) 'The Transmission of Religious Prejudice', (Editorial), *British Journal of Religious Education*, 14: 69–72.

—— (2000a) 'Religionism and Religious Education', in M. Leicester, C. Modgil and S. Modgil (eds) *Spiritual and Religious Education* (Education, Culture and Values Series vol. V), London: Falmer Press.

—— (2000b) 'Religion in the Service of the Child Project: The Gift Approach to Religious Education', in M. Grimmitt (ed.) *Pedagogies of Religious Education*, Great Wakering, Essex: McCrimmons.

Illeris, K. *et al.* (2002) *Ungdom, identitet og uddannelse*, Roskilde/Fredriksberg: Roskilde Universitetsforlag.

Jackson, R. (ed.) (2003) *International Perspectives on Citizenship, Education and Religious Diversity*, London: RoutledgeFalmer.

Øia, T. (1998) *Generasjonskløften som ble borte. Ungdom, innvandrere og kultur*, Oslo: Cappelen Akademisk Forlag.

Østberg, S. (1998) 'Pakistani children in Oslo: Islamic nurture in a secular context', unpublished Ph.D. thesis, University of Warwick.

Schweitzer, F. (1996) *Die Suche nach eingenem Glauben. Einführung in die Religionspädagogik des Jugendalters*, Güthersloh: Chr. Kaiser/Gühtersloher Verlagshaus.

Skeie, G. (1995) 'Plurality and pluralism: a challenge for religious education', *British Journal of Religious Education*, 17: 84–91.

—— (2002) 'The Concept of Plurality and its meaning for Religious Education', *British Journal of Religious Education*, 25: 47–59.

—— (2003) 'Youth: Who Are They and Why bother them with Religious Education?', *Panorama*, 14: 155–68.

Stafseng, O. (2001) 'Kunnskapsteoretiske perspektiver på forholdet mellom profesjonsutdanning og forskning i høgskolesystemet', *Norsk Pedagogisk Tidsskrift*, 2/3: 131–48.

—— (2002) 'Pedagogikkens ungdomsproblem – ungdommens pedagogikkproblem', *Norsk Pedagogisk Tidsskrift*, 4: 339–54.

Stafseng, O. and Frønes, I. (1987) 'Ungdomsforskning: Metodologi og teoritradisjoner', Stafseng/Frønes (ed.) *Ungdom mot år 2000*, Oslo: Gyldendal.

Ziehe, T. (1989) *Kulturanalyser. Ungdom, utbilding, modernintet*, Stockholm/Stehag: Symposion.

17 Religious education and the life-world of young people

Psychological perspectives

K. Helmut Reich

In a number of his writings, John Hull (e.g., Hull 1989, 1991a, b, 1998) has striven to make religious education (RE) relevant to children's and young people's experience whilst at the same time preserving the integrity of religion. Seen from my perspective, what stands out in this regard is John Hull's interest in the results of research in developmental psychology and their relevance for RE. This led to our collaboration and the publication of several articles in the *British Journal of Religious Education* (e.g., Reich 1989, 1994). However, our exchanges were no one-way street. John Hull (1999) opened at least one door for me: how children learn 'spontaneously' about money and its value, going through various knowledge and competence stages between the ages, say, of three and eleven years. The first message resulting from this for RE is to have confidence in children's 'self-learning' capacity and to build on it. The second message is more subtle: a parallelism between the development just indicated and the stages of *Religious Judgement* (RJ) according to Fritz Oser and Paul Gmünder (1991; Oser and Reich 1996), in particular regarding RJ stage 2, the 'bargaining' [with God] stage as Hull calls it.

My present purpose is to show what psychology can contribute to RE, given young people's life-world today. Before doing that, it should be made clear that the context in which the following considerations were developed is that of German state schools. If it exists, RE is denominational in these schools and its content is legally the responsibility of the established churches, in the case of my experience the Protestant church. Hence, while problem-orientated RE is also much in vogue in Germany, Christian teachings and the Bible form the curricular base. This is different from the situation in the UK (Hull 1989, 1991b). In this essay, I begin with some remarks on the relation between pedagogy/didactics and psychology, continue with the life-world of young people, then turn to the psychological dimensions of pupils' religiosity, and in each case look at their relevance for RE.

Pedagogy and psychology

Gifted teachers are often also good (intuitive) psychologists. For instance, Harold Loukes, the Oxford University Quaker religious educationist, more than four decades ago produced *Teenage Religion* (Loukes 1961). He centred RE on first identifying and exploring in their own terms problems of teenagers' present or future life-worlds such as friendship, sex and marriage, money, work and so on and then relating this to relevant biblical teachings. Thus, pupils' interest is captured and after the relevance of the Bible for their lives is established, it is hoped that they would be motivated to continue with the study of the Bible and its interpretation (cf. Reich 1996, 2003a, c; Schröder and Reich 1999). Timothy Arthur Lines argued for a 'systems approach' to RE: 'Systemic religious education is the search for, the attempt at, and creation of, an holistic nexus through the existential learning-adaptive process of transforming the heritage of the past into an actualised vision of the ideal future' (Lines 1987: 216).

Pedagogy has a long and successful history in the course of which it has accumulated a considerable body of knowledge about effective teaching methods in many subjects including RE (e.g., Grimmit 2000; Schweitzer 2003; Porzelt and Gurth 2000; Goldman 1964). Goldman, for example, at the time a lecturer at Westhill College, a free church teacher training college in Birmingham (UK), researched pupils' understanding of religious concepts from childhood to adolescence. Karl Ernst Nipkow and Friedrich Schweitzer (1991) studied adolescents' fulfilled and unfulfilled expectations of religious life. Given this flourishing state of affairs, it is questionable whether there is really a need or even room for a contribution to RE from psychology, considering also that psychological insights as a rule cannot be transferred as they stand, lock stock and barrel, into the classroom. For instance, Schweitzer points out that (a) no (psychological) theory can determine in advance what a given child or adolescent is going to think, what will arouse his or her interest, what will be disquieting or moving, and (b) it takes an appropriate setting for children and even adolescents to bring to bear their full creative and interpretive potential on the issue at hand (Schweitzer 1999b: 241–2).

The answer to the question of psychology's contribution to education is fairly straightforward for educational psychology. For instance, it is easy to see that understanding the detailed working of the human memory can be beneficial for effective teaching. The same goes for understanding and dealing with certain hurdles or even roadblocks in the case of RE (e.g., Reich 1997, 1998, 2005); but how about psychology in general and the psychology of religion in particular (cf. Bucher 1995)? A first hint is given by the research of Goldman (1964), and Nipkow and Schweitzer (1991) already referred to. As is well known, Goldman, an educational psychologist, based his work on Jean Piaget's findings on the development of worldviews and of logico-mathematical thinking; and Nipkow and Schweitzer made use of the theories of Erikson, Fowler, Glaser and Strauss, Kohlberg and Gilligan, Oser, Reich and Rizzuto. Thus, the first role of psychology is to furnish theories (and methods) that can be used by educationists for their own RE-related research.

A second role is to arbitrate between differing pedagogic proposals, for instance concerning the age at which biblical parables should be taught in order to be correctly understood. Contrary to the idea (not shared by Goldman!) that young children could fully benefit from parables, Anton A. Bucher's research, based on developmental psychology, showed that such an understanding may only arrive at the end of childhood or even later (Bucher 1991).This leads to the more general issue of RE and psychological developmental stages. Schweitzer (1999a and this volume) has explored this theme for many years and I have added two short 'footnotes' (Reich 2000, 2001) and recently a dynamic model (Reich 2003d). The main message is clear (cf. Hull 1991a): on the one hand, children and, to a lesser degree, adolescents need to be allowed to be free to develop their own developmental-stage-related religious images, ideas and conceptions which they are basically capable of doing. On the other hand, RE has the task of supporting the young seekers and fostering their religious maturity. Longitudinal studies show marked individual differences in the speed of (religious) development (e.g., Fetz, Reich and Valentin 2001). The resulting inter-individual developmental inhomogeneity of pupils present in the classroom makes this ideal RE objective not easy to reach.

Present-day life-worlds of young people

Studies show that:

(a)   each and every young person in practical terms lives in a different life-world. The individual characteristics even of identical twins differ – on average only half of their behavioural similarities are genetically inherited – and correspondingly their reaction to the 'same' life-world will not be identical in all details. Obviously, this is even truer of young people from different families, different social strata and different countries (e.g., Friesl and Polak 1999; Plesner 2002).

(b)   *Some* young people of the same age who live in the same neighbourhood, share interests and experiences and have frequent contact with each other, will have a number of features of their life-world in common.

(c)   At a more abstract level, all young people live in the same life-world in that their stage in the life course is situated between childhood and adulthood. These in-between years are the most formative years; not infrequently they leave traces still discernible much later in adulthood. Many wide-ranging studies concentrate on these shared aspects. Also, all young people experience (more or less) the same zeitgeist, for instance being aware of running the risk of being considered mentally unbalanced or even stupid when reporting a religious experience (e.g., Hay 2003). Nevertheless, even if they are not aware of it or do not take much interest in general issues, all are confronted with the basic religio-philosophical questions 'Where do I come from?', 'Where am I going?', 'Who am I here and now?' – even if the corresponding answers are not religious or even non-existent. Thus, from a psychological perspective, one expects some commonalities and many differences between pupils in an RE class (cf. Skeie – Chapter 16 in this volume).

Let us look at changes in the theory of education in the last hundred years or so which have affected young people's life-worlds related to their schooling. This is of course a vast subject (e.g., Schugurensky 2005) to which no justice can be done in a few lines. Four phases of development are identifiable (Speck 1991; EKD 2003): (a) the appearance, diffusion and increasing reception of Freudian psychoanalytical ideas and recommendations; (b) the anti-authoritarian movement of the 1960s and 1970s ('it is forbidden to forbid') and its impact; (c) the effects of post-modernism/relativism in the last quarter of the 20th century (Helsper 1999); and (d) the parallel trend toward individual self-realisation. Due to lack of space, we cannot expand in detail on them (cf. EKD 2003; Schweitzer [1996] 1998 for the current situation) but only indicate some of their consequences.

Although there are differences between them, the first three phases move in the same general direction: imposing a dominant, let alone a repressive authority on pupils is to be avoided because it limits personal freedom to achieve emancipation from the shackles imposed by a rigid traditional culture. After achieving many of their objectives, these trends are less marked now, yet still present. There is a true core to this argument but realising a full and healthy development needs external resistance and sparring partners besides encouragement and support. However, let not cultural pessimism prevail! A more permissive environment also opens up possibilities for a genuine self-realisation, which then have to be seized and implemented.

The outcome of the four trends indicated is an emphasis on personal rights and entitlements more than on duties and engagement for the common good, yet also the will (and the need) to take developing one's views, attitudes and actions, including religiosity, into one's own hands at a much younger age than previously. A spillover into RE appears to lead to the following: a demanding God, God's commandments, and the notion of sin are largely out of fashion; they are replaced by an idiosyncratic patchwork. Nobody wants to go back to nineteenth century society and its educational system, but the current life-worlds of young people are not entirely satisfactory either (e.g., EDK 2003; Porzelt 1999). We shall attempt to find out what could be improved, at least in RE classes.

Dimensions of personal religiosity

From the perspective of the psychology of religion, the dimensions of personal religiosity can be characterised as: (1) ritualistic/cultic practice;

(2) doctrinal/credal beliefs; (3) affective religious experience; (4) religious knowledge; (5) ethical and communal consequences of being religious. Ideally, a complete RE takes all five dimensions on board. However, at least in most Western countries, we no longer live in a Christian environment where the family, various institutions, the media and the culture together contribute to meeting RE's objectives. Being largely on its own, RE therefore needs to prioritise in order to seek effectiveness. Contemporary individualism implies that motivation, learning and change guided by religion (and more generally by ethics and values) are largely determined by individuals' choices. I argue that in this situation RE should focus on enabling pupils to decide in 'full' knowledge which kind of life they wish to live and how each of them answers the fundamental religio-philosophical questions previously listed, given the basic fact that we all have earthly lives limited in time span.

Ritualistic or cultic practice

Historically speaking, ritualistic or cultic practice could well constitute the beginning of religion. Its original purpose may have been to face up to particular situations such as healing disease, preparing oneself for hunting or fighting the enemy, burying the dead, marking life's transitions such as coming of age or marrying. One important effect of such rituals was and is to create a community, to establish a tradition that strengthened and strengthens group identity and can be transmitted to the next generation. What may one learn for RE from that state of affairs? Given the difficulty of RE – teaching pupils who are not necessarily interested in religion – it seems particularly important to create a kind of learning community in the class. This aim will presumably be the more difficult to achieve, the more the characteristics of the pupils and their life-worlds differ, but, then, it is also the more necessary and rewarding, both for each pupil and for RE.

Which rituals can help? Examples are: (a) to make it a practice that each pupil can express his or her opinion without fear of being laughed at and ridiculed (cf. Hay 2003); (b) to establish that emotionally gripping events such as the arrival of a living pet, or the death of a grandmother, or any other deeply moving personal occurrence can be shared. This can sometimes be done collectively while all sit in a circle (e.g., Berryman – Chapter 14 in this volume; Porzelt 1999: 81–118); (c) to *do* something *together*, even if it is just to have a cup of tea and a few biscuits during RE. More demanding projects would be to produce a religious play, to attend together a regional or even national religious gathering and so on, and obviously, where possible, to pray and worship together. As RE teachers know, the importance of creating a learning community can hardly be overestimated: it helps to create a good class ethos in which difficult issues can be approached, it fosters mutual acceptance, facilitates learning and opens up the mental and experiential horizons of the pupils.

Doctrinal and credal beliefs

Let us begin with the results of an empirical study of the acceptance of the (Christian) Apostolic Creed (Zwingmann, Frank and Moosbrugger 1996). The existence of God and of Jesus Christ as well as the crucifixion and death of Jesus Christ received the highest percentage affirmation (from about 60 per cent of representative Protestants to about 95 per cent of active Roman Catholics). The Immaculate Conception by the Holy Ghost met with the lowest percentage affirmation (from about 20 per cent of representative Protestants to about 40 per cent of active Roman Catholics). Clearly, credal beliefs nowadays are a matter of personal choice and not much more can be hoped for than an explanation as to why each pupil believes what he or she believes if indeed that can be done. When it comes to doctrines like those of the trinity or the two natures of Jesus Christ, the stage of cognitive development may come in as a further explanation (Reich 2002: 120–6). Given this situation, how is one to deal with it in RE? A possibility is to turn to present-day credal statements.

Affective religious experience

Since the 1970s much empirical work has been done in this area, particularly in England. If the definition of religious experience is drawn wide enough, and the interviewing is done in a confidence-inspiring and sensitive way, about three quarters of the persons interviewed report 'religious' experiences (Hay 2003). In the classroom it is presumably more a case of sharing such experiences (if it can be done) than actually having them there. However, it can also be quite fruitful (if accepted) to interpret jointly (Porzelt 1999) whatever experience is brought forward. Even if pupils may not be given to traditional religion they should be put in a position where they can contribute. The point is that they too have affective experiences of events that are central themes of religion (cf. Psalms 6: 6–7, 22: 12–18, 35: 11–16, 120: 5–7) even if they do not see them in that way. Examples are (a) dealing with contingencies and specifically with ephemerality and death, (b) feeling at home or as a stranger, (c) living psychosocially integrated or in isolation, (d) finding life and the world understandable or incomprehensible.

Hence, a major task is to bring out the common interest in the experience under discussion. The interpretation may again have to be personal yet could feed exchanges.

This dimension of religiosity is likely to be rather important for the development of resilience, which has much to do with psychic integrity; however, a split between one's cognition and emotions, between self and others, puts one in the 'at-risk' category. Hence anything that can be done to avoid such splits, or even to regain integrity in case splits occur is to be welcomed and hence to be striven for. A religion rich in spirituality can be of help to meet this objective. Once again, this dimension can be seen to contain elements that can make for mutual acceptance and the building up of a learning community.

Religious knowledge

This dimension is likely to be one where a given prescribed curriculum and a psychological perspective will have the greatest difficulties of meeting. What has priority from a psychological point of view? First, it is up to pupils to acquire knowledge through interaction with their environment, in many cases also by way of direct religious experiences (Hay 2003). Nobody else can do that for them but others can assist specifically in two ways: by presenting material (a) that is situated in the *Zone of Proximal Development*, and (b) doing so in a manner that is 'brain-compatible'. The 'Zone of Proximal Development' (ZPD 2000) is defined as: *'the distance between the actual developmental level as determined by independent problem solving* [without guided instruction] *and the level of potential development as determined by problem solving under adult guidance or in collaboration with more capable peers'*. 'Scaffolding' is any action taken by the 'guide' to ensure that the learner can properly navigate through the ZPD. This, then, means that not only has the content of the new material to be matched to the pupils' existing knowledge, but also the methods involved have to match the pupils' developmental level. Besides the role of the teacher as guide, the role of the peers should be given due emphasis, as is done, for instance, in group work, and systematically in RE in Jeshivas.

Attention needs to be paid to the nature of concept development. Basically, there are two kinds: filiation and substitution. An example of *filiation* is learning about money from coins to banknotes to credit cards and so on: what is learned later in no way limits or renders obsolete what was learned earlier. By contrast, *substitution* involves a replacement or at least a severe restriction of the domain of applicability of earlier conceptual knowledge or procedures. An example of substitution in RE concerns the God image: from an anthropomorphic maker and doer in childhood to the Ground of Being, a Higher Force, the Good and so on in adulthood. The issue is how to stay in the ZPD, yet not to support stagnation but help the (older) child to leave those early God images behind and see God in new ways.

An improved epistemic cognition constitutes a major ingredient for developing a more adult God image (Fetz, Reich and Valentin 2001; Reich 2002: 29–32). The decisive step is to reach the level of means reflection (reflecting on one's mental tools), to appreciate that God and my image of God are not necessarily identical. When that insight arises, adolescent pupils may say things such as: 'When I was a child, we built a house and that needed material and a blueprint. So I thought that God also needed material and a blueprint to make the world. In reality, we do not know how exactly God made the world'. To foster such a development while staying in the ZPD is particularly tricky in a developmentally inhomogenous class. All the same, means reflection is a precondition for a deeper understanding of nature, human nature and God (e.g., Barbour 2002). In that context, it seems wise to deal appropriately with issues that can potentially lead to cognitive dissonance such as Genesis 1–2. Another issue of that kind could be the claim that neuroscience can explain most of religion without residue (e.g., Boyer 2003). The idea is that even provoking a controversy in the classroom and clearing it up as much as possible within the learning community (cf. Reich 1996, 2003a, b and c) is preferable to letting the one or the other pupil ruminate in their corner getting confused.

What does *brain-compatible* mean? Learning most often means to 'reorganise' the brain. An outstanding example is learning to read. Nobody is born with a specialised neural reading circuit; it has to be formed. Even in less demanding learning tasks, the strength of the neural connections and the synapses usually need modification before new knowledge and skills are anchored for good. To help these processes along, material should be presented multimedially, and a number of variations experimented with. For instance, when it comes to the *Kingdom of God*, it is helpful for the embedding of the new knowledge in the brain to deal in succession with the various pertinent parables of the New Testament and to include the last book, Revelation.

In sum, a psychological perspective puts less emphasis on the complete curricular content and more on 'learning how to learn', and favours materials that are suitable for this end.

Ethical and communal consequences

Here is another dimension likely to benefit greatly from the existence of a learning community. In fact, Kohlberg's *Just Community* has as its sole purpose the improvement of moral reflection and action via a communal setting and appropriate procedures (Althof 2003). What does that mean in practical terms? In the section 'Ritualistic practice' above it was suggested that it be made a rule that each pupil should be able to express his or her opinion without fear of being laughed at and ridiculed. If this can be achieved, the greater the diversity of views in the classroom, the greater the progress. To achieve a fruitful exchange between fundamentalist believers and convinced atheists clearly is something to be remembered and used as a model for future social behaviour.

The basic question in this connection is 'Why be moral?' The answer is not obvious, especially in an era when a best-seller is entitled 'Honest people are dumb' (*Die Ehrlichen sind die Dummen*: Ulrich Wickert). How does one deal with this issue (cf. Hull 1998)? One way is to begin with a projection of Michelangelo's *The Last Judgement* whilst simultaneously playing Mozart's *Dies irae* from his Requiem. Perhaps it might also be opportune to present the Ten Commandments, which clearly do not enthrone an all-encompassing individual freedom; it is remarkable that they have lasted for three millennia. Karl Giberson (2003) argues that they enable a tribe, a society to flourish just as the (instinctive) behavioural rules of the ants ensure their survival. Recalling the situations depicted in the Psalms cited in the earlier section 'Affective religious experience', helps us to understand the need for social cohesion and solidarity (cf. Kelly 1998). There are of course those who will refuse to be compared with such 'lowly' animals as ants. However, is it not noteworthy that already in the Bible they are presented as a model of self-determined, socially valuable actors (Proverbs 6: 6–8)? Perhaps it might also be useful to compare humans with a jaguar, who runs faster than any enemy, sleeps alone in tree tops with no danger of being attacked while sleeping and so on. This might help to bring home the basic need for morality in the case of the more endangered human species.

History cannot (and should not) be turned back to an age where authority in its various forms was the key to an ordered society (a certain alliance between the Castle and the Cathedral, between the clergy and the teacher). Clearly *new* ways of living together as harmoniously and fruitfully as possible are required; in Switzerland 'authoritarian' traffic lights are being increasingly replaced by roundabouts. Maybe this could provide a clue as to how to engage everybody involved and make them more responsible when it comes to moral decisions and implementing them.

A different approach to 'teaching' solidarity is by way of exemplars (e.g., Oman and Thoresen 2003). There are of course model Christians such as Albert Schweitzer and Mother Theresa, but maybe sports heroes are closer to the heart of young people. For instance, how about introducing the concept of solidarity and facilitating its understanding through the case of a cyclist or a sailor, who risked foregoing his or her victory in the race on account of helping a co-racer who had an accident; this before coming to biblical examples such as Ruth, the Samaritan and so on?

Concluding remarks

Obviously, this is not a handbook article on the title theme, not an encompassing, systematic, balanced, neutral overview. There are many aspects which could have been included under the heading 'psychological perspectives'. For instance, we could have delved into relevant aspects of a well-meaning dialogue between psychology and religion (e.g., Jeeves 1997), or we could have studied how social cognition deals with mystical religious experiences, or we could have looked at the importance of religious attitudes and acts such as forgiving on mental health from the perspective of clinical psychology.

As it is, we have mainly dealt with the five dimensions of personal religiosity identified by the psychology of religion, namely ritualistic and cultic practice, doctrinal and credal beliefs, affective religious experiences, religious knowledge, and ethical and communal consequences; and we have considered how they relate to RE, or better, what RE can do to foster and enrich them as well as taking the cue from them for becoming more authentic and effective. In view of pupils' needs as conceived here, and the current possibilities of RE, the focus is on RE as a way to enable pupils to decide competently on how they want to answer for themselves the enduring, fundamental religio-philosophical questions. Thus, like numerous writings of John Hull, this is a personal programmatic essay with which presumably not everybody will agree, yet, it is hoped, in which they will find some food for thought.

References

Althof, W. (2003) 'Implementing Just and Caring Communities in Elementary Schools: a Deweyan perspective', in W. Veugelers and F.K. Oser (eds) *Teaching in Moral and Democratic Education*, Bern: P. Lang.

Barbour, I. (2002) *Nature, Human Nature, and God*, Minneapolis, MN: Fortress, London: SPCK.

Boyer, P. (2003) 'Religious thought and behaviour as by-products of brain function', *Trends in Cognitive Sciences*, 7: 119–24.

Bucher, A.A. (1991) 'Educational implications and application of the theory of religious judgement', in F.K. Oser and P. Gmünder *Religious Judgement: a developmental approach*, trans. N.F. Hahn, Birmingham, AL: Religious Education Press.

—— (1995) 'Religionspädagogik und Psychologie', in H.G. Ziebertz and W. Simon (eds) *Bilanz der Religionspädagogik*, Dusseldorf: Patmos.

EKD (2003) *Maße des Menschlichen. Evangelische Perspektiven zur Bildung in der Wissens- und Lerngesellschaft. Eine Denkschrift des Rates der Evangelischen Kirchen in Deutschland*, Gütersloh: Gütersloher Verlagshaus.

Fetz, R.L., Reich, K.H. and Valentin, P. (2001) *Weltbildentwicklung und Schöpfungsverständnis. Eine strukturgenetische Untersuchung bei Kindern, Jugendlichen und jungen Erwachsenen*, Stuttgart: Kohlhammer.

Friesl, C. and Polak, R. (eds) (1999) *Die Suche nach der religiösen Aura. Analysen zum Verhältnis von Jugend und Religion in Europa*, Graz/Vienna: Zeitpunkt.

Giberson, K. (2003) 'The ant colony on Mount Sinai', *Science and Spirit*, 14: 36–9, 52.

Goldman, R. (1964) *Religious Thinking from Childhood to Adolescence*, London: Routledge & Kegan Paul (also New York: The Seabury Press, 1968).

Grimmitt, M. (ed.) (2000) *Pedagogies of Religious Education: Case Studies in the Research and Development of Good Pedagogic Practice in RE*, Great Wakering, Essex: McCrimmons.

Hay, D. (2003) 'Why is implicit religion implicit?', *Implicit Religion: Journal of the Centre for the Study of Implicit Religion and Contemporary Spirituality (CSIRCS)*, VI: 17–41.

Helsper, W. (1999) *Das postmoderne Selbst*, in C. Friesl and R. Pollak (eds) *Die Suche nach der religiösen Aura. Analysen zum Verhältnis von Jugend und Religion in Europa*, Graz/Vienna: Zeitpunkt.

Hull, J.M. (1989) *The Act Unpacked: The Meaning of the 1988 Education Reform Act for Religious Education*, Derby: CEM.

—— (1991a) *God-talk with Young Children: Notes for Parents and Teachers*, Derby: CEM.

—— (1991b) *Mishmash: Religious Education in Multi-Cultural Britain: A Study in Metaphor*, Derby: CEM.

—— (1998) *Utopian Whispers: Moral, Religious and Spiritual Values in Schools*, London: Religious and Moral Education Press (RMEP).

—— (1999) 'Bargaining with God: Religious Development and Economic Socialization', *Journal of Psychology and Theology*, 27: 241–9.

Jeeves, M.A. (1997) *Human Nature at the Millennium: Reflections on the Integration of Psychology and Christianity*, Grand Rapids, MI: Baker.

Kelly, M.A. (1998) 'Solidarity: A foundational educational concern', *Religious Education*, 93: 44–64.

Lines, T.A. (1987) *Systemic Religious Education*, Birmingham, AL: Religious Education Press.

Loukes, H. (1961) *Teenage Religion: An Enquiry into Attitudes and Possibilities among British Boys and Girls in Secondary Modern Schools*, London: SCM Press.

Nipkow, K.E. and Schweitzer, F. (1991) 'Adolescents' justifications for faith or doubt in God: A study of fulfilled and unfulfilled expectations', in F.K. Oser and W.G. Scarlett (eds) *Religious Development in Childhood and Adolescence*, San Francisco, CA: Jossey Bass.

Oman, D. and Thoresen, C.E. (2003) 'Spiritual modeling: A key to spiritual and religious growth?', *The International Journal for the Psychology of Religion*, 13: 149–65.

Oser, F.K. and Gmünder, P. (1991) *Religious Judgement: A Developmental Approach*, trans. N.F. Hahn, Birmingham, AL: Religious Education Press (first German edition 1984).

Oser, F.K. and Reich, K.H. (1996) 'Religious development from a psychological perspective', *World Psychology*, 2: 365–96.

Plesner, I.T. (2002) 'Religio-political models and models for religious and moral education', *Panorama*, 14: 111–22.

Porzelt, B. (1999) *Jugendliche Intensiverfahrungen: Qualitativ-empirischer Zugang zur religionspädagogischen Relevanz*, Graz: Manumeder Verlag Schnieder.

Porzelt, B. and Gurth, R. (eds) (2000) *Empirische Religionspädagogik: Grundlagen – Zugänge – Aktuelle Projekte*, Munster: LIT.

Reich, K.H. (1989) 'Between religion and science: Complementarity in the religious thinking of young people', *British Journal of Religious Education*, 11: 62–9.

—— (1994) 'Can one rationally understand Christian doctrines? An empirical study', *British Journal of Religious Education*, 16: 114–26.

—— (1996) 'Relational and contextual reasoning in religious education: a theory-based empirical study', in L.J. Francis, W.K. Kay and W.S. Campbell (eds) *Research in Religious Education*, Leominster: Gracewing.

—— (1997) 'Indifference of pupils to religion: can anything be done about it?', *British Journal of Religious Education*, 20: 14–27.

—— (1998) 'Motivation by contents in religious education', in P. Nenninger, R.S. Jaeger, A. Frey and M. Wosnitza (eds) *Advances in Motivation*, Landau: Verlag Empirische Pädagogik.

—— (2000) 'Psychology of religion: Guidelines for priests, ministers, religious educators and parents', *Archiv fur Religionspsychologie*, 23: 278–94.

—— (2001) 'Ce que la psychologie de la religion peut enseigner et la catéchèse', in V. Saroglou and D. Hutsebaut (eds) *Religion et developpement humain: Questions psychologiques*, Paris: Harmattan.

—— (2002) *Developing the Horizons of the Mind: relational and contextual reasoning and the resolution of cognitive conflict*, Cambridge, UK: Cambridge University Press.

—— (2003a) 'Es nicht logisch, aber doch wahr!', *Katechetische Blätter*, 128: 8–13.

—— (2003b) 'Psychology of religion and neurobiology: which relationship?', presentation at the *Glasgow Conference for the Psychology of Religion*, University of Glasgow, 28–31 August.

—— (2003c) 'Teaching Genesis: a present day approach inspired by prophet Nathan', *Zygon: Journal of Religion and Science*, 38: 633–41.

—— (2003d) 'The person-God relationship: a dynamic model', *The International Journal for the Psychology of Religion*, 13: 229–47.

—— (2005) 'The stage-structural approach to religious education', in E.M. Dowling and W.G. Scarlett (eds) *Encyclopedia of Spiritual Development in Childhood and Adolescence*, Thousand Oaks, CA: Sage.

Schröder, A. and Reich, K.H. (1999) 'Eve's RE, not Adam's: a lesson about Zelophehad's daughters', *British Journal of Religious Education*, 21: 90–100.

Schugurensky, D. (2005) *History of Education: selected moments of the 20th century – a work in progress*, see http://www.fcis.oise.utoronto.ca/~daniel_schugurensky/assignment1/#00s.

Schweitzer, F. (1998) *Die Suche nach eigenem Glauben. Einführung in die Religionspaedagogik des Jugendalters*, 2nd edn, Gütersloh: Chr. Kaiser/Gütersloher Verlagshaus.

—— (1999a) *Lebensgeschichte und Religion: religiöse Entwicklung und Erziehung im Kindes- und Jugendalter*, 4th edn, Gütersloh: Kaiser, Gütersloher Verlagshaus.

—— (1999b) 'Kinder und Jugendliche als Exegeten?', in D. Bell with C. Reents (eds) *Menschen suchen – Zugänge finden: auf dem Weg zu einem religionspädagogisch verantworteten Umgang mit der Bibel: Festschrift fur Christine Reents*, Wuppertal: Foedus.

—— (2003) *Pädagogik und Religion: Eine Einführung*, Stuttgart: Kohlhammer.

Speck, O. (1991) *Chaos und Autonomie in der Erziehung: Erziehungsschwierigkeiten unter moralischem Aspekt*, Munich/Basel: M. Reinhardt.

ZDP (2000) 'How to use the Zone of Proximal Development', see http://www.wcer.wisc.edu/step/ep301/Spr2000/Constance-B/Our%ZPD%20Page.htm.

Zwingmann, C., Frank, D. and Moosbrugger, H. (1996) 'Der gemeinsame Glaube der Christen: Empirische Analyse zum Apostolischen Glaubensbekenntnis', in H. Moosbrugger, C. Zwingmann and D. Frank (eds) *Religiosität, Persönlichkeit und Verhalten: Beiträge zur Religionspsychologie*, Münster, Germany: Waxmann.

Appendix
The publications of John M. Hull

Books

Hellenistic Magic and the Synoptic Tradition {Studies in Biblical Theology}, London: SCM Press, 1974.

Sense and Nonsense about God {Senior Study Series}, London: SCM Press, 1974.
  Part reprinted in J. Churchill and D.V. Jones (eds) *An Introductory Reader in the Philosophy of Religion*, London: SPCK, 1979.
  2nd edition (revised), Scottish Higher Still/Support Material: RMPS Language, Philosophy and Religion, Scottish Consultative Council of the Curriculum, 1998.

School Worship: An Obituary, London: SCM Press, 1975.

Studies in Religion and Education, Lewes, Sussex: Falmer Press, 1984.

What Prevents Christian Adults from Learning?, London: SCM Press, 1985.
  US edition (with a new preface), Philadelphia: Trinity Press International, 1991.

The Act Unpacked: The Meaning of the 1988 Education Reform Act for Religious Education, Derby: CEM, 1989.

Touching the Rock: An Experience of Blindness, London: SPCK, 1990.
  Braille edition, 3 vols, Stockport: The National Braille Library, 1990.
  Large Print edition, Bath: Chivers Press, 1990.
  Australian edition, Melbourne: David Lovell Publishing, 1990.
  US Hardback edition, New York, Pantheon Books, March 1991.
  UK Paperback edition (with a foreword by Oliver Sacks), London: Arrow Books, June 1991.
  US Paperback edition (with a foreword by Oliver Sacks) New York: Random House, Vintage Books, 1992.
  Aylesbury: Calibre Cassette Library, 1991.
  London: RNIB Talking Book Library, 1991.
  Cassette Editions for the Blind, New Jersey: Recording for the Blind, 2 cassettes, 1991.
  US Commercial Cassette, New York: Random House (Sound Editions), abridged in two audio cassettes and read by David Purdham, October 1991.
  Dutch translation, *De dagen worden wel kouder maar niet korter: Leven met blindheid* translated by Joke Bomer with an introduction by Vincent Bijlo, Utrecht: A.W. Bruna Uitgevers, 1992.
  French translation, *Le Chemin vers la Nuit: Devenir Aveugle et Réapprendre à Vivre* translated by Donatella Saulnier and Paule Vincent, Paris: Robert Laffont, 1995.

German translation, *Im Dunkeln Sehen Erfahrungen Eines Blinden* trans. Silvia Morawetz, Munich: C.H. Beck'sche Verlagsbuchhandlung, 1992.

Book club edition (German), Frankfurt am Main: Buchergilde Gutenberg, 1992.

Paperback edition (German), Munich: Deutscher Taschenbuch Verlag, 1995.

Hebrew translation, translated by Shraga Gafni, Tel Aviv: Misrad Ha'bitahon (Israel Ministry of Defence Publishing House), 1994.

Italian translation, *Il Dono Oscuro, Nel Mondo di Chi non Vede* translated by Serena Lauzi with a preface by Oliver Sacks, Milan: Garzanti Editore s.p.a., 1992.

Japanese translation, translated by Shigeo Matsukawa, Tokyo: Shinkyo Shuppan-sha Publishing Company, 1996.

Spanish translation, *Ver en la Oscuridad, La Experiencia de la Ceguera* translated by Andrés Ehrenhaus with an introduction by Domingo Garcia, Sabell, Barcelona: Circulo De Lectores, 1994.

[With Michael H. Grimmitt, Julie Grove and Louise Spencer] *A Gift to the Child: Religious Education in the Primary School*, Teacher's Source Book, with Pupil's Pack and Cassette, Hemel Hempstead: Simon and Schuster, 1991.

God-Talk with Young Children: Notes for Parents and Teachers, Derby: CEM, 1991.

US edition (with a foreword by Maria Harris), Philadelphia: Trinity Press International, 1991.

German translation (with a foreword by Friedrich Schweitzer), *Wie Kinder über Gott Reden: Ein Ratgeber fur Eltern und Etziehende*, Gütersloh: Gütersloher Verlaghaus, 1997.

Mishmash: Religious Education in Multi-Cultural Britain, A Study in Metaphor, Derby: CEM, 1991.

On Sight and Insight: A Journey into the World of Blindness, Oxford: Oneworld Books, 1997.

Complex Chinese Translation (*Secret Garden in Heart of Blind Person*), Taiwan: Morningstar Publishing, 2000.

Cassette Edition for blind readers, Peterborough: RNIB Student Tape Library, Ref X-7169.

Korean translation, Seoul: Urikyoyuk, 2001.

Utopian Whispers: Moral, Religious and Spiritual Values in Schools, London: RMEP, 1998.

Glaube und Bildung {Ausgewahlte Schriften Band 1}, translated by Susanne Naumann and Sieglinde Denzel with an introduction by Prof. Dr Werner Kramer, Zurich: KIK Verlag, 2000.

Gott und Geld {Ausgewahlte Schriften Band 2}, translated by Silvia Morawetz, Berg am Irchel: KIK Verlag, 2000.

Holistic Education in the 21st Century (Taiwanese Lectures 2000, in Chinese), Taiwan, 2001.

In the Beginning There was Darkness: A Blind Person's Conversations With the Bible, London: SCM Press, 2001.

US Edition, Philadelphia: Trinity Press International, 2002.

Contributions to books

'The Integration of Religious Education and Some Problems of Authority' in I.H. Birnie (ed.) *Religious Education in Integrated Studies*, London: SCM Press, 1972.

Reprinted in *Studies in Religion and Education* (1984), 57–71.

'Agreed Syllabuses, Past, Present and Future' in Donald Horder and Ninian Smart (eds) *New Movements in Religious Education*, London: Maurice Temple Smith, 1975.

Reprinted in *Studies in Religion and Education* (1984), 73–92.

'Religious Education in a Pluralist Society' in Monica Taylor (ed.) *Progress and Problems in Moral Education*, London: NFER, 1975.

Reprinted in *Studies in Religion and Education* (1984), 45–55.

Chinese translation, *Hong Kong Journal of Religious Education*, 2, 87–92, 1990.

'The Birmingham Agreed Syllabus' in *Religious Education in the Government of Schools of Western Australia* (The Nott Report) Education Department, Western Australia, 1978.

Reprinted in *Studies in Religion and Education* (1984), 113–16.

'Christian Faith and the Open Approach to Religious Education' in The Integrated Education Committee (Newfoundland) *Religious Education for the 1980s: Implications for the Student*, St. Bride's College, St. John's, Newfoundland, 1980, 91–105.

Reprinted in *Studies in Religion and Education* (1984), 197–206.

'Religious Education in the 80s' in The Integrated Education Committee (Newfoundland) *Religious Education for the 1980s: Implications for the Student*, St. Bride's College, St. John's, Newfoundland, 1980, 1–18.

'Training the Religious Education Teacher' in The Integrated Education Committee (Newfoundland) *Religious Education for the 1980s: Implications for the Student*, St. Bride's College, St. John's, Newfoundland, 1980, 50–62.

'The Divergent Teacher, The Plural Society and the Christian Faith' in *Christians and Education in a Multi-Faith World* (Papers from the Joint World Council of Churches and Centre for the Study of Religion and Education in the Inner City Consultation 1–8 July 1981), Manchester: Sacred Trinity Centre, 1981.

Reprinted in *Studies in Religion and Education* (1984), 187–95.

'Open Minds and Empty Hearts: Commitment and the Religious Education Teacher' in R. Jackson (ed.) *Approaching World Religions*, London: John Murray, 1982.

Reprinted in *Studies in Religion and Education* (1984), 175–85.

'Can Theology have an Educational Role? A Response to Karl Ernst Nipkow' in M.C. Felderhof (ed.) *Religious Education in a Pluralistic Society*, London: Hodder and Stoughton, 1985.

'Kreatives Denken und die Bibel' in Herbert Schultze (ed.) *Erkundungen mit der Bibel*, Munster: Comenius Institut, 1987.

English edition, 'The Bible in the Secular Classroom' in J. Astley and D.V. Day (eds) *The Contours of Christian Education*, Great Wakering, Essex: McCrimmons, 1992.

'Menschliche Entwicklung in der Modernen Kapitalistischen Gesellschaft' in Karl Ernst Nipkow *et al.* (eds) *Glaubensentwicklung und Erziehung*, Gütersloh: Gütersloher Verlagshaus, 1988.

US edition, 'Human Development and Capitalist Society' in James W. Fowler, Karl Ernst Nipkow and Friedrich Schweitzer (eds) *Stages of Faith and Religious Development, Implications for Church, Education and Society*, New York: Crossroad, 1991.

UK edition, 'Human Development and Capitalist Society' in James W. Fowler, Karl Ernst Nipkow and Friedrich Schweitzer (eds) *Stages of Faith and Religious Development, Implications for Church, Education and Society*, London: SCM Press, 1992.

'Ideologien und die Bewusstseinsindustrien Religionsunterricht an den offentlichen Schulen einer spatkapitalistischen Gesellschaft' in R. Preul *et al.* (eds) *Bildung Glaube Aufklarung* (Nipkow Festschrift), Gütersloh: Gütersloher Verlagshaus, 1989.

English version, 'Religious Education in the State Schools of Late Capitalist Society' *British Journal of Educational Studies*, XXXVIII: 335–48, 1990.

Italian translation, 'Educazione religiosa nelle scuole di stato della societa tardo-capitalistica', *Religione & Scuola*, 5: 57–66, 1992.

'Church-Related Schools and Religious Education in the Publicly-Funded Educational System of England' in Dott. A. Giuffrè (ed.) *Church and State in Europe: Religion and the School* (European Consortium for Church-State Research, proceedings of the meeting Milan, Parma, 20–21 October 1989), Università Degli Studi Di Milano: Facoltà Di Guirisprudenza, 181–99, 1992.

Australian edition (adapted), 'Recent Changes in Religious Education in England and Wales', *Journal of Christian Education*, Paper 101, 1991.

'Curriculum and Theology in English Religious Education' in Johannes Lähnemann (ed.) *Das Wiedererwachen der Religionen als pädagogische Herausforderung: Interreligiöse Erziehung im Spannungsfeld von Fundamentalismus und Säkularismus* (Proceedings of the IV Nurnberg Forum, 25–28 September 1991) Hamburg: E.B. Verlag Rissen, 1992.

Reprinted in *Panorama: International Journal of Comparative Religious Education and Values*, 4: 36–45, 1992.

Reprinted in *Bulletin of the Association of British Theological and Philosophical Libraries*, 2: 3–15, 1993.

'Religion and Education in a Pluralist Society' in Dermot A. Lane (ed.) *Religion, Education and the Constitution*, Dublin: Columba Press, 1992.

'Theologische gesprekken met jonge Kinderen' in F.H. Kuiper and H.J.M. Vossen (eds) *Jonge Kinderen grootbrengen met geloof Zwolle*, Netherlands: Waanders Drukkers, 1992.

English version, 'Theological Conversation with Young Children', *British Journal of Religious Education*, 20: 7–13, 1997.

'Atheism and the Future of Religious Education' in Stanley E. Porter, Paul Joyce and David E. Orton (eds) *Crossing the Boundaries: Essays in Biblical Interpretation in honour of Michael D. Goulder*, Leiden: E.J. Brill, 1994.

'Critical Openness in Christian Nurture' in Jeff Astley and Leslie Francis (eds) *Critical Perspectives on Christian Education: A Reader on the Aims, Principles and Philosophy of Christian Education*, Leominster: Fowler Wright Books, 1994.

'Geschichte und Entwicklung des Lehrplans für den Religionsunterricht in Birmingham' in Ingrid Lohmann and Wolfram Weisse (eds) *Dialog Zwischen den Kulturen. Erziehungshistorische und Religionspädagogische Gesichtspunkte Interkultureller Bildung*, Munster: Waxmann, 1994.

'The Nature of Religious Education' in Hooshang Nikjoo and Stephen Vickers (eds) *Distinctive Aspects of Baha'i Education: Proceedings of the Third Symposium on Baha'i Education* (5–7 April 1991, Newman College, Birmingham), The Baha'i Publishing Trust, 1993.

'Can One Speak of God or to God in Education?' in Frances Young (ed.) *Dare We Speak of God in Public?*, London: Mowbray, 1995.

'Collective Worship: The Search for Spirituality' in *Future Progress in Religious Education: The Templeton London Lectures*, London: RSA, 1995.

'How Can We Make Children Sensitive to the Values of Other Religions Through Religious Education?' in Johannes Lahnemann (ed.) *Das Projekt Weltethos in der Erziehung. Proceedings of the 5th Nuremberg Forum on Religious Education* (28 September to 1 October 1994), Hamburg: E.B. Verlag, 1995.

'On Being a Whole-Body Seer: Blindness and Sight as Different Forms of Vision' in Uta Brandes (ed.) *Desire to See. E(ye)vent and Dis-Illusion. Changes in Visual Perception in the 20th Century* (Congress in the Forum der Kunst- und Ausstellungshalle der Bundesrepublik Deutschland, 22–26 September 1993), Gottingen: Steidl, 1995.

'The Ambiguity of Spiritual Values' in J. Mark Halstead and Monica Taylor (eds) *Values in Education and Education in Values*, London: Falmer Press, 1996.

'Christian Education in a Capitalist Society: Money and God' in David Ford and Dennis L. Stamps (eds) *Essentials of Christian Community: Essays in Honour of Daniel W. Hardy*, Edinburgh: T. & T. Clark, 1996.

'A Critique of Christian Religionism in Recent British Education' in Jeff Astley and Leslie J. Francis (eds) *Christian Theology and Religious Education: Connections and Contradictions*, London: SPCK, 1996.

'Freedom and Authority in Religious Education' in Brian Gates (ed.) *Freedom and Authority in Religions and Religious Education*, London: Cassells, 1996.

'Religious Education and the Conflict of Values in Modern Europe' in Aasulv Lande and Werner Ustorf (eds) *Mission in a Pluralist World*, Frankfurt: Peter Lang, 1996.

'Food for All' in Terence Copley *et al.* (eds) *Splashes of God-Light: Bible Stories Retold by Jews and Christians*, Swindon: Bible Society, 1997.

'From Primeval Passion to Tapered Discipline' (an interview on the nature of the research process with Professor Hull by Patricia Keiron) in H.B. Brown and G. Griffiths-Dickson (eds) *Passion for Critique: Essays in Honour of F.J. Laishley*, Prague: The Ecumenical Publishing House, 1997.

'Religion, Religionism and Education' in Johannes Lähnemann (ed.) *Interreligiöse Erziehung 2000*, Hamburg: EB, 1998.

'The shadow of my parents' in Joan King (ed.) *Family and All That Stuff*, Birmingham: NCEC, 1998.

'The Material Spirituality of Blindness and Money' in Ruth Harvey (ed.) *Wrestling and Resting: Exploring Stories of Spirit from Britain and Ireland* London: CTBI, 1999.

'Religionsunterricht und Muslime in England: Entwicklungen und Grundsätee' in Christoph Th. Scheilke and Freidrich Schweizer (eds) *Religion, Ethik, Schule: Bildunspolitische Perspektiven in der Pluralen Gesellschaft* (Karl Ernst Nipkow Festschrift), Munster: Waxmann Verlag, 1999.

English version, 'Religious Education and Muslims in England: Developments and Principles', *Muslim Education Quarterly*, 15, 10–23, 1998.

'Spiritual Education, Religion and the Money Culture' in James C. Conroy (ed.) *Catholic Education Inside-Out/Outside-In*, Dublin: Veritas, 1999.

'Blindness and the Face of God: Toward a Theology of Disability' in Hans-Georg

Ziebertz *et al.* (eds) *The Human Image of God* (Johannes A. Van Der Ven Festschrift), Leiden: Brill, 2000.

Reprinted in *The Baptist Ministers' Journal*, 281: 8–17, 2003.

'Religion in the Service of the Child Project: the Gift Approach to Religious Education' in Michael Grimmitt (ed.) *Pedagogies of Religious Education*, Great Wakering, Essex: McCrimmons, 2000.

'Religionism and Religious Education' in Mal Leicester, Celia Modgil and Sohan Modgil (eds) *Spiritual and Religious Education* (Education, Culture and Values Series Vol. V), London: Falmer Press, 2000.

'The Contribution of Religious Education to Religious Freedom: A Global Perspective' in Zarrín T. Caldwell (ed.) *Religious Education in Schools: Ideas and Experiences from around the World*, Oxford: International Association for Religious Freedom, 2001.

Reprinted in Peter Schreiner *et al.* (eds) *Committed to Europe's Future – Contributions from Education and Religious Education: A Reader*, Münster: Comenius Institut, 2002.

'Open Letter from a Blind Disciple to a Sighted Saviour: Text and Discussion' in Martin O'Kane (ed.) *Borders, Boundaries and the Bible*, Sheffield: Sheffield Academic Press, 2001.

Turkish translation, *Islamiyat* (Ankara), 3 part 4: 13–34, 2001.

'The Spirituality of Disability: The Christian Heritage as both Problem and Potential' in Johannes Lähnemann (ed.) *Spiritualität und ethische Erziehung: Erbe und Herausforderung der Religionen* (Nürnberger Forums 2000), Hamburg: EB-Verlag, 2001.

Adapted and enlarged in *Studies in Christian Ethics*, 16: 2, 2003.

'Wettbewerb und spirituelle Entwicklung' in Peter Biehl *et al.* (eds) *Gott und Geld* (*Jahrbuch der Religionspädagogik* 17), Neukirchen-Vluyn: Neukirchener, 2001.

English version, 'Competition and Spiritual Development' *International Journal of Children's Spirituality*, 6: 263–75, 2001.

'Practical Theology in Context: The Case of Europe' in Wilhelm Gräb and Brigit Weyel (eds) *Praktische Theologie und Protestantische Kultur* (PThK 9), Gütersloh, Chr: Kaiser/Gütersloh Verlagshaus, 2002.

Longer version: 'Understanding Contemporary European Religious Consciousness: an Approach through Geo-politics', *Panorama: International Journal of Comparative Religious Education and Values* 14: 123–40, 2002.

'Der Segen der Säkularität: Religionspädagogik in England und Wales' in Wolfrum Weiße (ed.) *Wahrheit und Dialog: Theologische Grundlagen und Impulse gegenwärtiger Religionspädagogik*, Berlin: Waxmann, 2002.

'Religious Education in Democratic Plural Societies: Some General Considerations' in *New Methodological Approaches in Religious Education: International Symposium Papers and Discussions 28–30 March 2001 – Istanbul*, Ankara: M.E.B., 2003 (including a Turkish translation).

'Viele Religionen – Eine Welt: Eine pädagogische Antwort auf religiöse Gewalt' in Christa Dommel *et al.* (eds) *WerteSchätzen: Religiöse Vielfalt und Öffentliche Bildung. Festschrift für Jürgen Lott zum 60. Geburtstag*, Frankfurt am Rhein: IKO, 2003.

'The World of Sight and the World of Touch' in Elisabeth Salzhauer Axel and Nina Sobol Levent (eds) *Art Beyond Sight: A Resource Guide to Art, Creativity, and Visual Impairment*, New York: AFB Press, 2003.

'Christian Education and the Reconstruction of Christian Faith' in Gloria Durka *et al.* (eds) *International Handbook on the Religious, Moral and Spiritual Dimensions of Education*, Dordrecht, Netherlands: Kluwer Academic Publishers, 2005.

'Religion, Violence and Religious Education' in Gloria Durka, Robert Jackson, Andrew McGrady, Marian de Souza and Kathleen Engebretson (eds) *International Handbook on the Religious, Moral and Spiritual Dimensions of Education*, Dordrecht, Netherlands: Kluwer Academic Publishers, 2005.

Journal articles and published lectures

'Training the Non-Specialist Teacher of Divinity', *Education for Teaching*, 73: 20–4, 1967.

'Making Student Teachers of Divinity Think', *Education for Teaching*, 77: 70–4, 1968.

'Worship and the Curriculum', *Journal of Curriculum Studies*, 1: 208–18, 1969.
   Reprinted in *Studies in Religion and Education* (1984), 5–16.

'Recent Developments in the Philosophy of Religious Education', *Educational Review*, 23: 59–68, 1970.
   Reprinted in *Studies in Religion and Education* (1984), 93–102.

'Worship and Education', *Educational Review*, 24: 26–33, 1971.
   Reprinted in *Studies in Religion and Education* (1984), 17–24.

'The Theology of Themes', *Scottish Journal of Theology*, 25: 20–32, 1972.
   Reprinted in *Studies in Religion and Education* (1984), 123–33.

'History, Experience and Theme in Religious Education', *Journal of Christian Education* (Sydney), Papers 53: 27–38, 1975.
   Reprinted in *Studies in Religion and Education* (1984), 149–61.

'Perennial Symbols: Preparing to Teach Religion Through Life Themes', *Education 3–13*, 104–9, 1975.
   Reprinted in C. Richards (ed.) *Education 3–13*, Nafferton Books, 1978.
   Reprinted in *Studies in Religion and Education* (1984), 163–72.

'Theme Teaching as a Method of Religious Education', *Lumen Vitae* (Brussels), XXX: 9–23, 1975.
   Reprinted in *Studies in Religion and Education* (1984), 135–48.

'Christian Theology and Educational Theory: Can there be Connections?' *British Journal of Educational Studies*, XXIV: 127–43, 1976.
   Reprinted in *Studies in Religion and Education* (1984), 229–47.
   Reprinted in Jeff Astley and Leslie Francis (eds) *Critical Perspectives on Christian Education: A Reader on the Aims, Principles and Philosophy of Christian Education*, Leominster: Fowler Wright Books, 1994.

'Religious Indoctrination in the Birmingham Agreed Syllabus?' *Faith and Freedom*, 30: 27–35, 1976.

'What is Theology of Education?' *Scottish Journal of Theology*, 30: 3–29, 1977.
   Reprinted in *Studies in Religion and Education* (1984), 249–72.
   Reprinted in Leslie Francis and Adrian Thatcher (eds) *Christian Perspectives for Education: A Reader in the Theology of Education*, Leominster: Fowler Wright Books, 1990.

'From Christian Nurture to Religious Education: the British Experience', *Religious Education* [USA], 73: 124–43, 1978.
   Reprinted in *Studies in Religion and Education* (1984), 27–44.

'The Value of the Individual Child and the Christian Faith', *British Journal of Educational Studies*, 28: 199–211, 1980.

Reprinted in *Studies in Religion and Education* (1984), 273–85.

'Christian Nurture and Critical Openness', *Scottish Journal of Theology*, 34: 17–37, 1981.

Reprinted in G.M. Castles and G.M. Rossiter (eds) *Curriculum Theory and Religious Education*, Sydney: Australian Association for Religious Education, 1983.

Reprinted in *Studies in Religion and Education* (1984), 207–25.

Reprinted in Leslie Francis and Adrian Thatcher (eds) *Christian Perspectives for Education: A Reader in the Theology of Education*, Leominster: Fowler Wright Books, 1990.

'Belemmeringen in het Leeproces van Volwassen Christenen', *Praktische Theologie*, 10: 298–313, 1983.

'Hva Hindrer Voksne Kristne i a Laere?' *Kirke Og Kultur*, 89: 174–87, 1984.

What Stops Christian Adults from Learning? [anniversary lecture], Manchester: The Centre for the Study of Religion and Education in the Inner City, 1984.

World Religions for Christian Children [presidential address], Redhill, Surrey: National Christian Education Council, 1985.

'On Being a Whole Body Seer: An Epistemic Condition for the Education of the Blind', *The British Journal of Visual Impairment*, 62–3, Summer 1990.

'Religious Education in the State Schools of Late Capitalist Society', *British Journal of Educational Studies*, 38: 335–48, 1990.

'Religious Education and Christian Values in the 1988 Education Reform Act: A Reply to J.D.C. Harte', *Ecclesiastical Law Journal*, 7: 69–81, 1990.

Agreed Syllabus Reform in Birmingham (CREDAR Lecture Series No. 3), Birmingham: Centre for Religious Education Development and Research, University of Birmingham, 1991.

Religion, Education and Madness: A Modern Trinity (an Inaugural Lecture delivered in the School of Education, University of Birmingham on 26 February 1991), CREDAR Lecture Series No. 2, Centre for Religious Education Development and Research: University of Birmingham, 1991.

Reprinted in *Educational Review*, 43: 347–61, 1991.

Reprinted in Peter Gordon (ed.) *The Study of Education: A Collection of Inaugural Lectures: The End of an Era?*, Vol. 4, London: Woburn Press 1995.

(With Michael H. Grimmitt, Julie Grove and Louise Spencer) *Religion in the Service of the Child: Interim Report* (CREDAR Lecture Series No. 4), Birmingham: Centre for Religious Education Development and Research, University of Birmingham, 1991.

Catholic Education Beyond 2000 – A Christian Perspective on Spiritual Education: Religion and the Money Culture (Occasional Papers in Education No. 3) Glasgow, St. Andrew's College, May 1995.

Reprinted in *Briefing: Education Special Edition* (The official documentation service of the Catholic Bishops' Conferences of England and Wales and of Scotland) 25–31, 1995.

Reprinted in James C. Conroy (ed.) *Catholic Education – Inside Out/Outside In*, Dublin: Veritas, 1999.

'Christliche Erziehung in einem Pluralistischen und Multireligiösen Europa', *Evangelisches Missionswerk in Deutschland (EMW)* (Monograph Series), 109: 1995.

Shorter version, 'Christliche Erziehung in einem Pluralistischen und Multi-religiösen Europa', *Feuervogel*, 1/95: 27–31.

The Holy Trinity and Christian Education in a Pluralist World (The National Society's RE Centre Annual Lecture 1994), London: National Society/Church House Publishing, 1995.

'Self-Deception as a Coping Strategy for Christians', *Christian Action Journal*, 19–21, Autumn 1995.

'The Theology of the Department for Education' (The 1993 Hockerill Lecture), *Educational Review*, 47: 243–53, 1995.

'Ministerial Education in a Post-Modern Society', *British Journal of Theological Education*, 7: 4–11, 1995/1996.

'Religion as a Series of Religions: A Comment on the SCAA Model Syllabuses', *From Syllabuses to Schemes – Planning and Teaching Religious Education*, Shap World Religions in Education Journal, 11–16, 1995/1996.

'Educational Values in the Money Culture', a paper presented to an education conference, CEM, Scotland, January 1996.

'Geld, Moderne und Moral: Einige Uberlegungen zur Christischen' *Der Evangelische Erzieher: Zeitschrift fur Pädagogik und Theologie*, 3: 277–91, 1996.

English version, 'Money, Modernity and Morality: Some Issues in the Christian Education of Adults', *Religious Education*, 95: 4–22, 2000.

'A Gift to the Child: A New Pedagogy for Teaching Religion to Young Children', *Religious Education*, 91: 172–89, 1996.

Chinese translation, *Hong Kong Journal of Religious Education*, 8: 40–49, 1996.

'Christian Education: Sufficient or Necessary? (1) The Sufficiency of Christian Education', *Epworth Review*, 24: 40–8, 1997.

'Christian Education: Sufficient or Necessary? (2) The Necessity of Christian Education', *Epworth Review*, 24: 38–46, 1997.

Encounter with Religion and Responding to Religion, Chester: Cheshire County Council Education Services, 1997.

'Karl Marx on Capital: Some Implications for Christian Adult Education', *Modern Believing*, 38: 22–31, 1997.

'Adult Religious Faith: Some Problems of Definition, of Research and of Education', *Modern Believing*, 40: 39–48, 1999.

'Bargaining with God: Religious Development and Economic Socialization', *Journal of Psychology and Theology*, 27: 241–9, 1999.

'Christian Boundaries, Christian Identities and the Local Church', *International Journal of Practical Theology*, 1: 1–13, 1999.

'Spirituality, Religion, Faith: Mapping the Territory', *Youth & Policy: The Journal of Critical Analysis*, 65: 48–59, 1999.

'Evangelische Religiöse Erziehung und der Pluralismus eines Multireligiösen Europa', *Schönberger Hefte*, 1/00: 4–12, 2000.

'Competition and Spiritual Development', *International Journal of Children's Spirituality*, 6(3): 263–75, 2001.

'From Experiental Educator to Nationalist Theologian: the Hymns of Isaac Watts', *Panorama: International Journal of Comparative Religious Education and Values*, 14: 91–106, 2002.

'"Sight to the Inly Blind"? Attitudes to Blindness in the Hymnbooks', *Theology*, CV: 333–41, 2002.

Reprinted as 'Those Who Won't See', *Church Times*, no. 7286: 16–17, 18 October 2002.

Reprinted in *EDAN* (Ecumenical Disability Advocates Network: World Council of Churches) January–March 2003, 20–1 (Part One); April–June 2003, 22–3 (Part Two).

'Spiritual Development: Interpretations and Applications', *British Journal of Religious Education*, 24: 171–82, 2002.

Turkish translation, *Journal of Values Education* [in Turkish], 1/2: 109–24, 2003.

'What Prevents Christian Adults from Acting' in Geoff Cornell (ed.) *Hugh Price Hughes Lectures 2002* (held at Hinde Street Methodist Church W1 February–June 2002), Hinde Street Methodist Church, 2002.

'The Blessings of Secularity: Religious Education in England and Wales', *Journal of Religious Education* [Australian Catholic University], 51: 51–8, 2003.

Norwegian translation, *Kirke & Kultur*, 5/6: 463–75, 2003.

'The Broken Body in a Broken World: A Contribution to a Christian Doctrine of the Person from a Disabled Point of View', *Journal of Religion, Disability & Health*, 7: 5–23, 2003.

'A Spirituality of Disability: The Christian Heritage as both Problem and Potential', *Studies in Christian Ethics*, 16: 21–35, 2003.

'Practical Theology and Religious Education in a Pluralist Europe', *British Journal of Religious Education*, 26: 7–19, 2004.

'Teaching as a Trans-world Activity' *Support for Learning* (Journal of the Association for Special Education) August 2004,103–6.

'Isaac Watts and the Origins of British Imperial Theology' *International Congregational Journal*, 4: 2, 2005.

'Religious Education in England and Germany: the Recent Work of Hans-Georg Ziebertz' *British Journal of Religious Education*, 27: 5–17, 2005.

Professional and popular publications

'Teaching Through Talking: The Role of Conversation in Christian Education', *Education in Church Today*, 1: 5–8, Summer 1989.

'Cathedrals and the Religious Experience of the Blind' in Christine Milligan (ed.) *Vision for the Nineties*, Salisbury: The Pilgrims Association, 1990.

'The Education of the Dreamy Christian', *React* [The Methodist Church Division of Ministries], 4–6, Autumn 1990.

The God of the Blind', *The New Beacon*, 74/877: 200–4, June 1990.

'Agreed Syllabus Revision and the Law', *Resource* (Professional Council for Religious Education), 14: 1–3, September 1991.

'Learning by Touch: RE and the Visually Handicapped Child', *Respect: A Journal for Teachers of Pupils with Special Educational Needs*, 3: 2–3, Summer 1991.

Reprinted in *Crosscurrent* (The National Society), 37: 4, Spring 1992.

'A Manifesto for Christian Education' in *Manifesto for Christian Education* (Association of Anglican Secondary School Heads, Annual Conference 19–21 September 1991, Chester).

'The Tactile Heart', *The Expository Times*, 102: 311–12, 1991.

'Insight and Outsight', *Foundations* (Association of Charitable Foundations), 2: 2–5, April 1992.

'Looking for a Meaning' in Paul Baker and Derek Jones (eds) *Disabling World*, London: Channel 4 Television, March 1992.

'A Critique of Religious Education Guidelines', *Islamia: National Muslim Education Newsletter*, 23: 10–11, March 1994.

'The Case Against Collective Worship in Schools', *Primary School Manager*, 3: 25, March 1995.

'Collective Worship and the Quest for Spirituality', *Summary of the 6th Annual Conference for Grant Maintained Schools*, 2: 56–7, March 1995.

'The Gifted Child in Religious Education', *Resource* [Professional Council for Religious Education], 17/3: 2–4, Summer 1995.

'A Touching Place', *Chariot Magazine*, 7: 62–3, April/May 1995.

'Good Religious Education – What will it be?' (Enfield SACRE Annual Lecture 1996), *Enfield SACRE Annual Report*, 9–14, 1995/96.

'Adult Faith Transforming Life: The Possibilities', *Caravan: a Resource for Adult Religious Educators* (Canadian Conference of Catholic Bishops, Ottawa), 9/7: 10–11, Winter 1996.

'God: The Idea That Will Not Go Away', *Teaching RE 5–11: God*, Derby: Christian Education Movement, 1996.

Reprinted in *Teaching RE 11–16: God*, Derby, Christian Education Movement, 1996.

'The Holy Trinity and the Educational Mission of the Church', *Viewpoints: Insights into Education and Training in Today's Church* (National Christian Education Council), 1: 14–16, September 1996.

'Money and God: Christian Education in a Capitalist Society', *PACT South West*, 5: 1–8, January/February 1996.

'Muslims in RE: What's Going On?', *Resource: the Journal of PCfRE*, 18: 11–12, Summer 1996.

'Spiritual Education and Money', *Summary of the 7th Annual Conference for Grant Maintained Schools*, 3: 51, March 1996.

'Why Learn? A Personal Response', *Report of an ATL Education Conference*, 8–10, 22 June 1996.

'Teaching the Apostle's Creed: Part 1', *Caravan: A Resource for Adult Religious Educators* (Canadian Conference of Catholic Bishops, Ottawa), 11/44: 8–9, Autumn 1997.

'The Bible as the Word of God in Christian Education Today', *Viewpoints: Insights into Education and Training in Today's Church* (National Christian Education Council), 4: 15, Spring 1998.

'The False Theology of the Post-Imperial Church', *Laity Newsletter* (Holland House), August 1999.

'Mission of God and Human Religion', *Grassroots*, 6–7, September 1999, Reprinted in *One: The Radical Christian Quarterly*, 27: 15, January 2000.

'Could a Blind Person have been a Disciple of Jesus?', *Viewpoints: Insights into Education and Training in Today's Church* (National Christian Education Council), 7: 4–5, Winter 1999/2000.

Reprinted: *Ministerial Formation* (World Council of Churches Education and Ecumenical Formation), 92: 20–1, January 2001.

Interview, *All People* (Changing Attitudes in the Churches to Disability), 85: 6–9, Spring 2000.

'Blind Disciple, Sighted Saviour' in Tim Woodcock and Irfan Merchant (eds) *Fleshing Out Faith: A Reflection on Bodies and Spirituality*, Birmingham: Student Christian Movement, 6–7, 2000.

'Faith and Disability: A Christian Perspective', *Ecumenical Disability Advocates Network*, 2–3, April–June 2000.

'My Story', *Ecumenical Disability Advocates Network*, 13–15, April–June 2000.

'Introduction', *An RE Curriculum for Global Citizenship*, Christian Aid, 2000.

Interview with Joseph Grigely, *Voilà*, 38, June–October 2000.

'Religious Education and the Future: Some Comments on Time', *World Religions in Education: Time* [SHAP Working Party on World Religions in Education], 75–6, 2000–01.

'Time and Blindness', *World Religions in Education: Time* (SHAP Working Party on World Religions in Education), 50–3, 2000–01.

'Declaration by Christian and Muslim Religious Educators in the University of Birmingham', *Panorama: International Journal of Comparative Religious Education and Values*, 13: 25–6, 2001.

'Do You Think I am Stupid?' in *Echoes: Justice, Peace and Creation News* (World Council of Churches), 19: 11–13.

Radio 4 interview (transcript), *Ecumenical Disability Advocates Network* (World Council of Churches, Nairobi), 7, January–March 2001.

'First Sunday in Lent: "I am the Gate for the Sheep"' and 'Second Sunday in Lent: "I am the Good Shepherd"' in Paula Clifford (ed.) *Jesus – Hope for Life* (The Christian Aid/Hodder Lent Book 2002), 10–11, 24–5, London: Hodder & Stoughton, 2001.

'In Darkness and in Light' in Nicola Slee (ed.) *Words for Today 2002: Notes for Daily Bible Reading*, 67–71, Birmingham: The International Bible Reading Association, 2001.

'Recognising Another World', *Access: The National Journal for People With a Disability* (Melbourne), 3/2: 23–6, April/May 2001.

'Sound: An Enrichment or State?' *Soundscape: The Journal of Acoustic Ecology*, 2/1: 10–15, July 2001.

'Borderlands – Margins and Meetings', *Annual Gathering of The Living Spirituality Network*, 5–8, April 2002.

(Notes on the Bible readings for Advent 2002) Pam Macnaughton (ed.) *Roots Children and Young People*, 2: *passim*, November/December 2002.

(Notes on the Bible readings for Advent 2002) Jean Harrison (ed.) *Roots Worship*, 2: *passim*, November/December 2002.

'Why should People of other Faiths visit our Cathedrals?', *MultiCulture? MultiFaith?* (The Pilgrims' Association Annual Conference 8–10 October 2002), 22–32, 2002.

'Religious Education after 11 September 2001', *World Religions in Education: Religion: the Problem or the Answer?* (SHAP Working Party on World Religions in Education), 43–7, 2002–03.

'Competition: Some Ethical and Theological Considerations', *Dialogue: A Journal of Religion and Philosophy*, 20: 21–5, April 2003.

'The Future Development of Christian Education', *EEF-NET* (Education and Ecumenical Formation: World Council of Churches) 12: 7–9, April 2003.

'Jesus: Who was he? Who is he? Who will he be?' in Rosemary Rivett (ed.) *Jesus:*

Who is He? (Developing Secondary RE), Birmingham: Christian Education Publications, 3–5, 2003.

'The National Association of SACREs: An Historical Note', *SACRE News* Special Issue 1993–2003, 2–3, Summer 2003.

'Is there a Spirituality of Money?', *World Religions in Education* (Shap Working Party): *Wealth and Poverty*, 81–4, 2003–04.

'How I Discovered my Blind Brother', *The Bible in Transmission: a Forum for Change in Church and Culture* (Bible Society), 9–12, Spring, 2004.

'Power in Religion: Editorial', *RE Today*, 21/2: 2, Spring 2004.

'Seeing through Words', *Magnet* (Methodist Church), 67: 4–5, Autumn 2004.

Other publishing activity

Contributions to encyclopaedias and dictionaries

'Demons in the New Testament' and 'Exorcism in the New Testament' *The Interpreter's Dictionary of the Bible: Supplementary Volume*, Nashville: Abingdon Press, 1976.

'Indoctrination', 'RE, Nature of' and 'Theology and RE' in John Sutcliffe (ed.) *A Dictionary of Religious Education*, London, SCM Press, 1984.

'Gran Bretagna: Il Educazione Religiosa Nelle Scuole Statali' *Dizionario di Catechetica*, Roma: Istituto di Catechetica dell' Universita Pontificia Salesiana de Roma, Editrice Elle Di Ci, 1986.

'School Worship (England and Wales)' in J.G. Davies (ed.) *A New Dictionary of Liturgy and Worship*, London: SCM Press, 1986.

'Nurture, Christian Nurture', in A.V. Campbell (ed.) *Dictionary of Pastoral Care*, London: SPCK, 1989.

'Inghilterra & Galles', in Flavio Pajer (ed.) *L'Insegnamento Scolastico della Religione Nella Nuova Europa*, Torino: Editrice Elle Di Ci, 1991.

'Adult Education' in Wesley Carr *et al.* (eds) *The New Dictionary of Pastoral Studies*, London: SPCK, 2002.

'School Worship (England and Wales)' in Paul F. Bradshaw (ed.) *The New SCM Dictionary of Liturgy and Worship*, London: SCM Press, 2002.

Membership of publishing working parties

City of Birmingham Education Committee, *Agreed Syllabus of Religious Instruction*, 1975.

City of Birmingham District Council Education Committee, *Living Together: A Teachers' Handbook of Suggestions for Religious Education*, 1975.

The British Lessons Council, *The Story of the People of God: A Basis for Christian Education in the Church Community* R.S. Matthews (ed.) London: BLC, 1976.

Schools Council Religious Education Committee, *A Ground Plan for the Study of Religion*, Spring 1977.

Works edited

Learning for Living: A Journal of Religion in Education 1971–78 (authorship of the editorials) including the special issues:

Islam (January 1972)

Pastoral Care in the School (January 1973)

Is School Dead? (January 1974)

Religious Education and the Slow Learner (January 1975)

The Birmingham Syllabus (Summer 1976)

Meaning and Method in Teaching Religion (Autumn 1976)

Religion in Childhood and Youth: A Research Report

Part I (Spring 1977)

Part II (Summer 1977)

Part III (Autumn 1977)

Consultant editor, *Character Potential: A Record of Research* (USA), 1975–81.

British Journal of Religious Education 1978–96 (authorship of the editorials) including the special issues:

Teaching Judaism Today (Summer 1981)

Religious Education Through Story (Summer 1982)

Can We Teach the Bible? (Summer 1984)

Teaching Hinduism Today (Summer 1984)

Spirituality Across the Curriculum (Summer 1985)

Teaching Buddhism in the Secondary School (Autumn 1986)

Religious Education and Language (Spring 1987)

Religious Education through Fantasy (Autumn 1987)

Religious Education and Personal, Social and Moral Education (Autumn 1988)

Women's Studies in Religious Education (Autumn 1989)

Science, Technology and Religious Education (Autumn 1990)

Religious Education after the 1988 Education Reform Act (Summer 1991)

Christianity in Religious Education (Autumn 1992)

Education in Europe: The Challenge of Religious Pluralism (Spring 1993)

(With Margaret Keys) *Religion in Education and Learning for Living, Index 1934–1978*, CEM, 1979.

The Child in the Church (Working Party Report), London: British Council of Churches, 1976.

Understanding Christian Nurture: a Sequel to 'The Child in the Church' (Working Party Report), London: British Council of Churches, 1981.

Both reports re-issued as *The Child in the Church*, London: British Council of Churches, 1984.

New Directions in Religious Education, Lewes, Sussex: Falmer Press, 1982 (with introduction and commentary).

'Introduction' reprinted as 'New Directions in Religious Education' *Religious Education*, 78: 391–7, 1983.

Forewords and introductions

'Foreword' to William A. Gent, *Living Centre: Assembly in the Secondary School*, London: CEM, 1984.

'Foreword' to Philip Cliff, *The Rise and Development of the Sunday School Movement in England 1780–1980*, Redhill, Surrey: NCEC, 1985.

'Preface' to Leslie J. Francis, *Making Contact: Christian Nurture Family Worship and Church Growth*, London: Collins, 1986.

'Foreword' to Leslie J. Francis and David W. Lankshear (eds) *Christian Perspectives on Church Schools: A Reader*, Leominster: Fowler Wright Books, 1993.

'Foreword' to Anthony Reddie, *Growing into Hope: Christian Education in Multi-ethnic Churches* [2 vols], Peterborough: Methodist Publishing House, 1998.

'Foreword' to Peter R. Hobson and John S. Edwards, *Religious Education in a Pluralist Society*, London: Woburn Press, 1999.

'Foreword' to *Global Citizenship Education*, London: Christian Aid, 2000.

'Foreword' to Leslie J. Francis, Jeff Astley and Mandy Robbins (eds) *The Fourth R for the Third Millennium: Education in Religion and Values for the Global Future*, Dublin: Lindesfarne Books, 2001.

Index